20 Ground-Breaking Directors of Eastern Europe

Kalina Stefanova • Marvin Carlson
Editors

20 Ground-Breaking Directors of Eastern Europe

30 Years After the Fall of the Iron Curtain

Editors
Kalina Stefanova
National Academy for Theatre
and Film Arts
Sofia, Bulgaria

Marvin Carlson
City University of New York
New York, NY, USA

ISBN 978-3-030-52934-5   ISBN 978-3-030-52935-2   (eBook)
https://doi.org/10.1007/978-3-030-52935-2

© The Editor(s) (if applicable) and The Author(s) 2021
This work is subject to copyright. All rights are solely and exclusively licensed by the Publisher, whether the whole or part of the material is concerned, specifically the rights of translation, reprinting, reuse of illustrations, recitation, broadcasting, reproduction on microfilms or in any other physical way, and transmission or information storage and retrieval, electronic adaptation, computer software, or by similar or dissimilar methodology now known or hereafter developed.
The use of general descriptive names, registered names, trademarks, service marks, etc. in this publication does not imply, even in the absence of a specific statement, that such names are exempt from the relevant protective laws and regulations and therefore free for general use.
The publisher, the authors and the editors are safe to assume that the advice and information in this book are believed to be true and accurate at the date of publication. Neither the publisher nor the authors or the editors give a warranty, expressed or implied, with respect to the material contained herein or for any errors or omissions that may have been made. The publisher remains neutral with regard to jurisdictional claims in published maps and institutional affiliations.

Cover illustration: rangizzz / Alamy Stock Photo

This Palgrave Macmillan imprint is published by the registered company Springer Nature Switzerland AG.
The registered company address is: Gewerbestrasse 11, 6330 Cham, Switzerland

The Life-Changing Theatre of Eastern Europe

"I read a book one day and my whole life was changed."[1] This is how the Turkish Nobel prize winner Orhan Pamuk begins his novel *The New Life*. Then he describes how the energy of the book overtook his soul so strongly that he felt as if his body was separating from the chair where he sat reading. At the same time, with his every particle, he remained anchored there, feeling the effect of the book not only on his soul, but on everything that made him what he was.

This is exactly how I felt while watching many productions by the directors included in our book. Their impact was so powerful that it was as if light was surging from the stage, its incandescence dazzling my intellect, but also endowing it with brilliant lucidity—I'm only slightly paraphrasing Pamuk here. "This was the kind of light within which I could recast myself; could lose my way in this light; I already sensed in the light the shadows of an existence I had yet to know and embrace,"[2] he continues.

I remember very clearly all these encounters, when sitting in the hall and eagerly experiencing the new reality on stage, my mind already barely aware that I'm watching theatre, and my whole life changing with every next minute there. (Again, I'm only slightly paraphrasing Pamuk.) Moreover, these productions have made me feel a transformation not only of my own life but of the whole world around me—exactly like his character feels, as described several sentences later.

---

[1] Orhan Pamuk, *The New Life* (London: Macmillan Publishers, 2014), p. 4.
[2] Ibid.

"The others experienced nothing like it even though they heard the same tales," Pamuk mischievously quotes Novalis as his book's motto.[3] Not the case with the theatre I am referring to. I dare say it has had a life-changing effect not only on me but on many other people, both in Eastern Europe and outside of it.

If one has seen the late Lithuanian Eimuntas Nekrošius' *Hamlet* (Meno Fortas, 1997), how can one ever forget the scene with the ice block, for instance? When the Father's ghost takes off Hamlet's shoes and rubs his naked feet and his hands with ice while telling him what happened—the ugly truth becoming palpably chilling in a very literal sense too. And then Hamlet smashing the ice block into pieces and vowing revenge on the dagger that falls from its very core and onto the flames of the rocking chair set on fire by his father just before he leaves the stage. All that amid omnipresent drizzle and chill, as if permeated into every fibre of the surrounding world...

Or another chilling scene of another take on the play: Ophelia's drowning in a canal at the Gdańsk Shipyard, and Hamlet and Laertes plunging to take her out with the background of piercing police and ambulance sirens—in *H.* by the Polish Jan Klata (2004, Teatr Wybreze). How can one forget the interweaving of so many historical layers and different references in that production? From the space—Warehouse 42A, a symbol of Solidarity and the coveted freedom, now empty and dilapidated, representing "Poland's painful past, disappointing presence and uncertain future."[4] To Hamlet and Horatio playing turbo-golf and the Ghost of the Father, clad in the attire of an eighteenth-century Hussar, solemnly entering the building on a horse. From the pretentious French language–peppered wine-tasting of the court (a hobby of today's Polish *nouveaux riches*), the White Stripes music, and multiple versions of "To Be or Not to Be" performed in a sort of reality casting, to the Bible as *the* book in Hamlet's hands hinting at a "To Revenge or To Forgive" interpretation of the main dilemma...

Or the beginning of the *Hamlet* of another Lithuanian, Oskaras Koršunovas (OKT, 2008): nine reflections of nine faces in nine dressing-room table mirrors in the darkness of the stage and the question "Who

---

[3] Ibid.

[4] Alexandra Sakowska, "The Politics of Space – Jan Klata's H. at Gdansk Shipyard, Warehouse 42A," *Romanian Shakespeare Journal*, issue 1, 2013, p. 98.

THE LIFE-CHANGING THEATRE OF EASTERN EUROPE   vii

Are You?"[5] resounding first in a hardly audible whisper, then gradually rising to a crescendo in nine voices. The actors who are to perform the play, sitting with their backs to us, staring at themselves and asking themselves, and as if us too, since the audience is also reflected in the mirrors... These dressing-room tables, the only set, being swirled around by the actors, would turn into a morgue table with the corpse of the Father who would tell Hamlet the truth and in the next minute would become Claudius (one actor speaking in the mirror and immediately afterwards directly to Hamlet); they would also turn into the "tapestry" behind which the court would witness the very real kiss of Hamlet and Ophelia, and then into screens, into the borderline between here and the beyond... How can one forget these mirrors not for mere looks but as "a mousetrap for our inner reality"[6]—mirrors for souls, that is?

Or the startlingly modern interpretation of the play by the Czech Daniel Špinar (Švanda Theatre, 2013), whose flights of imagination have invariably logical and at times even hyper-realistic springboards. In it Hamlet gets possessed by the Ghost after having a joint with Horatio: the lights blink, a door opens on its own and Hamlet falls into convulsions, speaks with another voice and then, still in delirium, writes his Father's message with his blood on a museum-type of glass case (where the usual attributes of the play—swords, a skull, a set of knight's armour—are exhibited). The mad Ophelia in this production, as if taken from the streets, will tear your heart: half-naked, in an oversize man's jacket and with a lipstick-smeared face, she yells and giggles, while masturbating with a microphone stick. Later on we see her sitting and playing with the dirt inside another museum-type of glass case, short and long, with the sign "mortal remains." "Whose is this grave?" asks Hamlet, getting out of the big glass case, meanwhile turned into his prison-madhouse. "Mine," she answers. While part of the grave-scene dialogue follows between them, he sits next to her and, like kids, they throw dirt at each other, and only when she tosses her dirty hair backwards does he realise who she is. Nearly vomiting because of the shock, Hamlet goes back—two glass cases with two exhibits of despondency in them. And while he says the lines about the river and the willow, she bends over her glass case, "drowns" and lies on

---

[5] In the Lithuanian translation of *Hamlet*, Horatio asks the Ghost "Who Are You?" Actually, in some Eastern European languages this is a way to ask "Who's There?"

[6] Oskaras Korsunovas, https://www.okt.lt/spektakliai/hamletas/ (accessed 22 March 2020).

viii   THE LIFE-CHANGING THEATRE OF EASTERN EUROPE

her back—already for real in her grave. "I've seen dozens of Ophelias," the Czech critic Richard Erml wrote, "but Zuzana Onufrakova has to be experienced—at your own risk."[7]

There is an even more overwhelming scene in this *Hamlet*: the very end, in which Špinar challenges the paradigm of Jan Kott. Hamlet not only revolts against his role, he literally refuses to play it out. This scene is a real masterpiece, without any exaggeration. Hamlet and Horatio are inside the lit glass case, the only object on a dark stage at that moment, right in the middle. "I'm not mad," Hamlet says, takes the exhibited sword, solemnly opens the doors, steps out followed by Horatio and, with his back to us, takes off his clothes, while the rest of the characters get into the glass case. Just a silhouette already, he lifts up the sword, as if giving a *Start* signal, and the three-dimensional people inside begin reciting the lines of the duel scene to a background of Bobby Vinton's song *Mr. Lonely*. The song is first hardly audible, then rises up and hushes down again, while the lines go on and, after Horatio pronounces Hamlet's words "I die, Horatio," the last refrain powerfully fills in the theatre: "Now I'm a soldier, a lonely soldier/Away from home through no wish of my own/ That's why I'm lonely, I'm Mr. Lonely/I wish that I could go back home." After the final chord, the sword slips out of Hamlet's hand; he goes to the glass case, still lit and with all the characters inside, and caresses it. This brief farewell caress is performed by the actor Patrik Dergel with such palpable sorrow that, despite being with his back to us and still just a silhouette, he makes us feel as if we ourselves are parting with life. "The rest is silence," he says then and the curtain falls.

It turns out that the implacable "great mechanism of history"[8] could be defied, that the "scenario" could be boiled down to "words, words, words" merely pronounced out loud. It turns out that there is a way out of what has always been deemed a no-way-out situation and that Hamlet can choose not only his motives, but his actions too. In the most crucial moment, at that: when it is his turn to perpetuate vengeance's vicious circle. He can choose then not to let the blinding rage get hold of him, to step aside and not take part in the carnage, and thus save his soul. This scene can, of course, have another interpretation: as an escape—a mere *Not-to-Be* choice. To me, though, it is rather a daring disassociating from the system—the "scenario" that has been presenting itself as the only

---

[7] Richard Erml, *Reflex*, as quoted by the program of the Pilsen Theatre festival, 2014, p. 84.

[8] Jan Kott, *Shakespeare Our Contemporary* (London: Methuen, 1965), pp. 52–55.

possible mode of life. That is why Hamlet's choice is an act of strength. One way or another, this *Hamlet* is a very modern and urgently topical SOS, pleading not just for the usual saving of our souls, but for saving our world for the sake of our souls.

And one more life-changing production that has to do with *Hamlet*—a "prequel" taking place during the night vigil after the King's death: *Hamlet – a Commentary* (2017) by the Polish Grzegorz Bral and his Song of the Goat Theatre. The dead king lies on an iron bed, his hand trembles, reaches up to the funeral mask on his face and removes it; he rises up and in the utmost dismay looks at all these people from the court, who obviously consider the death of his body as the very end of himself too. He tries to draw their attention by talking to them, shouting—in vain. His puzzlement transforms into amusement and he starts imitating them—the artificiality and falseness of their behaviour. It is the living ones who look like they are on a stage, whereas he does not for a moment look unnatural. Nevertheless, he starts to long for carnal warmth and caresses Gertrude, and tries to be caressed by her, putting his head under her palm. The visibility is, of course, in one direction only: it is us, the inhabitants of the visible, who remain blind and callous to the feelings of those already "on the other side." Only Ophelia senses his presence—maybe because she is to join him soon.

These scenes are heartrending and nostalgically philosophical. Yet, very much in the style of Song of the Goat Theatre, what this production is about has nothing to do with what might have happened that night. For the major reckonings in Shakespeare are between the human world and the invisible one; they are arranged on the territory of the human soul and only come out into the open in human destinies. So, despite the intense stage action in his plays, the most important action always takes place on the territory of the soul. And true to Shakespeare's essence, that is what *Hamlet – a Commentary* focuses on.

"It's a drama about energy that demands to be revealed and Hamlet is its medium," reads the show's programme. And like the rest of Bral's theatre, this energy is communicated in the first place via the fine frequencies of polyphonic music harmony, created by Jean-Claude Acquaviva and Maciej Rychły and sung, or rather enlivened, by the amazingly polytalented cast. There are indeed moments when it's as though the Song of the Goat's actors are not made of flesh, but are just sound vibrations extending far beyond the contours of their bodies.

It takes great courage to use the language of harmony to talk about disharmony, as Bral and his theatre have been doing when visiting Shakespeare; and in this very case when it comes to looking down into the abyss where we know the energies that are to torment and rule the world of Hamlet were possibly brewed. And it takes great courage to make it sound so poignantly contemporary, like it does in the powerful verses of Alicja Bral (the author of the show's libretto), which endow a near meta-physical experience with a topical edge. Just a sample—the lamentation hinting at the abusive treatment of Ophelia: "There is no fear/I despise the lies of your corrupted soul/Your filthy manhood drips onto the barren country/My beauty was repeatedly raped by weakness/I'm disgusted by every trace of your presence./In me/I die every night, to give life to revenge/There is no fear/I rise above the mud of this kingdom/Killers of nobleness/There is no more fear/You won't annihilate me/I tear apart the heart of your lies."

Back in 1992, the late American critic Jack Kroll pinpointed the trans-formational power of art even when people have not been its direct recipients: "Maybe they've never read *Ulysses*, nevertheless it has affected their life. Maybe they've never looked at Picasso, but he has changed their life, whether they know it or not."[9]

In the same vein, no matter whether people have seen the abovemen-tioned shows, of the mighty theatre of the directors included in this book and, as a matter of fact, of other compatriot-colleagues of theirs, they have anyway been affected by it. These directors have not only been changing the face of Eastern European theatre per se, they have also been enriching the territory of contemporary world theatre at large. In recognition of this, the second most important theatre award in Europe—for (New) Theatrical Realities—has markedly often been heading to the Eastern part of the continent. Seven of the directors included here are its recipients, quite a few of the rest have already been nominated for it,[10] and two are laureates respectively of the continent's main award (Europe Theatre Prize) and of a special edition of it.

---

[9] Kalina Stefanova-Peteva, *Who Calls the Shots on New York Stages?* (Reading, UK: Harwood Academic Publishers, 1994), p. 44.

[10] According to the rules of the Prize for (New) Theatrical Realities, the nominations are not just year by year; rather, the nominated or theatres enter a constantly expanding list, from which the next winners may get chosen.

From the above examples it may seem that the expansion of theatre's boundaries translates here into a rather free-wheeling handling of the classics. However, while most of the directors included in the book do indeed cut, edit and re-arrange texts, this is rarely done at the expense of the spirit of the work. The essence of the classics is usually not only kept, but gets even more accentuated exactly thanks to this focus not on the letter of the text but on what animates and enlivens it, on what makes the characters utter their words. As Bral says about his *Hamlet – a Commentary*, the aim is "to express what was merely mentioned and not said explicitly by the author."[11] Nekrošius, in turn, often used to have in his productions long scenes with nearly no text, yet via physical actions he made one feel much more palpably what the words had to say. Not that the text was for him of lesser importance, but he had an extraordinary talent for showing what precedes and shapes the words. For him it was not enough to have a character cry on stage and talk about it. He was a master of making the audience *live through* the very journey of this character's tears towards their eyes. In this sense, his theatre was something like psychoanalysis of emotions.

Grzegorz Bral and to some extent the Slovenian Jernej Lonenci even go one step further in this distilling of the classics to their quintessence. In their theatre, the material world, and in some cases the text too, is brought down to the minimum. They do not waste their time stripping life from its façades and appearances; they simply skip this process, aiming at directly entering the territory of the pure spirit. Thus they create, so to speak, a *vertical theatre reality* whose "body" occupies a very sparse horizontal space, in terms of sets, props and stage effects, in stark contrast to the materialism of our time and our sort of horizontal living.

This doesn't mean that Lorenci's *Iliad*, for instance, forgoes the epic of the ancient poem. Yet it is achieved in a stunningly minimalist, yet highly ingenious manner. The main characters—people and gods—sit on chairs, en face to the audience (a typical mise-en-scène of his), with mikes in front of them. These mikes are not there just to amplify their voices, when they pronounce or sing the words of the well-known Trojan war heroes. It is with them that the rumble of the war gets created, the clatter of hoofs, the banging of arms, the very flight of its ten pointless years. And this is done only via a slight finger-tapping on the mikes. This stunningly simple "trick," along with the mighty rhythm of Homer's hexameter and some

[11] From the programme of the show.

xii   THE LIFE-CHANGING THEATRE OF EASTERN EUROPE

brief "interventions" of music, played live on harp, piano and rebeck, creates an extraordinary epic feeling. And since there are no special visual effects (notably, only a few of the directors included here resort to an extensive use of multimedia), the epic becomes even more palpable. For the epic here is exactly on a vertical scale, coming to a large extent from the sound frequencies that attune the audience to special waves, as music does, and transport it to other-worldly dimensions.

At the same time, Lorenci's theatre doesn't entirely shy away from strong carnal accents. In *Iliad*, for instance, there is a real animal corpse on stage, as if taken right from a butcher's shop: it is this corpse that Achilles fiercely beats—a pile of meat left from the human being whom he punishes for the death of Patroclus. Also, for Lorenci the presence of text remains of great importance.

Unlike him, Bral casts the text in *Macbeth* (2008) and *Songs of Lear* (2012) in a role of just another component of the sound/musical score. Both productions are about an hour or so long, yet the energy of the plays remains intact. For Bral does not abridge Shakespeare, he delves deep into the Bard's works, identifies their very core and presents it in a highly intensified way, as if applying the whole-universe-in-a-drop-of-water principle. The final effect of this approach resembles the impact of an ancient Chinese four-line poem and in an inexplicable way manages to convey what the whole plays are about. What makes this possible is the aforementioned unique polyphonic music harmony in Bral's theatre, the way it shapes everything on stage and permeates everything both there and in the hall; not by chance is directing here close to conducting. "Words make you think. Music makes you feel. Song makes you feel your thoughts"[12] was the motto of *Macbeth*. The magnificent music and the way it is rendered in *Songs of Lear* do not only make one feel one's thoughts, but elevate us to an even higher territory—beyond feelings. That place, which the French writer and playwright Erik-Emanuel Schmidt so beautifully describes in his book *My Life with Mozart* as a place where there's just bliss and harmony is restored.

There is one unforgettable scene in *Songs of Lear*, which is a sample of how human bodies can become music itself. The actors, holding drum discs in their hands, form a semi-circle. Gradually the drums become as if extensions of their bodies and, at the same time, it is as if all the actors' bodies turn into one huge drum—a "drum" that also sings and sets the

---

[12] A common quote of E. Y. Harburg.

rhythm with ten pairs of feet. At that moment the musician, who is playing live on a set of instruments, leaves them and goes into the middle of the semi-circle and starts playing on the huge "drum" while it prompts him to quicken the tempo. It is like a metaphysical transformation—a trance-like type of moment for both the actors and the audience.

"Is Shakespeare in the room?" asks the Polish critic Pulka in his review of another breath-taking and fully non-traditional rendering of the Bard by Song of the Goat – *Island*, after *The Tempest*. And the very telling rhetorical answer is: "Yes, in a storm of breaths and loving gestures."[13] I would add that in all these productions, exemplary samples of *vertical theatre reality*, Bral and his team manage to go to the very core of Shakespeare's work and, as a matter of fact, of theatre at its best—that is, of both them being sort of a "tunnel" between the visible and the invisible worlds. This is theatre that catapults us high or deep (depending on the viewpoint) inside us where we can see with *the eyes of our heart* (Ephesians 1:18)—theatre with a distinctly harmonising effect, something truly life-changing in our increasingly disharmonious time.

The propensity of many of the directors included here, as well as of many of their colleagues in Eastern Europe, for looking beyond the text is also an attempt to overcome its limitations in principle—limitations so well captured by the Chinese term for Western drama, "spoken drama." Not by chance has the theatre of Eastern Europe become a frequent guest of the big Chinese theatre festivals.

The Lithuanian Alvis Hermanis sheds additional light on the reasons behind this propensity in the chapter on the directors' pedigree: "around this part of the world and among my generation, a major influence was most certainly the Lithuanian director Eimuntas Nekrošius. The linear theatre, staging plays, especially with our youthful go-getter attitude—it all seemed so senile and boring. Nekrošius offered a whole new ball game! Yes, we had extremely little trust in theatre as simply speaking text. The talking heads to us were just so yesterday."[14]

Actually, Hermanis made his international breakthrough with a production without a single word: *Long Life* (New Riga Theatre, 2003), which has toured the world over and is still on. It presents one day in the life of five pensioners sharing a three-room Soviet-style *communalka* apartment in Riga. The production is a fine blend between hyper-realism

---

[13] Leszek Pulka, "Treasure Island," *teatralny.pl*, 28 December 2016.
[14] See, page 267.

and an overt this-is-theatre approach. The rooms, the kitchen and the bathroom are packed with so many objects that create a stifling effect. Also, the acting is realistic, although, as Hermanis underlines, it follows that part of Stanislavski's theory that he formulated at the end of his life and that is largely an antipode of the well-known Method. At the same time, after entering the apartment through a long corridor with stifling air and hanging laundry, careful not to stumble over the objects piled down its length, the audience finds itself in a simple backstage space, through which it reaches several rows of seats. Then stagehands openly dismantle several painted windows in order to open the view towards the apartment, which is without walls between the rooms. In addition, throughout the show parallel actions take place on stage, none of them more important that the others, and it is the viewers who are to do the "internal editing" (Tarkovski).

While it is still dark, the feeling is as if we are witnessing the waking-up of the apartment: it snores, murmurs, grunts, tosses and turns in its bed, the mattresses squeak, clocks tick-tock. Then an alarm clock rings, a dim light bulb is lit, and another one. A snore breaks and heavy breathing calms down. Feeble hands stretch out of the blankets, thin legs reach out for slippers on the floor… When it is light enough, we see a very sad picture: five old people who are living their last years (or days) amid remnants of their life—presents, awards, idols, squeezed into these rooms—and who try to keep alive some remnants of dignity too by retaining the rituals of their everyday life. They dress very slowly. The clothes hang on their deformed bodies. With trembling hands, a woman gives her husband an injection. On a nail above a door, a neighbour exercises with a bottle of water hanging from elastic. In the kitchen they prepare their scanty food and sit over a slice of bread spread with the fat from yesterday's dinner pan, with eyes empty and hopeless.

We are paying a visit to old age. Yet we are paying a visit to poverty too, which old age translates to in some Eastern European countries. Everything is dismal and squalid. It is cold and the flat's inhabitants are in shabby coats and with hats on. Still, they are alive. One of them plays his almost non-working music player. A woman puts on a necklace before going out. There are even hints of adultery. And, despite all the unavoidable hostilities in this small space, they are fabricating gifts with what they have handy, because it's a neighbour's birthday. Something like a party is thrown, something like a song comes out of their mouths, lips are curved into something like smiles, bodies move into something like dance… Then all

THE LIFE-CHANGING THEATRE OF EASTERN EUROPE   xv

of them go back to their rooms, the outside world deigns to pay a brief visit via the TV news, the lights go off and the apartment again goes to sleep.

Finished is another day of people turned into refugees on their own land. Not by chance, they do not talk. What they have to say is no longer of any relevance. As Hermanis put it, "people of my parents' age became outcasts. In fact, society economically isolated them and put them under the conditions of an anthropological experiment that resembled a reality show with unclear game rules—whether the winner was the one who died first or last was not clear."[15]

Since *Long Life* is not created in the usual straightforward punching manner of political theatre, it has not been widely perceived as a political piece. To me, though, it initiated a wave of special political theatre that corresponds to the non-violent approach in real politics; theatre that is imbued with love and warmth, and prefers "punching with tenderness"—to use a phrase of Hermanis'.[16] It views the state of the world as a reflection of the state of our souls and is therefore not ordinary political theatre, but rather *politics-of-the-soul* theatre. The abovementioned Song of the Goat's four renderings of Shakespeare, for instance, are samples of it too, as well as *On the Edge* by the Bulgarian Alexander Morfov, about which you can read later on in the book. Or another extraordinary non-word production: *Pantagruel's Sister-in-Law* (Radu Stanca National Theatre Sibiu, 2003) by the Romanian Silviu Purcărete, who used Rabelais' classics as a springboard for creating a mighty metaphor of the spirit of our time of consumerism and refined demagoguery; warmth and love being applied there as an ironic counterpoint. In it people voraciously devoured not only food but their fellow kin too, while acting in a seemingly most humane manner. Among the many unforgettable scenes of this production, its culmination stands out. After a long and beautiful prelude of a homely bread-producing process—from dancing flour bags, collective sifting of the flour and kneading, all that accompanied with soothing and merry music—a man is prepared as a loaf of bread, while being taken notably good care of, caressed and consoled. He is then eaten in a similarly benign and also matter-of-fact fashion—after all, bread is the simplest of foods, not a whiff of gluttony there!

---

[15] From the show's programme.

[16] Ian Herbert and Kalina Stefanova, eds., *Theatre and Humanism in a World of Violence* (The Book of the 24th Congress of the IATC) (Sofia: St. Kliment Ohridski University Press, 2009), p. 35.

xvi THE LIFE-CHANGING THEATRE OF EASTERN EUROPE

Interestingly, most of these productions do not have singled-out protagonists. All the characters are of equal importance, forming something like a contemporary type of chorus-cum-main-character taking centre stage—sort of a dramatic (or tragic) hero in the plural. I wonder if this is a reflection of the increasing mass scale of real-life dramas and tragedies today. Certainly this phenomenon is not confined to Eastern European theatre. For instance, the eye-opening theatre installations *Exhibit B* and *Sanctuary* from the South African Brett Bailey and his Third World Bunfight company can certainly be viewed as a very powerful part of this trend.

Of course, along with *politics-of-the-soul* theatre, directly political theatre has also been very strong in Eastern Europe. From the unforgettable political cabaret *Black Land* (2004) by the Hungarian Árpád Schilling and his Krétakör Theatre, which went around the world, to his later socially charged happenings at home. From the poignant socio-political productions of the Romanian Gianiana Cărbunariu, both written and directed by her, to the deliberately provoking theatre of the Croatian-Bosnian Oliver Frljić, who has recently gone to unnecessary over-the-border extremes of the shocking... Most of this theatre is devised, using a combination of a we-do-not-present-ordinary-theatre type of frame/canvas and a true-to-life thread going through it, deftly playing on the edge between facts and fiction, and applying a daring montage to keep everything as an inseparable entity.

It is said that *Long Life* is expected to run until the actors, young at the time of the premiere, reach the age of their characters and do not any longer need make-up and pads. This "meeting" of different ages, or rather the theatre of age performed on the stage of our bodies and especially on the stage of one and the same body, is the focus of another unforgettable production by Hermanis: *Fathers* (2006, Zurich Schauspielhaus). Three men en face to the audience tell their life stories—to each other and to us—talking fondly about their life models, their fathers. While the stories unfold—one after another, interrupting each other, or at times even altogether, as if literally handed on to each other via themes or objects—portraits and photos of the fathers change behind them (brought by stage-hands). The three men first outright enact their fathers, then, gradually, the difference between them and the photos starts melting away and the resemblance becomes amazing. Importantly, the audience witnesses how this happens. For on the tables in front of them numerous objects may pile up, yet naturalism here, as in *Long Life*, is only part of the picture. In real open dressing rooms by the walls, there are real make-up and wig masters and, while a character tells his story, the others get transformed in front of us. So in the next scenes one of the sons would appear with an older cheek with hanging skin (only after several more scenes would the other cheek land on his face!), the other son would have a new, fattened nose, or grey hair... The theatre of life and the life of the theatre don't stop their dance for a minute from the very beginning to the end of the show! At the end, the three have grown even older than the photos behind them and, sitting next to each other, deformed and bent by age, they hold with shaking hands a small photo of a grandchild. However, at the same time, one of them "turns the tape back" and, again in the role of the son, talks about the birth of his daughter. And the production ends. Without having let the audience find out for sure whether the actors have been so fully immersed in the game of performing and have so credibly "become" their fathers, or simply in real life they have come to amazingly resemble their fathers; whether in the end the three are the fathers themselves or the sons after the years have gone by; or both the sons and the fathers have all that time been before us...

Fathers is an exemplary sample of a most refined dance between fact and fiction as well. It is based on the true stories of the three actors, the director and his assistants, which they told each other over the course of several weeks before the rehearsals and then Hermanis created a collage. Yet this is not documentary theatre, this is fiction, as he likes to underline. Again according to him, every human being's life is material for theatre. It is well known that in Berlin, a year before he created *Fathers*, he bet that a piece of theatre could easily be created about the first five people entering a bar, if it were to tell their real stories. In the same vein, he is also famous for having said that what's important for a theatre-maker is not so much being interested in theatre as being interested in life. *Fathers* is Hermanis' hats-off to Life as the greatest playwright in whose dramas we so convincingly act throughout our lives.

* * *

I can continue telling you about more productions by the directors included here that have made me feel like Pamuk's character. Of course, not all of them have created theatre that has had such an effect on me. Yet other people have in turn been in the shoes of Pamuk's character when watching their productions. And, of course, there are many other directors in Eastern Europe who have created memorable theatre that has changed lives and has also changed the face of their nation's theatres. To bring the final number of directors for this book down to twenty, after consultations with a lot of colleagues I've come up with the current choice. I would like to underline that the aim of the book is not to present a detailed analysis of the theatre in each and every country of the region—such an aim would require a far larger number of chapters and a different, more inclusive approach. Therefore there are countries not "represented" here. Or vice versa, there are six directors from Poland—more than from any other nation. For the aim of the book is not to pursue a national "quota" within the selection either. The directors included here have been major catalysts for a change in the face of Eastern European theatre at large during the last three decades—this is the main criterion for selection. So hopefully, a general picture of the theatre there will emerge from the book too. As already mentioned earlier, they have exerted a substantial influence on the overall European theatre as well and, by pushing theatre ahead into new territories, they have enriched and enhanced the perception of theatre as an art form in principle on the world stage. Their very names have been drawing audiences in their countries, on the international festival circuit and in theatres beyond national borders alike.

* * *

While I'm writing these lines, theatres around the world are dark, the pandemic rages and the final song of Lorenci's *Iliad* resounds in my mind: "We will die/Today or tomorrow/Life is what we borrow." At the end of the production's first part, Achilles' mother, appearing as a vision, outlines two possible paths for her son—a short life and immortal death or a long life without any trace of him left afterwards. Fully appropriate to the modern nuance of this choice, Achilles sits at this moment in front of a bulb-framed, modern dressing-room table mirror. After she disappears, he remains there, alone and silent, with a background of the rhythm created by the narrator on the mike—as if a fading echo of the sorrow in the mother's voice and, in her face, of an invisible Chorus who's been trying to guide people, blind to the right path from days of yore.

"Whenever there's a playhouse, the world will not go on amiss,"[17] wrote William Hazlitt about 200 years ago in his essay *On Actors and Acting.* Hopefully, when you are reading this book, the playhouses will have already been re-opened and we will start paying more heed to what great theatre has always been trying to do for us: to lift up the invisible curtains before our eyes, so that we can see through into the immaterial and get an insight into the essence of our seemingly only material world—into what really matters. This is the mission the directors included here have been trying to contribute to with their work.

Sofia, Bulgaria   Kalina Stefanova

REFERENCES

Erml, Richard, *Reflex*, as quoted by the programme of the Pilsen Theatre festival, 2014.

Herbert, Ian and Kalina Stefanova, eds., *Theatre and Humanism in a World of Violence* (The Book of the 24th Congress of the IATC) (Sofia: St. Kliment Ohridski University Press, 2009).

Hinchliffe, Arnold P., ed. *Drama Criticism: Developments since Ibsen* (London: Macmillan, 1979).

Korsunovas, Oskaras, https://www.okt.lt/spektakliai/hamletas/ (accessed March 22, 2020).

Kott, Jan, *Shakespeare Our Contemporary* (London: Methuen, 1965).

Pamuk, Orhan, *The New Life* (London: Macmillan Publishers, 2014).

Pulka, Leszek, *Treasure Island, teatralny.pl,* 28 December 2016.

Sakowska, Alexandra, "The Politics of Space – Jan Klata's H. at Gdansk Shipyard, Warehouse 42A," *Romanian Shakespeare Journal,* issue 1, 2013.

Stefanova-Peteva, Kalina, *Who Calls the Shots on New York Stages?* (Reading, UK: Harwood Academic Publishers, 1994).

[17] Arnold P.Hinchliffe, ed., *Drama Criticism: Developments since Ibsen,* Macmillan, 1979.

THE DIRECTORS OF EASTERN EUROPE

During the 1960s, the theatre of the European continent between Germany and Russia, almost totally ignored by Western European and American theatre historians for the past several decades, once again began to attract the attention of Western scholars. Directors like Grotowski, Kantor, Ciulei and Svoboda and dramatists like Mrożek, Havel, Różewicz and Kohout became a much more familiar part of the international theatre scene. A clear illustration of this was the appearance in Spring 1967 of a special issue of the *Tulane Drama Review*, at that time the most important reflector of current trends in theatre scholarship, devoted to Eastern Europe. All of the names I have just mentioned (except Kantor) were discussed in that important issue, and the leading article, by Henry Popkin, began boldly: "Right now, the Eastern European theatre is the most exciting in the world."[1]

Since the 1960s much more attention has been devoted to Eastern Europe, especially Poland, and international tours and festivals have enabled audiences outside this area to gain some idea of the continuing depth, innovation and variety of the theatre it offers. Even so, there remain far fewer sources of information on this rich theatrical culture than in the historically better represented theatre traditions of Western Europe. The most significant contributions in recent years are two important collections of essays: the 2007 *Theatre and Performance in Eastern Europe:*

---

[1] Henry Popkin, "Theatre in Eastern Europe," *Tulane Drama Review* 11:3 (Spring, 1967), 23.

The Changing Scene[2] and *Eastern European Theatre after the Iron Curtain*.[3] Both of these volumes, with slightly different mixes of countries, survey this part of Europe since the key modern event, the Fall of the Iron Curtain in 1989. Both consider a variety of aspects of theatre in Eastern Europe, predominantly directing, theatre organisation and playwrighting.

The present volume, in addition to presenting a more up-to-date survey of this rapidly changing region, focuses, as neither of these previous collections did, on a particular but central part of modern theatrical culture, the director. Ever since the beginning of the previous century, the director has served as a central creative power in the modern theatre, and nowhere has this been more evident that in the theatres of Eastern Europe. Those with an interest in international theatre will almost certainly be familiar with the names of distinctly more theatre directors from Eastern Europe during the past half century than they will with the names of playwrights from these same countries, and this is not at all surprising, seeing that it is the directors who have created the most innovative and memorable theatre experiences in recent theatrical memory.

Innovation is a key term here, since closely connected with the concept of the modern director, especially in Europe, has been the idea of innovation, of taking the art of the theatre in often surprising new directions. Again, the leading directors of Eastern Europe have for decades been particularly noted for expanding the boundaries of our theatrical experience. This is as true for the current generation of directors as it was for their predecessors at the end of the last century and the opening of this one. The present selection has focused upon this quality, selecting twenty East European artists who have been particularly noted for their contributions to change and innovation in this art.

Unlike my co-editor, I have unfortunately not seen a great number of the productions discussed in this informative collection, but those I have been privileged to see I count among the most memorable of my international theatre experiences. I was fortunate enough to see Eimatus Nekrošius' stunning *Hamlet* in 1998 at the Teatro Fabbricone in Prato, Italy, one of Europe's major centres for international experimental theatre, and the density, complexity and sheer beauty of its visual images made me all too aware of how much I was missing by not seeing more of the work of this Baltic artist and of his Eastern European contemporaries.

---

[2] Dennis Barnett and Arthur Skelton, eds. (Plymouth: Scarecrow Press, 2007).
[3] Kalina Stefanova, ed. (London: Routledge, 2010).

The present collection can only suggest the richness of this work, but it does provide a much-needed opportunity for theatre lovers like myself to gain a better knowledge of the most recent work in this fascinating, but all too little reported part of the theatre world.

New York, NY   Marvin Carlson

References

Dennis Barnett, Dennis and Arthur Skelton, eds. *Theatre and Performance in Eastern Europe: The Changing Scene* (Plymouth: Scarecrow Press, 2007).

Popkin, Henry, "Theatre in Eastern Europe," *Tulane Drama Review* 11:3 (Spring, 1967), 23.

Stefanova, Kalina, ed. *Eastern European Theatre after the Iron Curtain* (London: Routledge, 2010).

Acknowledgements

I'd like to express my deepest gratitude to Prof. Marvin Carlson for standing by me from the first day I suggested to him we do this book. Special thanks go to Tomas René, Palgrave Macmillan's editor, who believed in and backed our proposal, as well as to the current editor Eileen Srebernik and the editorial assistant Jack Heeney for their support. This book is a result of the truly collective work of all contributors. Moreover, this work is done entirely for love both figuratively and literally, in the usual spirit of Eastern Europe. I cannot thank them enough that they agreed to participate in this endeavour and did it very eagerly and with true zest. Many thanks also go to the directors who were so kind as to agree to contribute to the book by sharing their views. Finally, a thank-you to the organisers of festivals throughout Eastern Europe who have kindly given me the chance to keep up with the developments in the fascinating, ever-changing and life-changing theatre of our part of the world.

Kalina Stefanova

CONTENTS

Grzegorz Bral: Cosmopolitan Experiments in Theatre 1
Tomasz Wiśniewski

My Name Is Gianina Cărbunariu: I'm a Lioness 17
Maria Zărnescu

Oliver Frljić or the Theatre of Provocation 31
Kim Cuculić

Alvis Hermanis: "To Be Everything and Nothing at All" 43
Edīte Tišheizere

**Grzegorz Jarzyna's Theatre of Post-Dramatic Joy and
Recognition** 57
Artur Duda

Jan Klata: The Social-Identity DJ of the Polish Theatre 71
Katarzyna Kręglewska

**"What Is Hecuba to Him or He to Hecuba?" or the Theatre of
Oskaras Koršunovas** 85
Rasa Vasinauskaitė

xxvii

xxviii CONTENTS

Jernej Lorenci: "People Are the Key" 97
Blaž Lukan

Krystian Lupa: The Maestro They ~~Criticise~~ Love 109
Katarzyna Waligóra

Dark Visions of Jan Mikulášek 123
Kamila Černá

Alexander Morfov, the Game-Changer, and His Collective Theatre 135
Kalina Stefanova

Eimuntas Nekrošius: The Poetics of Paradise and Hell 147
Rasa Vasinauskaitė

Béla Pintér and His Postmodern National Theatre 159
Noémi Herczog

Silviu Purcărete: The Master of Rich Theatre 171
Octavian Saiu

From the Theatron to the Agora: Changing Concepts of Theatricality in Schilling Árpád's Oeuvre 185
Gabriella Schuller

Andrei Şerban: The Search for 'New Forms' 197
Ion M. Tomuş

Beauty by Instinct or Daniel Špinar's Theatre of Style 207
Michal Zahálka

Włodzimierz Staniewski: (Re-)Constructing Traditions and Archetypes 221
Tomasz Wiśniewski

Rimas Tuminas: A Poetic View of Theatre   237
Dmitry Trubotchkin

Krzysztof Warlikowski: A Beautiful Shock Therapy   249
Małgorzata Jarmułowicz

An Attempt at Drawing an Artistic Family Tree   263
Marvin Carlson, Kamila Černá, Kim Cuculić, Artur Duda,
Katarzyna Kręglewska, Blaž Lukan, Octavian Saiu, Kalina
Stefanova, Edīte Tišheizere, Dmitry Trubotchkin, Rasa
Vasinauskaitė, Tomasz Wiśniewski, and Michal Zahálka

The Stakes Today   279
Marvin Carlson, Kamila Černá, Kim Cuculić, Artur Duda,
Katarzyna Kręglewska, Blaž Lukan, Octavian Saiu, Kalina
Stefanova, Edīte Tišheizere, Dmitry Trubotchkin, Rasa
Vasinauskaitė, Tomasz Wiśniewski, and Michal Zahálka

Index   295

Notes on Contributors

Marvin Carlson is a theatre, drama and performance studies scholar. He is a Distinguished Professor of Theatre, Comparative Literature and Middle Eastern Studies and holder of the Sidney E. Cohn Chair at the Graduate Center of the City University of New York. He has received an honorary doctorate from the University of Athens, the ATHE Career Achievement Award, the ASTR Distinguished Scholarship Award, the George Jean Nathan Award for Dramatic Criticism, and the Calloway Prize for writing in theatre. He is the founding editor of the journals *Western European Stages* and *Arab Stages*. He is the author of twenty-three books, translated into seventeen languages. Among these are *Theories of the Theatre* (1993), *Places of Performance* (1989) and *Performance: A Critical Introduction* (1996). His most recent books are *10,000 Nights* (Michigan, 2017) and *Theatre and Islam* (Macmillan, 2019).

Kamila Černá is a theatre journalist, editor and cultural manager. She is a graduate of the Theatre and Film Studies Department at Charles University in Prague. Since 1993 she has worked as an editor of the Arts and Theatre Institute's Publishing Department and since 2001 she has also been the head of this department. She manages the book series Contemporary Drama and World Theatre and is the editor-in-chief of *Czech Theatre* magazine. In her scholarly and journalistic work, she focuses on contemporary Czech and European theatre. She publishes in theatre journals in the Czech Republic and abroad (*World and Theatre, Theatre News, Puppeteer, Lidové noviny, Teatrul, Teatr Polski*

xxxi

xxxii NOTES ON CONTRIBUTORS

et al.). She has taken part in numerous publishing projects, was the leader of the Visegrad Drama grant project of Czech Theatre and Drama, a project aimed at the German cultural context. As a dramaturg she prepared two showcases of Czech theatre, and has been on the programme board of the International Festival DIVADLO (Theatre) in Pilsen; she also served as the festival's dramaturg-in-chief (2007–2014).

Kim Cuculić is a culture columnist, journalist, theatre critic and editor at *Novi list*, a daily paper from the city of Rijeka in Croatia. She graduated in Croatian language and literature from the University of Rijeka, Croatia. Apart from *Novi list*, she has cooperated with a number of other Croatian newspapers and magazines, as well as European Stages, CUNY, USA. As a journalist and critic she has covered all major cultural events in Croatia, as well as some in Poland, Slovenia, Hungary, Germany, Italy, the UK, Austria and South Korea. She was a member of the editorial board of *Rival*, a literature magazine that was published in Rijeka. She has authored the books *Peti red, parter/The Fifth Row, Stalls* and *The Classics, Our Contemporaries*. She is a member of the Croatian Association of Theatre Critics and Theatre Scholars, the Croatian Journalist Association, ITI and AICT.

Artur Duda is a theatre and performance researcher. He teaches at the Faculty of Humanities of Nicolaus Copernicus University Toruń, Poland. He is co-leader of the Research Team—Performance and Drama Translation Studies. His main academic interests are Eastern European contemporary theatre, theatre and other live performances as human media, and theories of theatre and performance. He is author of the books *Teatr realności/ Theatre of Reality* (2006), *Performans na żywo jako medium i obiekt mediatyzacji/Live Performance as Medium and Mediatized Object* (2011), *Teatr w Toruniu 1904–1944. Opowieść performatyczna/Theatre in Toruń 1904–1944. A Performative Story* (2020), and a co-editor of a collective monograph, *Teatr wśród mediów/Theatre among Media* (2015). He is a DAAD Fellow (Free University Berlin, 2001, supervisor: Prof. Erika Fischer-Lichte), theatre reviewer and constant collaborator of the Polish journals *Teatr, Pamiętnik Teatralny, Didaskalia* and *Litteraria Copernicana*. A member of IFTR, Gesellschaft für Theaterwissenschaft (GTW) and Polish Society for Theatre Research (PTBT), he is a constant collaborator of the Centre for Eastern European Theatre, founded in 2018 by the Shanghai Theatre Academy.

Noémi Herczog is a critic, editor and scholar working in Budapest (Hungary) and Cluj (Romania). She is a faculty member at Babeş–Bolyai University, Theatre and Film, Cluj, an editor of the oldest Hungarian theatre journal, *SZÍNHÁZ/Theatre*, and has a theatre column in the Hungarian cultural-political weekly *Élet és Irodalom/Life and Literature*. She is a former activist of One Million for the Freedom of Speech—a Hungarian civic movement (Milla). Since 2013, she has regularly given classes to applied theatre students at the University of Theatre and Film, Budapest. She is co-editor of the theatrical book series *SzínText*, and co-curator of projects in the field of Hungarian independent theatre, such as dunaPart Hungarian Platform and the Péter Halász Award. In 2018 she received a CITD grant for a lecture tour in the USA. Her first book is to come out in 2021: *The Lawyer, The Prosecutor and the Escapologist: The History of Reporting Theatre Criticism (Criticism of Denunciation) in Hungary (1956–1989)*.

Małgorzata Jarmułowicz is a theatre, drama and performance studies scholar. She is Head of the Department for Drama, Theatre and Performance Studies, University of Gdańsk, and Deputy Head of the Institute of Polish Philology. Her research concentrates on performative arts, particularly on the issues of evil and totalitarian regimes in contemporary theatre and drama, Polish and foreign theatre of the absurd, the ritual sources of theatre and traditional Asian performance. She has authored and edited several books, including *Sezony błędów i wypaczeń. Socrealizm w dramacie i teatrze polskim/The Seasons of Errors and Misrepresentations* (2003), *Teatralność zła/The Theatricality of Evil* (2012), *Teatr—terytorium terroru/Theatre as a Territory of Terror* (2008), *Ogród sztuk Indonezji—Taman Seni Indonesia/The Garden of Art—Taman Seni Indonesia* (2015) and *Ogród sztuk. Maska/The Garden of Art. The Mask* (2017), as well as reviews and essays in journals and collected volumes.

Katarzyna Kręglewska is a theatre studies scholar and translator. She works as an Assistant Professor in the Department of Drama, Theatre and Performance at the University of Gdańsk, Poland. She has authored *Polskie pamiętniki teatralne. Teoria—historia—teksty/Polish Theatre Memoirs: Theory—History—Texts* (2017) and co-edited several books on Polish theatre and literature. Since 2016 she has been Deputy Director of Research at the Between.Pomiędzy Festival.

xxxiv   NOTES ON CONTRIBUTORS

Blaž Lukan received his PhD from the Academy of Theatre, Radio, Film and Television of the University of Ljubljana in 2006. In addition to working as a dramaturg in theatre and film, he writes theatre reviews, texts accompanying published plays by Slovenian and foreign authors, as well as scientific papers in the field of drama and the theory of performing arts. He was the artistic director of the Glej Experimental Theatre (1985–1988) and Celje People's Theatre (1989–1993). From 2008 to 2012 he was the president of the Association of Theatre Critics and Researchers of Slovenia. He is the author of numerous books, among them *Gledališki pojmovnik za mlade/Theatre Glossary for Young People* (1996), *Slovenska dramaturgija: dramaturgija kot gledališka praksa/Slovenian Dramaturgy: Dramaturgy as Theatre Practice* (2001), *Performativne pisave: razprave o performansu in gledališču/Performative Gestures: Essays on Performance Art and Theatre* (2013) and *Turški lok/Turkish Bow: Essays on Slovenian Drama* (2019).

Octavian Saiu is a scholar and professional theatre critic. He holds a PhD in Theatre Studies from the National University of Theatre and Film in Romania and a PhD in Comparative Literature from the University of Otago in New Zealand. He completed his Post-Doc in Modern Literature at the University of Otago. Currently, he teaches on the postgraduate programmes of various universities in Europe and Asia. He has been Chair of the Conferences of Sibiu International Theatre Festival, and has given talks and chaired conferences at Edinburgh International Festival, the Theatre Olympics (Wroclaw and Toga), etc. He is Adjunct Secretary General of the International Association of Theatre Critics (IATC) and President of the Romanian Section—Theatre Studies of IATC. He is the author of eleven books on theatre. He received the Critics' Award in 2010, the Award of the Union of Theatre Artists (UNITER) in 2013, and the Order of Cultural Merit from the President of Romania in 2020.

Gabriella Schuller is a theatrologist who has authored many articles on contemporary Hungarian theatre, theatre history of the socialist era and visual studies. Between 2000 and 2016 she worked as a Lecturer on Theatre History at the University of Pannonia and Karoli Gaspar University of the Reformed Church. Since 2016 she has been a researcher and archivist at Artpool Art Research Center—Museum of Fine Arts, Budapest. She is a member of the Theatre and Film Studies Committee of the Hungarian Academy of Sciences.

NOTES ON CONTRIBUTORS   xxxv

Kalina Stefanova is author/editor of sixteen books: fourteen books on theatre, some of them launched in New York, London and Wroclaw, and two fiction ones, published in nine countries, in two editions in China. She was a Fulbright Visiting Scholar at the New York University and has been a Visiting Scholar at the University of Cape Town, South Africa, Meiji University, Japan, and the Shanghai Theatre Academy, China, among others. In 2016 she was appointed as Visiting Distinguished Professor of the Arts School of Wuhan University, China, as well as Distinguished Researcher of the Chinese Arts Criticism Foundation of Wuhan University. She served as Vice President of the International Association of Theatre Critics (IATC; 2001/2006) and as its Director Symposia (2006–2010). In 2007, she was the dramaturg of the highly acclaimed production of *Pentecost* by David Edgar, directed by Mladen Kiselov, at the Stratford Festival of Canada. Since 2001 she has regularly served as an evaluation expert for cultural and educational programmes of the European Commission. Currently she teaches at the National Academy for Theatre and Film Arts, in Sofia.

Edīte Tišheizere is a Latvian theatre scholar and critic. She graduated from the State Institute of Theatre Arts in Moscow (GITIS, 1976–1985). She is senior researcher at the Institute of Literature, Folklore and Art, University of Latvia, and editor-in-chief of the theatre magazine *Teātra Vēstnesis*. In 2017, she received Normunds Naumanis' National Award for Art Criticism. Her publications include two books: *Abpus rāmjiem. Sarunas par dzīvi un mākslu/Beyond Frames: On Life and Art* (2015) and *Režijas virzieni un personības Liepājas teātrī/Directors and Directing in Liepaja Theatre* (2010). She has contributed to numerous collective monographs on directing, set design, the history of Latvian theatre and the historical avant-garde. Her research interests are interaction between directing and set design, the historical avant-garde and the neo-avant-garde.

Ion M. Tomuș teaches at "Lucian Blaga" University, Sibiu, Department of Drama and Theatre Studies (courses in History of Romanian Theatre, History of Worldwide Theatre, Text and Stage Image and Drama Theory). He is a member of the Centre for Advanced Studies in the Field of Performing Arts (Cavas). In 2013 he finished a postdoctoral study together with the Romanian Academy, focused on the topic of the modern international theatre festival, with case studies on Edinburgh International Festival, Festival d'Avignon and Sibiu

International Theatre Festival. He has published studies, book reviews, theatre reviews and essays in prestigious cultural magazines and academic journals in Romania and Europe. Since 2005, he has been part of the staff at Sibiu International Theatre Festival.

Dmitry Trubotchkin is Head of the Department of Classical Art at the State Institute for Art Studies, Moscow, teaches at the Russian Institute of Theatre Arts (GITIS) and is Assistant to the Artistic Director of the Vakhtangov Theatre. He is also a member of the Board of the Theatre Union of the Russian Federation and Head of the Department of Art Studies at the Russian Fund of Basic Research. He has published extensively (in Russian, English and Italian) and made presentations at conferences around the world on European classical theatre and on contemporary Russian theatre. His monographs, in Russian and published in Moscow, include *Ancient Greek Theatre* (2016), *Rimas Tuminas: Moscow Productions* (2015), *Understanding the Theatre of Arkady Raikin* (2011), *Ancient Literature and Dramaturgy* (2010) and *Roman Palliata in Action* (2005).

Rasa Vasinauskaitė studied at Saint Petersburg State Theatre Academy (1987–1992). Her PhD thesis is on "The Mask and Its Influences on Theatre of 20th Century and on Systems of Acting." She is Head of the Department of Music and Theatre History at the Culture, Philosophy and Arts Institute. She is also Professor at the Department of Art History and Theory of Lithuanian Music and Theatre Academy. She has authored *Theatre of Impermanence. Outline of Lithuanian Directing in 1990–2001* (2010) and has taken part in collective monographs on the Lithuanian theatre and theatre history, among which are *Post-Soviet Lithuanian Theatre: History, Identity, Memory* (2014), *Theatre of Eimuntas Nekrošius: Interviews, Articles, Reviews* (2012) and *Lithuanian Theatre History 1929–1990* (2002, 2006, 2009). She has written numerous scholarly and popular articles on contemporary theatre and Lithuanian theatre history. She is a member of the International Association of Theatre Critics and the Lithuanian Association of Performing Arts Critics.

Katarzyna Waligóra is a PhD candidate at the Theatre and Drama Department at Jagiellonian University in Cracow. She authored the book *Koń nie jest nowy (O rekwizytach w teatrze)/It's Not a Brand New Horse (on Theatrical Props)*, 2017, and is a regular contributor to the Polish theatrical magazine *Didaskalia*. She is the curator of the XVIII edition of theatre Festival Prapremiery in Bydgoszcz. As a theatre teacher she teaches contemporary theatre, performance art and performance studies in various Polish institutions for both adult and young students. Her current research interests lie in embarrassing female performances—a specific form of emancipatory women's participation in the public sphere.

Tomasz Wiśniewski is Head of the Performing Arts Division at the University of Gdańsk. In 2016–2019 he was Deputy Director for Research in the Institute of English and American Studies at the University of Gdańsk. He is the founder of the Between.Pomiędzy Festival, and the Beckett Research Group in Gdańsk. He has published *Complicité, Theatre and Aesthetics* (Palgrave Macmillan, 2016), a monograph on Samuel Beckett (Universitas, 2006) and (co-)edited several academic publications, including a bilingual edition of *The Historie of Lord's Glorious Resurrection* (Teatr Wierszalin, 2017) and interviews and articles that celebrate the fortieth anniversary of Włodzimierz Staniewski's OPT "Gardzienice" (Konteksty, 2018). Since 2018 he has been a member of the board of the Polish Association for the Study of English and of the Program Board of the Gdańsk Shakespeare Theatre.

Michal Zahálka is a theatre scholar, translator, book editor and dramaturg, and a graduate of the Theatre Studies Department at the Faculty of Arts of Charles University. Originally a theatre critic, he covered many of Daniel Špinar's productions in regional theatres and has already published a shorter English-language study about several of them in the *Czech Theatre* magazine, of which he was one of the editors from 2013 until the magazine's final 2019 issue. In the 2018/2019 and 2019/2020 seasons, he worked as dramaturg at Prague City Theatres. He works as editor at the Arts and Theatre Institute's publishing department and as one of the programmers of the International Festival THEATRE/DIVADLO in Pilsen. He regularly translates French and English drama and does research on the subject of theatre translation. Currently he is translating John Dryden's *All for Love* as part of a large publishing project dedicated to English Restoration drama.

Maria Zărnescu is a Romanian theatre theorist and critic. She graduated from the Theatre Faculty, Department of Theatre Studies at the National University of Theatre and Cinematography UNATC "I.L. Caragiale" Bucharest (2005) and the Chemistry Faculty of the Polytechnic University of Bucharest (1993). Her doctoral thesis is "From Theatre Play to

xxxviii   NOTES ON CONTRIBUTORS

Musical." She is Associate Professor and, since 2017, Head of the Theatre Studies Department of UNATC. She has published studies, essays and theatrical reviews in national and international magazines, like *Critical Stages*, *European Stages*, *Yorick*, *Teatrul Azi* and *Concept*. She is the author of the books *Music and Muses* (2015) and *The Sound of Theatre Music* (2016). She is a member of the Board of the International Association of Theatre Critics (IATC)—Theatre Studies and a member of the Romanian Association of Theatre Professionals (UNITER). She holds the UNITER Award for Best Theatre Critic in 2015.

LIST OF FIGURES

Grzegorz Bral: Cosmopolitan Experiments in Theatre

Image 1   *Hamlet—a Commentary*, directed by Grzegorz Bral, Song of the Goat Theatre, 2017. From the left: Julianna Bloodgood, Natalia Voskoboynikov, Jenny Kaatz, Olga Kunicka, Magdalena Szczerbowska, Dimitris Varkas, Volodymyr Andrushchak, Peyman Sichani, Julien Touati, Łukasz Wójcik. (Photo by Mateusz Bral)   14

My Name Is Gianina Cărbunariu: I'm a Lioness

Image 1   *Common People*, directed by Gianiana Cărbunariu, National Theatre Sibiu, 2017. (Photo by Adi Bulboacă)   28

Oliver Frljić or the Theatre of Provocation

Image 1   *Turbofolk*, directed by Oliver Frljić, National Theatre of Ivan pl. Zajc, Rijeka, 2008. (Photo by Dražen Šokčević)   40

Alvis Hermanis: "To Be Everything and Nothing at All"

Image 1   *Long Life*, directed by Alvis Hermanis, New Rīga Theatre, 2003. (Photo by Jānis Deinats)   54

Grzegorz Jarzyna's Theatre of Post-Dramatic Joy and Recognition

Image 1   *We Are Pretty Good*, directed by Grzegorz Jarzyna, TR Warsaw, 2009, Lech Łotocki as Gloomy Old Biddy. (Photo by Natalia Kabanow, from TR Warsaw Archive)   67

xl   LIST OF FIGURES

Jan Klata: The Social-Identity DJ of the Polish Theatre

Image 1   *H.* directed by Jan Klata, Teatr Wybrzeże, 2004. (Photo by
Wiesław Czerniawski)   83

"What Is Hecuba to Him or He to Hecuba?" or the Theatre of Oskaras Koršunovas

Image 1   *Hamlet,* directed by Oskaras Koršunovas, OKT, 2008,
Gertrude—Nelė Savičenko, Hamlet—Darius Meškauskas,
Claudius—Dainius Gavenonis. (Photo by Dmitrij Matvejev)   95

Jernej Lorenci: "People Are the Key"

Image 1   *The Iliad,* directed by Jernej Lorenci, Slovenian National Theatre
Drama Ljubljana, Ljubljana City Theatre and The Cankar
Centre, 2015, from left to right: Aljaž Jovanović, Marko Mandić,
Jette Ostan Vejrup, Gregor Luštek. (Photo by Peter Uhan)   107

Krystian Lupa: The Maestro They Criticise Love

Image 1   *CAPRI—the Island of Fugitives,* directed by Krystian Lupa,
Powszechny Theatre, 2019. (Photos by Natalia Kabanow)   119

Dark Visions of Jan Mikulášek

Image 1   *Golden Sixties* by Pavel Juráček, Jan Mikulášek, Dora
Viceníková, directed by Jan Mikulášek, Divadlo Na zábradlí
(Theatre on the Balustrade), 2013. (Photo by Viktor Kronbauer)   134

Alexander Morfov, the Game-Changer and His Collective Theatre

Image 1   *On the Edge,* directed by Alexander Morfov, National Theatre,
Bulgaria, 2015. (Photo by Elena Nikolaeva)   145

Eimuntas Nekrošius: The Poetics of Paradise and Hell

Image 1   *Hamlet,* directed by Eimuntas Nekrošius, Meno Fortas Theatre,
1997, Hamlet—Andrius Mamontovas. (Photo by Dmitrij
Matvejev)   157

Béla Pintér and His Postmodern National Theatre

Image 1   *Kaisers TV, Ungarn,* directed by Béla Pintér, Béla Pintér and
Company, 2011, Béla Pintér in the production. (Photo by
Zsuzsa Koncz)   168

LIST OF FIGURES   xli

Silviu Purcărete: The Master of Rich Theatre

Image 1   *Faust*, directed by Silviu Purcărete, 'Radu Stanca' National
Theatre, 2007. (Photo by Mihaela Marin)   183

From the Theatron to the Agora: Changing Concepts of Theatricality in Schilling Árpád's Oeuvre

Image 1   *Pansion Eden*, directed by Árpád Schilling, Zagrebačko kazalište
mladih (Zagreb Youth Theatre), 2018. (Photo by Marco
Ercegovic)   194

Andrei Șerban: The Search for 'New Forms'

Image 1   *Richard III*, directed by Andrei Șerban, Bulandra, 2019.
(Photo by Mihaela Marin)   204

Beauty by Instinct or Daniel Špinar's Theatre of Style

Image 1   *Hamlet*, directed by Daniel Špinar, Švanda Theatre, 2013,
Patrik Děrgel as Hamlet and Marek Pospíchal as Horatio,
(Photo by Alena Hrbková)   218

Włodzimierz Staniewski: (Re-)Constructing Traditions and Archetypes

Image 1   *The Wedding*, directed by Włodzimierz Staniewski,
"Gardzienice," 2017, Photo by Bartłomiej Górniak   234

Rimas Tuminas: A Poetic View of Theatre

Image 1   *Eugene Onegin*, directed by Rimas Tuminas, Vakhtangov
Theatre, Moscow, 2013. (Photo by Valery Myasnikov, Courtesy
of the Vakhtangov Theatre, Moscow)   246

Krzysztof Warlikowski: A Beautiful Shock Therapy

Image 1   *We Are Leaving*, directed by Krzysztof Warlikowski, Nowy
Teatr, 2018. (Photo by Magda Hueckel)   260

An Attempt at Drawing an Artistic Family Tree

Image 1   A drawing by Krystian Lupa of his artistic family tree   270

Grzegorz Bral: Cosmopolitan Experiments in Theatre

Tomasz Wiśniewski

INTERNATIONAL STATUS

Born in 1961 in Gdańsk, Grzegorz Bral works in the city of Wrocław, where Teatr Pieśń Kozła—internationally known as Song of the Goat Theatre—has been based ever since it was established in 1996 by him and Anna Zubrzycki. Over the years, the company has intensely explored the wealth of performative skills, exploited the potential of polyphonic vocal traditions, cultivated powerful physical training and mastered the precision of collaborative ensemble formation. Bral's innovative treatment of twentieth-century experimental theatre has been firmly manifested, not least by the decision to establish the company in the city commonly associated with the legacy of Jerzy Grotowski. There is a critical consensus that Bral's productions are marked by a distinctive artistic signature that interweaves archetypal universality with formal experiments.

T. Wiśniewski (✉)
University of Gdańsk, Gdańsk, Poland
e-mail: tomasz.wisniewski@ug.edu.pl

© The Author(s), under exclusive license to Springer Nature Switzerland AG 2021
K. Stefanova, M. Carlson (eds.), *20 Ground-Breaking Directors of Eastern Europe*, https://doi.org/10.1007/978-3-030-52935-2_1

Global recognition of Song of the Goat Theatre has been confirmed by international tours—in the USA, South America, Great Britain, Georgia, Italy, Israel and China, among others. Frequent presentations at the Edinburgh Fringe resulted not only in awards (e.g. Scotsman Fringe First, 2004 and 2012; Performance and Stage Award for Acting Excellence, 2007; Herald Archangel, 2012), but also in a two-year project focused on exploration of Scottish and Gaelic vocal traditions. Commissioned by Eleven and Summerhall performative arts programme, the project resulted in *Return to the Voice*. The production was originally staged in St Giles Cathedral at the Edinburgh Fringe in 2014, weeks before the independence referendum.[1]

Other distinctive honours include the audience award at the MESS Festival in Sarajevo (2006), the International Theatre Institute (ITI) Award for promoting Polish culture abroad (2010) and numerous awards in Poland.[2] In 2019 alone, productions of Song of the Goat Theatre were presented in Berkeley (University of California), London (Shakespeare's Globe), Shanghai, Jerusalem (Israel Festival) and at the Grotowski Fest in Warsaw. In the latter case, Bral's monumental production of *Anty-Gone* concluded—to enormous applause from the audience—the festival, which was a major global celebration of the twentieth anniversary of the death of Jerzy Grotowski.[3]

Formative Experience and the Company's Formation

Notwithstanding the frequent association with Grotowski, Bral stresses that his sole personal link with him was the formative experience of watching *Apocalypsis cum figuris...* at the age of 16. It was this production that fostered his life-long vocation as a theatre-maker. After studying in Gdańsk, Lublin, Wrocław and Warsaw, he joined Włodzimierz Staniewski's "Gardzienice," where he worked from 1988 to 1991, soon to become one of the leading actors and trainers. Given the chance to collaborate with the Royal Shakespeare Company and the Living Theatre, he gained indispensable performative experience that was to be later developed in his

---

[1] See http://www.elevenhq.com/tg_portfolios/return-to-the-voice/ (accessed on 28 June 2019).

[2] For further details see http://piesnkozla.pl/en/our-theatre#170-history (accessed on 28 June 2019).

[3] See Ewa Bąk's review, "39. WST Anty-Gone Tryptyk Teatr Pieśń later everybody" http://www.e-teatr.pl/pl/artykuly/274285.html (accessed on 28 June 2019).

idiosyncratic way. Bral's work for Staniewski's "Gardzienice" may be seen as the formative experience for his artistic career.

In 1991, Bral left "Gardzienice" and he was followed in 1993 by Anna Zubrzycki, also an actress there, in what was then seen as an artistic "schism," so as to pursue their independent professional paths. Their profound interest in the ancient Greek tradition of dithyramb—a choral hymn praising the god Dionysus—was to determine the direction of their artistic pursuit and motivated an innovative exploration of archetypal vocal traditions. They moved to Wrocław where in 1997 they founded a company that was initially referred to as "Tragos," and since 1998 as Song of the Goat Theatre. Initially hosted by the newly founded Grotowski Institute and the Institute of Theatre–Culture Findings in Wrocław, in 2002 the company was offered unusual premises in the refectory of the thirteenth-century monastery building where it rehearsed and performed till June 2019.[4]

BRAVE, THE TIBETAN LINK AND OTHER INITIATIVES

Apart from strictly theatrical entrepreneurship, Song of the Goat Theatre has been involved in other forms of activity. One major project was the "Brave Festival—Against Cultural Exile." Established in 2005, this annual event was set to counterbalance the dominant cultural models promoted by commercial mass culture and was "devoted to various cultures and traditions from all over the world, particularly those that are rare, marginalised or almost extinct."[5] The Brave Festival was organised in Wrocław till 2018.[6]

In 2009, Bral, inspired by Dr Akong Tulku Rinpoche, a Tibetan lama, established an educational project Brave Kids, whose "mission is to bring together children from all over the world" and "to nurture cross-cultural understanding amongst the next generation."[7]

Both of these projects hint at the Tibetan Buddhist inspirations for various of the company's activities, which are further confirmed by its long-lasting support of the charity organisation ROKPA. Reflecting on this

---

[4] https://culture.pl/en/artist/song-of-the-goat-theatre (accessed on 28 June 2019).
[5] https://culture.pl/en/event/brave-festival (accessed on 28 June 2019).
[6] http://www.bravefestival.pl/ (accessed on 28 June 2019).
[7] www.bravekids.eu (accessed on 6 June, 2019). See also: https://www.tygodnikpowszechny.pl/zrodlo-radosci-16655 (accessed on 17 March, 2020).

inspiration, Grzegorz Bral states: "Many years ago [in 1993] I met the Tibetan lama and meditation master Dr. Akong Tulku Rinpoche—a refugee, a doctor, a teacher, and founder of the 'ROKPA' charity organization that helps people throughout the world. I became fascinated with his human qualities, with his compassion, wisdom, and understanding of the roots of happiness and success."[8]

In spite of his unorthodox education as a theatre-maker—obtained in "Gardzienice" rather than in conventional theatre schools—Grzegorz Bral has also gained more traditional, institutional experience. Between 2004 and 2012, Song of the Goat cooperated with the drama department of the Manchester Metropolitan University on a joint MA Acting Programme, and between 2010 and 2012 Bral was appointed artistic director of Teatr Studio in Warsaw. Given the chance to probe his innovative methods of work in a regular repertoire institution, Bral produced plays by playwrights such as Eugene Ionesco and Eugene O'Neill, and produced a stage adaptation of Fyodor Dostoyevsky's *The Idiot.* As he comments at present, working in one of the major theatres in the capital of Poland was indispensable experience that enabled him to recognise and develop the specificity of the ensemble formed by Song of the Goat Theatre.[9]

Anna Zubrzycki's essential and unquestionable participation in developing the performative language of Song of the Goat Theatre finished in 2014, when she assertively left the company and commenced her independent career as an actress, producer and trainer.[10] Her departure led to far-reaching consequences, not only for the company as a whole but also for the individual artistic signature of Grzegorz Bral.

"Bral Acting Method"

Since 2013, Bral's pedagogical interests have focused on exploring the so-called Bral Acting Method within the framework of the Bral School of Acting. Based on the practice of Song of the Goat Theatre,[11] the training

[8] www.bralschool.com (accessed on 29 March, 2019).

[9] Personal communication (conversation on 24 May, 2019).

[10] See: www.annazubrzycki.com (accessed on 29 March, 2019).

[11] The "Bral Acting Method" approaches from a new perspective earlier pedagogical interests of the company that were originally developed with Anna Zubrzycki, Marcin Rudy, Rafał Habel and others as "The Coordination Method" (e-mail correspondence on 14 March 2020).

is offered in Wrocław, London and elsewhere,[12] and it ranges from concise two-day workshops to nine-month intensive courses.[13]

When discussing the training, one needs to bear in mind its practical and physical character, which somehow obscures any attempt at describing it verbally. Promotional materials succinctly define the method as "an original practice based on the integration of all acting tools [i.e. voice, text, energy, and imagination] into one common and organic unity"[14] and provide its emblematic qualities.

First, when assuming that "mind, voice and imagination are truly connected," the Bral Acting Method approaches the performer as "the centre of actor's craft and training." It encourages finding a connection between the inner world of a performer and the "external environment" so as to add and contribute "to a common aim—performance of a highest quality."

Second, Bral does not prioritise "intellectual understanding," but aims at achieving performative "confidence [that is] similar to a well-trained musician." For this reason, "presence, magnetism and energy on stage" are of greatest prominence, just as "precision, energy, and sharpness" are. His objective is to foster "an effort of perpetual refinement" in "a process requiring hard work and commitment." As he claims, his obsession with incessant improvement is rooted in techniques of Tibetan meditation.

Third, Bral is explicit that "preservation of human heritage" and interculturalism are central to his method. Not only does he insist on learning from other—frequently marginal—cultures, but he also stresses his fascination with Buddhism. As we read in the promotional materials, on the one hand the method "combines Western traditions of dramatic practices, with ancient performance techniques originating from indigenous cultures," and, on the other hand, it makes use of the observation that "the ancient wisdom of Tibetan enlightened and sacred wisdom [supports] our modern theatre."

All in all, the international reputation of Bral's training becomes a professional threshold for graduates from various parts of the globe. Some of them find their way into the company's projects and this is one of the ways

---

[12] Bral delivered courses in the USA, Brazil, Chile, the UK, Taiwan, Turkey, Greece, Sweden and Norway. Between 2015 and 2018 he did over 100 workshops, mainly in the UK (e-mail correspondence on 14 March 2020).

[13] This section is based on www.bralschool.com (accessed on 6 June 2019).

[14] All quotations in this section after www.bralschool.com (accessed on 6 June 2019).

6   T. WIŚNIEWSKI

in which its main slogan comes true: "Together we aim for the impossible. Only the impossible is worth achieving."

EARLY PRODUCTIONS

Unlike many contemporary theatre-makers in Poland (e.g. Jan Klata, Paweł Demirski, Monika Strzempka and Krzysztof Garbaczewski), Grzegorz Bral has given priority to formal experiments and exploration of the grand myths of European and global culture rather than to socially engaged theatre. Following principles canonised by Jerzy Grotowski, each production has been treated as a strenuous and long-lasting process that involves a long rehearsal phase and evolves well after its premiere. It is striking that within the initial ten years, Song of the Goat produced no more than three one-hour-long productions—*Song of the Goat—Dithyramb* (1997), *Chronicles—A Tradition of Mourning* (2001), and *Lacrimosa* (2005)—yet each one was praised for its exceptional performative quality. The long-lasting creative process was a consequence of the unstable organisational and financial situation of the newly founded ensemble; at the same time, though, the challenging rehearsal conditions created an environment for unusual creativity. The successful presentations of these early productions around the world—at the Edinburgh Festival Fringe in particular—established an international reputation for the company that lasts till today.

The eponymous *Song of the Goat—Dithyramb* (*Pieśń Kozła—Dytyramb*) comprised many of the features that later became trademarks of the company. Even though the plot was inspired by Euripides' *Bacchae*, the central axis of the production was of musical rather than dramatic character. Adaptations of traditional songs, "discovered" during expeditions to Greece (Epiros), Albania and Romania in the early phase of rehearsals, successfully constructed a contemporary image of the ancient performative spirit. Conventions that were frequently mentioned included Greek lamentations and the Madinados traditions ("musical poetry improvisations from Crete").[15] What was of particular importance for the ensemble was an attempt "to summon up the spirit of ancient audiences."[16] The festive, if mournful, spirit of the production was perhaps best reflected in the following description:

[15] https://culture.pl/en/artist/song-of-the-goat-theatre (accessed on 28 June 2019).
[16] https://culture.pl/en/artist/song-of-the-goat-theatre (accessed on 28 June 2019).

How far are we from the world of Greek myth? A few million light years. But with Song of the Goat it's all so close, as if the actors had just come from some kind of Balkan banquet, from tables adorned with wine, olives, meat and paprika. [...] They come in order to dance, (amazingly) act, sing, sigh and moan. Holding each other by the hand, they wandered around and stamped out an unusual tale ... [17]

Another factor that should be mentioned at this point is that while producing *Song of the Goat—Dithyramb,* Grzegorz Bral's role somehow evolved. Being initially just one of the performers who had to contribute to the creation of an ensemble, he finally developed into the leader who became responsible for the final shape of the production. This was, as he sees it now, a natural process that echoes the way in which the function of the director emerged in the history of theatre: "Others just needed someone to look at their work and tell them what works and what does not."[18] As the title of the second production—*Chronicles—A Tradition of Mourning* (*Kroniki—Obyczaj lamentacyjny*) suggests, at this early stage the mood of lamentation was set as pivotal for the company. The programme suggests that the dramatic plot—this time inspired by the story of Gilgamesh's "unsuccessful initiation into eternal life"[19]—was again subordinate to the sonic tissue of the performance. Its frequently praised polyphonic quality originated in the company's two-year "search for the tradition of lamentation in various countries"[20] and extensive exploration by the ensemble consisting of seven performers and the director. Further justification for the fascination with mourning may be found in this statement: "Lamentation seems to be a very primary form of human expression, and the link between theatre and feasts of the dead has long since been a subject for debate."[21] Critics observed "the musical and vocal structure of the song" as well as "the physical proficiency" of the ensemble, which won the company the reputation of a leading representative of physical theatre.[22] What was particularly appreciated was the intensity of this short production and the value of a contemporary pursuit of the experience of catharsis.

---

[17] Barbara Sola, *Literary Journals,* 2002, no. 4 (translated as in the archive of the company).

[18] Personal communication (conversation on 24 May 2019).

[19] Quotation from the programme.

[20] Quotation from the programme.

[21] Programme in the company's archive.

[22] See https://culture.pl/en/artist/song-of-the-goat-theatre (accessed on 28 June 2019).

8   T. WIŚNIEWSKI

Inspired by Andrzej Szczypiorski's novel *A Mass for Arras, Lacrimosa* was the third production directed by Grzegorz Bral for Song of the Goat Theatre. In the mode already established by the company, a "metaphoric and poetic"[23] exploration of the story of the plague and pogroms in the fifteenth-century French city forms the background for extensively vocal and intensively physical, if multilingual, performance. Mark Brown recognises three "disparate elements"[24] of the production: the story inspired by the novel, the choral music that was based on *Requiem* by Wolfgang Amadeus Mozart, and "the physical movement of practitioners of the ancient Greek fire-walking cult of Anastenaria."[25] All these elements were interconnected "by the idea of the human mind being 'possessed'."[26]

These are all vital features of *Lacrimosa*. Yet, Grzegorz Bral insisted on "'the ultimate goal of' [the creative process being] 'to build a performance which speaks about the poetry of violence'."[27] And he referred not only to the medieval story of a plague, but also to "crises of the twenty-first century: 'I am interested in the growing madness in the contemporary world; a terror which grows inside the mind, not only in the world outside, and, so, people become increasingly violent'."[28] The subtext of anti-Semitism and xenophobic scapegoating was commented upon in a prominent review by a leading Polish performance scholar, Dariusz Kosiński. Sceptical about perceiving *Lacrimosa* as a mere adaptation of the novel, Kosiński lays emphasis not only on "the theme of an innocent victim that is sacrificed for the sake of community,"[29] but also on revaluating the energy of Mozart's *Requiem* with a vigour indebted to Polish experimental theatre. Most notably, for Kosiński, the entire performance developed into a communal "confession and a request for forgiveness."[30] He stressed the particular role of this aspect in view of "the mechanisms of scapegoat"[31] that were revealed by the brutality of history in the twentieth

[23] Mark Brown, "Festival that showcases the theatre of poetry," *New Statesman*, 2 August 2007, https://www.newstatesman.com/arts-and-culture/2007/08/goat-theatre-poland-song (accessed on 17 February 2020).
[24] Ibid.
[25] Ibid.
[26] Ibid.
[27] Mark Ramsey, *The Scotsman*, 4 August 2007 (archive materials).
[28] Ibid.
[29] Dariusz Kosiński, "Prawa i lewa strona kobierca," *Didaskalia*, Oct 2005, p. 66.
[30] Ibid.
[31] Ibid.

century, the Holocaust included. For Kosiński the main question was that "of relation between the cruel world and God, of His presence and possibilities of finding God in the surrounding darkness."[32]

The role of the three plays—*Song of the Goat*—*Dithyramb, Chronicles*—*A Tradition of Mourning* and *Lacrimosa*—in laying the foundation for Grzegorz Bral's international reputation and his stage language is unquestionable; yet one needs to remember that these formative productions were created by an ensemble where the contribution of Anna Zubrzycki and others was strong. Since then, Grzegorz Bral's method of work has significantly shifted and acquired more personal shape, becoming much less indebted to the roots of his working style obtained in "Gardzienice."

INSPIRATION BY SHAKESPEARE

The 2008 production of *Macbeth* was pivotal for Grzegorz Bral since it was the first in a sequence of productions based on Shakespeare. Originating in the company's cooperation with the Royal Shakespeare Company, it was created by an ensemble of five actors and two actresses from Poland, England, Wales, Scotland and Finland. Profound exploration of the sonic potential of Shakespeare's play was paired with achieving the mastery of physical performativity. The company refreshed its intensely integrated ensemble and managed to lay the foundation for its remarkable stage interpretations of Shakespeare.

Macbeth, a seventy-minute piece, employed neither ornamental props nor spectacular stage design. The visual devices were reduced to basic black-and-white costumes that resembled "martial arts outfits or the down part of men's kimono,"[33] candlelight, screens, plain wooden tables and wooden sticks. The latter functioned not only as useful props that ignited the audience's imagination, but also as rudimentary instruments producing sounds. In a manner typical of the company, the stage language was dominated by intense exploration of the sonic tissue that was created by spectacular choral songs and several instruments operated by one performer.

---

[32] Ibid.

[33] Kalina Stefanova, "Theatre for Sounds and Souls, or The Quest of the Polish Song of the Goat Company into the Impossible, Inspired by Shakespeare," http://piesnkozla.pl/en/news#363-kalina-stefanova-about-song-of-the-goat-theatre (accessed on 6 June 2019).

10 T. WIŚNIEWSKI

Like the previous productions of Song of the Goat Theatre, *Macbeth* achieved critical acclaim both in Poland and abroad, and it was generally praised for providing an innovative approach to the ancient notion of catharsis. As Anna Tarnowska puts it: "If catharsis is to be experienced in contemporary theatre, this notion may be exercised in *Macbeth* by Song of the Goat Theatre. Actors perform in a very suggestive and clear—practically non-theatrical—way since there is no typical role-play. Here emotions have to be true. [...] This theatre proves that Shakespeare's play is onomatopoeic and words serve to extract emotions through music. It is a birth of tragedy out of ancient mysteries and what accompanies this delivery is the Nietzschean spirit of music."[34] A similar view is proposed by Kalina Stefanova, who insists that *Macbeth* "not only further expand[s] the very notion of what theatre could be," but also "brings us back to what theatre essentially is, or at least is supposed to be, at its very core: an experience with an overwhelming and purifying catharsis—something which contemporary stages very rarely, alas, dare to aspire to or, for that matter, manage to achieve."[35]

Songs of Lear, the second production inspired by Shakespeare, premiered at the Edinburgh Festival Fringe in August 2012 and, in spite of major shifts in the cast, is still presented in various parts of the world. The production takes the form of a performative "oratory" and challenges audience's expectations concerning the linear arrangement of the dramatic action. The sequence of songs framed by Grzegorz Bral's introductory comments provides a contemporary response to Shakespeare's *Lear* and as such is not bound to reflect the classical storyline. Rather, it explores "the world of subtle energies and rhythms" through "gestures, words and music."[36] Such a loose treatment of the play has developed into one of the main features of Bral's working style.

Inspired by Corsican rhythms and medieval Georgian polyphonic singing, the music was composed by Jean-Claude Acquaviva and Maciej Rychły, who have since then become steady collaborators of Grzegorz Bral. In fact, in *Songs of Lear* the conventional dialogue has been completely substituted by singing, which brings profound consequences. As Stefanova puts it: "The result is a condensed *King Lear* not in terms of being abridged but of being intensified. It has the effect of an ancient

---

[34] Anna Tarnowska, "Gazeta Wyborcza—Bydgoszcz," 9 May 2011.
[35] Stefanova, op. cit.
[36] Quotation after promotional materials.

Chinese four-line poem which in a mysterious way conveys what the whole play is about. Namely: a paradise that gets segmented, then lost and, finally, regained."[37]

The lot of the two productions that premiered in 2016—*Crazy God* and *Island*—was very different. Whereas the former was quickly suspended, *Island* developed into a complete piece that introduced a new quality to the company's stage language. Inspired by Shakespeare's *The Tempest*, *Island* involved collaboration with a Dutch-based company called INNE. That company's leader, Iván Pérez, was responsible for choreography, since this time Grzegorz Bral decided to integrate the performative/sonic tissue with modern dance. The result of such multidimensional and intercultural cooperation reshaped the stage language of Song of the Goat Theatre. Interaction between thirteen performers/singers and six dancers succeeded in balancing the mastery of polyphonic singing and performative intensity with the visual integrity of the dynamic ensemble. A number of striking images were inspired by familiar paintings, such as Edvard Munch's *The Scream*.[38] An equally memorable *tableau* was created by means of a shadow-play formed by the entire collective towards the end of this one-hour spectacle. Additionally, a textual dimension was added and integrated by Alicja Bral, who thus firmly confirmed her position as the company's dramaturg.

When discussing his involvement in the creative process, Iván Pérez provides some insight into the rehearsal practice of Song of the Goat Theatre. He was surprised that during rehearsals Grzegorz Bral

> was ready to talk about other dimensions of understanding the world. For example, from an energetic perspective, from a perspective of vibration, of expansion of our bodies, and ways that our energies communicate beyond the physical or whatever we can see. He really dares to talk about matters that are invisible. [...] There's a mystical element of his perception of life that comes into the work. The way he articulates this to his people is quite fascinating. I can connect to many of these ideas, but I tend to intellectualise them. [...] We can learn a lot from the subconscious, intuitive, sensorial knowledge that we can perceive through the body.[39]

---

[37] Stefanova, op.cit.

[38] I owe this observation to Professor Jerzy Limon.

[39] Tomasz Wiśniewski, "Conversation With Iván Pérez," posted on 17 March 2017, https://thetheatretimes.com/conversation-ivan-perez-founder-inne-choreographer-song-goat-theatre (accessed on 28 June 2019).

Pérez's observation of Bral's fascination with the irrational, the invisible and the bodily seems particularly apt when one confronts it with the intense experience of performative liveness that dictates the transmission of energy in the course of the productions directed by Grzegorz Bral. When introducing his pieces to an audience, he usually mentions the length of a spectacle, which generally does not exceed sixty minutes. He claims he does so in order to strengthen the intense duration of his rather short performances.[40]

LATEST PRODUCTIONS

Even though Shakespeare remains a constant point of reference for Grzegorz Bral (*Hamlet: A Commentary* premiered in 2017 and at present he is considering an adaptation of *Titus Andronicus*[41]), in recent years Song of the Goat Theatre has also produced performances based on other dramatists and other types of material. Based on a play by Anton Chekhov, *Portraits of the Cherry Orchard* (2014) is a multilingual production that laments the loss of a paradise and does so in neither a linear nor a strictly rational manner.[42] Similarly, the twelve songs that constitute *Return to the Voice* (2014) were inspired by ancient songs and other musical material that the company members explored during their expeditions in Scotland. Then, more dialogical in nature, *The Grand Inquisitor* (2018) is based on a fragment of Dostoyevsky's *The Brothers Karamazov* and explores the existential confrontation of an individual with his internal daemons and the Other, who is ultimately represented by God. Although these pieces are based on varied material and represent different performative styles, they confirm not only the integrity of the stage language that has been developed by Grzegorz Bral, but also his fascination with formal experiments.

This is equally true in the monumental production of *Anty-Gone* (2018), a triptych consisting of *Seven Gates of Thebes*, *Anty-Gone* and *Ecstasy*. By the standards of Song of the Goat Theatre this is an unusually grand-scale spectacle, with over thirty performers/singers and dancers involved. The conflict between civil obedience and loyalty to personal

---

[40] Personal communication (conversation on 10 February 2017).

[41] Personal communication (conversation on 15 April 2019).

[42] Mateusz Węgrzyn, "Teraz marzę", www.dwutygodnik.com, 05-12-2013, www.e-teatr.pl (accessed on 28 June 2019).

values is, on the one hand, embedded in an archetypal confrontation of female and male elements and, on the other hand, acquires particular resonance in the surrounding world. Bral frequently refers to this production as to a hybrid one, since it is capable of functioning as independent performances and transforms from one presentation to another.[43]

What is more, *Cassandra's Report* (2018) makes use of songs—but not dancers—that were composed for the second and third parts of *Anty-Gone* and develops them into an autonomous performance. In summer 2019, when performed at the open air Enter Enea Festival, *Cassandra's Report* transformed into a partly improvised concert conducted together with a renowned Polish jazz pianist, Leszek Możdżer.

Throughout the years, Grzegorz Bral has succeeded in establishing his idiosyncratic artistic language. Rooted in the tradition of Polish experimental theatre, the aesthetics of Song of the Goat Theatre make extensive use of performative and singing traditions adapted from various parts of the world. Bral's cosmopolitan aspirations seem insatiable. This is visible not only in his latest theatre production, *The Warrior*—labelled by Mirosław Kocur a masterpiece[44]—but also in the contribution of the company to the sixth season of *Vikings*, a popular series directed by Michael Hirst. There are strange, if intriguing, implications in such a collaboration of an experimental theatre with the world of global mass media. As Grzegorz Bral puts it, "we have never had an opportunity to reach such a broad audience all around the world."[45] This is certainly an interesting way of adapting ambitious artistic aspirations to the current situation of this nomadic theatre.

---

[43] Personal communication (conversation on 20 November 2018).

[44] http://teatralny.pl/recenzje/uwaga-arcydzielo,2892.html?fbclid=IwAR2_qqR-RQWQQLiUnxBEse1vTNHo2ltGLKls86KtSMBwc4AxuejJwtoMFgwI (accessed 23 November 2019).

[45] Personal communication (conversation on 14 November 2019).

Image 1 *Hamlet—a Commentary*, directed by Grzegorz Bral, Song of the Goat Theatre, 2017. From the left: Julianna Bloodgood, Natalia Voskoboynikov, Jenny Kaatz, Olga Kunicka, Magdalena Szczerbowska, Dimitris Varkas, Volodymyr Andrushchak, Peyman Sichani, Julien Touati, Łukasz Wójcik. (Photo by Mateusz Bral)

References

Bąk, Ewa, "39. WST Anty-Gone Tryptyk Teatr Pieśń Kozła," http://www.e-teatr.pl/pl/artykuly/274285.html (accessed on 28 June 2019).
Bral School of Acting, Official Website, www.bralschool.com (accessed on 29 March 2019).
Brave Festival, Official Website, http://www.bravefestival.pl/ (accessed on 28 June 2019).
Brave Kids, Official Website, www.bravekids.eu (accessed on 6 June 2019).
Brown, Mark, "Festival that showcases the theatre of poetry," *New Statesman*, 2 August 2007.
Kocur, Mirosław, "Uwaga, arcydzieło," http://teatralny.pl/recenzje/uwaga-arcydzielo,2892.html?fbclid=IwAR2_qqRRQWQQLiUnxBEse1vTNHo2lt-GLKls86KtSMBwc4AxuejJwtoMFgwI (accessed on 23 November 2019).
Kosiński, Dariusz, "Prawa i lewa strona kobierca," *Didaskalia*, Oct 2005.
Ramsey, Mark, The Scotsman, 4 August 2007.

Song of the Goat, Official Website, http://piesnkozla.pl/en (accessed on 28 June 2019).

Stefanova, Kalina, "Theatre for Sounds and Souls, or The Quest of the Polish Song of the Goat Company into the Impossible, Inspired by Shakespeare," http://piesnkozla.pl/en/news#363-kalina-stefanova-about-song-of-the-goat-theatre (accessed on 6 June 2019).

Tarnowska, Anna, Review, "Gazeta Wyborcza—Bydgoszcz," 9 May 2011.

Wiśniewski, Tomasz, "Conversation with Iván Pérez," posted on 17 March 2017, https://thetheatretimes.com/conversation-ivan-perez-founder-inne-choreographer-song-goat-theatre (accessed on 28 June 2019).

Wiśniewski, Tomasz, "The conditions are never ideal. In conversation with Melanie Lomoff," posted on 16 April 2020, https://thetheatretimes.com/the-conditions-are-never-ideal-in-conversation-with-melanie-lomoff/ (accessed on 17 July, 2020).

Węgrzyn, Mateusz, "Teraz marzę," www.dwutygodnik.com, 05-12-2013, www.e--teatr.pl (accessed on 28 June 2019).

Zubrzycki, Anna, Official Website, www.annazubrzycki.com (accessed on 29 March 2019).

My Name Is Gianina Cărbunariu: I'm a Lioness

Maria Zărnescu

Had she been born in another time or another space, Gianina Cărbunariu (b. 1977) would have been one of those rebels who changed the history of the arts. Nowadays she is one of the most important Romanian contemporary theatre-makers—director and playwright—her productions and plays frequently staged at home and abroad.

Gianina Cărbunariu embraces the mission of re-shaping Romanian theatre through a new way of writing and using the stage to convey comments and oppose the state and society—much like the individual's right to whistle-blow or to throw a stone. Her shows originate from contemporary themes, inspired by present-day topics or by recent history. Her documentation process (through interviews and archive research) is followed by improvisation with actors (from her own generation or younger), resulting in a fictional script where real-life elements are sometimes integrated. "Every fiction is EXPERIENCE-DOCUMENTARY-IMAGINATION,"

M. Zărnescu (✉)
National University of Theatre and Cinematography "I.L. Caragiale",
Bucharest, Romania

© The Author(s), under exclusive license to Springer Nature Switzerland AG 2021
K. Stefanova, M. Carlson (eds.), *20 Ground-Breaking Directors of Eastern Europe*, https://doi.org/10.1007/978-3-030-52935-2_2

emphasises Cărbunariu.[1] It's her way of focusing on contemporary local creations and rejecting any expression of formal and ideological conservatism. "Her approach to post-1990's controversial issues has become her signature style,"[2] wrote Cristina Modreanu.

Since 2017, she has been the manager of the Theatre of Youth in Piatra Neamț (her native city), one of the most important cultural institutions of the country, a true landmark in Romanian theatre.

The Beginnings: "dramAcum"—Stop the Tempo

Born on 9 August 1977 in Piatra Neamț, Gianina Cărbunariu studied Letters at the University in Bucharest (2000–2004). Then she graduated from the National University of Theatrical Arts and Cinematography "I.L. Caragiale," Bucharest, majoring in Theatre Directing (2004). She also has a Master's degree in Playwriting (2006) and a PhD from the same university, with the thesis "The Playwright Director."

Along with the advent of the new millennium, something was changing in the Romanian contemporary theatre environment. Together with three fellow students, in 2002 Cărbunariu co-founded a drama competition that soon became an important active platform for new playwrights, generating novel dramaturgy and innovative dramaturgical techniques. This group, called "dramAcum," offered a fresh look at the Romanian theatre, the strongest since the fall of Communism, in 1989.

At the beginning of her career, the director Cărbunariu was stronger than the playwright. Her shows were based on contemporary texts, with stories inspired by immediate reality, written by her or by other authors. Her graduation production, *My Name Is Isborg. I'm a Lioness* (2003), was based on a play by Icelandic Hávar Sigurjónsson. But this was also one of the last shows based on a text that was not written by her.

Cărbunariu's first play, *Stop the Tempo* (2004), represented also the start of her international career, the text being considered the "cream" of the generation of new playwrights. It was originally staged at the Green Hours Club in Bucharest and featured three actors and three lanterns. The story

---

[1] Gianina Cărbunariu, *Written text—the script for a show* (foreword / *mady-baby.edu*) (Bucharest: "Cartea Românească" Publishing House, 2007), p. 11.

[2] Cristina Modreanu—*Gianina Cărbunariu: Documentary Theatre with Political Focus*, "The Theatre Times," 29 September 2016 (https://thetheatretimes.com/gianina-carbunariu-documentary-theater-with-political-focus/) (accessed on 10 August 2020).

of three young people, lonely and lost in space, who want to blow up the night clubs, supermarkets and theatres in their town, was considered a manifesto of the young generation whose existence is expropriated and who are protesting through self-destruction. That same year the show was invited to the Wiesbaden Biennale, Germany. Since then, the play has been performed on stages in Paris, Berlin, Dublin, New York, Istanbul, Vienna, Nice and Leipzig.

Stop the Tempo was going to transform Romanian theatre decisively. As Iulia Popovici wrote, "It was to become the starting point of a small revolution in the contemporary dramaturgy of this land, Gianina Cărbunariu introduced a new way of writing and a non-conformist esthetics of staging in the Romanian theatre."[3] The playwright-director confesses: "As an artist I am inspired by books, by the work of other artists, but mostly by my personal experience and by self-inflicted experiences based on meetings, interviews, the study of archives a.s.o."[4]

Her second play, *Kebab* (*original title: mady-baby.edu*), which was conceived at the Royal Court Theatre in London, where Cărbunariu stayed as an international artist-in-residence, was banned by a private theatre in Bucharest, a few days before the premiere, because of its "indecent language." It tells another story of three young Romanians, who are hoping that Ireland is the land of opportunity. Only once they get there, their life quickly turns to dust. The pimp, the prostitute and the victim-customer devour each other under the impact of their own choices. Cărbunariu analyses an item from the five o'clock news, but she is looking neither for the sensational nor for the horror, but for the hidden causes that triggered the story.

After having been supported in 2005 by the Very Small Theatre in Bucharest (an institution that also encouraged Cărbunariu's career as a director), *Kebab* became one of the most frequently toured productions abroad; it caught the attention of theatres around the world, from Japan to the UK, and from Denmark to Greece, with an important stop at the famous Schaubühne of Berlin.

---

[3] Iulia Popovici, *Romania of Daily Nightmares* (foreword / *mady-baby.edu*) (Bucharest: "Cartea Românească" Publishing House, 2007), p. 5.

[4] Gianina Cărbunariu—"*I'm scared by the polarization of the speeches*" (interview by Maria Cernat), "Baricada," 9 April 2019 (https://ro.baricada.org/carbunariu-teatru-munca-interviu/) (accessed on 10 August 2020).

20   M. ZĂRNESCU

The "secret" of the huge European attention granted to Gianina Cărbunariu's first two texts lies in their marked specificity. "Displaying a sense of humour that ignores the temptation of satire and without manifest critical-moralistic intentions, the plays are the theatrical expression of a kind of *Weltanschauung*[5] belonging to a special generation of the special first decade of the new millennium in the special space called Romania,"[6] wrote Iulia Popovici.

NATIONAL AND INTERNATIONAL RECOGNITION: FESTIVAL D'AVIGNON—*SOLITARITY*

But the tempo didn't stop there for Cărbunariu's career—on the contrary. Tens more of her author-productions followed, staged within the country and abroad. Documenting some Romanian stories from the present or the recent past, she fuels the collective memory. She picks topics avoided by authorities, not enough or not at all analysed by historians or sociologists, themes that are aesthetically treated and focusing on small histories, real facts forgotten by researchers, facts that are pointed out through theatrical expressiveness.[7] Many of them have been translated and staged by other directors, and the shows won high recognition by the theatrical world.

Over the years, the prevailing role of Cărbunariu in the theatre has changed: from being solely a director she has become the complete author of shows; yet both roles have brought countless national nominations and awards, among them the award of the Romanian Section of the International Association of Theatre Critics for the project "dramAcum," as well as for original directing and playwriting; and the UNITER[8] Senate

---

[5] *Weltanschauung* (literally "a look at the world") is a term consecrated by German philosophy and indicates the systematic way in which an individual understands and interprets the meaning of the world and of life as a whole.

[6] Iulia Popovici. *Romania*, p. 6.

[7] A well-documented review on this matter is signed by Oltița Cîntec, the President of the Romanian Section AICT/IATC.ro of the International Association of Theatre Critics: *Gianina Cărbunariu's Theatre, a Form of Memory in Recent History* (*STUDIA UBB DRAMATICA*, LXII, 2, 2017, pp. 131–141). The study is built around the methodology developed by the French philosopher Paul Ricoeur in his book *Memory, History, Forgetting* (2004) and is based upon the most successful shows created by Gianina Cărbunariu.

[8] The Romanian Association of Theatre Professionals, UNITER, was founded in 1990 as a professional, apolitical, non-governmental and non-profit organization, and resulted from the free association of artists from the theatre industry. The UNITER Awards Gala is one of its most important programmes, organised every year since 1991.

Award for *Typographic Capital Letters* (co-production of Odeon Theatre Bucharest, "dramAcum" Association and the International Theatre Festival Divadelna Nitra, as part of the project "Parallel Lives—Twentieth Century through the Eyes of Secret Police," 2013). The presence of her shows (Romanian or co-productions) at festivals all over the world has earned her international recognition.

In 2014, with the presentation of her show *Solitarity* (a co-production of the National Theatre "Radu Stanca" Sibiu, the National Theatre of the French Community in Brussels and the Avignon Festival) in the official selection of the Avignon Festival, as part of the project "Cities on Stage," the playwright-director Cărbunariu formally became the most famous Romanian female theatre artist abroad. The show was a critique of national hypocrisy—as encountered in such environments as politics, family or religion, or even in the theatre world.

Of *Solitarity*'s five scenes, a few stand out: the wall built by the municipality of a Romanian town in order to isolate the Roma community or the building of the new National Cathedral in the capital city, a very delicate issue in a country where schools and hospitals tend to close, but hundreds of millions of euros are spent on such an initiative. The name of the show is a coined word, but it is quite expressive, starting from *solidarity*, but actually suggesting its opposite: *solitude*: "I have been under the impression, lately, that it is increasingly difficult for us to achieve solidarity and that this failure brings about a certain type of isolation, of *solitarity*."[9]

However, the texts that Cărbunariu has written over time are not just reports of serious situations, not just wake-up calls made in order to obtain visibility. Her strong point is a sharp sense of humour, which creeps behind the straight faces. Thus, the reception of her shows becomes less intricate; the militant shuddering is absent from her work, and the artistry is most certainly present. "Cărbunariu is not just enumerating 'slices of life' displayed hastily and alarmingly, but finds the most creative artistic means— both from the point of view of the situations created for the characters, as well as for the expressive capabilities of the actors in the cast,"[10] wrote Alina Epîngeac.

---

[9] Gianina Cărbunariu—"*Because we care*" (interview by Medana Wident), "Deutsche Welle," 28 January 2016 (https://www.dw.com/ro/pentru-c%C4%83-ne-pas%C4%83-despre-altruism-curaj-civic-%C8%99i-sim%C8%9Bul-datoriei-pe-scena-teatrului-sibian/a-19010467) (accessed on 10 August 2020).

[10] Alina Epîngeac—*The Manipulation through Theatre* (PhD thesis), UNATC Library, Bucharest, 2019, p. 156.

TIGERN

Yet it is mostly the playwright Gianina Cărbunariu who has enjoyed international recognition. Her writings have been translated into many languages and staged on three continents. As she says: "In all the places I have worked as an artist I have been interested in knowing who the community which I am addressing is, who the audiences are. When I worked in München, I was thinking about the spectators who were coming to Kammerspiele. When I worked in Italy, I went to see other shows in order to find out who the people coming to watch theatre were. I was also thinking about those who I wished would come to the show. The same thing happened in Târgu Mureş, in Sibiu... This is why, after the show, I have talks with the audience."[11]

In 2016, the same official selection of the Avignon Festival included *Tigern*, a production of the Swedish Jupither Josephsson Theatre Company, directed by Sofia Jupither. The performance was based on *Mihaela, the Tiger of Our Town (A Mockumentary Play)*. The history of the play is, however, somewhat longer. The original title was *The Sibian Tiger*, after the name of Sibiu, a city in the middle part of Romania, of approximately 150,000 inhabitants—one of the most important cultural centres of the country, designated as a European Capital of Culture in 2007 and hosting the annual Sibiu International Theatre Festival since 1993.

Just like other Cărbunariu plays, *Mihaela, the Tiger of Our Town* is based on a real fact that became news: a tiger escaped the zoo in Sibiu in 2011. Actually, it simply ran free as a consequence of human negligence: the zookeeper had forgotten to lock the cage after leaving the food. After a few hours spent in freedom in the woods near the zoo, the female tiger named Mihaela was found by the search teams and shot dead.

So "*Sibian*" in the original title meant "originating from Sibiu," but was also intended as a pun: "*Sibian*" sounding like "*Siberian*." However, the name of the city is not mentioned in the play. It may be any contemporary town.

In one prologue and eleven scenes, the writer re-makes the facts of that day of the Sibian tiger's freedom through a series of imaginary interviews with people who, in one way or another, had interacted with the feline: a

---

[11] Gianina Cărbunariu—"*The theatre can't save the world, but it can provoke thinking*" (interview by Medana Weident), "Deutsche Welle," 30 September 2018 (https://www.dw.com/ro/gianina-c%C4%83rbunariu-teatrul-nu-poate-salva-lumea-dar-poate-provoca-g%C3%A2ndire/a-45691408) (accessed on 10 August 2020).

talkative taxi driver; two homeless persons using dirty language in Central Park; a Japanese tourist and a French one, each of them demonstrating the typical psychology of their respective nationality; representatives of the populations of pigeons, crows and sparrows; a pensioner who easily succumbs to manipulation; a school (as a building, but also as an institution of tradition); an owner of a very expensive car, as well as the car itself; a young female emergency room doctor; the manager and one employee of a bank; the depressive new zookeeper; and three different animals, former "fellows" of Mihaela, the tiger.

These imaginary interviews are made by a number of "documentary makers"—the same number of the actors in the production. (At the Romanian premiere there was a cast of three actors, each of whom played a number of different roles.) The outcome isn't a documentary play but a false one, therefore: a *mockumentary play*, as Cărbunariu's sense of humour breaks through each cue, each situation. She uses the means of documentary theatre, but they are ironically turned inside out. Thus the fundamental themes of present-day society are brought to the forefront: captivity versus freedom, "system errors," the centre's fear of the periphery and the periphery's fear of the centre.

"We tried to capture the way in which 'the foreigner's' look meets the realities of a contemporary town: the look of the minority member, of the different one, of the outsider, of the one who breaks the rules," declares the author. All of them speak about the others whom they blame. In fact, they all speak about themselves, telling their own stories and their own guilt. "Hell is other people" would have said Sartre the existentialist in the mid-twentieth century. Nowadays, and with much humour, Cărbunariu takes a totally unflattering magnifying glass and examines the human errors of certain individuals and communities, no matter where they might find themselves.

The Romanian premiere of the show took place in 2012, as a co-production of "dramAcum" and the Comedy Theatre in Bucharest. Since then the text has been translated into English, French, Spanish, Bulgarian, German, Swedish, Italian and Chinese.

Artists Talk

In 2017 Cărbunariu was the artist selected to represent Romania at the Festival de Liège, with her show, *Artists Talk*, co-produced by Bucharest Cultural Center ARCUB together with the Association "Piese refractare."

"The role of the artist is to ask questions, not to answer them." One of the most quoted of Chekhov's statements seems to contradict the habit of organisers to include in cultural events' programmes famous discussions between artists and spectators (be it journalists or critics). The mission of these Q&A sessions is, in theory at least, to build a bridge between the creative team and the target public, sometimes providing "that missing link" in their relationship. In practice they may reveal the artists' intentions and thoughts (unknown otherwise) or, on the contrary, they may develop into an alternation of diluted truisms and neologisms: big talk versus small talk. "Artistic approach," "collaborative projects," "artistic concept," "challenge," "artistic message," "transparency," "social/political art," "empathy," "performing arts," "syncretism," "eclecticism," "interesting," "captivating," "wonderful," "splendid"… Words, words, words… Big words versus small words. All sorts of words.

In the last few years "we have witnessed interesting situations, where the social and political context has strongly impacted on the way the artistic discourse was delivered and received. Being an opinion-former an artist has a certain responsibility. Since we are living in a world that is less and less inclined towards dialogue, what are now the artistic tools to operate with?"[12] This is the question Cărbunariu is asking herself. Just like Chekhov, she affirms that the role of the artist is to ask questions. As far as the answer is concerned, this role might be taken over by the viewers—involved in the performance and, possibly, in solving the problems raised by the text. This is exactly the case with *Artists Talk*, which, inspired by discussions with spectators or documented by interviews, asks questions. "As a part of this system, we were interested to understand how the artist's responsibility (or the absence of it) shows through from the discourse about their approach and about the world the artist lives in," the author confesses.

In five scenes and a prologue that sets the show's protocol, artists from all fields are (self) incited to discussions. The general action takes place "somewhere in Europe," even though the stories take us to TV shows, theatre and film festivals and public venues—identifiable or not. The small stage of the ARCUB hall is horizontally outlined by a shiny floor on which the actors walk wearing shoe covers (as in museums or hospitals) and vertically by a background of glittering fringes (as at the cabaret or music-hall).

---

[12] Gianina Cărbunariu—*The Artists Talk* (https://arcub.ro/eveniment/artists-talk-3/) (accessed on 10 August 2020).

The predominantly black costumes are adorned with coloured or sparkling applications, by means of which every self-respecting artist boosts their personalities. (Between the episodes, the actors change clothes almost within sight, in one of the stage wings.) The whole set exudes "casual glamour," supplemented by electro dance music—rhythmic, abrupt and, due to its varied characteristics, ironically pointing to different stories.

"Irony" and "self-irony" are, in fact, the words that best describe this show. Sometimes accused of thesisism in her productions dedicated to social issues, Cărbunariu seems to get even this time, through the humour both in the extremely hilarious text and in the performance of the Romanian actors. This is perhaps because all of them are part of and only too familiar with this "artistic system," whether they like it or not.

And the *artists talk*… in their own language, the artistic one, whether it is Romanian, English, French or even a little Czech. The *artists talk* sometimes the language of sincerity, at other times that of the sacred ignorant naivety, and most of the time that of hypocrisy. The rhetorically claimed honesty keeps hidden other interests and flaws such as vanity, indifference or artistic self-conceit. They are revealed as answers to the endlessly (that is, stupidly) repeated questions of the media people: "What was the author's intended meaning? / What was the creative drive? / What are your future plans?" Sometimes the developing discussions are sterile, sometimes they are thrilling. Although the resemblance to real persons is not coincidental, the identification of a certain artist having a specific rhetoric is not at stake in this fiction. The particular becomes universal. Even if the particular is represented by a Romanian mayor who built a wall (sorry: a fence!) between two ethnic city communities, inviting afterwards a group of Visual Arts students to paint and turn it into a work of street art (revisiting the main theme of *Solitarity*). Or if the particular could have had the name of the Lithuanian director Alvis Hermanis, who refused to work in a theatre, one of the reasons being the institution's position as "Refugees-Welcome-Center." And even if, in the last scene of the show, the particular actually bears the name of Irène Némirovsky, a novelist of Ukrainian Jewish origin. Born in the Russian Empire, she lived more than half of her life in France, wrote in French, but was denied French citizenship. Arrested as a Jew under the racial laws, she died in Auschwitz at the age of 39 and became famous posthumously, by means of modern marketing.

Questions about anti-Semitism, about individual destiny versus the collective one, about responsibility and artists' freedom, about the reception of a work of art... Questions about the world's refugees or those from one's own country, about country borders, about walls between us and the rest of the world. Questions about "art for art's sake" versus "art with a message"... What does "mainstream" mean today? What does it mean to be "fashionable" today? Is it better to remain "a fly on the wall" or must you commit yourself as an artist? These are all questions that Cărbunariu has not proposed to answer, nor does she intend to formulate verdicts; she only presents the issues. Excellently balanced, delivered with much humour and (self-)irony, the answers reach their target. Due to the range of problems tackled and the high-quality acting, ARCUB's *Artists Talk* is a production that meets the standards of Europe. A Europe redefining not only its borders, but also its artistic tools... A Europe that is seeking to find itself...

THE THEATRE OF YOUTH: *FRONTAL*

The Theatre of Youth in Piatra Neamț is one of the most important Romanian cultural institutions, with an over sixty-year history and a special artistic approach. It has won renown as a launch pad for young actors, directors, theatre designers and composers, who have developed outstanding professional careers. Just like any older theatre in Romania, it went through all kinds of periods—auspicious or not—due to changes of political regime, managers' replacements or never-ending building renovations. But the Theatre of Youth has always been reborn, just like the phoenix, and since 2017 has been living a renewed youth under the management of Gianina Cărbunariu. She left Piatra Neamț more than twenty years ago, yet it was the Theatre of Youth and its rebellious spirit has to a large extent shaped her as a spectator and a theatre-maker. This theatre has always had an aura, suggesting a place where atypical, non-conformist things were happening, addressed to a special audience that can be described as articulate, civilised, curious, capable of nuanced discussions, somewhat reserved in its reactions during a performance, but extremely generous with applause if appreciative of the show.

The coordinates of Cărbunariu's management plan, *The Theatre of Youth—Creative Co-laboratory*, are Cooperation, Contemporary, Community, Co-production. All of these are aiming at a re-invented relation between the theatre and its audience, as well as opening up to other national and international institutions and contexts. The young manager considers that "in the twenty-first century a theatre should not simply provide services under the form of shows, but it should also be a place where the artists, alongside the spectators, imagine a possible future while confronting themes of the present."[13] And she keeps her word—as proven by the Theatre of Youth's repertoire (inviting artists who have something to say in this respect), by its related activities (various programmes dedicated to raising and educating new audiences), but above all by the contents of the annual international festival that takes place in Piatra Neamț.

In 2019 it was half a century since the first edition of this festival. It too has gone through difficult times (being censored, or even stopped completely for periods), but is now living a second youth, just like the theatre itself. The programme of the anniversary edition included also the latest show from Cărbunariu, *Frontal*, staged at Piatra Neamț. This intends to revisit one of the best-known Romanian prose-fables, *The Story of a Lazy Man*, written at the end of the nineteenth century by one of the main figures of the national literature, Ion Creangă. Even the original story has a plurality of levels: fed up with the protagonist's proverbial indolence, which has led him as far as to view chewing food as an effort, his fellow villagers organise a lynching. This upsets the sensibility of a noblewoman who happens to witness the incident. When she offers to take the lazy man into her care and feed him breadcrumbs, he seals his own fate by asking: "But are your bread crumbs soft?" The production of the Theatre of Youth in Piatra Neamț suggests new meanings inspired by interviews done by the entire artistic team, sociology and anthropology studies, and on-line comments on social inequity. The fiction tries to reveal contemporary mechanisms criminalising poverty, the role of the media in constructing stereotypes associating "poverty" with "laziness," as well as the social consequences of such narratives.

Cărbunariu confesses: "I have been concerned by work as a theme, for a few years now. I am annoyed, frustrated and sometimes depressed by the fact that humble people in a poor country are fighting the poor people, instead of fighting poverty. I am outraged by the fact the poverty is associated with laziness."[14] And she refers then to the intention of her shows, but also to their impact on the audience: "I am not one of those who

---

[13] Gianina Cărbunariu—"*I'm a product of relevant theatrical experiences on the stage of the Theatre of Youth*" (interview by Cristina Modreanu), *Scenaro*. Nr. 39, 1 (2018), p. 22.

[14] Gianina Cărbunariu—"*There comes a generation of artists interested in the reality*" (interview by Cristina Rusiecki), "B-Critic," 22 November 2019 (https://www.b-critic.ro/spectacol/teatru/vine-o-generatie-de-creatori-interesati-de-real/) (accessed on 10 August 2020)

believe that theatre can change the world overnight. It seems to me that a show must ask questions of which I do not have the answers myself. A show can make me—not to change my position, because this is more difficult—but ask myself questions, nuance my opinions."[15]

It is said that "les enfants terribles" are ageless. Gianina Cărbunariu is one of them. Born under the sign of Leo, she displays the strong, fiery characteristics bestowed by her zodiac sign. With terrifying candour and irreverent humour, she puts things plainly both in the theatre and in society through her productions and plays, frequently staged at home and abroad. She was the first woman director to win the Romanian Association of Theatre Professionals UNITER Award for Best Show (*For Sale*, Odeon Theatre Bucharest, 2014) and she was short-listed by the Romanian media as one of the 100 most influential women in Romanian society today.

Image 1 *Common People*, directed by Gianiana Cărbunariu, National Theatre Sibiu, 2017. (Photo by Adi Bulboacă)

[15] Ibid.

"Theatre as practiced by Gianina Cărbunariu is not meant for contemplation, but for debate,"[16] writes Cristina Modreanu. This reflects a trend existing on the international stage. She is the first in her generation to introduce the idea that she was guided in her work by ethical values rather than aesthetics: "Very early in the rehearsals questions emerged about how could we approach this issue, this material, these 'characters' (real people like us), and how could we deal with the audience. These are questions which are connected with its ethics."[17]

But her greatest achievement is the remarkable balance between ethics and aesthetics. Socially committed theatre reaches its goal when it doesn't become theist, activist, manipulator. Cărbunariu's shows have such a powerful aesthetic content to preserve theatrical convention; the message conveyed by the characters does not overcome it in an intentional or ostentatious way. The audience "manipulation" is done in artistic ways, not political, and the emotion keeps its own sense. So it seems that Gianina Cărbunariu has found the alchemical secret through which she has discovered the philosopher's stone of twenty-first-century theatre.

References

Cîntec, Oltița, *Gianina Cărbunariu's Theatre, a Form of Memory in Recent History*, STUDIA UBB DRAMATICA, LXII, 2, 2017.

Epîngeac, Alina, *The Manipulation through Theatre* (PhD thesis), Bucharest: UNATC "I.L. Caragiale" Library, 2019.

Modreanu, Cristina, *Gianina Cărbunariu: Documentary Theatre with Political Focus*, The Theatre Times, 29 September 2016.

Popovici, Iulia, *Romania of Daily Nightmares* (foreword / *mady-baby.edu* by Gianina Cărbunariu), Bucharest: "Cartea Românească" Publishing House, 2007.

---

[16] Cristina Modreanu—*Three Photos with Gianina Cărbunariu* / vol. *Romanian Theatre Directing: From Authorship to Collaborative Practices* (coord. by Oltița Cîntec) (Iași, "Timpul" Publishing House & The International Theatre Festival for Young Audience, 2016), p. 43.

[17] Gianina Cărbunariu, quoted by Cristina Modreanu—*Gianina Cărbunariu: Documentary Theatre with Political Focus*, "The Theatre Times," 29 September 2016 (https://thetheatretimes.com/gianina-carbunariu-documentary-theater-with-political-focus/).

Oliver Frljić or the Theatre of Provocation

Kim Cuculić

Oliver Frljić, born in 1976 in Travnik, Bosnia-Herzegovina, arrived in Croatia as a refugee at the age of 16. Nine years later he enrolled to study at the Academy of Dramatic Art in Zagreb and graduated, in 2001, with a degree in philosophy and religious culture as well as in theatre directing and broadcasting. Soon afterwards, he started creating shows that began polarising audiences. Since then, in his capacity as a director, writer and actor, and a general manager of the Croatian National Theatre Ivan pl. Zajc in Rijeka (2014–2016), Oliver Frljić has pointed out the blind spots and festering wounds in society. His main topics include the war in Yugoslavia and fascist tendencies in contemporary Europe. A critic in *The Guardian* called him "one of the continent's most controversial theatre directors—and one of its most necessary;" the critic went on to describe his theatre as "nothing more and nothing less than the search for the right artistic tool to stop the descent into national hell."[1]

---

[1] Matt Trueman, "Move over Ivo van Hove: Europe's hottest theatre directors," *The Guardian* (3 September 2018). https://www.theguardian.com/stage/2018/sep/03/move-over-ivo-van-hove-europe-hottest-theatre-directors (accessed 4 December 2019).

K. Cuculić (✉)
Novi List Newspaper, Rijeka, Croatia

© The Author(s), under exclusive license to Springer Nature Switzerland AG 2021
K. Stefanova, M. Carlson (eds.), *20 Ground-Breaking Directors of Eastern Europe*, https://doi.org/10.1007/978-3-030-52935-2_3

32   K. CUCULIC

Although Frljić's often controversial shows have won numerous national and international awards, making him a major figure in the theatre of Eastern Europe, he has also been the target of vicious attacks by critics in the conservative media, both in Croatia and abroad.

Frljić's theatre work actually began before he entered the Academy of Dramatic Arts: in the mid-1990s he founded an amateur theatre troupe, Le Cheval, which participated in festivals of amateur theatre. Later on, after graduation from the Academy, he collaborated with many independent troupes in Zagreb and also directed children's plays. His first major success was the production *Turbofolk*, which premiered in 2008 and received several major international directing awards. In one form or another it has been in the repertoire of the Croatian National Theatre ever since.

This production, created without a fixed play text and relying heavily on the actors' improvisation, analyses the phenomenon of "turbofolk" music, which has penetrated all aspects of society in the Balkans and has become one of the most popular modern musical forms there. *Turbofolk* is one of the most-awarded productions in the history of the Croatian National Theatre. It was originally designed to be performed on the main stage of the theatre, representing a clash between the traditional concept of the theatre and the phenomenon of turbofolk, which isn't just a musical expression. The fluid form of the show allows for new political and social content to be continually added, with ever-new meanings. The show has also been adapted to the audiences of other countries to which it has toured (Austria, Germany, Poland).

His next major directorial work was *Damned Be the Traitor to His Homeland!* in 2010 at the Mladinsko Theatre in Ljubjiana. The show received two Borštnikov Awards at the Maribor Theatre Festival that year and broke the Slovenian record for the greatest number of international performances of a single production. During the same year, Frljić directed *Spring Awakening* at the Zagreb Youth Theatre. At the end of 2010, he directed *Cowardice* at the Narodno pozorište, Subotica, which was considered the theatrical event of the year by many critics.

Frljić received extensive media coverage with his next major project, the dramatisation of the novel *When Father Was Away on Business*, by Abdulah Sidran, which was performed early in 2011 at the theatre Atelje 212 in Belgrade. The production won over thirty awards and made Frljić the unofficial directorial star of the region. He confirmed his star status with *The Lexicon of Yu Mythology*, premiered in 2011 in Ljubljana and co-produced by six countries (Kosovo, Macedonia, Slovenia, Croatia, Serbia and Montenegro). In the same year, at the prestigious regional festival MESS in Sarajevo, his production *Letter from 1920* caused a great stir by using excerpts from the war monodrama *Years of Deception* (by the Bosnian/Herzegovian actor Emir Hadžihafizbegović) in which he calls for a *Jihad*. The actor threatened Frljić in the media, but nothing came of it and the production won great critical acclaim.

Many of Frljić's productions have caused public outrage, shock and disbelief and there have been attempts to stop them from being performed both in Croatia and abroad (Bosnia and Herzegovina, Serbia, Poland). On several occasions, actors refused to perform in his shows. In a number of his works, such as *Zoran Đinđić* (2012), *Aleksandra Zec* (2014) and *Our Violence and Your Violence* (2016), he has represented extreme scenes and has been accused of blasphemy, provocation and violation of the religious and ethnic rights of citizens, as well as Catholics and Muslims in particular. This had led to calls for boycotts, attempts to take the shows out of the repertoire and even criminal charges. His very first show at the Stary Teatr in Poland, an adaptation of Krasinski's *Non-Divine Comedy*, was taken from the repertoire mere days before the premiere. The administration and a number of the actors rejected Frljić's attempt to make the production a reflection on anti-Semitism in contemporary Polish society as well as on the role of the Polish people in the Holocaust.

One of his best productions so far, in my opinion, was definitely *I Hate the Truth!* at the Zagreb Teatar &TD, in 2011. Here Frljić utilised his own family history by placing it into a theatrical context, thus writing a sort of a psychological diagram of his family. Of course, it all should be taken with a grain of salt, since the play is a blend of fact and fiction and not an autobiographical narrative that can be trusted. Still, Frljić bravely revealed at least a part of his family's story by playing with the fine line between reality and theatrical illusion. As Pirandello once did, Frljić is apparently trying to expose the fiction behind the "real thing" that precedes and substantiates the theatrical game. The actors play members of the playwright's family, constantly breaking out of and re-entering their characters, as in Pirandello. This creates a mesh of fiction and reality where real life and theatre keep changing places, bringing forth only one question: what is more real—acting or life?

The actors are self-referentially aware of the process, speaking to the director and giving him feedback on the play itself. In some situations they—that is, their characters—protest because they think something happened differently from the way Frljić portrays it. Questions of subjectivity and the uncertainty of memory crop up, undermining the certainty of the story. The plot takes us back before 25 April 1992, which is the day Frljić left his parental home. The play dissects his family's situation, but touches on the broader social and political context of Bosnia before the war. Frljić does not treat the family as a separate entity, but as a community on which the waves of social circumstances break. Building on the relationships of family members, whose last real connection is the moment of gathering around the dining table, Frljić tackles many topics—domestic violence, nationalism, homophobia, racism, Bosnian multiculturalism, language, taboos about parents' sexuality, the death of a child and so on. Many important topics he wants to discuss are left unsaid or are lied about, while some other family truths become unbearable. But in order to prevent the play from coming off as pathetic, he incorporates a degree of humour.

In turn, Frljić's *Hamlet*, at the Zagreb Youth Theatre in 2014, is an example of a contemporary rendering of a classical piece. Frljić approached Shakespeare's text from a modern-day viewpoint, turning it into a chamber play while still keeping all the main motifs, protagonists and their relations to each other. In this somewhat reduced version, the dramatic starting point is the "Mousetrap" scene, which frames the entire play. The mousetrap here is not set to reveal the foul crimes of Claudius, but is instead sinisterly woven around Hamlet himself. Actors and roles create a synaesthesia and it's as if we are watching "a play within a play." The scenography, composed of an elongated table and a few inclined chairs, resembles actors' reading rehearsals. We get the same impression from their costumes: they seem unfinished and as if they belong to the actors themselves. Books with several translations of Hamlet are used as props. And although the play is still set in Denmark, which is a synonym for dungeons and rotting states, the hardcore turbofolk rhythm of the introductory scene evokes images of today's society burdened by an upstart political elite.

By making *Hamlet* so topical, Frljić made some themes and motifs even more radical. In his version, Hamlet strangles Ophelia and Gertrude slits Hamlet's throat with a knife. Knives and poison are replaced by firearms that Polonius uses to kill Horatio, making the crime even more brutal. The ruling elite gathered around the black table, wearing black blazers, seems like a gang of criminals hell-bent on doing Hamlet in. *Hamlet*, as seen by Frljić, is a dark image of the world today where every attempt at rebellion is brutally extinguished and various characters such as Claudius and Gertrude remain in power despite having blood on their hands. Thus interpreted, Shakespeare's protagonists seem like our contemporaries, devoid of tragic pathos. This *Hamlet* can be seen as an actors' play where, on the ritualistic table of Hamlet's slaughter, it is still only stage blood that is being shed.

In 2015, *The Trilogy of Croatian Fascism* premiered, directed by Oliver Frljić while Marin Blažević created the text. In fact it combined three productions by Frljić—*The Bacchae, Aleksandra Zec* and *The Croatian Association of Dramatic Artists.* Performances of *The Trilogy* were heavily guarded by the police, especially *The Bacchae,* which was presented in front of the National Theatre in Rijeka. By combining the already performed pieces as a whole, one could follow the developmental line of these connected productions.

The Trilogy of Croatian Fascism started in 2008, when the production of *The Bacchae* (at the theatre in Split) was banned, but was eventually performed, when Ivo Sanader (the then Croatian Prime Minister) issued a decree allowing it to carry on. It could be seen during the International Small Scene Theatre Festival in Rijeka. Then Frljić directed another production of *The Bacchae* at the Croatian National Theatre Ivan pl. Zajc in Rijeka. In comparison with the original version, it was drastically changed, with a new cast that brought forth a new kind of energy. Yet the dramatic essence of *The Bacchae* remained the same: through the fabric of Euripides' tragedy, Frljić and Blažević talked about war and crime, as well as asking what the relationship between an artist and the government really is. In the Rijeka production, the focus was shifted to Croatian Homeland War veterans; that is, to Croatian politics, which—according to Frljić—betrayed them. In 2018, the dramatist remarked: "I used to say that theatre should be the mirror of society. But one that we can smash on the head of that same society."[2]

By staging *The Bacchae* in front of the National Theatre, Frljić and Blažević made the topic of the relationship between politics/ideology and the theatre even more pronounced. During the first scene, actors in camouflage uniforms emerged from body bags, each carrying name tags and

---

[2] Quoted in Nick Awde, "Meet Oliver Frljic, the Croatian provocateur with neoliberal theatre in his sights," *The Stage* (25 July 2018). https://www.thestage.co.uk/features/interviews/2018/meet-director-oliver-frljic-the-croatian-provocateur-with-neoliberal-theatre-in-his-sights/ (accessed 15 August 2019).

Croatian flags: Milan Levar, Josip Reihl-Kir and Aleksandra Zec. This was a reminder of the darker parts of recent Croatian history: Milan Levar was a former officer in the Croatian Army during the Homeland War for Independence, known for willingly testifying in the mid-1990s before the Hague tribunal along with two other veterans. They testified about the massacre of Serbian nationals perpetrated by Croatia military and paramilitary forces in the autumn of 1991. Levar received death threats and was eventually killed in a bombing in Gospić in 2000. The perpetrators as well as those who had Levar killed were never caught or persecuted. Josip Reihl-Kir was a police commissioner in Osijek who was murdered in an ambush in 1991. The murder itself, despite subsequent trials, was never truly explained. This wasn't an accidental killing, though. He was killed because he was anti-war. The murder of Aleksandra Zec, a young girl, is an example of the most extreme of crimes—she was killed after witnessing both her mother and her father being murdered. Her executioners, despite confessing and despite material evidence, remained free.

The Bacchae depicted the hiding and denial of war crimes committed during the war in Croatia, and Euripides' tragedy was boiled down to a repetitive report of the Messenger on the murders that took place off the stage; that is, away from the public's eye. Frljić and Blažević prudently blended ancient Greek tragedy and contemporaneity. Euripides' Messenger recounted the story of the fervent dances of the Bacchae and the bloody finale where Pentheus' drunken mother Agave, having failed to recognise her son, impaled his head on Dionysus' staff and took it home as a hunting trophy. In accordance with the brutal details of the dismemberment of Pentheus' body, the scene props in this minimalistic scenography were broken down to a single white circle, pieces of meat and details of a suit composed of raw meat. This was a prelude to a scene where one of the characters in a miniature theatre box minced meat, while actors with baroque-style wigs ritualistically burned a cardboard model bearing a photograph of the Croatian National Theatre in Zagreb. The exalted style of Euripides' tragedy in *The Bacchae* was interwoven with excerpts from TV news, while the scattered meat was forensically gathered by the actors and placed in buckets. Remaining pieces of meat were stacked into a swastika—all while drinking wine, providing an ironic link to Dionysus' (Bacchus') companions. In the final scene of the Split production, the actors joined the public and merged with them in a polyphonous rendering of the text by the Messenger, which created a much stronger cathartic effect than was the case in the Rijeka production.

The production *Aleksandra Zec* was developed at the HKD Teatar in Rijeka. Frljić and Blažević here portrayed the fate of a young girl—an innocent war casualty and a victim of a brutal crime. In this production she becomes a contemporary Antigone. The production is dedicated to all children who perished as war casualties. The girl Aleksandra Zec who, in the final act, points a gun at the participants of the Croatian theatre award ceremony is the link between all three parts of *The Trilogy*. She points the gun but doesn't shoot ....

The Croatian Association of Dramatic Artists was performed as the third part of *The Trilogy*, where the duo Frljić/Blažević became even harsher towards the Croatian theatre scene, since some contemporaries were directly and publicly called out. This production, among other things, recollected concentration camp victims during World War II as well as the genocide in Srebrenica in the mid-1990s. While *The Trilogy* caused a great deal of controversy among parts of the public, *The Croatian Association of Dramatic Artists* was even protested against by the Croatian Catholic church. One critic wrote:

> I associate the following keywords with Frljic: Croatia, nationalism, radical, provocative, a story about a beheaded chicken whose blood creates the image of a Croatian flag on stage.[3]

"This scene was made while the government kept the film in their possession"—this is the sentence that ends *The Ristić Complex*, directed by Frljić in 2015 and co-produced by CNT Ivan pl. Zajc, Slovensko mladinsko gledališče, Ljubljana, BITEF, Belgrade and MOT, Skopje. It interrogated the artistic and political activity of the theatre director Ljubiša Ristić, who greatly influenced the former Yugoslav art scene. This production did not deconstruct this director's biography, it rather focused on the way Frljić is preoccupied with the relationship between art and politics, the artist and the government. In a way, Ristić was a metaphor for Yugoslavia.

The theatrical method used by Frljić in *The Croatian Association of Dramatic Artists* is the same one he relied upon in *The Ristić Complex*, but with a different ideological underpinning. While the previous work dealt with the Ustashe regime, this production dissected the failed Yugoslavian

---

[3] Quoted in Aljoscha Begrich, "Who's afraid of Oliver Frljić?", *Contemporary Theatre Review*, Issue 28.2 (2018). https://www.contemporarytheatrereview.org/2018/begrich-whos-afraid-of-oliver-frljic/ (accessed 12 February 2020).

38   K. CUCULIC

state and its totalitarian ideologies. The quote from the beginning of *The Ristić Complex* was a commentary on a scene from a film that really did vanish. The film in question is *Plastic Jesus* by film director Lazar Stojanović from 1971, where a documentary scene of the wedding between Ljubiša Ristić and the painter Višnja Postić was included. The film was taken down and upon subsequent showings the scene in question was gone. This scene must have been questionable to the regime because it showed not only the newlyweds but their fathers as well (who both happened to be generals in the Yugoslav army), in addition to a number of their friends—officers and high officials of the national security department/ministry.

The film *Plastic Jesus* is a controversial portrait of a rebellious film-maker and a harsh criticism of the Yugo-establishment of the time. The film contains archive footage of the Croatian Ustashe, the Serbian Chetnics and of Hitler and Tito, which the author uses to compare the regimes. The missing wedding scene was the starting point of *The Ristić Complex* by Frljić, which also referred to the Ljubiša Ristić play and the production *Missa in A-Minor* (performed at the Slovenian Youth Theatre in Ljubljana in 1980). It was because of this play that Danilo Kiš, author of the play *A Tomb for Boris Davidovič*, became so angry at Ristić that he refused to speak to him. There was a lot of discussion about the play, which was created using motifs from Kiš's play. *A Tomb for Boris Davidovič* was also involved in a literary scandal and another play by Kiš, *An Anatomy Class*, was a response to these controversies. A scene in *The Ristić Complex*, where the actors put on masks with the image of Stalin, was a reference both to Kiš and to the famous painting by Rembrandt, "The Anatomy Lesson of Dr. Nicolaes Tulp" (1632). Frljić's production made several other references to works of art. Thus, the allegory of Yugoslavia was a young woman with a naked breast, wrapped in the Yugoslav flag (a reference to "Liberty Leading the People" by Delacroix, 1830). Frljić questioned the boundaries of freedom in the ex-Yugoslav state, while the "revolution" was ironically reduced to a Coca-Cola bottle and cowboy boots, which are seen as symbols of the West.

Similar to some effects in *The Croatian Association of Dramatic Artists*, Frljić used a few attached tables and chairs in *The Ristić Complex*. The only difference was that the actors in the *Complex* wore partisan uniforms, as opposed to Ustashe ones. The stage had a map of Yugoslavia outlined in red paint on which the actors later—accompanied by a religious hymn—urinated, after which it would be gathered up and enshrouded like a corpse by a forensic team.

The Ristić Complex was an example of non-verbal, iconic theatre based on expressive images, with music also having a prominent role. Other than the song lyrics, the show had no spoken words and the public was left to interpret and make associations on the basis of symbols and images. Similar to his methods in *The Croatian Association of Dramatic Artists*, Frljić used the motif of Oedipus' blindness in *The Ristić Complex*, indicating ideological blindness and fallacy. Orgies in wedding dresses worn by both men and women provided a social commentary on the perversion of the former social system and the ideas presented by the far left.

In 2016, inspired by the novel *The Aesthetics of Resistance* by Peter Weiss and also by Bertolt Brecht, Frljić and Blažević created another production together: *Our Violence and Your Violence*—an attempt to give a direct answer to "the here and the now," to the current socio-political crisis in both Europe and the world. This premiered at the Wiener Festwochen as an international co-production with other European theatres. It has been performed all over Europe and its topic is widely familiar and well known. In a mere seventy or so minutes, Frljić and Blažević tackle many current topics, like immigration, fundamentalism, terrorism, and the growing trend of fascination in European societies with the problem of East/West relations throughout a history that has been violent and exploitative.

With a series of brutal scenes and heinous actions, the production is a theatrical portrayal of the history of violence; that is, of the fact that violence begets violence. And so we find ourselves in contemporary times, when the arrogant post-colonial relationship between America and Europe and the Middle Eastern countries comes back like a boomerang, bringing with it the immigration crisis and terrorist attacks. At the beginning of the show, in the form of a confession, refugees who arrived in Europe a very long time ago are seen as an example of "successful" integration. The audience is addressed many times and, from a blissful silence and passivity, it is asked to participate in a minute of silence for terror attack victims in France, Belgium and Germany, and then, in another minute of silence, for the four million people killed by Europeans and Americans in Afghanistan, Iraq and Syria since the 1990s.

In *Our Violence and Your Violence* there are statements like: "Europe, I am ashamed of your name for it is my own. I am ashamed of Europeans who would rather go to the theatre than barge into the headquarters of their fascist governments and demand basic human rights. I am ashamed of humanitarian relief that is trying to wash away the scum of its own guilty conscience. I am ashamed of European democracy." These words attempt to make the viewer feel guilty or to provoke resistance. This politically active production keeps referring to theatre that is raising questions and pointing to problems yet again, but gives no answers and remains helpless before the horrors that transpire.

Our Violence and Your Violence is laden with quotations. The naked bodies of the performers, marked with Arabic letters, are a reference to the works of the Iranian artist Shirin Neshat. But the most controversial scene is when a woman wearing a hijab pulls out a flag from her vagina (it is always the flag of the country where the production is presented). At the premiere in Rijeka, it was the Croatian flag used during the Nazi Independent State of Croatia. Another controversial scene is when a man resembling Jesus climbs down from a cross made of oil cans and rapes a Muslim woman. This has disturbed religious spectators in some countries. Images that are present in everyday media are transformed into theatrical scenes, with music providing an ironic commentary, like when prisoners in orange jumpsuits and hoods are being decapitated. Also, icons of Islam

Image 1 *Turbofolk*, directed by Oliver Frljić, National Theatre of Ivan pl. Zajc, Rijeka, 2008. (Photo by Dražen Šokčević)

and Christianity are opposed, making relevant the problems of a clash between civilisations as well as the growing issues of intolerance and racism.

In 2014, Oliver Frljić became the artistic director of the Croatian National Theatre (CNT) in Rijeka, but held that position for only two years before becoming a member of Rijeka 2020—the European Capital of Culture project team. During this period, he perceived the CNT as a sort of artistic project, questioning and relativising the concept of a national theatre house. At the very beginning of his mandate, he hung a rainbow flag on the theatre and, on the eve of the Croatian Independence Day, he proclaimed the CNT in Rijeka to be a lesbian, gay, bisexual and transgender (LGBT) theatre. This was just an introduction to a number of activities that stirred up the police, the Catholic church, homeland war veterans, sports fan groups and right-wing political parties. During these activities and projects that took place in the course of Frljić's mandate, neither art nor theatre aesthetics were placed front and centre; what was central was his desire to incite activism and social commentary about events in Croatia, Europe and further abroad.

It may be that the theatrics and methods used by Oliver Frljić in his last few productions have been depleted and become somewhat mannerist. Yet the problems he addresses remain as serious as ever. It is to be hoped that this ever-innovative and barrier-breaking director will continue to provide us with different creative challenges and breakthroughs in the future.

References

Awde, Nick. "Meet Oliver Frljic, the Croatian provocateur with neoliberal theatre in his sights," *The Stage* (25 July 2018). https://www.thestage.co.uk/features/interviews/2018/meet-director-oliver-frljic-the-croatian-provocateur-with-neoliberal-theatre-in-his-sights/ (accessed 15 August 2019).

Begrich, Aljoscha. "Who's afraid of Oliver Frljić?" *Contemporary Theatre Review*, Issue 28.2 (2018). https://www.contemporarytheatrereview.org/2018/begrich-whos-afraid-of-oliver-frljic/ (accessed 12 February 2020).

Trueman, Matt. "Move over Ivo van Hove: Europe's hottest theatre directors," *The Guardian* (3 September 2018). https://www.theguardian.com/stage/2018/sep/03/move-over-ivo-van-hove-europe-hottest-theatre-directors (accessed 4 December 2019).

Alvis Hermanis: "To Be Everything and Nothing at All"

Edīte Tišheizere

Perhaps the most accurate definition of just who Alvis Hermanis (b. 1965) is may well be something he himself said many years ago in an interview: "It seems to me that for a human the most ideal path is if he goes on and on, [and] connects with [something] … it's an opportunity to be everything and nothing at all at the same time."[1] Hermanis has pointed out repeatedly that he does not have his own distinctive style, that every material requires its own directing approach and often a new type of acting as well.

THE BEGINNING

Hermanis says in an interview that he was lucky enough to be born at the right moment to finish his theatre studies in the late 1980s and start working professionally at a time when previous theatre experience was not relevant in Eastern Europe anymore and everything had to be started from

[1] Juris Zvirgzdiņš, "Alvis Hermanis Free Lance," *Liesma* 4:12 (1990), p. 1.

E. Tišheizere (✉)
Institute of Literature, Folklore and Arts of the University of Latvia, Riga, Latvia

© The Author(s), under exclusive license to Springer Nature Switzerland AG 2021
K. Stefanova, M. Carlson (eds.), *20 Ground-Breaking Directors of Eastern Europe*, https://doi.org/10.1007/978-3-030-52935-2_4

44   E. TIŠHEIZERE

scratch: "An electrician comes and turns the counter to zero. That was exactly the moment in the Eastern European theatre in the early nineties. A zero point. Everything that had been before was effectively erased. It didn't work anymore, it was drained out."[2]

Hermanis got his first impulses towards theatre as early as his high school years, at the "Rīga pantomime" led by Roberts Ligers. This was possibly the most free-thinking art organism of the Soviet era, which could not be subdued by censorship. He failed to enter the directors' course at the State Conservatory of the Latvian SSR, so he graduated from the actors' course in 1987. As early as his student years and right after that, Hermanis played some important roles in cinema. Disabled veteran of the Afghan war Kārlis (*A Photo of a Woman and a Wild Boar*, dir. A. Krievs, 1987), explorer of artificial intelligence Navarzin (*Autumn, Chertanovo*, dir. I. Talankin, 1988) and magician Toms (*Eve's Garden of Paradise*, dir. A. Krievs, 1990) are all parts with certain similarities: a young man living in his own mysterious and mystical inner world, existing on the verge of overstrung nerves. With these roles Hermanis made it clear that he was an introverted actor who can achieve the needed characteristics of the role with minimal exterior means. The young actor did not join any theatre.

This was the period of *perestroika* and the Latvian National Awakening; Hermanis was explicitly, even demonstratively apolitical during this time. He visited the USA, because "it seemed completely absurd to me that a land can be free, I thought that only people could be free. You can only save yourself individually."[3] According to him, the two years spent in the States had not provided anything in terms of understanding theatre, yet they changed him as a person. "The world within myself has opened up,"[4] he said upon returning to Rīga.

THE FIRST PRODUCTIONS

At the beginning of 1993 the New Rīga Theatre (NRT) opened with Hermanis' first production, *Like a Calm and Peaceful River Is the Homecoming*. Based on the script for Steven Soderbergh's *Sex, Lies and Videotapes*, it was shocking in terms of content—four people talking about

[2] Sarmīte Ēlerte, "Hermaņa pasaules rasas pilienos" in: Laima Sava (ed.), *Alvis Hermanis* (Riga: Neputns, 2015), p. 625.

[3] Uldis Tīrons, "Lāčplēša atgriešanās," *Rīgas Laiks* 12:12 (1995), p. 1.

[4] Gita Valtenberga, "Pilnīga neintervija," *Latvijas Jaunatne*, (23 Oct. 1992), p. 6.

their sexuality, urges, desires, the unreachable—and, possibly even more so, due to the style of acting. These were actors much like himself (because he was still acting at the time and, thus, looking for congenial partners): introverted, submerged into scrutinising their own sensations, seemingly indifferent to what impression they would make on the audience, and therefore very daring. The erotic tension was huge, but it was achieved by a spiritual openness instead of a physical one. The performance was painful, but also tender and merciful; if mercy could be perceived as a daring way for one to express the most hidden things about oneself and not to judge others—the audience, the partners—for their possible secrets.

Fifteen years later, in his address to the participants of the Congress of the International Association of Theatre Critics (2008), Hermanis said he sought a theatre language removed from aggression, except in the case of necessity, that would "punch with tenderness."[5] This particular, non-sentimental tenderness could be traced back as early as his first production.

Almost immediately afterwards, another substantial characteristic of Hermanis' directing became apparent: beauty as the goal and justification of art. *Madame de Sade* by Yukio Mishima (1993) was a manifestation of this. In the theatre foyer, among the white columns, a beautiful ritual took place, where the director used the unrealistic expressiveness of traditional Japanese No and *butoh* dance, and the unconscious grace of wild animals.

During the first four years of his work, Hermanis staged about ten productions, experimented with the actors' (himself being one of them) sexuality and psyche, and pushed the boundaries of openness and exploration of the subconscious, sometimes doing so in a self-admittedly cruel and provocative manner, mixing art with life in its most extreme displays. However, this "dark" stage was natural and necessary in order for him to look for a professionally secure and stable basis for the actors' work later on.

For his first productions, Hermanis chose an empty white room. This was the optimal solution in the destitution of theatre and, to a certain extent, a symbolic gesture: "The space was empty, like a blank page. That is what my white stage looked like."[6] Space and its fluidity under the influence of the actor's acting have formed an important component of his stage language ever since and are becoming more and more refined.

---

[5] Alvis Hermanis, "Teātris un humānisms mūsdienu vardarbības pasaulē," *Teātra Vēstnesis* 2:4 (2008), p. 103.

[6] Laima Slava (ed.), *Alvis Hermanis* (Riga: Neputns, 2015), p. 17.

46   E. TIŠHEIZERE

In May 1997, Hermanis became the artistic director of the NRT and took a radical step. After a period of projects-based theatre, he returned to a stable, closed company, thus ensuring the continuous development of the actors' professional level. He came up with his own concept of theatre directing, which clearly proposed that the NRT would be a "profitable theatre loved by the audience, at the base of which there is a solid acting company."[7]

Hermanis carried out these reforms in anticipation of much greater, global changes—the NRT was preparing for the coming of the new millennium, connecting it to new aesthetic qualities, among other things. This period marked the beginning of themes and creative techniques that would go on to develop and mature in the following century.

Among these themes of Hermanis' directing is that of time and the theatre as a peculiar time machine. Such a time-machine model could be seen in the production *XX Century. Поезд-призрак. Vision Express* (1999). In this production about a ghost train that is said to have entered a tunnel and disappeared in 1911, only to haunt people in various places of the world for the rest of the century, two new techniques were used that proved to be fruitful in the future. First, it was a production without a previously written dramaturgical basis, since the director had compiled the text himself, using various sources. Second, being the stage designer as well, he marked the acting space with authentic Soviet-era objects—a soda vending machine, radio lamps, a gas stove and the like. In the new century, the authenticity of the object space as a documentary witness of a certain era was to become one of the most prominent "trademarks" of Hermanis' productions.

According to critics, "such modern anti-theatre experiments are practiced by several prominent figures in the new European directing, thus achieving a suggestive, hypnotic, even magical effect. Anti-theatre (no characters, no action, no plot ...) turns into theatrical poetry, an event of high sensual capacity. For example, that is how the Swiss Christoph Marthaler works, or the Belgian French Jan Fabre. And it dictates the theatre style of the new century—the theatre as a phantom of engaged sensations."[8] A "phantom of engaged sensations" is a precise definition for Hermanis' following productions as well.

---

[7] Dita Rietuma, "Dzīve pēc citiem likumiem," *Diena* (20 Sept. 1997) p. 4.

[8] Normunds Naumanis, "Dejas uz teātra kauliem," *Diena* (23 Sept. 1999), p. 12.

The theme of time continued in Tom Stoppard's *Arcadia* (1998). The stage design and costumes, created by Andris Freibergs, were made from paper to save expense. Yet this material made for beautiful metaphors and could be changed in the blink of an eye. In the end, the paper got set on fire and perished, just like the world that was created from it.

This production marked the rise of Hermanis' directing technique that one might call a *material metaphor*. He used it also in *The Story of Caspar Hauser* (2002). While in *Arcadia* diverse metaphors stemmed from paper as a special material, the space-creating, metaphorical material in *Caspar Hauser* was sand. A mysterious foundling emerged from heavy, wet sand, and that was where he would return as well—society buried him again—the grave was his beginning and his end. Paper and sand would later be joined by ice in *The Ice. Collective Reading of the Book with the Help of Imagination* (2005, three versions: in Rīga, Gladbeck—Ruhr Triennale—and the Frankfurter Schauspielhaus) and straw in *Die Soldaten* at the Salzburger Festspiele (2012). All of it served the purpose of creating the "phantom of engaged sensations."

Entering the International Arena

Hermanis had worked for approximately ten years when he earned international acclaim in 2002 by taking part in the Salzburg Festival Programme for Young Directors with a staging of Nikolai Gogol's *The Inspector General*. He won the competition and received a Max Reinhardt Pen. Since then, Hermanis has received the Europe Theatre Prize for (New) Theatrical Realities in 2007, a Nestroy-Preis as Best Director in Austria and a Konrad Wolf Award for his work in German-speaking countries (2010); was included among the ten most influential European theatre personalities of the last ten years by *Du* (a Swiss culture magazine) based on the opinion of experts from twenty countries (2012); and was awarded with a Star on the Sibiu Walk of Fame, Romania (2016). His productions have been awarded with the Grand Prix at prominent festivals all over the globe.

The Inspector General literally exploded the auditorium. The play was hilariously funny from the first moment to the last. Hermanis transported the story of nineteenth-century civil servants in a provincial town to the 1970s, which was the time of his childhood, choosing a Soviet-era cafeteria for his set. The set design was recognisable for anyone who had ever visited such an eatery, with tin bowls and utensils, and an immediately

48   E. TIŠHEIZERE

identifiable stench that involved fried onions and chlorine disinfectant. The hyper-realistic set design was made grotesque by chickens that freely wandered all over the stage. Also grotesque were the characters: the actors wore padded costumes; they were literally sinking into their own "flesh." These vividly individualised characters came to form for the audience a collective hero—*Homo Sovieticus.*

With less than a month between them, two premieres took place that marked an entirely new period in Hermanis' directing and became hits at international festivals—*Long Life* (which is still in the repertoire of the New Rīga Theatre) on 9 December 2003 and *By Gorky* (an adaptation of Maxim Gorky's *The Lower Depths*) on 2 January 2004. Despite critical acclaim, Hermanis himself believed that a certain crisis and routine had set in in his theatre, made even more serious by reality shows, which had just come into fashion: "Reality shows have absolutely disrupted the purpose of theatre and cinema actors. They lost the monopoly on imitating reality; the level of credibility has changed drastically."[9] Hermanis staged both these productions together with the set designer Monika Pormale, because space is a quintessential component there.

Long Life is a very refined manifestation of reality. The "fourth wall" is brought down right in front of the audience, revealing an environment realistic to the finest detail, where nothing is a copy or a prop. However, this environment is a deliberately arranged "very complex symphony of real, live objects."[10] In this space of "live objects," one day in the life of five people takes place. Each moment in the action is as lifelike as possible, and the choice and composition of these moments give one the illusion that an entire day has passed, from dawn to the evening news, although what the audience has seen is not reality, but a concentrated version of it. Also, this meticulously observed, researched life, presented in the smallest physical and physiological detail, is actually enacted by actors who were precisely half a century younger than their protagonists were at the time of the premiere.

The production has been on for over sixteen years. The space created by Monika Pormale gets disassembled and reassembled, yet it has been living for all these years precisely because the actions taking place in it are not imitation, but the actual energy of the five people filling the space. If the production will, as promised by the director, continue until the actors

---

[9] Ieva Zole, "Jaunais reālisms—kas tas tāds?" *Forums* (23 Jan 2004) p. 4.
[10] Reinis Suhanovs, "Maigā nežēlība," *Teātra Vēstnesis* 3:4 (2013), p. 44.

reach the age of the characters, their existence will gradually turn into their own physical reality instead of acting. That would be an unprecedented experiment in the interaction of theatre and reality.

With *Long Life*, what were called the "Latvian times" started at the NRT. From 2003 to 2010, Hermanis staged more than ten productions, all examining the Latvian mentality, character, history and daily life, and which largely fit into the context of verbatim theatre. The actors were very independent in collecting material about real people in order to put these stories into action together with the director, based on improvisations. However, Hermanis himself stresses the difference from the verbatim mainstream: "We might have been unique in the sense that we stayed with professional actors. By using our acting technologies, taking real prototypes, we tried to create some sort of a third reality, where a real prototype overlaps with the actor's personality."[11] This method of the actors' and director's work was further advanced both at the NRT—in *Latvian Love* (2006), *Grandfather, Martha from the Blue Hill* (2009), *Black Milk* (2010)—and abroad—*Väter* (Schauspielhaus Zürich, 2007), *Kölner Affäre* (Schauspiel Köln, 2008), *Die schönsten Sterbeszenen in der Geschichte der Oper* (Schauspielhaus Zürich, 2015) and *Insgeheim Lohengrin* (Residenztheater, München, 2017).

Hermanis and Pormale applied an alternate concept of reality and space in *By Gorky*. Using the reality show aesthetic, together with actors from the NRT, they created a performance structure where everything took place in several parallel spaces, times and forms of existence. One version of space was the glass box of a reality show, where actors existed under their own names, but in situations set by the play. In the other one, exiting onto a small forestage square in direct proximity to the audience, the actors were themselves, but in a double manifestation; namely, the female actors were reading magazines, the glamorous covers of which featured their own Photoshopped portraits. Three parallel screens showed first, a not-so-distant past—fragments of rehearsals; second, a dimension beyond time—a graphic virtual ritual transforming the faces of several protagonists into ornaments; and third, the actors' "inner space"—close-ups captured on video by Monika Pormale as she moved freely among the actors.

A further advancement of this principle could be observed in the three versions of *The Ice. Collective Reading of the Book with the Help of*

---

[11] Sarmīte Ēlerte, "Hermaņa pasaules rasas pilienos" in: Laima Sava (ed.), *Alvis Hermanis* (Riga: Neputns, 2015), p. 629.

50   E. TIŠHEIZERE

Imagination in Rīga, Frankfurt and Gladbeck (Ruhr Triennale)—especially in Gladbeck, in the engine room of an abandoned coal mine, where several processes took place on different levels. Each of these productions featured a space that remained constant, yet developed and changed in the audience's perception.

"Russian Seasons"

Since 2007, Hermanis has been working regularly in German-speaking countries. In 2011–2012 he staged several classical Russian works—Ivan Goncharov's *Oblomow* (Schauspiel Köln), Anton Chekhov's *Platonov* (Wiener Burgtheater), *Eugene Onegin*, after Pushkin (Berliner Schaubühne), all in 2011, and Maxim Gorky's *Wassa* (Münchner Kammerspiele) and *Sommergäste* (Berliner Schaubühne), both in 2012. These productions comprised a cycle of sorts, united by the concept of space and the type of actors' existence. They caused a conflicting reaction on the part of critics, some of whom questioned the "old-fashioned," "dusty" naturalism, others finding this "new sense of reality" to be an important inspiration for contemporary theatre.

Starting with *Oblomow*, Hermanis staged Russian classics seemingly following Stanislavsky's principles from the early Moscow Art Theater—with historically accurate decorations and costumes, and the atmosphere of the performance created by the lighting designer, the score and so on. However, as Normunds Naumanis, a specialist and documentarian of Hermanis' productions, wrote, the staging of *Oblomow* was, on the one hand, a hyperbolised, meticulously detailed psycho-realism, on the other hand an artistic hyperbole close to the grotesque.[12] The actors' "natural" acting could easily become grotesque when friends were rolling on the floor out of the joy of seeing each other and the reality of the interior was challenged by a lilac bush that had suddenly "grown" into it.

In *Platonov*, the set designer Monika Pormale created a fantastic and accurately "realistic" glass cage, a 1:1 model of the manor interior and a pavilion, where, through the many windows, one could see the woods, the veranda, the antechamber to the dining room, and which "is occupied literally to the last inch within the five hours of the performance."[13] Martin

---

[12] Normunds Naumanis, "Ceriņu simfonija minorā," *Diena* (18 Feb. 2011), p. 7.
[13] Normunds Naumanis, "Līdz mielēm un pilnībai," *Diena* (20 May 2011), p. 6.

Wuttke acted Platonov with astonishing artistry, his portrayal reaching a "quasi-documentary existence"[14] in its psychological realism.

Outlining Hermanis' concept of space and acting, seemingly so much in conflict with contemporary theatre, the researcher of his foreign productions Margarita Zieda concluded that the "Russian cycle" productions "still connect, in a unique manner, with the most current phenomena in modern theatre and cinema art—with a strong demonstration of authenticity. In works of other modern artists, authenticity is achieved through an uttermost approximation of acting to natural human behaviour or a total abandonment of actors altogether and fitting non-professionals into the work of art [...], but Alvis Hermanis' actors remain in a definitely art territory without even trying to imitate something, without trying to pretend to be someone they are not. And it is not even about today's authenticity, but that of an entirely different era. It is like the total sum of all the elements of theatre, including the stage existence of characters, the material culture surrounding them, the poetry texts of, and historical comments on, their era, which allows an intellectual cosmos of another era to gradually come together in the spectator's mind. [...] Alvis Hermanis' production turns into a 'time machine,' creating a bridge that lets you 'zoom' into the consciousness of a person from another era."[15]

OPERA DIRECTING

In 2012, Hermanis took on opera directing, which became his main field of work in the following years. He outlined the crucial reason for such a decision in an interview before the premiere of *La Damnation de Faust*: "Trends in European theatre in the last 30 years have tended to have a mentality of destruction. Opera, on the other hand, allows you to focus on harmony, giving us a chance to put things back together."[16]

Over the course of five years (2012–2017) Hermanis staged more than ten operas, among them Alois Berndt Zimmermann's *Die Soldaten* at Salzburger Festspiele (2012), Leoš Janáček's *Jenůfa* at La Monnaie, Brussels (2014), Verdi's *I Due Foscari* and Giacomo Puccini's *Madama*

---

[14] Ibid.

[15] Margarita Zieda, "Jevgeņijs Oņegins. Komentāri," *Studija* 1:12 (2012), p. 3.

[16] *La Damnation de Faust by Alvis Hermanis*: A Fairy Tale and a Voyage of the Mind. http://www.euronews.com/2015/12/10/center-stage-opera-national-de-paris [accessed 8 March 2017].

Butterfly at Teatro alla Scala (2015, 2016), Hector Berlioz's *La Damnation de Faust* at Opéra Bastille (2015) and Richard Wagner's *Parsifal* (Wiener Staatsoper, 2017).

The Salzburg production of *Die Soldaten* gained broad recognition and became an important event in the life of European opera theatre. Hermanis shifted the plot from the middle of the eighteenth century to the early twentieth century, the moment before World War I. This period, very significant to European culture and history—oversaturated, desperate and full of inequality—was embodied by early erotic photography projected on the windows. The contrast between the eroticism of the photography, the openly sexual behaviour of the soldiers and the cliff walls created a truly dramatic tension and simultaneously revealed its time—the moment of stasis and anticipation before the Great War.

In the production of Leoš Janáček's opera *Jenůfa* the archetypical passions of the protagonists—brotherly competition, hatred of a stepmother towards her stepdaughter and her bastard—were literally transformed by the director into a mythical frame. The stage designers were Hermanis and Uta Gruber-Ballehr, the costume designer Eva Dessecker and the video designer Ineta Sipunova. Hermanis staged the production with the use of art nouveau motifs, inspired by Moravian nature, on exquisite decorative panels and on video projections. The singers acted in this manner too, in stylised costumes and with contingent movement. A "river"—a line of dancers—flowed as a continuous live ornament. The middle act—the birth and death of the child and the mother's grief—he depicted completely realistically, yet it was also enclosed in an ornamental frame: both above the space of the action and behind the frozen windows, where the "river" was still flowing and nursing the drowned child in its "waves." An extraordinary mythological beauty encircled the death of one human's world.

Hector Berlioz's dramatic legend *La Damnation de Faust* was Hermanis' most complex production. He created his own narrative and it revolved around the frustration of the human mind and a search for escape. The escape from an intellectual and spiritual crisis he found in the fantastic project "Mars One." The director had also found the appropriate modern-day analogue of Faust—the explorer of space and time Stephen Hawking. Actually, this was a story of two Fausts: the pure soul, incarnated by the opera megastar, German tenor Jonas Kaufmann, and the pure mind—the motionless Hawking, embodied by Dominique Mercy, the principal dancer of Pina Bausch. In the finale, when the expedition to Mars had begun, Hawking–Faust floated upwards from the hands of ballet dancers as if in a state of weightlessness. In the meantime, the other Faust had fallen into a wheelchair and become still in a paralytic's pose. The resurrection was possible only for the Mind, not for the Soul. Such is the sceptical outlook of the modern-day European.

THEATRE OF POETRY

The theatre of poetry has become a specific element of Hermanis' directing. This started in 2006 with a production based on the poetry of the Latvian romanticist Fricis Bārda—*Fricis Bārda. Poetry. Ambient*—a meditation in which great importance was placed not only on poetry, but also on voice modulation, the rhythm of speech and music. All this turned "poetry into time and space," as the critics wrote.

Poetry was the source of both time and space in the internationally famous *The Sound of Silence* too, staged the same year. It was dedicated to Hermanis' parents and the generation of '68 Latvia—the flower children behind the iron curtain—and poetry existed there as Simon and Garfunkel lyrics.

Nearly ten years later, Hermanis returned to the theatre of poetry, staging two one-person shows at the NRT for two exceptional actors—*Brodsky/Baryshnikov* (2016) for Mikhail Baryshnikov and *The Tipsy God* (2018) for Guna Zariņa. Both productions had a firm documentary basis, although interpreted differently.

In the case of *Brodsky/Baryshnikov*, the work concerns the actor himself, his real persona and life—his long-standing friendship with Joseph Brodsky. The production is a ceaseless dialogue, sometimes between the actor and the poetry he is reading; sometimes between Baryshnikov, the dancer, and Brodsky, the poet; sometimes between contemporaries on both sides of the border of life, or between movement and the poet's voice from an old tape recorder; between the body and space, flesh and word, man and death. The protagonist of the show is the word, made visible by Baryshnikov.

The documentary quality of *The Tipsy God* is created by the actress (Guna Zariņa) fully possessing the exterior image of the poet, avant-gardist and hippie Aivars Neibarts. However, the performance begins when the real person has died, choking on fumes from a fire. This is the journey not of a real person, but of the poetic *alter ego* or the poet's soul, between life, poetry and heaven. Hermanis, also the set designer of the piece, has divided the stage into three parts. The first is sort of a watch-house of language: there the protagonist captures words resounding in his head and on the tape recorder between hissing tapes, assessing the words and using them in a verse or forgetting them. The next room is an almost real (albeit hyperbolised) poet's room with an iron bed, a typewriter and countless bottles. There the protagonist lives a bohemian life and drinks until he becomes unconscious, whereas the actress behaves like a marionette, clearly separating herself from the character, staggering and falling with the most acrobatic agility during the craziest drunkenness. The third room is heaven, or maybe the space of creation itself. This space of creative existence unites *The Sound of Silence*, *Brodsky/Baryshnikov* and *The Tipsy God*. It is a very personal theme that can be read from these productions of Hermanis: creation in any form is offered as the only feasible mode of existence.

With *The Tipsy God* Hermanis returned entirely to his own theatre after fifteen years of sharing his time between the NRT and productions abroad. Since the autumn of 2017, the NRT has been working in temporary

Image 1 *Long Life*, directed by Alvis Hermanis, New Rīga Theatre, 2003. (Photo by Jānis Deinats)

premises, waiting for its historic building to be renovated. Hermanis is working with student actors because the theatre needs a restart after twenty years under his leadership.

Hermanis' productions are still a constant and multifaceted challenge—to his actors as well as to his audiences and reviewers—that has lasted nearly thirty years. It is a challenge to accept unprecedented rules of the game, to be able to see theatre from whatever standpoint, to hear silence and to see poetry; and, most importantly, to get used to the fact that nothing will be as expected and to give in to Hermanis' provocations.

Translated by Kristina Guste.

References

Hermanis, Alvis, *La Damnation de Faust by Alvis Hermanis:* A Fairy Tale and a Voyage of the Mind. http://www.euronews.com/2015/12/10/center-stage-opera-national-de-paris [accessed 8 March 2017].

———, "Teātris un humānisms mūsdienu vardarbības pasaulē," *Teātra Vēstnesis* 2:4 (2008), p. 103.

Kelleher, Joe, *Illuminated Theatre: Studies on the Suffering of Images* (London & New York: Routledge, 2015).

Laera, Margherita, *Theatre and Adaptation: Return, Rewrite, Repeat* (London: Bloomsbury Methuen Drama, 2014).

Mauro, Margherita, *Le Signorine di Wilko* (Rome: Ponte Sisto, 2010).

Naumanis, Normunds, "Ceriņu simfonija minorā," *Diena* (18 Feb. 2011).

———, "Dejas uz teātra kauliem," *Diena* (23 Sept. 1999).

———, "Līdz mielēm un pilnībai," *Diena* (20 May 2011).

Rietuma, Dita, "Dzīve pēc citiem likumiem," *Diena* (20 Sept. 1997).

Slava, Laima (ed.), *Alvis Hermanis* (Riga: Neputns, 2015).

Suhanovs, Reinis, "Maigā nežēlība," *Teātra Vēstnesis* 3:4 (2013).

Tīrons, Uldis, "Lāčplēša atgriešanās," *Rīgas Laiks* 12:12 (1995).

Valtenberga, Gita, "Pilnīga neintervija," *Latvijas Jaunatne*, (23 Oct. 1992).

Zieda, Margarita, "Jevgeņijs Oņegins. Komentāri," *Studija* 1:12 (2012).

Zole, Ieva, "Jaunais reālisms—kas tas tāds?" *Forums* (23 Jan. 2004).

Zvirgzdiņš, Juris, "Alvis Hermanis Free Lance." *Liesma* 4:12 (1990).

Давыдова, Марина, *Культура Zero: Очерки русской жизни и европейской сцены* (Москва: НЛО, 2018).

Grzegorz Jarzyna's Theatre of Post-Dramatic Joy and Recognition

Artur Duda

Some critics and theatre researchers claim that the newest Polish theatre was born on the day of two Warsaw premieres: Grzegorz Jarzyna's *Tropical Craze*, based on two Stanisław I. Witkiewicz plays, and Krzysztof Warlikowski's *Electra*, by Sophocles, in Teatr Dramatyczny/Drama Theatre Warsaw.[1] It was 18 January 1997. Both heroes of the day created the extraordinary status of Teatr Rozmaitości (Theatre of Rarities), or just TR, Warsaw, during the next few years and became symbols of contemporary Polish theatre. They launched brand new and controversial texts and issues, both to the theatre and to public life. In Warlikowski's performances there was a naked Prince of Denmark (Jacek Poniedziałek) vising

---

[1] *Wątroba. Słownik polskiego teatru po 1997 roku*, ed. Maciej Nowak, (Warsaw: Krytyka Polityczna Press, 2010), p. 7; see also Beata Guczalska, *Aktorstwo polskie. Generacje*, (Cracow: Państwowa Wyěsza Szkoła Teatralna Press, 2014), p. 369.

A. Duda (✉)
Nicolaus Copernicus University, Toruń, Poland
e-mail: dudaart@umk.pl

© The Author(s), under exclusive license to Springer Nature Switzerland AG 2021
K. Stefanova, M. Carlson (eds.), *20 Ground-Breaking Directors of Eastern Europe*, https://doi.org/10.1007/978-3-030-52935-2_5

58   A. DUDA

his mother (Stanisława Celińska, *Hamlet*, 1999), pieces of raw meat on the table as the abject remains of Pentheus in *Bacchae* by Euripides (2001), and the monstrous body of Grace, a woman with a taped-up chest after the resection of her breast and sewing on her brother's penis (Sarah Kane's *Cleansed*, 2002)—all of these scenes depicted problems of forbidden, psychoanalytically motivated love and madness, traumatic experiences of the human body.

Jarzyna's journey to the theatre was a logical one. It started with studying philosophy at Jagiellonian University in Cracow, then he enrolled at the Cracow Theatre Academy to study directing and there, later on, was Krystian Lupa's assistant during his mentor's work on Hermann Broch's *Sleepwalkers* (1995). Jarzyna's theatre debut in 1997 was thoroughly brilliant and catapulted him to a very rapid career. After staging three productions—the aforementioned *Tropical Craze*, as well as *Ivona, the Princess of Burgundia*, by Witold Gombrowicz, and *Unidentified Human Remains and the True Nature of Love*, by Brad Fraser—in 1998 Jarzyna became the artistic director of TR in Warsaw—a post he has held ever since.

His career as the most promising theatre superstar of Poland seems to be similar to the early start of Thomas Ostermeier in Germany or Oskaras Koršunovas in Lithuania. From the beginning it was a succession of victories. Jarzyna won all the essential festival prizes: for the best staging of Polish classic drama (Opole 1999), the best director of the season (Katowice 1999), first ever Grand Prix for Polish director during the International Theatre Festival "Kontakt" (Toruń 2000), the prestigious prize of the monthly "Teatr" (Konrad Swinarski Prize 1999, once again in 2009) and the Passport of "Polityka" (1999). Then, he started international collaborations both in theatre and in opera.

Tropical Craze was an example of a sophisticated post-dramatic playing with conventions of cinema, television, video clips and popular music. Relationships between protagonists who love and hate each other were presented in an ironic way, typical of the postmodern culture of quotations. Some critics claimed it was reminiscent of the iconic, cinematic style of David Lynch or Quentin Tarantino, but staged by a "natural born" master of theatre pastiche and parody. Unlike Warlikowski, Jarzyna did not aim at representing tragic features of human existence on stage or at creating an author's "theatre for neurotic spectators"[2] or a "phantasm

---

[2] Grzegorz Niziołek, *Warlikowski extra ecclesiam* (Cracow: Homini Press, 2008), p. 53.

theatre which combines therapeutic and social impact."[3] His approach was also intellectual, but it led to a theatre of joyous recognition. *Tropical Craze* made viewers from the older generations angry and irritated because it was addressed to city *flâneurs* with the greatest sense of humour, recognising both the aesthetic filters used by Jarzyna and variable, blurred images of the contemporary world and of their own existential status.

Not by chance did Jarzyna choose in the beginning plays by masters of the Polish grotesque and absurd drama: Witkacy and Gombrowicz. Maja Ostaszewska—beloved by the audience for her exaggerated attitudes and general affectation—created in the *Tropical Craze* a model figure of an interwar-period *femme fatale*. There is a striking contrast between her and another of Jarzyna's favourite actresses (and fiancée at that time), Magdalena Cielecka, who, in *Ivona, the Princess of Burgundia* impersonated an alien and alienated girl, neither beautiful nor ugly, but still irritating everybody in the king's court and making them laugh at her, hurt her and in the end kill her. In her general aura of independence, provocative primacy and being nobody, she resembled Marina Abramović's performance *Rhythm 0*, where the artist invited the audience to act on her as they wished. Ivona impersonated by Cielecka, unlike Abramović, was killed after all the human demons were set free.

Magdalena Cielecka also played in Jarzyna's *4:48 Psychosis*. The second case in this comparison is the story of Sarah Kane's autobiographical figure of a woman shortly before committing suicide. If Ivona was impersonated in accordance with the rules of the sophisticated conventions of realistic playing, Kane's heroine seemed to be represented in terms of corporeal acting and performance art. Here's how Beata Guczalska described this creation:

> On the edge of the stage, turned to the audience, an almost naked woman is standing—wearing only flesh-coloured pants, bandages on her wrists and knees. There are marks of tears and internal mutilations, grief and determination on her face. She is in a do-or-die situation, exhausted by the psychical fight. She is praying a litany—to God (?), to her lover (?), to the spectators (?)—"Touch me! See me! Love me, set me free. Talk to me!" However, nobody is talking, neither God, or man, or any spectator tied by the theatrical convention. The woman is turning back and running to the iron wall; she darts towards it in a suicidal way; a loud crash of sheet metal is heard. She is bleeding from hardly blocked wounds on her wrists, from her smashed

---

[3] Ibid., p. 16.

60   A. DUDA

face. This sequence is repeated a few times; there is more and more blood, tears and screams; following attempts of destroying the body, breaking it, become stronger and stronger.[4]

Jarzyna's *4:48 Psychosis* could be interpreted as following the path of Warlikowski. Here's what Niziołek wrote about the corporeality of Warlikowski's theatre: "[he] reverses the values of the spiritual and the corporeal. He makes the body a locus of truth and sanctity. He does not believe in transcendence, because the greatest mystery is for him the physical entity which could be a camouflage of rebellion against all incarnations of bourgeois reality, and derives power from an individual protest, creates ephemeral, unsustainable social constellations. [Warlikowski] does not fear syncretism; he appropriates religious symbols from different times and cultures."[5]

However, *4:48 Psychosis* was one of a few exceptions in Jarzyna's work. There he chose a more aesthetic strategy of "taming" the audience, whose members were in many cases not at all familiar with the art of the theatre. From a philosophical point of view, Jarzyna's theatre is not as atheistic as Warlikowski's. From the very beginning there were elements of ritual in it, hints of a belief in the existence of the sacred or the transcendental. This is, in fact, the hidden thread between Jarzyna and his mentor Krystian Lupa: discovering mystical dimensions of the world after and despite the ultimate victory of capitalism and globalisation. As a young student and artist, Jarzyna used to embark on journeys to exotic countries. First of all in Asia, where he experienced Balinese dance as a spectator, and then to Australia and Papua New Guinea, in the steps of Bronisław Malinowski and Witkacy. It was his journeys to the tropics that inspired his debut *The Tropical Haze*—a grotesque and narcotic meeting of white Europeans with the indigenous cultures of Others. As Roman Pawłowski claimed, "tropics are here not only as a witty stylization. Ecstatic dance, perverse love and drugs become symbols of Witkacy's obsession: insatiability, 'strangeness of existence,' degeneration of a man who fights the deprivation of spiritual experience back."[6]

---

[4] Guczalska, *Aktorstwo polskie*, pp. 364–365.

[5] Niziołek, *Warlikowski*, p. 75.

[6] Roman Pawłowski, *Chichot tropików*, "Gazeta Wyborcza" no. 16 (20 Jan. 1997), http://www.e-teatr.pl/pl/artykuly/134377.html (accessed 19 May 2020).

Twenty years after this debut, in an interview for the monthly *Teatr*, Jarzyna commented on the different contexts of his successful staging of Pier Paolo Passolini's *T.H.E.O.R.E.M.*:[7]

> I do not believe in astrology, in any prophecies, but I believe in miracles. I believe in the existence of an irrational dimension of our life. A miracle is everything which I cannot understand, which goes beyond my consciousness. The stelliferous heaven is a miracle for me.[8]

And he added briefly:

> I believe in the Absolute.[9]

Moreover, in some performances Jarzyna used to apply Far Eastern techniques of using the body, for example Cezary Kosiński preparing himself for the role of Mr Price trained in martial arts and Balinese ritual dance; Magdalena Cielecka together with a Korean master improved her ability to be more present on stage while not doing anything. The impact of the East was noticeable for the audience not only in the music, but also in the unclear status of Ivona onstage. Cielecka commented:

> *Mun Gun Sung* is a master of Korean dance. He came not to set my stage movement, although he thought this was his duty at the beginning, when he had heard I was impersonating a mute person. It was important for Grzegorz to create a kind of deep concentration. There are a few scenes in the performance when I am completely disabled. People from the Far East have got a great equilibrium; just being with my trainer, perceiving him, gave me confidence that it is possible to live in tranquility, in harmony with myself. Technically, we were working on a passage regarding my walking before the banquet scene—how to take breaths and restrain the body.[10]

---

[7] See also Maryla Zielińska, *Warszawski spleen, czyli fin de siècle i Grzegorz Jarzyna*, in: *20-lecie. Teatr polski po 1989*, ed. Dorota Jarząbek, Marcin Kościelniak, Grzegorz Niziołek (Cracow: Korporacja Ha!Art Press, 2010).

[8] Grzegorz Jarzyna, *Wierzę w cuda*, the interview by Jacek Kopciński, *Teatr* no. 2 (2010), http://www.e-teatr.pl/pl/artykuly/88859.html (accessed 20 May 2020).

[9] Ibid.

[10] Magdalena Cielecka, Anna Polony, Mieczysław Grąbka, Marek Kalita in the interview entitled "Jarzyna czy jak go tam zwą," *Notatnik Teatralny*, no. 17–18 (1998), p. 114.

Cielecka's statement acknowledges the specificity of Jarzyna's work in the field of acting; namely, his ability to use conventions borrowed from different types of theatre—the traditionally realistic, the post-dramatic corporeal (leaning towards performance art) and, as mentioned above, the anthropological as well.

Interviewed by the critic Jacek Kopciński, here's how Jarzyna outlines his notion of theatre:

> [Theatre] is a tool for recognizing the essence of reality. What are we doing in the theatre? We analyze daily life events by repeating them in such a way that allows defining the phenomenon of these events in a thoroughly precise manner. This theatrical analysis is safe because even the most extreme, painful events are repeated painlessly. Theatre refines life from different casual features, material or psychological, it extracts the very essence. When the lights go out, the darkness in the hall deprives you of what you came to the theatre with; your social position in reference to the other people. Critical theatre makes this place an agora, while I prefer [...] the kind of theatre as it was in Epidauros.[11]

"[A] theatre-sanctuary of a god and healer," adds Jacek Kopciński, revealing something important: the adhesion of Jarzyna to the traditional, long-lasting, "bourgeois" and "municipal" theatre of illusion.

How could Jarzyna's theatre be at the same time artistic and avant-garde? Since the very beginning the director and his ensemble have had to feed this omnivorous "monster," so they have tried to construct an image of the theatre as a brand—just like "Coca-Cola." This is a new strategy in a Poland in transition from the Communist to the (post-)capitalistic system. Some new descriptions were needed, like "cool theatre," "young theatre," "theatre for youngsters wearing Dr. Martens' boots." And Jarzyna and his team have delivered by building a new visual identity for TR; they have linked theatre with popular culture and the Internet. They still need commercial success and controversies; they are pioneers of educational theatre in Poland, having created a cultural spot open to kids, students, disabled people (audio-description). The cultural spot is also open to foreign tourists (for whom English subtitles are needed). They know that in Warsaw all arts institutions have to fight for visibility, for being perceived as the most attractive choice.

---

[11] Jarzyna, *Wierzę w cuda*, op. cit.

That is why in Grzegorz Jarzyna's productions there are so many audio-visual effects and elements taken from life outside of the theatre. His theatre resounds with Mexican or Indonesian folk rhythms, Rammstein, Sepultura, pop hits or techno, motifs from Oliver Stone's *Natural Born Killers* soundtrack, Nat King Cole's standard *When I Fall in Love* sung by Marilyn Monroe, operatic arias taken from Donizetti's *Tosca* and *Elixir of Love* (*Tropical Haze*) or Verdi's *Don Carlos*, performed by Maria Callas (*Unidentified Remains*).

For the same reasons, Jarzyna himself used to reconstruct his own image, applying many witty nicknames. *Tropical Haze* was signed by Grzegorz Horst d'Albertis (allusion to the German name of Jarzyna's Silesian father and the surname of the Italian traveller who discovered Papua New Guinea). His Thomas Mann's *Doctor Faustus*, by Thomas Mann, was signed by Das Gemüse ("a vegetable" in German, which corresponds to the ordinary Polish meaning of "Jarzyna"), Thomas Vinterberg's *Festen* by H7, and *4:48 Psychosis* just with a cross (+). As he got older, the director abandoned his postmodern game of changing identities, but went on for years with changes in his clothing style and hairstyle, challenging the traditional artist's image in post-war Poland—limited to the patterns of "an old public servant" (in a grey suit) and "an experienced intellectual" (in a black turtleneck, impersonating the existentialists).

Via his clothing patterns, Grzegorz Jarzyna demonstrated self-confidence, and at the same time they were a symbol of an ironic self-reflection, mirroring the fears and nightmares of postmodern people. These fears and nightmares form a list without end: psychoses, neuroses, drug addiction, perversions, escapism, unbelief, weakness, depression, violence, aggression, suicidal tendencies, crises and so on, and so on. They are very well described by the critic Rafał Węgrzyniak, who quoted Krystian Lupa when commenting on Jarzyna's work:

> After the premiere of the [*Tropical*] *Haze*, Lupa realized immediately that there are [in this adaptation of two of S. I. Witkiewicz's plays] "people of the end of the 20th century," with their "experience of alienation and narcotic escapism," striving for "losing their identity and looking for a place totally elsewhere and for a primordial rhythm," that there was revealed "the dark energy of a new primitivism, a new primordiality hidden in today's man" and "eruptions of dark, ecstatic motifs in people, which are like jumps in the darkness." In the *Haze* "a new primitivism, a new primordiality" are results of an encounter of the European culture with the Far East one.

64   A. DUDA

> Affected by this culture, Europeans get into the trance, dancing to the aboriginal music, consuming drugs and taking part in sexual orgies. [...] In a state of deep trance, dancers lose their mind, try to kill themselves or at least hurt [themselves].[12]

Paradoxically, Jarzyna's more than twenty-year career both in Poland and elsewhere in Europe can be described in equal measure with the words "success" and "crisis." The latter meant in his case "becoming a general director and losing the artistic power to seduce the audience and critics." After the premieres of his *Doctor Faustus* (1999), *The Prince Myshkin*, based on Dostoyevsky's *Idiot* (2000), and *2007: Macbeth*, after Shakespeare (2005), many critics were prophesying the director's ultimate decline. However, he lost much more in those years: the best collaborating director and the core of the actors' ensemble. During the autumn of 2007, Krzysztof Warlikowski left TR Warsaw with a considerable group of prominent actors (e.g. Maja Ostaszewska, Jacek Poniedziałek, Andrzej Chyra and Magdalena Cielecka) to establish The New Theatre. The youngest in this group, called by even professional researchers "the TR generation"[13] and defined as a new school of acting, challenging the taboos of corporeality—seemed to be indispensable. One of the established critics proclaimed "the death of the great TR myth."[14] Jarzyna survived against all odds, trying to replace "renegades" in different ways. In the first place he hired representatives of the hottest German-style political theatre, importing some of them successfully (Rene Pollesch), others not at all (Jan Klata).

Another crisis involved the site of Jarzyna's theatre. Situated on Marszałkowska Street, in a prestigious and busy neighbourhood, the building was not intended for modern art projects. Also, it had a small auditorium of only 168 seats and the scene had technical limits. Jarzyna faced the challenge and started looking for new places for TR productions. In 2005 he launched the Warsaw Terrain Project, dedicated to young, talented theatre lovers and beginners interested in working with TR artists on contemporary rather than already well-known plays, without money for set design and music. Site-specific theatre was not new in Poland, but

---

[12] Rafał Węgrzyniak, "Grzegorz Jarzyna vel Horst D'Albertis vel Leszczuk, vel Brokenhorst," *Notatnik Teatralny*, no. 16–17 (1998), p. 127.

[13] Guczalska, *Aktorstwo polskie*, pp. 363–418.

[14] Tomasz Plata, "Śmierć wielkiego mitu Teatru Rozmaitości," *Dziennik*, no. 266 (2007), http://www.dziennikteatralny.pl/artykuly/smierc-wielkiego-mitu-teatru-rozmaitosci.html (accessed 19 May 19).

in this case TR started revealing step by step the capital city of Poland in a rapid transition. Productions directed by different artists were presented in the Warsaw pub at the Central Train Station before renovation (*Risk It All*, 2003), an old tenement house (Ivan Vyrypaev's *Oxygen*, 2004), an old printing house (Neil La Bute's *Bash*, 2004) and so on. Along with discovering new theatre territories and new groups of spectators, in the course of the Terrain Warsaw Project Jarzyna found a few new collaborators, like Jan Dravnel. Also the Warsaw municipal authorities promised to find a new place for TR in the centre of the city: in the brand new building for the Museum of Modern Art.[15]

In 2005 Jarzyna started one more project, called TR/PL and devoted to a quest for new contemporary Polish plays. A series of workshops with a group of young playwrights were held and their texts were published in an anthology.[16] The most significant discovery was Dorota Masłowska, whose 2002 debut, at the age of 19, with the novel *Wojna polsko-ruska pod flagą biało-czerwoną* (*White and Red*), catapulted her to the status of the golden girl of Polish literature. Masłowska was never enthusiastic about drama and theatre, but she did write some texts when she was invited by Jarzyna. Her first drama was *Dwoje biednych Rumunów mówiących po polsku* (*A Couple of Poor Polish-speaking Romanians*), whose world premiere took place in TR in November 2006, directed by Przemysław Wojcieszek.[17]

For the audience, it was an outstanding opportunity to experience Masłowska's gift of story-telling by quoting street slang, ordinary people's speech, commercials and other popular culture texts and genres. Yet the production was not a success. The director oversimplified Masłowska's fantastic story about two drunken and stoned party participants in the disguise of poor Romanians, roaming through the Polish provinces. Elements of the theatre of the absurd and a multilingual cacophony were turned into a chain of cabaret-like routines. There was no place in it for the problem of social exclusion, which is of importance, since playing Romanian in Poland means mocking the poorest (in street language "Romanian" equals "Gypsy"—i.e. "thief, cheater, outcast").

In contrast, Masłowska's second play—*Między nami dobrze jest* (*We Are Pretty Good*, 2009), directed by Jarzyna at the Schaubühne in Berlin—was

---

[15] The date of opening is still delayed.

[16] *TR/PL. Antologia nowego dramatu polskiego* (Warsaw: TR Press, 2006).

[17] See one of many reviews: Roman Pawłowski, "Królowa w rumuńskim przebraniu," *Gazeta Wyborcza* no. 120 (24 May 2006).

66   A. DUDA

a great hit from the very beginning. It is a multidimensional story. In the first place it is an ironic portrait of a Warsaw family where the "real" Polish identity is mocked: a Small Metal Girl (Magdalena Popławska) lives together with her mother Halina (Magdalena Kuta) and Grandmother in a wheelchair (played by the brilliant Danuta Szaflarska, and after her death Lech Łotocki, a male actor in drag). At the same time, it is a tragic story of the non-existent capital of Poland—a ghost city destroyed by Hitler and Stalin. Then, it is a postmodern story of (post-)capitalism with its desires, joys, phantasms, instant products, promised lands, commercials and commercialisation in a Second World aspiring to be more than what it is. Finally, it is an auto-thematic story of a theatre that cannot establish any believable image of the real world and, thus, it becomes an embodiment of theatre in principle, unmasked as a medium applying all techniques used by public relations and marketing specialists. It's important to note that the title of the play alludes to a song by the Polish punk group Siekiera (The Axe) about a girl raped by four men in a forest.

In his work on the play, Jarzyna decided to underline the auto-thematic dimension. "[I]nstead of a lumber room in an old Warsaw tenement house, there is a black and white TV studio closed with three walls as screens," wrote Łukasz Drewniak. "The setting of the performance is a house, which doesn't exist."[18] This made all figures and events in the production unreal—zombies, phantasms. The only real thing left there was language.

The audience—whether in Germany or in Poland—enjoyed all the auto-ironic fragments regarding the Polish discourse of an innocent victim of History, such as a bizarre radio monologue about the world that at the very beginning was Poland and all people were Polish. However, after effectively seducing all spectators with a liberating laugh at national stereotypes, clichés and simply lies, Jarzyna's production came to a shocking finale. Łukasz Drewniak claimed that "on the screens, there are houses of bombed Warsaw which come down. It turns out that the Grandmother died on the first day of WW2, so her daughter was never born, and the Small Metal Girl never existed. The world, which we were staring at, never existed; it was from the very beginning in an absolute negation, as Neverland. The war destroyed one world, and the one built later was from

---

[18] Łukasz Drewniak, "Sukces sztuki Masłowskiej w Berlinie," *Dziennik*, no. 75 (2009), http://www.e-teatr.pl/pl/artykuly/70040.html?josso_assertion_id=D3A5763C6FD8EB4D (accessed 20 May 2020).

the beginning fake—a façade. People who lost their lives were never born or didn't have any chance to come into existence, yet they still live in a certain, 'negative' Poland. They are so numerous that the phantom of Poland covers the non-existence of a real Poland. [The façade] is a shelter of phantasms, cheatings, mirages, lies, affectation."[19]

All in all, the production of Masłowska's *We Are Pretty Good* is an excellent example of Jarzyna's theatre's dwelling between post-dramatic joy and intellectual recognition.

What can be seen at Jarzyna's TR Warsaw at the end of the season 2018/2019? On the home stage at Marszałkowska Street it is the dark musical *Rechnitz. Opera—The Angel of Holocaust*, based on the horrifying text by Elfriede Jelinek and directed by Katarzyna Kalwat as a concert for six actors and a string quartet. Also Georg Büchner's *Woyzeck*, directed by Grzegorz Jaremko—the third winner of the TR Debut Prize. At the same

Image 1 *We Are Pretty Good*, directed by Grzegorz Jarzyna, TR Warsaw, 2009, Lech Łotocki as Gloomy Old Biddy. (Photo by Natalia Kabanow, from TR Warsaw Archive)

[19] Ibid.

68 A. DUDA

time, the "evergreen" *4:48 Psychosis* was performed at the Macao Culture Centre and *California/Grace Slick* (directed by Rene Pollesch) visited an international festival in Bratislava.

As for Grzegorz Jarzyna himself, he has directed Masłowska's third play, *Inni ludzie* (*Other People*), written especially for him. This is a "musical and multilingual poem" portraying Poland after thirty years of transformation, and a story about the people living in Warsaw. The production is an example of trendy participatory theatre, realised by professional artists, rappers and common citizens of Warsaw. The set is a green box with three corrugated metal sheets as screens, borrowed from the numerous construction sites in the Polish capital today. The production abounds in videos and hip hop music. Is it a commercial mockery of poor people? Or just the opposite: creating a free space for social outsiders? Exploitation or support? Perhaps it is both. Recently, Grzegorz Jarzyna turned 50 and got married. He is still waiting for TR to have a new building.

REFERENCES

Drewniak, Łukasz, *Sukces sztuki Masłowskiej w Berlinie*, "Dziennik" 2009 no. 75, http://www.e-teatr.pl/pl/artykuly/70040.html?josso_assertion_id=D3A5763C6FD8EB4D (accessed 20 May 2020).

Guczalska, Beata, *Aktorstwo polskie. Generacje*, Cracow: Państwowa Wyěsza Szkoła Teatralna Press, 2014.

Gruszczyński, Piotr, *Ojcobójcy. Młodsi zdolniejsi w teatrze polskim*, Warsaw: W.A.B. Press, 2003.

Cielecka, Magdalena, Anna Polony, Mieczysław Grąbka, Marek Kalita (Jarzyna's actors) in the interview entitled *Jarzyna czy jak go tam zwą, Notatnik Teatralny* 1998, no. 17–18.

Jarzyna, Grzegorz, *Two Swords in Beijing. Premiere*. The interview by P. Cieślak, "Rzeczpospolita" 18 January 2018, https://www.rp.pl/Teatr/301189927-Grzegorz-Jarzyna-o-premierze-spektaklu-Dwa-miecze-w-Pekinie.html (accessed 19 May 2020).

———, *Wierzę w cuda*, the interview by Jacek Kopciński, "Teatr" 2010, no. 2, http://www.e-teatr.pl/pl/artykuly/88859.html (accessed 20 May 2020).

Kosiński, Dariusz, *Teatra polskie. Historie*, Warsaw: Instytut Teatralny Press, 2010.

Krakowska, Joanna, *Demokracja. Przedstawienia*, Warsaw: Instytut Teatralny Press, 2018.

Niziołek, Grzegorz, *Warlikowski extra ecclesiam*, Cracow: Homini Press, 2008.

Nowak, Maciej (ed.), *Wątroba. Słownik polskiego teatru po 1997 roku*, Warsaw: Krytyka Polityczna Press, 2010.

Pawłowski, Roman, *Chichot tropików*, Gazeta Wyborcza no. 16, 20.01.1997, http://www.e-teatr.pl/pl/artykuly/134377.html (accessed 19 May 2020).

———, *Królowa w rumuńskim przebraniu*, Gazeta Wyborcza 2006, no. 120, 24.05.2006.

Plata, Tomasz, *Śmierć wielkiego mitu Teatru Rozmaitości*, Dziennik 2007 no. 266, http://www.dziennikteatralny.pl/artykuly/smierc-wielkiego-mitu-teatru-rozmaitosci.html (accessed 20 May 2020)

TR/PL. *Antologia nowego dramatu polskiego*, Warsaw: TR Press, 2006.

Węgrzyniak, Rafał, *Grzegorz Jarzyna vel Horst D'Albertis vel Leszczuk, vel Brokenhorst*, Notatnik Teatralny 1998, no. 16–17.

Zielińska, Maryla: Warszawski spleen, czyli fin de siècle i Grzegorz Jarzyna, in: 20-lecie. Teatr polski po 1989, ed. Dorota Jarząbek, Marcin Kościelniak, Grzegorz Niziołek, Korporacja Ha!Art Press, Cracow 2010.

Jan Klata: The Social-Identity DJ of the Polish Theatre

Katarzyna Kręglewska

It was six years after finishing his studies to become a director that Jan Klata mounted his first fully independent production: Nikolai Gogol's *The Government Inspector* (at the Jerzy Szaniawski Theatre in Wałbrzych, 2003). However, after this late debut, the director moved forward at lightning speed. Indeed, a section of critics named the 2004/2005 theatre season "the year of Klata"—a year crowned by a festival, *KLATA FEST*, organised in December 2005 by the Theatre Institute in Warsaw, and by the "Paszport *Polityki*" award, in 2006, from one of the most influential Polish weeklies. The prestigious award for promising young artists, offered every year since 1993, in Klata's case was for "innovative and bold interpretations of the classics, for the passion and pertinacity with which he

---

K. Kręglewska (✉)
University of Gdańsk, Gdańsk, Poland
e-mail: katarzyna.kreglewska@ug.edu.pl

© The Author(s), under exclusive license to Springer Nature Switzerland AG 2021
K. Stefanova, M. Carlson (eds.), *20 Ground-Breaking Directors of Eastern Europe*, https://doi.org/10.1007/978-3-030-52935-2_6

diagnoses the state of Polish reality and the strength of national myths."[1] He successfully directed his subsequent productions (winning multiple awards), which not only struck a loud chord in theatrical circles but also frequently enjoyed huge public acclaim.

The repertoire that Klata aimed at can be described as unusually rich (if not eclectic): he directed both Polish and world classics—especially plays by Shakespeare and also ancient Greek drama.[2] In parallel with his work on a series of productions, the director consistently built up his public image: that of an outsider, an opposition figure, dressed in the Doc Martens of a rebel with a Mohawk hairdo.[3] However, despite these fringe-theatre attributes, Klata was able successfully to direct productions at the leading theatres in Poland. And in January 2013, he accepted the post of Head of Helena Modrzejewska Narodowy Stary Teatr (National Old Theatre) in Cracow, one of the oldest and most important theatres in Poland.

But let's start from the very beginning. The director's theatrical experiences go back to his youth: when barely 12 years old, he wrote a play entitled *Słoń zielony* (*The Green Elephant*), which won a drama competition, organised by the periodical *Dialog*, and had a premiere in the Stanisław Ignacy Witkiewicz Theatre in Zakopane. The play was also translated into English and presented at a theatre festival in Australia.[4] Immediately after leaving high school, Klata was accepted as a student at the Faculty of Directing of Aleksander Zelwerowicz National Academy of Dramatic Art in Warsaw. After two years there (as a result of some conflict or in search of a new mentor) he transferred to Cracow, where he was able

---

[1] See: "Jan Klata," *Polityka*, 3 November 2009, https://www.polityka.pl/tygodnikpolityka/kultura/paszporty/173243,1,teatr-jan-klata.read (accessed 6 May 2019).

[2] It is worth mentioning, in particular, two productions staged at the Narodowy Stary Teatr in Cracow: *Oresteja* (The Oresteia; 2007) and *Król Edyp* (Oedipus the King; a production of Igor Stravinski's opera *Oedipus Rex* from 1927; 2013). Małgorzata Budzowska writes about these productions in "Jan Klata. Muzyczność rewolucji" [in:] *Sceniczne metamorfozy mitu. Teatr polski XXI wieku w perspektywie kulturowej* (Łódź: Wydawnictwo Uniwersytetu Łódzkiego, 2018), pp. 233–88.

[3] The director's self-creation is most fully discussed by Monika Kwaśniewska in *Pytanie o wspólnotę. Jerzy Grzegorzewski i Jan Klata*, (Cracow: Wydawnictwo Uniwersytetu Jagiellońskiego, 2016). See also: A. R. Burzyńska, *The Classics and the Troublemakers. Theatre Directors from Poland* (Cracow: Wydawnictwo Uniwersytetu Jagiellońskiego, 2014); O. Śmiechowicz, *Lupa, Warlikowski, Klata. Polski teatr po upadku komunizmu*, (Warsaw: Wydawnictwo Naukowe PWN, 2018).

[4] Cf. M. Zielińska, "Prowokator," *Ozon* 2005, no. 1.

to study (including as an assistant) the work of Jerzy Grzegorzewski, Jerzy Jarocki and Krystian Lupa. His fellow student there was Grzegorz Jarzyna. When they both graduated in 1997, Jarzyna immediately began a stunning career, while Klata did not.

During the next five years Klata undertook several part-time jobs, including that of a music critic writing about alternative music, a copywriter and a director of television talk shows. His professional position altered radically from the moment when his play *Uśmiech grejpruta* (The Gripefruit's Smile)[5] was accepted for the final stages of a drama competition organised by *Dialog* and Teatr Polski (Polish Theatre) in Wrocław. In December 2002, Klata prepared a well-received workshop production of the play at Teatr Polski, which he turned into a full stage production five months later. At the same time, he worked on Nikolai Gogol's *The Government Inspector*, and a little later on André Gide's *The Vatican Cellars* (premiere 9 January 2004). In *The Gripefruit's Smile*, Klata presented journalists impatiently awaiting the Pope's death, in order to send their reports over the media. The action of *The Government Inspector* he transferred to Poland and the Gierek years of the 1970s, showing this period as a time shaping the country's national consciousness. In *The Vatican Cellars* he asked questions about the sense of religious feelings (setting extreme nihilism alongside religious fanaticism).

2.

From the beginning of his work in the theatre, Klata has created a *théâtre engagé*—one that is, above all, socially and also politically engaged. This is why Roman Pawłowski calls him a "rebel with a cause," one who practises a "high-risk theatre"[6] and even—probably unfortunately—a Polish Frank Castorf.[7] Klata's priority is neither an aesthetic theatre nor a theatre that is a pretext for philosophical considerations, but theatre dealing with topics that are deeply rooted in contemporary reality. In his productions a very important role is played by Poland and its complex history that is not subject to simplified diagnoses. Klata considers what constitutes the nation. He examines the nature of social relations and seeks features that form the (majority of) commonly shared world-views in Polish society. He asks questions about religious confession and affiliation, and about the manner of grasping and implementing morality. He explains his vision

---

[5] The spelling mistake in the Polish word *grejpfrut* and the English is deliberate.

[6] R. Pawłowski, "Teatr 2004," *Gazeta Wyborcza* 2004, no. 300.

[7] Idem, "Tow. Horodniczy," *Gazeta Wyborcza* 2003, no. 89.

74 K. KRĘGLEWSKA

of the theatre's obligation to the public as follows: "because it happens 'here and now,' the theatre has to have a high temperature. The theatre has to happen, it has to be blood, sweat, and tears. That's simply the kind of medium it is, a bit of a circus, a bit of a psycho-drama."[8] He admits that what really gets him going is "the challenge to do something with the crumbling world, to give an order to this chaos, to give it a rhythm. To prove that, where the theme doesn't hold together, important questions are being raised; that under the layer of form and a so-called specific sense of humor, there is truth."[9]

But descriptions like "theatre of engagement" and "political theatre" do not exhaust the image of Klata's theatrical language. There is no doubt that an extremely important role in his work is played by the way in which he shapes theatre space and—which may be the most important role—by music. Indeed, it is from music that Klata most frequently starts working on a given production; it is music that often forms the key to interpreting the whole.

3.

The seeds of the director's personal signature and his later theatrical aesthetics can perhaps be found in Klata's fourth production. The premiere of *H.* (after Shakespeare's *Hamlet*) took place in the Gdańsk Shipyard on 2 July 2004.[10] Performed in the "home of Solidarity," the production was met with extreme responses on the part of critics. However, from the perspective of the over fifteen years that have elapsed since the premiere, it is possible to see clearly that this production has passed into history as one of the most important pieces of work in the Polish theatre from the beginning of the twenty-first century.[11] There is no space here to examine the production in detail, but it is worth bringing forward two

---

[8] "Dorosnąć do widowni," J. Klatą in conversation with D. Kardasińska, *Notatnik Teatralny* 2004, no. 32–33, p. 63.

[9] J. Klata, "O prawdzie i nieprawdzie, etyce i estetyce," edited by M. Kuźmiak, *Notatnik Teatralny* 2004, no. 32–33, p. 76.

[10] *H.* after *Hamlet* by William Shakespeare, translated by Stanisław Barańczak, directed by and with sampling and scratching by Jan Klata, spatial arrangement, costumes, lighting by Justyna Łagowska, movement by Maćko Prusak, premiere 2 July 2004 in Production Hall No. 42 A of the Gdańsk Shipyard. See: K. Kręglewska, "Hamlet w Stoczni. "H." według Szekspira w reżyserii Jana Klaty" [in:] *Teatr Wybrzeże w latach 1996–2016. Zjawiska-ludzie-przedstawienia,* ed. J. Puzyna-Chojka, K. Kręglewska, B. Świąder-Puchowska, (Gdańsk, 2019)—In the present essay, I refer to that discussion.

[11] Two years after the premiere, the production was recorded, see: http://ninateka.pl/film/h-spektakl-teatr (accessed 7 May 2018).

extremely important elements of it: the choice of place for the production and the music.

The decision to use a non-theatrical place is a performative act of a sort, one that significantly influences the play's reception and the audience's perception of it. As Josette Féral suggests, theatrical place can be understood as a mental sphere, which is an evocation, perhaps an image, in the actor's mind, as in the audience's minds.[12] Thus, the manner in which a play is received by the audience is also determined by its manner of experiencing space and the experience that is connected with a given mental sphere.

The director explains his choice of space for *Hamlet* by his "experience of the shipyard." He was inspired by his reading of *Studium o Hamlecie* (A Study of Hamlet) by Stanisław Wyspiański, who made his interpretation of the play dependent on how Elsinore is understood and presented.[13] According to him, Shakespeare, "whenever he presented what happens, had, of course, before his eyes the terrain where that happens."[14] Wyspiański himself intended to locate the action of *Hamlet* on Wawel Hill and Castle in Cracow—"he wanted a place where the spirit of the nation, society, history is focused, whatever we call it."[15] Klata declared that for him:

> The Gdańsk Shipyard is an ideal place to perform this play: the production hall with Anna Walentynowicz's gantry, not far from where the history of Europe and the world changed. When you go into that space—gigantic, post-industrial, a bit sacred, as it were—[...] you have the impression that a moment earlier the shipyard workers left to take part in a demonstration. To fight for their own and for my fate.[16]

Thus, the production of *H.* emerged out of a feeling of gratitude for what happened at the shipyard, but also in consternation at what happened afterwards—out of a need to reflect on where the changes begun

---

[12] Cf. J. Féral, "Miejsce teatralne jako przestrzeń fascynacji: "Wieża" Anne-Marie Provencher" [in:] *Teatr w miejscach nieteatralnych*, ed. J. Tyszka, (Poznań, 1998), p. 190.

[13] See: "Wawel na mnie nie działa," *Didaskalia* 63 (2004), p. 17.

[14] S. Wyspiański, *Hamlet*, [in:] idem, *Dzieła zebrane*, vol. 13 (Cracow, 1961), ed. L. Płoszewski etc., pp. 13–14. See also: pp. 15–17.

[15] "Myślę, że Hamlet jest Polakiem," J. Klata talks with M. Wąsiewicz, *Gazeta Wyborcza— Trójmiasto* 153 (2004), http://encyklopediateatru.pl/artykuly/127328/mysle-ze-hamlet-jest-polakiem (accessed 6 May 2019).

[16] Ibid.

here have led Poles.[17] And it must be acknowledged that the image of the state a decade and a half after transformation did not inspire either pride or optimism. On the contrary, it was an image of a ruin, which was perfectly echoed in the neglected (and abandoned) space of the shipyard, covered in rust and overgrown with weeds. In the ruined interiors, the new "elites" gave themselves over to consumption. Klata has stated that the choice of location had an important influence on shaping the layers of meaning in the production.[18] As he explains it, *H.* was an attempt to tell of "a young person who rejects the existing, rotten world, and, at the same time, the only thing he has to offer is a somewhat senseless rebellion. And he matures to the point where he can lose beautifully. That is so hugely Polish. [...] We always preferred to lose beautifully than to set out our lives normally."[19]

*

Many critics blamed Klata for explicitly limiting the play's meaning to a socio-political dimension. It should be stressed that politics is an important point of reference in many of his other productions. In *The Government Inspector*, he pitilessly evaluated the actions and character of politicians. In the city of Wałbrzych, when representatives of the local authorities attended one of the performances of the production, the cast and the director had good reason to fear their reaction and tried to foresee "the consequences of what will happen if you hold up a mirror to people."[20] There were no immediate consequences: every politician present in the audience pretended that the depictions on the stage were of the other political party. Klata remarks:

> when I saw something like that, I thought: Holy Jesus! it's true the system absorbs every revolt. In any case, it's like with pop culture. Those are my two passions: politics and pop culture. Pop culture is also able to absorb every kind of revolt, every opposition, even if it comes from a position that is absolutely alternative and combative, with a certain constellation of the stars it suddenly is apparent that every kind of revolt in relation to pop culture sells fantastically well—think of Nirvana.[21]

*

[17] Cf. "Wawel na mnie nie działa," op.cit., p.17.
[18] Cf. "W Polandzie," J. Klata talks with K. Mieszkowski, *Notatnik Teatralny* 38 (2005), p. 36.
[19] Ibid.
[20] "Dorosnąć do widowni," op. cit., p. 60
[21] Ibid, p. 60.

One of the most characteristic features of Klata's directorial strategy is the dramaturgical techniques that make it up, which he himself calls "sampling" and "scratching." "Sampling" is a musical term meaning the use of an excerpt from an earlier recording as an element in a newly created piece of work. "Scratching" in DJ practice is the scratching of vinyl records with a gramophone needle, while in the theatre it refers to an operation carried out on the audience's consciousness, one that shakes fixed models and stereotypes of reception.[22] These are techniques carried over directly from a world dominated by consumption and pop culture.

Working on the principle that every element of reality can be subjected to deconstruction, re-construction, re-making and recycling, Klata draws freely from his surroundings and mixes signs drawn from different aesthetics, thus shattering the viewers' habits of reception.[23] "No one in Polish theatre has employed references to mass culture on such a scale—to concerts, video techniques, music videos, and advertisements," comments Paweł Sztarbowski.[24] He also notes that Klata has an absolutely uninhibited relation to dramatic texts (which he treats like musical works; that is, as material for remixing) and every so often "protests are raised and [there are] complaints about [his] flattening out masterpieces, the reduction of meanings, or an undoing of the action that goes too far."[25] At the same time, it is worth stressing that when Klata considers his interference in the text to be significant, "he faithfully changes the titles so that it is clear that he is creating plays in new 'arrangements', according to a story and words drawn from someone else's repertoire."[26]

How did Klata treat Shakespeare's play and the myth of Hamlet that functions in general consciousness? Above all, he added a lot to Shakespeare. At the same time, there were elements exceptionally strongly rooted in the tradition of producing the play that the director abandoned. His Hamlet did not give the famous "To be or not to be" monologue that is the dream of many actors. It was also in vain that one would wait for the extended scene of Ophelia's madness. In general, Klata quite consistently gave up

---

[22] Quoted from: "Słownik pojęć dramaturgicznych," *Notatnik Teatralny* 58–59 (2010), pp. 78–95.

[23] Cf. J. Kowalska, "Egzorcysta," *Notatnik Teatralny* 38 (2005), pp. 82–85.

[24] P. Sztarbowski, "Teatr mój widzę masowy," *Newsweek Polska* 2007, no. 9.

[25] J. Kowalska, "Egzorcysta," op. cit., p. 82.

[26] P. Sztarbowski, "Teatr mój widzę masowy," op. cit.

78   K. KRĘGLEWSKA

on an in-depth presentation of characters. It was difficult to find detailed motivations behind their actions and there was a lack of clear, logical connection among individual scenes. Klata simply relinquished traditional narrative structures.

The constructional axis of events in the production was not the play. The director created "a wholly autonomous order of events beyond the text, sometimes, indeed, contrary to it. These parallel narratives take shape, above all, in image and music."[27] In any case, Klata has frequently clearly indicated that "the director may do as he likes, but a good show has to come out of it."[28] By reducing the text in *H.*, Klata transferred its meanings onto some other element of the production, like the stage movement and music.

*

For Klata, music is "uber-important." According to him, today music is the dominating form of expression in culture, "a code that makes it possible for a group of people to identify themselves."[29] So it is no surprise that a "play list" is an exceptionally important element of Klata's productions. Justyna Łagowska (in private life the wife of the director) says that when Klata begins work on a production, he first thinks up an appropriate convention in which he can root the text, and immediately afterwards chooses the music: "he gives me the text, plays music, and I have to find my way with those guidelines."[30] In turn, Klata describes his way of working as follows:

> the very construction of my productions is musical. The staging devices that I use, for example, sampling comes from cutting excerpts of one material and using those in constructing something new. And scratching is giving a roughness to what happens on stage. [...] The more conscious member of the audience will know what I took from where; the less conscious ones will just get the emotions.[31]

---

[27] J. Kowalska, "Egzorcysta," op.cit., p. 82.

[28] "W Polandzie," op.cit., p. 38.

[29] Cf. "W oku salonu," J. Klata talks with Ł. Drewniak, *Przekrój* 8 (2005).

[30] Cf. "Intensywne życie z szachistą," op.cit., p. 45.

[31] "W oku salonu," op.cit. It is worth noticing that the musical pieces woven into the dramaturgy of Klata's productions often fulfil a similar role in the play's structure as Brechtian songs do. See, for example, Anna R. Burzyńska, *The Classics and the Troublemakers. Theatre Directors from Poland*, op. cit.

In *H.*, too, samples, in the form of cited musical works, had an exceptionally important role. They functioned not only as signs drawn from the aesthetics of mass culture (and they usually appeared in arrangements that differed from the original), but they were also embedded in appropriate places in the dramatic structure in a careful and well-thought-out manner.

In Klata's productions, musical samples implement the tasks once ascribed to the chorus. They serve as a means of characterising a given character, as a commentary on particular events or as a prefiguration of events to come. Finally, samples and mental scratching mean that at times Klata's entire staging brings to mind an extended music video, made up of edited scenes, the value of which lies, above all, in exceptionally spectacular, suggestive images.[32]

*

There is no doubt that in *H.* Klata wrote his own story based on the motifs of Shakespeare's tragedy, a story the main theme of which was an image of contemporary Poland.[33] The choice of space, just like the techniques of sampling and scratching, meant that the audience had an opportunity to get close to the "mental sphere" called into being or signalled by the director in the staging—moving the action "outside the theatre" led to an increase in its emotional impact on the spectator. The abandonment of the hegemony of a traditional narrative model meant that the spectator could immerse her/himself in the story presented. The strategy chosen by Klata was all the more justified by the fact that the question of what we did with the freedom gained in 1989 sounded exceptionally relevant in 2004, and—what is worse—has lost none of its relevance today. Just like discussions of whether anything still unites us (history? martyrology? religion? custom?), there are discussions over whether—as a nation—we still in general form some sort of community.[34]

4.

The deconstruction of national myths and the painful considerations of the shape(lessness) and (non-)presence of community certainly have an important place in Klata's work. The director has frequently "dealt with" the topic of national identity, for example, through adaptations of works

---

[32] Klata has often referred to the aesthetics of the music video, and the strategy achieves perhaps its strongest expression in the production *Witaj/Żegnaj*, which is based on the cycle *365 Days/365 Plays* by Suzan-Lori Parks (Teatr Polski in Bydgoszcz, 2008).

[33] See: R. Pawłowski, "Duński książę w cieniu stoczni," *Gazeta Wyborcza* 155 (2004).

[34] Cf. R. Pawłowski, "Głosujcie na Klatę!", *Notatnik Teatralny* 38 (2005), pp. 26–33.

from the Polish classical canon, such as *Trylogia* after Henryk Sienkiewicz (Trilogy, Narodowy Stary Teatr in Cracow, 2009) and *Ziemia obiecana* (The Promised Land, Teatr Polski in Wrocław, 2009). Special mention should be given to *Transfer!* (Wrocławski Teatr Współczesny, 2006). The production, described by the director as a "history lesson," told of the fates of Poles and Germans who were the victims of post-war transfers of population. Its script was based on the accounts of real people (some of whom later appeared onstage), participants in and observers of the events recounted—"of people caught up in the machinery of history, pawns on the great political map."[35]

There is no doubt that Klata's productions grow out of the space in which he creates them and out of which they emerge. However, it is impossible to define his work as simply local. It is a body of work deeply rooted in a contemporary, deconstructed, postmodern, fragmented world. On the one hand, it draws freely on the world of pop culture, while on the other hand, it addresses important issues of a moral nature and raises questions concerning individual and collective identity. Klata's reflections on contemporary reality often become a pretext for asking universal questions—about human beings, their nature, their duty in relation to the world and their fellow inhabitants. That is certainly the case with regard to *Córka Fizdejki* (The Daughter of Fizdejka), after the play by Stanisław Ignacy Witkiewicz (Jerzy Szaniawski Teatr Dramatyczny in Wałbrzych, 2004), in which a tale of Poland's accession to the European Union became a pretext for reflections on relations with the Other. In *Szewcy u bram* (The Shoemakers at the Gates, TR Warsaw, 2007, based on *Szewcy* by Stanisław Ignacy Witkiewicz) and *Sprawa Dantona* by Stanisława Przybyszewska (The Danton Case, Teatr Polski in Wrocław, 2008), Klata considered the mechanisms that accompany revolution. In a later production, *Witaj/Żegnaj* (Greetings/Farewell, Teatr Polski in Bydgoszcz, 2008), based on *365 Days/365 Plays* by the American dramatist Suzan-Lori Parks, he offered a description of the contemporary world, one that evades clear diagnosis and that it is impossible to perceive save in fragments.

Almost from the start, the decision to appoint Klata to the post of Head of the Narodowy Stary Teatr in Cracow aroused extreme reactions, above

---

[35] Cf.: ""Transfer!" Jana Klaty," https://culture.pl/pl/dzielo/transfer-jana-klaty (accessed 6 May 2019). The production can be seen online on the Ninateka page; see: https://ninateka.pl/film/transfer-jan-klata

all in right-wing circles.[36] The situation shortly became more embittered after the first production directed by him, August Strindberg's *To Damascus* (autumn 2013). As a response to the production's presentation of seemingly indecent, "pornographic" scenes, there was a demonstration during one performance, which expressed opposition to "the left-wing attitudes and the blasphemous treatment of national-theatrical monuments by Director Jan Klata"[37] and led to an interruption of the show. After the change of government in Poland in 2015, the controversies around Klata grew ever greater; more and more voices were heard calling for his dismissal. Subsequent productions consistently inflamed the tensions surrounding him, including Ibsen's *An Enemy of the People* (Narodowy Stary Teatr in Cracow, 2015), not just a tale of the timeless stupidity of small-town authorities, but also one that touches on the current issue of the migrant crisis and xenophobia. The earlier production of *King Lear* (Narodowy Stary Teatr in Cracow, 2014), the action of which Klata transferred to the cellars of the Vatican, presented a discussion about the contemporary Roman Catholic Church and mechanisms of power. Ultimately, Klata was not dismissed, but when his term of office ended in the summer of 2017, a search for a new Director was announced. The members of the appointment committee (largely composed of representatives of the authorities) decided against Klata's re-appointment, and thus he left the post on 30 September 2017.

Klata's last premiere as Director in Cracow was a production of *Wesele* (The Wedding) by Wyspiański (12 May 2017). One can say without exaggeration that it was a symbolic premiere—*Wesele* is one of the most important of all Polish plays, a fundamental statement on national identity. The production was called a masterpiece.[38] In response to public demand, it was for a period of time performed twice a day in the Stary Teatr. However, after the staff changes in the theatre, there was no place for the production in its repertoire, although guest performances were presented on many Polish stages (not always theatrical ones, e.g. *Wesele* was presented during the Open'er music festival in Gdynia in 2018 and elsewhere).

---

[36] Of his directorship much has been written: see, above all: J. Targoń, "Klata i po Klacie," *Dialog* 9 (2017).

[37] M. Kęskrawiec, "Tajne przez jawne na widowni Starego Teatru," *Dziennik Polski* 2013, 14 November.

[38] See, for example: D. Kosiński, "Teatr z tej i nie z tej ziemi," *Tygodnik Powszechny* 21 (2017).

5.

After leaving Cracow, Klata worked on a production of Shakespeare's *Measure for Measure* at the Theatre pod Palmovkou in Prague (premiere 27 January 2018). The director had already worked several times abroad, above all in Germany—at the Düsseldorfer Schauspielhaus he directed *Shoot/Get Treasure/Repeat* by Mark Ravenhill (2010); and in Bochum *Amerika* by Franz Kafka (2011), *The Robbers* by Friedrich Schiller (2012) and *Hamlet* (2013). He also had an opportunity to work at the Moscow Arts Theatre (*Macbeth*, 2016).

More recently, in Poland, Klata directed *Wielki Fryderyk* (Fryderyk the Great) based on a play by Adolf Nowaczyński (Teatr Polski in Poznań, premiere 5 May 2018) and Eurypides' *The Trojan Women*, which had its premiere on 8 September 2018 in Teatr Wybrzeże in Gdańsk. And his latest production is *Długi* (Debt, Teatr Nowy Proxima in Cracow, premiere 14 September 2019). A theatrical essay inspired by David Graeber's book *Debt: The First 5000 Years*,[39] it has been very successful. The production is a collage, constructed in the poetics of a videoclip. Music performed live by the four-actor cast is entwined with dramatic scenes based on various classical texts concerning the issue of debt in both literal and metaphorical senses (e.g. Dostoevsky's *Crime and Punishment*, Goethe's *Faust* or Shakespeare's *The Merchant of Venice*). And again, in this very energetic, arresting and intelligent work, Klata offers a diagnosis of our contemporary reality, characterised by one of the recurring lines: "Each man is a debt. Each day is a loan."

In November 2018, Klata was given one of the most important theatrical awards in Europe—the Award for (New) Theatrical Realities as part of the eighteenth edition of the Europe Theatre Prize. With this, he joined a company of artists that includes, among others, Anatoly Vasiliev, Eimuntas Nekrošius, Oskaras Koršunovas, Alvis Hermanis, Guy Cassiers and Katie Mitchell.[40]

Translated by David Malcolm

---

[39] See: D. Graeber, *Debt: The First 5000 Years* (New York: Melville House, 2011).

[40] A full list of prize-winners, recognised for creative innovation, is available on the web page of Premio Europa per il Teatro; see: http://www.premio-europa.org/open_page.php?id=250 (accessed 7 May 2019).

Image 1 *H.* directed by Jan Klata, Teatr Wybrzeże, 2004. (Photo by Wiesław Czerniawski)

References

Budzowska, Małgorzata, "Jan Klata. Muzyczność rewolucji" [in:], *Sceniczne metamorfozy mitu. Teatr polski XXI wieku w perspektywie kulturowej* (Łódź: Wydawnictwo Uniwersytetu Łódzkiego, 2018).

Burzyńska, Anna R., *The Classics and the Troublemakers. Theatre Directors from Poland* (Warsaw: Zbigniew Raszewski Theatre Institute, 2008).

"Dorosnąć do widowni," Jan Klata in conversation with Dorota Kardasińska, *Notatnik Teatralny* 2004, no. 32–33.

Féral, Josette, "Miejsce teatralne jako przestrzeń fascynacji: "Wieża" Anne-Marie Provencher" [in:] *Teatr w miejscach nieteatralnych*, ed. J. Tyszka, (Poznań: Wydaw. Fundacji Humaniora, 1998).

Graeber, David, *Debt: The First 5000 Years* (New York: Melville House, 2011).

Kęskrawiec, Marek, "Tajne przez jawne na widowni Starego Teatru," *Dziennik Polski* 2013, 14 November.

Klata, Jan, "O prawdzie i nieprawdzie, etyce i estetyce," edited by Marta Kuźmiak, *Notatnik Teatralny* 2004, no. 32–33.

Konopko, Aleksandra, "The Theater of Jan Klata. Struggling for a New Audience," *Journal of Education, Culture and Society*, 2 (2010).

84 K. KRĘGLEWSKA

Kosiński, Dariusz, "Teatr z tej i nie z tej ziemi," *Tygodnik Powszechny* 21 (2017).

Kościelniak, Marcin, *"Młodzi niezdolni" i inne teksty o twórcach współczesnego teatru*, (Cracow: Wydawnictwo Uniwersytetu Jagiellońskiego, 2014).

Kwaśniewska, Monika, *Pytanie o wspólnotę. Jerzy Grzegorzewski i Jan Klata*, (Cracow: Wydawnictwo Uniwersytetu Jagiellońskiego, 2016).

"Myślę, że Hamlet jest Polakiem," Jan Klata talks with Mirella Wąsiewicz, *Gazeta Wyborcza—Trójmiasto* 153 (2004), http://encyklopediateatru.pl/artykuly/127328/mysle-ze-hamlet-jest-polakiem (accessed 6 May 2019).

Notatnik Teatralny [special number], 2005, no. 38.

Pawłowski, Roman, "Duński książę w cieniu stoczni," *Gazeta Wyborcza* 2004, no. 155.

———, "Tow. Horodniczy," *Gazeta Wyborcza* 2003, no. 89.

Puzyna-Chojka, Joanna, Kręglewska, Katarzyna, Świąder-Puchowska, Barbara, "Hamlet w Stoczni. "H." według Szekspira w reżyserii Jana Klaty" [in:] *Teatr Wybrzeże w latach 1996–2016. Zjawiska-ludzie-przedstawienia*, (Gdańsk: Uniwersytet Gdański, 2019).

"Słownik pojęć dramaturgicznych," *Notatnik Teatralny* 2010, no. 58–59.

Sztarbowski, Paweł, "Teatr mój widzę masowy," *Newsweek Polska* 2007, no. 9.

Śmiechowicz, Olga, *Lupa, Warlikowski, Klata. Polski teatr po upadku komunizmu*, (Warsaw: Wydawnictwo Naukowe PWN, 2018).

Targoń, Joanna, "Klata i po Klacie," *Dialog* 2017, no. 9.

"Wawel na mnie nie działa," A conversation with Jan Klata, *Didaskalia* 2004, no. 63.

"W oku salonu," Jan Klata talks with Łukasz Drewniak, *Przekrój* 2005, no. 8.

Wyspiański, Stanisław, *Hamlet*, [in:] idem, *Dzieła zebrane*, ed. Leon Płoszewski etc., vol. 13 (Cracow: Literackie, 1961).

Zielińska, Maryla, "Prowokator," *Ozon* 2005, no. 1.

RECORDINGS OF PERFORMANCES DIRECTED BY JAN KLATA AVAILABLE ONLINE

Transfer: https://ninateka.pl/film/transfer-jan-klata
H.: http://ninateka.pl/film/h-spektakl-teatr

"What Is Hecuba to Him or He to Hecuba?" or the Theatre of Oskaras Koršunovas

Rasa Vasinauskaitė

Although already belonging to the middle generation, Oskaras Koršunovas (born in 1969) will probably always be referred to as a young director in the history of Lithuanian theatre. If the new history of Lithuania itself began in 1990, it also began with the biography of his theatre. Still a student, the 21-year-old Koršunovas made his debut with a production of *There to Be Here,* based on texts by Daniil Kharms (1990). Unlike other Lithuanian productions of the time, permeated with the theme of national independence, his show featured Chaplinesque tricks and black humour pouring out in dreamlike, deformed, nightmarish, yet funny images that had nothing in common with reality. Koršunovas gained immediate fame as *the* Lithuanian theatre director and has been boldly moving towards international recognition ever since.

Importantly, unlike another famous Lithuanian colleague—Eimuntas Nekrošius—Koršunovas is unique in his ability to change his theatre with the times. This attests to his having not only a style and a theatrical language of his own, but also to his ability to feel "the fashions" of the theatre

---

R. Vasinauskaitė (✉)
Lithuanian Music and Theatre Academy, Lithuanian Culture Research Institute, Vilnius, Lithuania

© The Author(s), under exclusive license to Springer Nature Switzerland AG 2021
K. Stefanova, M. Carlson (eds.), *20 Ground-Breaking Directors of Eastern Europe*, https://doi.org/10.1007/978-3-030-52935-2_7

85

86   R. VASINAUSKAITĖ

world in principle, as well as the pulse of life, culture and politics. His productions are avant-gardist and experimentalist, yet always in tune with mass culture. Hence Koršunovas' theatre can be called "postmodernist," due to its critical and deconstructive attitude, and "transitional," since it has been reflecting the transitions in Lithuanian context from Soviet to post-Soviet times, society and theatre. Notably, by being a transitional director Koršunovas also embodies the most important feature of his generation[1]—the critical and ironic perception of (contemporary) reality.

After his debut, Koršunovas staged two more productions based on texts by Daniil Kharms and Alexander Vvedensky.[2] In the first version of *The Old Woman* (1992), red-and-white stripes flooded the stage, in the middle of which was a coffin. In the second version, *The Old Woman 2* (1994), red was replaced by black and instead of the coffin there was a huge suitcase-box: black-and-white stripes traversing the space recalled a prison in which a solitary light bulb was switching on in a ghostly manner (set designer Žilvinas Kempinas). On this occasion, the theatre critic Rūta Vanagaitė wrote: "The theatre of Eimuntas Nekrošius undulates like air—with wind, rain and an evening coolness. The theatre of Oskaras Koršunovas is constructed and cold like the inside of an empty coffin. 'The world is a corpse'—this postulate sounds almost like mockery. The world is a corpse! So, let's have some fun and shave off the beard that continues to grow on that corpse."[3] What followed in 1994 was *Hello Sonia New Year*, after Vvedensky's play *Christmas at the Ivanovs* and Jean Anouilh's *The Lark*, which Koršunovas, the set designer Kempinas and the composer Gintaras Sodeika called "a Dadaistic opera."[4]

Reality and unreality, life and death, crime and punishment, drama and farce, tragedy and eccentricity, lyricism and buffoonery—these were the departure points for Koršunovas when he was choosing the themes for this trilogy and was creating their inimitable forms pulled out somewhere from the corners of the subconscious. All the characters were prisoners of their own fears, nightmares and apprehensions, and it was not so much the paradoxical and the absurd but their own cruel and insolent efforts to

---

[1] The "turning-point" generation, which was born and raised in an occupied country and started independent life in conditions of freedom.

[2] Members of the group of Russian avant-garde artists "OBERIU" (an acronym for the Society for Real Art in Russian), active in the 1920s and 1930s.

[3] R. Vanagaitė, "Teatrinio sezono įvykis: mirusios Senės pabučiavimas." *Lietuvos rytas*, 13 January 1995.

[4] The playbill of *Hello Sonia New Year*; the premiere took place on 17 March 1994.

"WHAT IS HECUBA TO HIM OR HE TO HECUBA?" OR THE THEATRE... 87

liberate themselves that provoked outbursts of laughter in the audience. This was what left individual marks of the possibility of inner freedom on every one of us. So it was not only the form of Koršunovas' theatre but also his characters that differed from the usual stage characters and the poetic language of Lithuanian theatre at the time.

The Classics as (Post)Modernists and Vice Versa

Lithuanian theatre approached the threshold of the twenty-first century believing in its inherent creative flight of imagination and, at the same time, having found a new mission and new forms of interaction with the public. This "new openness" reflected the ties between the metaphorical school of Lithuanian directing and the aesthetics of another type of theatre, called "post-dramatic" by the Western theatre historians and theoreticians of the 1980s and 1990s. Hans-Thies Lehmann's book, translated into Lithuanian in 2010,[5] has allowed a re-evaluation of the stage phenomena of the 1990s and beyond, and the calling of many different theatrical examples "post-dramatic." However, the post-dramatic with its different features has been characteristic of the Lithuanian stage already since 1980, thanks to the theatre of Eimuntas Nekrošius, both in terms of directorial handling of dramatic texts and theatrical elements and, even more importantly, the theatre's connection with reality and its way of communicating with the audience. For Koršunovas this communication was always very important, and his theatrical language was constantly gaining new features, reacting quickly to the significant changes in reality and (world) theatre alike. So after staging the OBERIU texts, he began his reflection on his breakthrough generation via both classic and contemporary drama.

In 1997, critics wrote that Koršunovas was no longer considered among the ranks of his fellow young directors, but had risen to equal Jonas Vaitkus (Koršunovas' teacher[6]), Eimuntas Nekrošius and Rimas Tuminas in importance, thus becoming one of the big four of Lithuanian directing. His most important productions of the turn of the century were *P.S. File*

---

[5] H.-T. Lehmann, *Postdraminis teatras*, iš vokiečių kalbos vertė Jūratė Pieslytė (Vilnius: Menų spaustuvė, 2010).

[6] Koršunovas belongs to the first generation of directors who graduated in Lithuania, not in Russia. His teacher at the Lithuanian Academy of Music and Theatre was the director Jonas Vaitkus (born in 1944), a prominent creator of political theatre during the Soviet period.

88 R. VASINAUSKAITĖ

O.K., by the Lithuanian writer and playwright Sigitas Parulskis (1997); *Roberto Zucco*, by Bernard-Marie Koltès (1998); *Shopping and Fucking*, by Mark Ravenhill (1999); Shakespeare's *Midsummer Night's Dream* (1999); *The Face of Fire*, by Marius von Mayenburg (2000); Mikhail Bulgakov's *The Master and Margarita* (2000); and Sophocles' *Oedipus Rex* (2002). They all focused on the state of the young—their inner self, the conflicts between them and society. Initially still using the language of symbols and paradoxes, Koršunovas gradually turned towards the "new realism,"[7] yet in his hands it also had an important subtext—it spoke about tragic traumatic memory and rebellion. In 1999 he founded the independent Oskaras Koršunovas Theatre (OKT)[8] and chose as its sign the Kharms hieroglyph, a point in the centre of several circles.

In all Koršunovas' productions, two layers can be detected: symbolic, born out of the respective production's aesthetics; and realistic, focused on the identification of reality. And in all of them, it is the visual rather than the verbal that carries the meaning of the action, regardless of the choice of literary or dramatic work. Another common feature is that all Koršunovas' productions have an "open structure" that, in Umberto Eco's words, is based on the active perceptual and receptive activities of the audience; this liberates the productions from the frames of the dramatic structure and releases a multifaceted interpretive potential.

Roberto Zucco sounded like Koršunovas' discussion/argument with Nekrošius: it was as if the young director was creating the *Hamlet* of his time and generation. (Ten years later, in 2008, he would create his own *Hamlet*.) Lithuanian theatre critic Valdas Vasiliauskas wrote that *Roberto Zucco* was directed like a movie thriller, with vibrant montage and surtitles of the episodes (of violent film scenes on a huge screen), with a cast of actors and non-actors[9] and, most importantly, for the first time in Lithuanian theatre, a generation of rockers, bikers, skateboarders, DJs and prostitutes spoke in their own language. "Koršunovas is a theatre

---

[7] O. Koršunovas, Teatru per laika *OKT: būti čia* (Vilnius: VšĮ "Oskaro Koršunovo teatras," 2009), pp. 21–22.

[8] Koršunovas announced that OKT will be a repertory theatre in which classics will be played as contemporary drama, and contemporary drama will gain classical value. That is, he would aim to discover in classical dramaturgy what is relevant for a contemporary audience and find what is universal in contemporary plays.

[9] Several well-known and well-recognized Lithuanian cultural figures also appeared on the stage, not only putting the actor–role relation in an unusual perspective, but also bringing the events of the play closer to the Lithuanian context.

terrorist,"[10] wrote Vasiliauskas. The reality on stage was the reality of the city and its nightlife. And the city inevitably acquired the features of mass culture: most of the characters wore street and club clothes, techno music resounded, dazzling lights flashed and a real skateboard ramp (for a real skateboarder) stood on stage. The set design was created by Jūratė Paulékaitė (1965–2011), who became Koršunovas' regular collaborator and co-author of the best productions of OKT, as did the composer Gintaras Sodeika.

At first glance, it seemed that the Lithuanian stage version of *Shopping and Fucking* covered every possible field of perception. An extensive advertising campaign was organised and after the premiere there were meetings with the audience. The production was influenced by postmodern cinematic stylistics, there was a rapid episode montage, emotionally and energetically intense acting. The novelty of the performance was elsewhere, though: in a new way of acting that "freed" the actors from the characters and allowed for a direct connection between the stage and the audience. Through the contrast between mass culture clichés, stereotypical images and extreme life situations, the theatre of Koršunovas spoke of a reality in which, in Baudrillard's words, "[t]he impossibility of rediscovering an absolute level of the real is of the same order as the impossibility of staging illusion. Illusion is no longer possible, because the real is no longer possible."[11] The actors turned into a "modern" counterweight to postmodern stage visuality; it was important for Koršunovas to keep the actors natural and suggestive even in the most shocking episodes. This way of working with actors was going to be especially important in his future productions *Hamlet* (2008), *The Lower Depths*, by Maxim Gorky (2010), and Anton Chekhov's *The Seagull* (2013). Particularly in the latter two, each actor was to become at once "a story" and "a stage," "the action" and the meaning of the production.[12]

---

[10] V. Vasiliauskas, "Teroristas O. Koršunovas dar nėra suimtas," *Lietuvos rytas*, 20 January 1998.

[11] J. Baudrillard, *Simulacra and Simulation*, trans. by S. F. Glaser (Ann Arbor, Michigan: University of Michigan Press, 1994), p. 19.

[12] Such acting can be called post-Brechtian: the actor gets immersed in the stage action, but at the same time the actor models/steers this action (or character) in the eyes of the audience. There is maximum overlap between the actor and the character, or the actor is a real character. All Koršunovas' productions are characterised with conceptual selection of the actors for the roles.

90 R. VASINAUSKAITĖ

A fanatic who never tired of searching and experimenting, Koršunovas naturally became a regular guest at international festivals. In 2000 he got involved in the Avignon project *Theorem* and showed his own version of *Hotel Europa* and Bulgakov's *The Master and Margarita*. In 2002 he was awarded the Lithuanian National Prize for Culture and Art. In 2006 he received the Europe Prize New Theatrical Realities. So far, his international festival prizes and state awards are close to forty in number. OKT touring itineraries have run from Europe to Latin America and from Australia to Asia. Still, Koršunovas' theatre is primarily designed for his native Lithuanian audience and his city. He himself feels that he is first of all a director from Vilnius. Moreover, the audience in Vilnius, according to him, is special: like a midwife, it receives each new play of his with love.

Indeed, in his *Oedipus Rex* by Sophocles, the playground on stage was a traditional Lithuanian one—gloomy and dead, it caused fear rather than attraction, so children played there only occasionally. Today there are no such playgrounds remaining from the Soviet years, but in 2002 this was instantly recognisable. Koršunovas' Oedipus (a contemporary man of power—a politician and businessman) was a child in such a playground, with a sandpit that was at once an altar, the bed of Oedipus and Jocasta, the sacred soil of the town and the shelter of the grown-up Oedipus. It was the embodiment of the very fate of this cursed Oedipus-child: in the sandpit he "found" Teiresias; and it was there to which he returned after he was blinded, and there he extinguished the last beams of light in the sand. However, *Oedipus Rex* was interesting not only because of its recognisable story of a contemporary authority figure, but also, and maybe more importantly, because the very form of the tragedy was interpreted in a (post)modern way. The form was created as a musical score (by the composer Sodeika and the percussionist Arkadijus Gotesmanas) in which everything—intonations and movements—was measured by rhythm and it was the rhythm that shaped the content.

In Koršunovas' words, "Every person potentially is an Oedipus, but not everyone takes this path."[13] In 2002 this production was the closest to his philosophy, maybe even the most intimate, opening the door to that passionate desire for cognition that inevitably brings one closer to a tragic self-awareness.

---

[13] O. Koršunovas, "Oidipas karalius" *OKT: būti čia* (Vilnius: VšĮ "Oskaro Koršunovo teatras," 2009), p. 32.

"What Is Hecuba to Him or He to Hecuba?"

Koršunovas is a theatre director to the marrow of his bones. That is why the characters of his productions and the productions themselves undergo a paradoxical metamorphosis: creating a powerful "shadow" reality. Everyday situations on his stage expand into metaphorical generalisations, a nearly photographic realism grows into an abstract and symbolic one, and a regular social space becomes mythopoetic. Here probably lies the secret of the new realistic dramaturgy's popularity: some directors use it as a device for social criticism and an instrument for active struggle; others employ it as one of the possible means for diagnosing the illnesses of civilisation; still others treat it as material for creating new tools for theatrical expression and acting. I would place Koršunovas in the latter group, even though he himself is convinced that his productions have the extremely important mission of bringing to the fore the topical problems of our time.

The OKT functions as a creative laboratory and a way of life: Koršunovas' concern is not merely to stage a play, but to follow its life, to steer it and make continuous changes. Theatre for him is an organism that functions every day and that develops fantasies and emotions; his faithful actors are generators of ideas who, incidentally, have created and are creating their best roles. Although the OKT is a stage for extreme feelings and experience both for the creators and the audience, this experience is an expression of a particular aesthetics rather than a pure imitation of a "hyper-real" reality.

The changing language of Koršunovas' theatre has retained both the phantasmagory found in the OBERIU trilogy, which deforms stage reality, and the specificity and truthfulness of the "new realism," which provokes an active dialogue between the stage and the audience via recognisable situations and characters. Perhaps that is why the director easily combines modernist and postmodernist aesthetics, "unifies" classics and contemporary drama. For him what is important is the metaphysics of the imagination and the theatricalisation of life, rather than a mere stage depiction of the world of a concrete play. Koršunovas has not changed his opinion that a stage work exists only according to its own rules as a unique reality, and that it can be comprehended only through one's subjective "self."[14]

---

[14] His most famous performances staged in Lithuania were *The Most Excellent and Lamentable Tragedy of Romeo and Juliet* (2003), *Cold Child* by Marius von Mayenburg

92 R. VASINAUSKAITĖ

In *The Master and Margarita*, Koršunovas focused on the act of creation in principle and on acting in particular as an embodiment of the search for truth and the interplay between truth and lie. This theme resounded in an even more prominent way in *Hamlet*. At the beginning of the production, all the actors sat in front of dressing-room mirrors and asked their reflections "Who are you?" This questioning continued through all the subsequent narrative lines. Shakespeare's *Hamlet* was turned into a story about the relationships between actors, between actors and a director, between actors and roles. The dressing rooms with make-up tables and the backstage (the set was created by Koršunovas himself), as well as theatre and life as a whole, were so well intertwined that fiction could hardly be separated from reality. Koršunovas blended the "stories" of Shakespeare and of a theatre, and Hamlet became the director of his own tragedy. In 1997, Nekrošius' *Hamlet* was a fierce *theatrum mundi*. In 2008, Koršunovas' *Hamlet* was a theatre for the febrile consciousness of a person for whom it was vital to reveal the truth—to uncover the truth in a theatre where everyone is always in the process of playing roles.

Steps towards revealing the truth were undertaken also in *The Lower Depths* and *The Seagull*—two fully laboratory works; as well as in *Expulsion* (2011)—a huge five-and-a-half hour production about the Lithuanian emigration to Great Britain, by the Lithuanian playwright of the same generation Marius Ivaškevičius—and in *The Cathedral* (2012), by Justinas Marcinkevičius, one of the 1970s' most important texts for the formation of Lithuanian national identity.

The Lower Depths and *The Seagull* demonstrated a completely "naked" acting style. Both were performed not on a stage but in a rehearsal hall—a medium-size room in the theatre. In the first, the actors sat on one side of a long table and the seats for the viewers were simply on the other side of the table. In *The Seagull*, the audience sat slightly farther from the actors, but the actors too were sitting on chairs, lined along the walls, and, as spectators, were watching their colleagues before "playing" their role. Theatre disappeared or rather became a condensed depiction of relationships and events, in which live, natural people, here and now, "act." As

(2004), *To Damascus* by August Strindberg (2007), *Miranda*, based on *The Tempest* by William Shakespeare (2011), *Krapp's Last Tape* by Samuel Beckett (2013), *Cleansed* by Sarah Kane (2016), *Wedding* by Bertolt Brecht (2016), *Attempts on Her Life* by Martin Crimp (2018) and *Russian Romance* by Marius Ivaškevičius (2018). In all these different productions Koršunovas worked as an author who modified/transformed the possibilities of the play via theatrical means.

Lithuanian critic Alma Braškytė wrote, "the director sought to explore the very preconditions of participating in a theatrical action—renouncing a complex set-design, theatre machinery, use of video images, complicated soundtrack and the actors' protective armour—their professional mastery. The aim of these laboratories was the actors' self-exploration, a test of their personal and professional abilities through the themes of the play and the meeting with the audience."[15]

The Lower Depths and *The Seagull* put an end to a long and important period of Koršunovas' oeuvre.

AND ABOUT POLITICS …

Politics is always "contained" in the subtext of Koršunovas' productions. Moreover, his theatre is always in a state of confrontation, both with the dominant theatrical aesthetics and with the political and social system. It opposes everything that restricts the freedom of thought, "normalises" and turns a human being into a cog within a system. In this regard, his choices of plays by the Lithuanian playwrights Parulskis and Ivaškevičius are important. Their texts are characterised by a non-linear narrative, transformations of time and action, non-standard language and intertextuality (slang, social dialect, Russian swear words, collage of artistic and non-artistic texts). Also, *P.S. File O.K.* by Parulskis was the first play reflecting the Soviet reality as trauma, and Ivaškevičius' *Expulsion* is focused on the ideology, identity, politics and history of independent Lithuania.

Importantly, in Koršunovas' productions of the last decade, politics emerged as a subject/object of debate and laughter, leading to a tragic farce. In *Expulsion* the scenes were connected with live music and the action was duplicated with video projections. A gallery of different national, religious and social types was presented, along with the themes of the adaptation of emigrants to a foreign environment and the possibility of creating an authentic identity in a global, multicultural space, where linguistic, bodily or spiritual freedom is constantly manipulated. So the focus shifted from emigration to integration, which leads to sacrificing language, history, religion and even human dignity. In other words, the production asserted a new subjectivity in contrast with the universal ethical and aesthetic norms, social and political hierarchy. This subjectivity was

---

[15] A. Braškytė, Oskaras Koršunovas: Real-Time Theatre. *Contemporary Lithuanian Theatre. Names and Performances* (Vilnius: TKIEC, Tyto Alba, 2019), pp. 113–114.

based on the theatre's responsibility to a small nation—a responsibility that is taken for granted in Lithuania and post-Soviet countries, where theatre is still the most important place for discovering reality and for creating identity.

In turn, in Molière's *Tartuffe* (2017), the politics represented by Tartuffe was portrayed as manipulation, compulsion and lies, while the politics represented by Orgon was mere blindness, stupidity and selfishness. Intense, with a strong musical score, full of eccentric and comic episodes, multiplying the characters' images with video projections, the production ended without Molière's final episode; that is, without the intervention of the king. So Tartuffe was presented as a contemporary demon, obsessed by desire for power, conquering the house of Orgon. The laughter and the horror were integral to Koršunovas' *Tartuffe*, as they are to his latest production—*Our Class*,[16] a tragic play/testimony about the Holocaust by Tadeusz Słobodzianek (2019).

Lithuanian critics call Oskaras Koršunovas' theatre a *Real Time Theatre*. In its form and content, it is not only post-dramatic but post-traumatic too. It encodes not only the visible or recognisable reality, but the real one in a Lacanian sense. It is *the* real that does not exist in our reality, which is not signified but which can somehow be discerned within our symbolic order and even named as the real of death, the real of the traumatic past, the real of the uncompromising truth of our existence.

A new generation of actors, stage designers and composers has emerged with the independent Oskaras Koršunovas Theatre and a new generation of spectators has also grown up with it. Over the last two decades, the OKT has managed to relate the new understanding of the Lithuanian theatre tradition to contemporary global culture. After twenty years of work and touring both nationally and internationally, the OKT has become one of Lithuania's leading theatre companies. (Meanwhile, in 2004, it received the status of a Vilnius City Theatre.) All this time Koršunovas has been staging productions both in Lithuania and abroad and has been working with students at the Lithuanian Academy of Music and Theatre. He is still one of the most productive Lithuanian directors, who easily manages drama and opera, theatre and performance art, easily combines reality and imagination and creates his own theatrical world.

"I have always been interested in one aspect of the theatre: the possibility to express what cannot be expressed in words, to create a mysterious

---

[16] Koršunovas staged *Our Class* also at Oslo's National Theatre, Norway, in 2015.

Image 1 *Hamlet*, directed by Oskaras Koršunovas, OKT, 2008, Gertrude—Nelė Savičenko, Hamlet—Darius Meškauskas, Claudius—Dainius Gavenonis. (Photo by Dmitrij Matvejev)

inner communication between spectators and actors. The inadequacy between a word and an action, a word and a view, are very important to me. The discrepancy helps new meanings to appear,"[17] said Koršunovas in 1998. Today his work continues to respond to the changing world and the new possibilities for theatre.

REFERENCES

Baudrillard, Jean, *Simulacra and Simulation*, translated by Sheila Faria Glaser, Ann Arbor, Michigan: University of Michigan Press, 1994.
Braškytė, Alma, ed., *OKT: būti čia*, Vilnius: VšĮ: "Oskaro Koršunovo teatras," 2009.

---

[17] *The Theatre of Oskaras Koršunovas*, ed. by R. Vasinauskaitė (Vilnius: Baltos lankos, 2002), pp. 65–66.

———, "Oskaras Koršunovas: Real-Time Theatre," *Contemporary Lithuanian Theatre. Names and Performances*, edited by Ramunė Marcinkevičiūtė and Ramunė Balevičiūtė, Vilnius: TKIEC, Tyto Alba, 2019.

Koršunovas, Oskaras, *The Theatre of Oskaras Koršunovas*, edited by Rasa Vasinauskaitė, Vilnius: Baltos lankos, 2002.

Lehmann, Hans-Thies, *Postdraminis teatras*, iš vokiečių kalbos vertė Jūratė Pieslytė, Vilnius: Menų spaustuvė, 2010.

Jernej Lorenci: "People Are the Key"

Blaž Lukan

Jernej Lorenci (b. 1973) belongs to a generation of directors known in Slovenian theatre as "the fourth generation." It includes directors like Tomi Janežič, Sebastijan Horvat, Diego de Brea and the slightly older Mateja Koležnik and Ivica Buljan. Most of them are internationally renowned. Lorenci himself was the 2017 recipient of the prestigious Europe Theatre Prize for (New) Theatrical Realities. At the beginning of his career he did direct some productions on alternative and experimental stages, yet since then he has been working predominantly at major theatre institutions, to which he brings new, alternative forms of theatre or of functioning of the creative team. Lorenci is also a mentor to young directors and actors at the University of Ljubljana Academy of Theatre, Radio, Film and Television (ULAGRFT) and in addition to this directs opera.

B. Lukan (✉)
Academy for Theatre, Radio, Film and Television, University of Ljubljana, Ljubljana, Slovenia
e-mail: blaz.lukan@guest.arnes.si

© The Author(s), under exclusive license to Springer Nature Switzerland AG 2021
K. Stefanova, M. Carlson (eds.), *20 Ground-Breaking Directors of Eastern Europe*, https://doi.org/10.1007/978-3-030-52935-2_8

THE BACCHAE: ANTIQUITY AND MYTH

To get a notion of the fundamental characteristics of Jernej Lorenci's theatre, a look must be taken first at his fondness for ancient and mythological themes or scripts. His 1996 ULAGRFT graduation production was Sophocles' *Antigone*. The same year he veered from that thematic course with Brecht's *Baal* (Drama SNT Maribor), but returned to it in 1998 with Eliot's poetic *Murder in the Cathedral* (Ljubljana City Theatre), which certainly contains something "ancient," and with *The Bacchae* by Euripides (Drama SNT Maribor). This is indeed a topic to which Lorenci keeps coming back.

The Bacchae marked the beginning of his first, decade-long directorial phase, which ended in 2009 with another classical text, Aeschylus' *Oresteia*. Between *Bacchae* and *Oresteia*, there were some twenty productions originating from ancient and mythological themes (e.g. *Medea*, *The Epic of Gilgamesh*), although in theme and expression Lorenci also touched upon other dramatic or textual contexts. The central productions of his second phase are definitely *Wind in the Pines*—Noh plays based on Kan'ami, Zeami and Zenchiku (Drama SNT Maribor, 2009)—and Witkiewicz's *The Crazy Locomotive* (SNT Drama Ljubljana, 2012). The shift to his third creative phase came in 2015 with the staging of Homer's *The Iliad* (with some previous productions anticipating it)—not a dramatic but an epic text, which inaugurated Lorenci's "narrative theatre" phase, in which he still is today.

Lorenci's most obvious directorial move in *The Bacchae* was formalising the action and its declarative turn. He believes in a frontal monologue more than a "profile" dialogue and thus—with a single directorial gesture—"negates" all the effort that has been "invested" in the development of Greek tragedy since Aeschylus. Then he radicalised this move even further in *Oresteia*. The heroes of *Bacchae* (gods and kings) were onstage alone, wandered "the world" alone, and even performed the (rare) ritual acts—by definition collective—alone. Their presence onstage was not accidental or sporadic, it was organised into an oratorical set—into an orchestrated dramatic recital with dithyrambic accents. In principle Lorenci is not interested in the pure form of replicas—in his theatre they are always lined with complicating tones: tics, signs, shifts, multiplications, echoes. The same directorial move could be seen later, for example in *The Iliad*, where a microphone is important for expression, not only as an intermediary of the voice, but as an autonomous generator of sound.

In *Bacchae* Lorenci did not care about searching for a (new) god or even quarrelling with that god (he proclaims himself an atheist); neither was he searching for human harmony that a sacrifice supposedly leads to: perhaps he was only catching energy lines from the ether, in waiting— probably in a New Ageistic manner—for the arrival of a new era. The most reliable element in his work was the feeling that by providing the cruel and "chaotic" ancient world with a sophisticated form, he was re-arranging (this) world and giving it a meaning. The effect was a performance of cold energy nipping any attempt at identification in the bud and settling for restraint of its own formal invention.

Bacchae was a good example of a model production whose complexity announced Lorenci's further development. It included themes that keep on intriguing him: gods or divine, human, a confrontation between "beauty" and "horror" within the mythological dramatic structure, and then an invention of performing signs with poetic ("energetic") value, suitable for a dramatic script. Lorenci continued formalising action for a while, as could be observed in his *Dom Juan* by Molière (SLG Celje, 1999), in which he also searched for authentic human material in the play itself as well as in the actor and—perhaps most important—in himself, the director, as the initiator of the theatre event.

THE EPIC OF GILGAMESH: A THEATRE SEARCH FOR THE HUMAN

In addition to being focused on mythological or poetic themes, Lorenci's first directorial phase was marked by a desire to manifest the human. But what is the human to Lorenci? He says: "People are the key because theatre is about people, for people, among people."[1] Lorenci tries to answer the basic question: *What makes us who we are?* This is an old question that demands new answers. One of them is outlined by Giorgio Agamben: "The humanity of humans," for him, is a principle that "erases all the differences [...] the ultimate difference beyond which no further division is possible."[2] At the base of everything is the human, or even humanity, the tribe, group, genus from which everything emerges and to which it

---

[1] Ana Perne, "Zame se predstava nikdar ne zgodi na odru." Interview with Jernej Lorenci. *Literatura*, Vol. 30, No. 326 (August, 2018), p. 94.

[2] Giorgio Agamben, *Čas, ki ostaja: Komentar k Pismu Rimljanom* (Ljubljana: Študentska založba, 2008), p. 69.

returns, the tiniest speck of matter that is guaranteed a place in the periodic table of existence. The human is indestructible and can thus be destroyed into eternity, says Agamben with Maurice Blanchot: "there isn't a single human essence that can be destroyed or found, it means a human is a being that endlessly misses himself, who is always already separated from himself. But if a human is what can be endlessly destroyed, it means that beyond this destruction and in this destruction something always remains, it means that what remains is a human."[3]

In Lorenci's theatre, the human is what remains and beyond which there is nothing. The human is the eternal residue, that one-and-the-other, that "not-all"[4] that we cannot avoid in life or in art (see *The Iliad*, 2015).

Among the productions from Lorenci's first phase that swirl around the notion of the human and find a suitable performative formula are *Male Fantasies* (KGB Maribor, 1999), *Cleansed* after Sarah Kane (SNT Drama Ljubljana, 2001), Gombrowitz's *The Marriage* (Mladinsko Theatre, 2004) and the 2005 stagings of the Tibetan mystery *Tchrimekundan or The Unblinded* (SNT Drama Ljubljana) and *The Epic of Gilgamesh* retold by Nebojša Pop Tasić (Mladinsko Theatre). *Cleansed* was staged as a poetic metaphor that avoided drastic action; instead, Lorenci invented performing signs that created an autonomous performative structure, at one point removed from the text, although they were—paradoxically—its most authentic expression. The production was just physical enough to evoke pain and disgust in the spectator.

Lorenci's direction of *The Marriage* brought to the surface the dream-like rhythm of a pathetic episode about the destruction of some absurd will for power. Yet he made sure this episode did not succumb to the superficial absurdisation characteristic of the ready-made interpretations of dreams. He linked the scenes with almost Aristotelian preciseness. Dreams in this marriage evoked a deeper order, where absurdity faded into melancholy and the crudeness and directedness first cut to the quick, the flesh, and only then developed a halo of the sublime and the beautiful. *Marriage* carried the director's intense questions about establishing oneself in a world where everything can be said, yet that does not lighten our emotions; about standing on your own two (theatre) feet, which themselves are the artificial creations of an endless chain of predecessors; about

[3] Ibid., p. 70.
[4] Ibid., p. 72.

being visible in a world where practically everything is visible, yet remains consistently within the invisible and only presumed.

Lorenci offered his first complex answer to these questions in *The Epic of Gilgamesh*. The undisputable quality of this production was that the epic broadness of the ancient work was intensified in the limited space of the Mladinsko chamber stage. It was turned into a kind of primordial sandpit, where the fateful drama of the combat between gods or the initiators of the human and the drama of the human took place. Lorenci did not care for an economic bare theatre, but sought to dip into the essence of this 4000-year old "matrix" of a human (read: acting) figure performing in front of the spectators. A good example of evoking his "memory" of Gilgamesh was actor Dario Varga: particularly in the third "human" part, the audience could see a searching human who tries to find the true nature of the humane, a true explanation for the fateful captivity in one's own transient existence—that connection with space and time that alone guarantees his existence and that of the world around him. One needed only to reflect on the illuminated darkness in the actor's eyes or his (Beckettian) breathing that submerged into silence, leaving traces like deep scars.

In *Gilgamesh*, there were Lorenci's specific, already recognisable performative means: an empty stage, covered in sand, "natural" elements, such as a log or a dry branch; the set designer for almost all of his productions is Branko Hojnik. A concentrated and contemplative acting interpretation is used that defines the rhythm of the performance: in part melancholic and in part incantation. There is the constant presence of music (Lorenci's permanent composer is Branko Rožman) and an attempt to establish communicative closeness with the spectator. In Lorenci's directing it's as if nothing comes from the outside but only from the inside—not only from the dramatic (or mythological or poetic) script, but from his passionate search for the human in mythology, history, the pure present and himself.

When reflecting on theatre and its original material, Lorenci was quickly aware of the danger of becoming hermetically closed into his own world, in which the (intimate) thought itself could become more important than its (theatre) form. Until his 2009 *Oresteia* his productions thus seemed increasingly quieter, inward looking and forgetful of the key dimension of the theatre event—the spectator. Two productions then came as milestones: *Oresteia* and *Wind in the Pines*. They still "followed" a text, but Lorenci was already opening new performative and philosophical spaces.

It was then when he learnt a fundamental life truth, as he says in the already mentioned interview: namely, that working in theatre or art means to "open oneself wide." For theatre does not grow only from searching for the humanity of the (drama) script, its characters or actors, but also from the director as the basic initiator of this search.

ORESTEIA: OPENING NEW THEATRE SPACES

Oresteia and *Wind in the Pines* each articulated a new kind of contact with the theatre material and the spectator. Lorenci's most noticeable directorial move in *Oresteia*—already an anthology of different (postmodern) directorial moves—was duplication, double exposition of the performative actions that metaphorically pulled one skin over another, covered one form with another and then slowly took them off and mixed them at will, merged and extracted. Then and now, formally, Lorenci's direction does not illustrate or symbolise; it interrupts situations, actions or images before they can turn into symbols, or repeats them so many times that it empties them out.

Deep down, Lorenci's take on *Oresteia* was more than just staging the known mythological material—a tragedy of a family torn between loyalty and revenge, a seeming discrepancy between free will and divine order. It looked as if he had found a universal code in Aeschylus and his world: the demise of sovereign power. This demise happened in total: the former hierarchy of gods and people was collapsing, as were/are the universal human rights and even democracy as the universal (non-)hierarchical system. Last, the immanent dramaturgical structure of the script could no longer be staged without a chaotic distance, only with the memory of Aeschylus' essential pure sequence of dialogues or the exchange of choral strophes with monologues. The powerlessness of sovereignty (including the supreme power) appeared as the inevitable entrapment in the crisis that spared nobody: an entrapment in the vicious circle of shifting responsibility and endless transmissions, where authorities and their sovereign powers no longer reign but instead rule as non-government, which requires nothing from the one authorised and hides fully as the supreme force, concealing itself (*deus absconditus*) and leaving behind devastation and empty space that only arbitrary and irresponsible play can fill. This is the end—the endgame—of any play.

Wind in the Pines was a much more intimate production. It was closer to the spectator, whom it addressed with Aeschylus' divine irony, beautifully staged in a scene with a naked actress, Nataša Matjašec, on a wooden table, who was merely breathing in front of the spectator, thus evoking endless associations with human life.

Oresteia and *Wind in the Pines* were followed by a series of productions in a similar rhythm of alternating striking "spectacle" with intimate, chamber plays: Strniša's *Frogs* (Ptuj City Theatre, 2010), Ostrovsky's *The Storm* (Ljubljana City Theatre, 2011), Witkiewitz's *The Crazy Locomotive* (2012), Šeligo's *The Wedding* (SNT Drama Ljubljana, 2013) and Shakespeare's *Othello* (Ljubljana City Theatre, 2013).

Perhaps the situation before the new turning point was best represented by *The Crazy Locomotive*, most strongly in its relationship with the spectator, whose emotional imagination, according to Lorenci, had to be evoked by the performance or who had to be provoked to identify their life with the theatre event. In directing *Crazy Locomotive*, Lorenci moved between three conceptual segments. The first was craziness in principle, which interested him the least. The second was the "crazy world" rushing past the passengers on this metaphorical locomotive. The third was the "emptiness in the head" that one of the protagonists discussed and offered the greatest possibility of stage and semantic dynamics. Yet Lorenci found a fourth option: it is not about whether we or the world are crazy, and not about us being too full or too empty, but about the fact that we are basically defined by the crashes between emptiness and fullness, ratio and craziness, speed and stillness; our nature (and the nature of the world) is actually elusive; while we are at the end of something, we are only at the beginning; when we feel we are rushing into the future, we are returning to the past. As soon as we get used to our identity, it becomes different; we accept everything that happens to us with a smile, but this does not protect us from horror ...

The Iliad: An Anthology of Directorial Moves

The shift to Lorenci's new, still ongoing, directorial phase came with the productions of *The Dead Man Comes for His Sweetheart* by Svetlana Makarovič (Prešeren Theatre Kranj, 2014) and *The Iliad* after Homer (co-production of SNT Drama Ljubljana, Ljubljana City Theatre, Cankarjev dom, 2015). *The Dead Man Comes for His Sweetheart* is a grotesque poetic-musical piece, full of ecstatic orchestrated passages, whose course moves from one performative level to another. It introduces the principle

104   B. LUKAN

of frontal organisation of performers, who present their dramatic narrative directly addressing the audience.

In *The Iliad* the notion of the human undergoes a form of specific and paradoxical disfiguration: although there are actual, human figures on stage, they merge into a single non-body, into a sketch of humanity emerging from the emptiness behind their backs. (The production is staged on the proscenium of the grand Gallus Hall in Cankarjev dom and the audience can barely sense the vast empty hall behind the iron curtain, which gets revealed for a brief moment in the second part.) However, it is not about the voice coming from the void and Lorenci is aware of this: the voice comes from Homer's book, which is already an organisation of traces, of historical records. Lorenci's whole *Iliad* emerges from the background of nothingness, whether a space, history, a book, the stage edge, or simply an imaginary semicircular line that separates thought from phenomenon, idea from execution, eternal sleep or humankind's childhood from its contemporary existential spectacle. Lorenci is a mediator between the audience and this nothingness/emptiness in the process of *The Iliad*'s emerging from there.

With *The Iliad*, Lorenci's new understanding of the director's role is almost fully formed. As he explains, the director is a medium who does not consider his position to be exclusive, because at the beginning of the study "he doesn't know about it" himself. His primary task is establishing a safe space and a creative expression for the entire team, and he must constantly retain awareness and recognise the value of the gathered material that is a result of the actors' tasks in the process. From the completion of these tasks and the moments of improvisation and presentation of personal stories, he must in the end form a production following certain (dramaturgical) principles of stage composition, at the "intersection of imaginations of the actor and the spectator."[5]

In *The Iliad*, Lorenci is a mediator also between humans and gods, even though both play the written score that is not the director's—here, he does not identify with the legacy of the creators of twentieth-century directing—as the author is someone else. In fact, every new reality is written into it, so it is at the closest to the audience, the "humankind" gathered in the theatre—the stage has entered the auditorium, succumbed to its dictates. Lorenci's theatre in *The Iliad* is Aristotelian "archi-theater" as

---

[5] Ana Perne, "Zame se predstava nikdar ne zgodi na odru." Interview with Jernej Lorenci. *Literatura*, Vol. 30, No. 326 (August, 2018), p. 95.

Philippe Lacoue-Labarthe understands it, "a pious wish," "ideality doomed to crashing time and again into the harsh reality of the stage (space, actors and audience),"[6] which shows the way from epos to tragedy. *The Iliad* thus does not say that everything has happened, but rather that everything is still waiting to happen, despite the closing song about the transience of everything! Or because of it: it is what will come—death as the formatting of humanity, as its translation into a book, a poem, a stuttering verse on the verge of suffocating and strangulation, the loss of contact with reality.

Bible: The Narrative Theatre

The time after *The Iliad* is marked by Lorenci's realisation that the text is "one possibility of the theatre, but not the single or only one." His theatre from then on can be described as narrative theatre ("tale-acting"), as already mentioned. His next productions are more or less authorial. They are often still tied to a chosen textual script (e.g. Molière, Jarry, Shakespeare, Mayakovsky). Yet the scripts are no longer necessarily dramatic (e.g. *Bible* or *The Visoko Chronicle*). One way or another, based on this, the creative team carves out a new performance script. It might at times still lean on the original text (in *Ubu the King* only a few original lines remain in the final version), but often deviates from it completely, so that any link between the original and the performing scripts is arbitrary. Lorenci calls these productions "variations on a theme." The most characteristic ones are *Learned Women* after Molière (SLG Celje, 2015), *Ubu the King* after Jarry (SNT Drama Ljubljana, 2016), *Bible, first attempt* (SNG Drama Ljubljana, 2017), *Bedbug* after Mayakovsky (Prešeren Theatre Kranj, 2017) and *The Visoko Chronicles* after the novel by Slovenian author Ivan Tavčar (SNT Drama Ljubljana, 2018).

Ubu the King was a macabre Rabelais-like fresco, a depiction of debauchery rooted in the bases of acting. The centre of the production was the actor Jernej Šugman, the emblematic figure of Ubu and Actor, and at the same time a prototype of a contemporary individual, busy with his own greedy pleasure, or the "ego" that in the absence of all the norms is becoming a norm of everything and ascribes to itself the absolute virtue of "sincerity." Everything in the production was grotesque, including the

---

[6] Philippe Lacoue-Labarthe and Jean-Luc Nancy, *Scène* (Villeneuve-d'Ascq: Christian Bourgois editeur, 2013), p. 23.

final image—an extremely blown-up photo of the naked and perversely exposed director, who does not exclude himself from this *danse macabre* in any way.

Lorenci's *Bible* was an attempt at theatralisation of the book of books, without megalomaniac expectations and illusions, and it originated from the presumption that the Bible is primarily a book of human words rather than divine ones, a worldly book rather than a holy one. And the production was dedicated to the words—the holy words, which, spoken through the mouths of the actors, become merely human. *Bible* was first a production of deep concentration on words, and then the words themselves became an event, particularly in the sequence of the Book of Job. Lorenci staged the Bible outside a religious context, as far as this is at all possible. He de-contextualised and de-constructed it, and in the end the production focused on the words' source—the body. The denied, tortured, bullied body, which perhaps needs precisely such an elementary performative gesture to become awakened and free itself from the layers and bandages of holiness and to glow in front of the audience or congregation in its naked, authentic image. God in the production was reduced to the presence of light—a bare (and antiquated) tungsten filament light bulb hanging powerless above the scene, not strong enough even to illuminate itself. Nevertheless, the production as a whole was neither "critical" nor polemic to the (Christian) religion, perhaps only in the moments of exposing certain basic human characteristics, for example vanity. Neither did it challenge tradition or posed as superior to it. It was mostly a poetic stage metaphor for the recognition of our true value, best represented by the biblical ashes, or dust, used in Job's scene. The principle of Lorenci's *Bible* was not negation but creation: what can the human word from the beginning of all tell a human at the end?

The Visoko Chronicle is a story based on a novel-chronicle following the life of a family from the seventeenth century, yet from the beginning it is set in the present. Some of Lorenci's post–third turn directing characteristics can be observed in it. Actors, seated at a table, trade witty comments to describe the beginning of the work—the director's idea and his wishes, as well as their own attitude to the written material. This instantly sets up a "domestic" situation of authenticity in a theatre event, conceived as a stage narrative. But as is known from Lorenci's previous post-dramatic productions, as well as from similar ones by foreign directors, like Alvis Hermanis, Tim Etchells and Evgeny Grishkovets, the narrative never remains simply a narrative, despite being the starting point, but at a certain moment grows into an action; that is, *drama* (which etymologically means *action*). In *The Visoko Chronicle*, improvisation thus alternates with readings of the script, personal stories with novelistic episodes, performers' private relationships with the relationships between the fictive characters. The audience witnesses theatre in its creation: a table that becomes a stage the moment an actor steps on it, but also becomes some "real" distant set, with the spectator "adding" everything that is missing in one's imagination. The narrative brings the material closer to the spectator and simultaneously distances it in the staging of a body of sensual sensations. But they return into the spectator's imaginary consciousness after a strange turn, so that they are at the same time here and there, present and absent. And the spectator is at the same time the one who listens and the one audible, the creator and the consumer of the world, the original initiator of which is (merely) the human word. For "people are the key," as Lorenci puts it.

Image 1 *The Iliad*, directed by Jernej Lorenci, Slovenian National Theatre Drama Ljubljana, Ljubljana City Theatre and The Cankar Centre, 2015, from left to right: Aljaž Jovanović, Marko Mandić, Jette Ostan Vejrup, Gregor Luštek. (Photo by Peter Uhan)

REFERENCES

Agamben, Giorgio, *Čas, ki ostaja: Komentar k Pismu Rimljanom,* Ljubljana: Študentska založba, 2008.

Lacoue-Labarthe, Philippe and Jean-Louis Nancy, *Scène,* Villeneuve-d'Ascq: Christian Bourgois editeur, 2013.

Perne, Ana, "Zame se predstava nikdar ne zgodi na odru," interview with Jernej Lorenci, *Literatura*, vol. 30, no. 326 (August, 2018).

Krystian Lupa: The Maestro They ~~Criticise~~ Love

Katarzyna Waligóra

The cries of the passing demonstration barge into the room through the open window. It's impossible to distinguish the shouted words, but we know there is a huge crowd in the streets, whistling, screaming, drumming. The cries carry no joy, only blunt frustration and fury. The people of different ages in the room listen to the sounds from the street: they are a group of artists, madcaps, oddballs or just wanderers who have not found their place anywhere else. They are listening with curiosity to the voices from outside the window: worried, but not frightened. What happens in the street is of no concern to them; it doesn't yet penetrate their world. A moment later a man enters the room: he is stark naked but wearing shoes. Arkadina, an elderly woman played by Maria Maj, introduces him: "This is Janek—a poet and fetishist." "And you were walking in the street like that?" "What did they say?" the others ask. "Nothing. When they saw my shoes they were lost for words," Janek answers slyly.

This is the opening scene of *The City of Sleep*, one of the most thought-provoking and also most underappreciated productions directed by

---

K. Waligóra (✉)
Jagiellonian University, Kraków, Poland

© The Author(s), under exclusive license to Springer Nature
Switzerland AG 2021
K. Stefanova, M. Carlson (eds.), *20 Ground-Breaking Directors of Eastern Europe*, https://doi.org/10.1007/978-3-030-52935-2_9

Krystian Lupa. The play premiered at the TR Warszawa Theatre in 2012. Lupa reached for Alfred Kubin's novel *The Other Side*; many critics believe he failed to measure up to it and created a production that was too long, stammering, incoherent and unoriginal—there was no end to the list of critiques. And yet, although appreciated by few, the 2012 version of *The City of Sleep* might have been the most surprising production in the director's oeuvre, full of dazzling scenes and innovative ideas. It was also a production that closed a certain chapter in Lupa's work and opened a new one in his complicated, four decade–long career.

THE BEGINNINGS

From the earliest days, Krystian Lupa's achievements in the theatre were accompanied by the critics' alternating admiration and disillusionment, and *The City of Sleep* is but one of many of his productions that were dismissed. Still, the theatre was not Lupa's first stop. In 1969 he graduated from the Academy of Fine Arts in Kraków. Having obtained his diploma in painting, he embarked on another course of studies, this time at the Łódź Film School. He was there for a few years until he was expelled on the excuse of his allegedly poor films, yet Lupa often insists that the institution's aversion to him was on homophobic grounds. Homosexuality was not forbidden in the People's Republic of Poland (PRL) in the early 1970s, but it stayed in society's and the state's blind spot. So although gays and lesbians usually were not subject to official systemic repression, they were forced to conceal their sexual identity and the public realm was rife with homophobic prejudice. In the 1970s Krystian Lupa went through a rebellious period, as he himself admits:

> Suddenly, I felt being myself, I accepted myself. [...] I felt an explosion inside myself unexpectedly. [...] I behaved provocatively and scandalously during my studies.[1]

As a student of directing, his professors found homosexual tropes in the etudes he prepared for his exams. Many years later, Lupa reminisced:

---

[1] Krystian Lupa, Łukasz Maciejewski, *The End of the World of Values*, (Łódź, 2017), p. 513.

KRYSTIAN LUPA: THE MAESTRO THEY ~~CRITICISE~~ LOVE   111

I had other intentions … It was a film about a mutual influence of two bodies, misfits, sharing the same room in a dormitory. […] The commission saw what it had wanted to see.[2]

Although being thrown out of the Film School was a difficult experience for the director, he decided to take the entrance exam to the State Higher Theatrical School in Kraków, today known as the AST Academy of Theatre Arts. However, the fascination with film, not unlike his earlier painting studies, made their mark and often returned as afterimages in successive productions.

Krystian Lupa's exceptional talent manifested itself straightaway, in his second independent production in 1977, when he directed *Dainty Shapes and Hairy Apes, or The Green Pill* (by the eminent Polish writer, painter and photographer Stanisław Ignacy Witkiewicz) as a diploma work with fourth-year students of the Acting Faculty at the School. The production was generally commended and opened many doors for the young director. He decided to accept a full-time job at the C.K. Norwid Theatre in Jelenia Góra, a small town in the west of Poland. The seemingly surprising decision to reject the opportunity to work in a major theatre seems to make sense if you consider what that backwoods theatre was known for. Its director, Alina Obidniak, knew how to run the institution, balancing its repertoire between the popular and the ambitious. The first earned the theatre the favour of the audience, ticket revenues and satisfied the authorities, while the second allowed artistic development. Lupa worked with a fairly permanent actors' troupe on the theatre's Studio Stage, which was designed for experimental pursuits. This is when he started working with Piotr Skiba, who became his favourite actor and to this day is cast in nearly all Lupa's productions. The theatre in Jelenia Góra also offered him comfortable conditions for laboratory work, with extended rehearsal periods and full availability of the actors. The group of artists who gathered around Lupa were united not only by their work, but also by private friendships and the need to spend time together. Lupa spent ten years in Obidniak's theatre, preparing a total of ten premieres. He left Jelenia Góra as the acting troupe began to fall apart.

[2] Ibid., p. 514.

K. WALIGÓRA

SUCCESSES AND FAILURES

During and after his Jelenia Góra period, Lupa worked also for the Stary Theatre in Kraków, and it was there that he created some of his most renowned works. Grzegorz Niziołek writes in his book about Lupa's directing style:

> Lupa's theatre shows the human in the act of experiencing and getting to know himself and reality—not in action. [...] His productions consist of series of scenes, each a repeated attempt at the same act of transgression [...]. In trying to define this type of dramatic construction, Lupa makes reference to a form of musical variation which is based on repetitions and developments of a theme [...], and although the thread of the plot is never fully broken, it becomes secondary to the variation-based composition of the play.[3]

This variation-based composition is manifested not only within a single production, but also in general repertoire decisions: Lupa loves returning repeatedly to the same text. That was the case with *The Other Side*, Alfred Kubin's novel that provided the grounds for *The City of Sleep*. The first version of the production premiered at the Stary Theatre in Kraków in 1985, and it was completely different from the one he would produce in Warsaw twenty-seven years later. It was in 1985 that Lupa for the first time reached for a novel rather than a dramatic text. He did not adapt it, but rather treated Kubin as the inspiration and starting point for a complex, five-hour-long production that always ran over two nights. The drama about a country of radical dreamers was met with a complete lack of understanding. After over 120 rehearsals, it was only performed fifteen times. Grzegorz Niziołek wrote that the reason for such a poor reception of *The City of Sleep* could be the fact that Lupa violated the theatrical principles that were considered unchallengeable at the time, primarily the rule of coherent dramatic construction, the principle of clarity of the message, and the principle of performing the piece only when it is fully completed and unchangeable. And as Niziołek claims, "the reviewers' opinions were only the tip of the iceberg of judgements of the same ilk, albeit not expressed in writing, that Lupa's theatre triggered, particularly within the theatre world."[4]

---

[3] Grzegorz Niziołek, *Sobowtór i utopia. Teatr Krystiana Lupy* (Kraków, 1995), p. 71.

[4] Idem, "Klęski Krystiana Lupy," *Didaskalia*, No. 57 (2003), http://www.didaskalia.pl/57_niziolek.htm.

KRYSTIAN LUPA: THE MAESTRO THEY ~~CRITICISE~~ LOVE   113

Despite this type of reception, novels took a permanent place in Lupa's oeuvre, on a par with dramas. Throughout the years, the authors whom the director most readily reached for were Robert Musil, Hermann Broch and, above all, Thomas Bernhard. Interestingly, Lupa's productions from the 1980s and early 1990s that today are considered his greatest achievements often met a degree of indifference from the audience. For example, a year after the premiere of Robert Musil's *The Dreamers* in 1989, theatre critic Jacek Sieradzki noted:

> The drama was hardly ever played after the premiere, there were long pauses between the short series of performances. That production did not, and could not, become a dazzling success, but it gathered quite an unusual group of aficionados; people who knew what they were coming to, in many cases repeatedly. [...] There were not too many of them, however, perhaps just several dozen people in the audience.[5]

In contrast, the premiere of Thomas Bernhard's *The Lime Works*, staged at the National Stary Theatre in Kraków in 1992, was a spectacular success that was hailed as one of the most important theatrical events of the 1990s. It captivated viewers with its intimate portrayal of the drama developing in the relationship between Konrad, haunted by the desire to write a memorable study *On Hearing*, and his sick wife. The ingenious direction of the actors, and especially Małgorzata Hajewska-Krzysztofik and Andrzej Hudziak in the leading roles, was amazing. The drama was televised in 1998, and it could still be seen live on stage even sixteen years after its premiere.

The Krystian Lupa legend is built not only by his productions, but also by the often-repeated information and anecdotes about the very process of their creation. The director is famous for extending rehearsal time: although it takes an average of two months to prepare a production in Polish theatre, Lupa may work on a single production for as long as a year. He also knows how to secure far larger budgets for his productions than other Polish directors usually have at their disposal. He always designs the sets himself, because the visual setting is an integral part of his artistic vision. He also selects the text himself, usually also arranging it and proposing the musical score.

---

[5] Jacek Sieradzki, "Kłopoty z teatrem powaěnym," *Polityka,* No. 8 (1998), http://www.e-teatr.pl/pl/artykuly/120210.html?josso_assertion_id=98E086C61EEDE961.

Whether in Jelenia Góra, in the Stary Theatre in Kraków or later in the Polski Theatre in Wrocław and the Dramatic Theatre in Warsaw, there is a group of actors fascinated by Lupa who are ready to work on his terms. His theatrical visions require an appropriate approach to acting method. This is how Monika Żółkoś describes it:

> The process of building a role develops through introspection, deepening self-awareness, looking within for emotions and experiences from which a character may emerge. It must be said that what triggers the privacy of the actor's performance in Lupa's theatre and, at the same time, makes it credible, is the attitude of the director. In working on a production, Lupa uses his own experience and childhood memories. He identifies with certain characters in his theatre, sharing with them a similar understanding of the world. [...] In this way Lupa inspires actors to show the role from their own privacy, while not letting them slide into exhibitionism.[6]

Lupa does not deny that he is so strongly involved in his productions that he can become hysterical. He says: "I often can't bear my theatre. I can't look at the actors when I see that they're not doing something with the courage they could be using."[7] And adds: "Sometimes I wonder myself whether those dissatisfactions of mine aren't just accidental whims. Maybe so, it does happen that sitting in the audience I step over some threshold of frustration. [...] I must instantly leave the performance because I feel that I am not able to stand what is happening physiologically."[8]

THE WATERSHED

The premiere of *Factory 2* in 2008 was a watershed for Krystian Lupa's work. The eight-hour drama was performed on the Kameralna Stage of the National Stary Theatre in Kraków: the outcome of a fascination with Andy Warhol's Factory, the characters who visited it and Warhol himself. When working on it, for the first time Lupa decided to create a script while rehearsing without a literary base. He invited two dramaturgs, Iga Gańczarczyk and Magda Stojowska, as well as a group of actors to cooperate with him. The key element in working on the production was the

---

[6] Monika Żółkoś, "Podróě do granic aktorstwa w teatrze Krystiana Lupy," *Przestrzenie Teorii*, No. 7 (2007), p. 302.

[7] Krystian and Maciejewski, *The End*, p. 296.

[8] Ibid, p. 374.

KRYSTIAN LUPA: THE MAESTRO THEY ~~CRITICISE~~ LOVE   115

preparation of screen tests; that is, actors' improvisations that were shot with a camera, some of which were later used in the production. Spending time together, talking, watching films, browsing through photographs, reading biographies and memoirs, and the organisation of parties, modelled on those held at the Factory, were also an integral part of the work on the production. This meant that the whole theatre had to align its schedule with the production of a single drama. And the work on *Factory 2* lasted for over a year! The Kameralna Stage has only one rehearsal room, so its regular use was disrupted for that whole period. Its walls were painted silver, a colour alluding to Warhol's Factory. The costumes were very important for the process of developing the characters, and Piotr Skiba, who was responsible for them, imported some of the fabrics from Paris. Soon there were so many costumes made for the production that they required a separate room in the warehouse, and some of them were never used on the stage. (This kind of appropriation of the theatre, as well as this type of work with actors, rightly raise ethical doubts among some researchers.[9]) The best actor improvisations were written down, edited and included in the script. It was the first time Lupa had earmarked so much space in his production for video projections: not only the screen tests but also live transmissions from stage activity were included.

Factory 2 made its mark on the imagination of the younger generation of artists and caused a change in the approach to work on dramatic material in the theatre. It was during that period, also thanks to *Factory 2*, that Polish theatre slowly began to liberate itself from the embrace of literature and opened up avidly to texts, often written during rehearsals.

Lupa continued to be interested in the possibilities created by actors' improvisations. He went on to draw inspiration from biographies of influential figures like Warhol: people who, to quote the director, live by their dreams. While at the Dramatic Theatre in Warsaw, he decided to start working on a theatre triptych devoted to three iconic characters: the American actress Marilyn Monroe, the French-Jewish philosopher Simone Weil and Armenian thinker and guru George Gurdjieff. The first part— *Persona. Triptych/Marilyn* (2009)—presented a fantasy about Monroe escaping from the set and hiding in an abandoned sound stage to engage in a series of conversations with visitors, including her acting teacher Paula

---

[9] For further information see M. Kwaśniewska, "Between Freedom and Manipulation: The Situation of Actors in Factory 2," *Polish Theatre Journal*, No. 1:7 (2019), http://www.polishtheatrejournal.com/index.php/ptj/article/view/195/945.

116   K. WALIGÓRA

Strasberg, photographer Andrew de Dines and therapist Ralph Greenson. The extremely powerful connection that developed between Sandra Korzeniak, the leading actress, and the character she played was very moving. In his review, Jakub Papuczys put it directly: "Korzeniak did not play Marilyn, she became her. Now the audience have the opportunity to admire, for three hours, the unbelievable effects of this transformation."[10] This illustrates perfectly the course of Lupa's quest: the desire to incarnate the character in the person of an actor. Marilyn suffered constantly: she spoke about her pain but also showed it in her bodily expression, and, similar to *Factory 2*, this was an important point in the show. Also similar to *Factory 2*, an important point in the production was the projection of the screen test. Presented towards the end of the play, just before the final scene, the recording in which Marilyn's body is symbolically offered as a sacrifice shows Sandra Korzeniak without any make-up. The video is semiprivate, as the actress knew that the camera was running but she spoke as herself, and not as her character. She spoke of how much effort it was for her to take on the role of Marilyn, and how imperfect she felt being confronted with the Hollywood icon.

While *Persona. Triptych/Marilyn* was widely acclaimed by critics, *Persona. Simone's Body* received a very cold welcome. It was considered too long, monotonous and even incomprehensible. Whether it was because of this reception or for other reasons, Lupa lost interest in continuing work on the triptych. Instead, the director started working on two parallel productions with similar titles: *The Waiting Room* at the Théâtre Vidy-Lausanne and *Waiting Room.0* at the Polski Theatre in Wrocław. He used Lars Noren's novel *The Human Circle 3:1* for the actors' improvisations in the Swiss production. The production was set in an underground passage, presented in a beautiful set design, and its heroes were young drug addicts portrayed as people refuting the accepted principles of social interactions. In turn, the Wrocław *Waiting Room.0* was presented at a train station—almost literally, as the theatre stage on which it was performed was developed in an old train station. In this production the passengers on a broken-down train disembark at an abandoned station, not knowing where they are and how long they will have to wait. Lupa tried to think about a specific experiment caused by coincidence: to be forced to stay together in an enclosed room for longer than expected, and

---

[10] Jakub Papuczys, *Walka z personą*, e-teatr.pl, 1 May 2009, http://www.e-teatr.pl/pl/artykuly/72039,druk.html.

without the option of leaving. *Waiting Room* and *Waiting Room.0* were received badly by most Polish critics and again for the usual reasons: that the productions were incoherent, convoluted and stammering.

That was precisely when *The City of Sleep* premiered at TR Warszawa. Lupa again invited the *Factory 2* dramaturg Iga Gańczarczyk to cooperate with him, and again his subject was a community that develops around a dream. However, this time, as Joanna Wichowska wrote:

> The island of the castaways […] is situated on the outer perimeters of reality, and the micro community that populates it is not so much a group of outsiders who disclose chips of unwanted truth to us, but incurable egotists, whose thoughts and experiences are non-transparent, and untranslatable into any known or assimilated language.[11]

The method of creating the text was similar to previous productions. Kubin's novel provided inspiration for actors' improvisations, which were written down and transformed by Lupa into a dramatic text. Its construction was complicated and favoured fragmentary reception. The production lasted six hours and the director was not afraid of moments of stagnation, slumps in energy or inaction. However, there were scenes in the play that vibrated with innovative energy, lined with wild humour and freedom of experimentation. In one of them, the citizens of the utopian dream city looked out at the audience, stating that they felt they were being watched. On the suggestion "Let's take a snapshot with our collective hallucination [i.e. the audience]," the actors lined up on the edge of the stage. One of them took a camera, started taking pictures of the rest, and a photo of the actors and the audience appeared on the screen above the stage. Then, when it looked like the same photo was taken again, the screen showed instead only the actors against the background of the empty hall.

As mentioned in the beginning, *City of Sleep* was not received well by critics, in contrast to Lupa's next production: *Woodcutters,* which was based on Thomas Bernhard's text and produced successfully at the Polski Theatre in Wrocław in 2014. Here, the director returned to the subject of a meeting of *la bohème*, ridiculing the poor condition of the cocksure egotistic artists. The key moment was the monologue of Thomas Bernhard, played by Piotr

---

[11] Joanna Wichowska, "Mistrz zaprasza do konfesjonału," *Didaskalia* No. 112 (2012), p. 54.

118   K. WALIGÓRA

Skiba, which criticised the system of artistic production that slavishly depended on the proceedings of state authorities. The words were exceptionally topical, especially as the sense of an imminent threat to the independence of Polish art was already very strong at the time. Especially in the glamour of its premiere, *Woodcutters* seemed dazzling and that resulted in an all-encompassing admiration. However, it would be difficult not to notice that with this production Lupa went back to his previous, well-known position: into the arms of his favourite author, with a sophisticated and safe acting style on stage, and coherent narrative constructions. And the critics sighed with relief that the period of worrying experiments was over.

No Surrender

In 2011, more or less when Lupa was working on *The City of Sleep*, some 20,000 people walked the streets of Warsaw in the March of Independence: a demonstration with a nationalistic character, organised by extreme right, bordering on fascist, organisations. There were clashes with the police, brawling in the streets and attacks on journalists. It is quite likely that these were the events that influenced the scene of listening to the street demonstration that I described at the beginning of this chapter. Incorporating it into the production was a sign of another change taking place in Lupa's theatre, which is evidenced by the concern for artistic independence expressed in *Woodcutters*. The March of Independence became a regular event in Poland on 11 November each year. In 2015, the right-wing Law and Justice party, which is infamous for aligning with the Catholic Church in encouraging homophobic attitudes and a distaste for art that will not allow itself to be subjected to state power, won the Polish election and formed a government.

The strengthening of nationalistic sentiments in the public and political realms in Poland had a very strong impact on Krystian Lupa. In November 2015, on the occasion of working on the production *SPI->RA->LA*, he wrote a long manifesto, which including the following passage:

> I am afraid of the red-and-white flag, can you imagine what that means? So yes, I have indeed been left alone, if I yearn to leave, I am left alone ... I don't feel a Pole, like Thomas Bernhard who, towards the end of his life, was sick with the unabating need to escape the place where he had to be an Austrian.[12]

---

[12] Krystian Lupa, "Iznowu się na coś strasznego zgodzimy," *Tygodnik Powszechny* No. 47 (2015), http://www.e-teatr.pl/pl/artykuly/213037.html.

Lupa also began to give many interviews in which he expressed his concern with the situation in Polish politics.

In 2016, he started work on an adaptation of Franz Kafka's *The Trial* for the Polski Theatre in Wrocław. At the same time, the Minister of Culture and National Heritage decided it would not extend the contract of the previous, long-term director of the theatre and a call for a new director was announced. The selection panel was made up mostly of public servants, who rejected the candidates supported by the Polish theatre community, choosing instead a candidate who was incompetent and irresponsible. This development resulted in an unprecedented and intense protest by actors and audience alike that lasted several months, which was nonetheless ignored by the new authorities.[13] Lupa, in protest against the Minister's decision, immediately decided to suspend work on *The Trial*. The play was eventually put

Image 1 *CAPRI—the Island of Fugitives*, directed by Krystian Lupa, Powszechny Theatre, 2019. (Photos by Natalia Kabanow)

---

[13] For further information see Monika Kwaśniewska, "The Actor in the Deadlock of Contemporary Folwark Relations," *Polish Theatre Journal* No. 12:4 (2017), http://www.polishtheatrejournal.com/index.php/ptj/article/view/108/574.

on stage by him in 2017 with the actors of the Wrocław theatre; however, it premiered in Warsaw as a co-production of a number of local theatres and with the financial support of foreign theatres. Even before its premiere, the production became a symbol of the struggle for artistic independence.

The Trial has much in common with Krystian Lupa's latest production, *Capri—the Island of Fugitives*, which was produced for the Powszechny Theatre in Warsaw. Both productions are monumental, lasting many hours, aesthetically refined stage treatises. *The Trial* was perceived as a production "on being exhausted with Poland, world, and humanity [....] On the hopelessness and lack of ideas for a better tomorrow."[14] *Capri—the Island of Fugitives*, based on the prose of Curzio Malaparte, is a voyage through images from World War II. The drama is a meticulous study of various forms of cruelty, a vivisection of catastrophe and various emanations of fascist ideology.

Krystian Lupa's theatre was never a political theatre: for many years it was even perceived as ostentatiously apolitical. The director's latest productions are eagerly anticipated and received with an unheard-of enthusiasm, but also decoded through the prism of the current political situation in Poland. Thanks to this, Lupa's theatre, although ever more strongly returning to already known motifs and conventions, remains valid and popular.

REFERENCES

Burzyńska Anna, Róëa, *Mały słownik trudniejszych rekwizytów*, "Didaskalia" 2008, nr. 84.

Dzieciuchowicz, Iga, Herbut, Anka, Gańczarczyk, Iga, Stojowska, Magda, *Wyobraźnia, intuicja, potrzeba kreacji*, "Didaskalia" 2008, nr. 84.

Kluzowicz, Julia, *Faktoryjka*, "Didaskalia" 2008, nr. 84.

Kościelniak, Marcin, Teatr śmierci Krystiana Lupy, "Didaskalia" 2008, no. 84.

———, *Regions of Negotiation. Factory 2, Persona. Marilyn, Persona. Simone's Body*, "Didaskalia" 2010, nr 96.

Kwaśniewska, Monika, *Between Freedom and Manipulation: The Situation of Actors in Factory 2*, "Polish Theatre Journal" 2019, nr. 1 (7).

———, *The Actor in the Deadlock of Contemporary Folwark Relations*, "Polish Theatre Journal" 2017, nr. 1–2 (4).

---

[14] Witold Mrozek, "'Proces', czyli okrutna kpina Krystiana Lupy," *Gazeta Wyborcza*, 16:11(2017), https://wyborcza.pl/7,112395,22656180,proces-czyli-okrutna-kpina-krystiana-lupy-siedmiogodzinny.html.

KRYSTIAN LUPA: THE MAESTRO THEY ~~CRITICISE~~ LOVE   121

Lupa, Krystian, *I znowu się na coś strasznego zgodzimy*, "Tygodnik Powszechny" 2015, nr. 47.
Lupa, Krystian, Maciejewski, Łukasz, *The end of the world of values*, Łódź 2017.
Łuksza, Agata, *Glamour, kobiecość, widowisko*, Warszawa 2016.
Niziołek, Grzegorz, *Sobowtór i utopia. Teatr Krystiana Lupy*, Kraków 1997.
———, *Klęski Krystiana Lupy*, "Didaskalia" 2003, nr. 57.
———, *Anty-Jung*, "Didaskalia" 2008, nr. 84.
Sieradzki, Jacek, *Kłopoty z teatrem poważnym*, "Polityka" 1998, nr. 8
Wasztyl, Waldemar, *Krystian Lupa as a Student*, "Didaskalia" 2010, nr 100.
Wichowska, Joanna, *Mistrz zaprasza do konfesjonału*, "Didaskalia" 2012, nr. 112
Żółkoś, Monika, *Podróż do granic aktorstwa w teatrze Krystiana Lupy*, "Przestrzenie Teorii" 2007, nr. 7

Dark Visions of Jan Mikulášek

Kamila Černá

Eight actors and actresses on stage present an unstable "matter:" a mass of bodies, which, in an endlessly repetitive movement, collapses to the ground, gets up, falls again, for a moment lets one member perform an individual action, but then immediately clusters together and falls again and again to the ground, in a wild rhythm. This is a scene from *Europeana*, one of the most highly praised productions of Czech theatre director Jan Mikulášek.

Patrik Ouředník's novel that served as the production's base is structured as a seemingly objective list of historical facts, where events with at first sight nothing in common are linked. The combination of encyclopaedic and statistical data is sometimes comical, but elsewhere the tragedy of history prevails. Gradually, the image of European history in the twentieth century is being created, in all its absurdity and instability. Mikulášek's stage adaptation was more animated, manic in its tempo, rapidly speeding through the changing world, yet at the same time it was more emotionally

K. Černá (✉)
Arts and Theatre Institute, Prague, Czech Republic
e-mail: kamila.cerna@idu.cz

© The Author(s), under exclusive license to Springer Nature Switzerland AG 2021
K. Stefanova, M. Carlson (eds.), *20 Ground-Breaking Directors of Eastern Europe*, https://doi.org/10.1007/978-3-030-52935-2_10

124 K. ČERNÁ

urgent, referencing not only the horrors of the wars but also the sexual revolution, broken taboos, new possibilities, new restrictions, new worries... From the combination of humour, irony, mystification and precise facts a bizarre testimony about Europe arose: a captivating theatre commentary on the last century, where banalities and historical milestones were given the same amount of space, and alongside the destructive wars and political conflicts an important role was played by the invention of the bra or perforated toilet paper. Individual images culminated emotionally; they were a suggestive metaphor of the madness of war, but also of the inability of humankind to learn from its own history.

For Mikulášek and his dramaturg Dora Viceníková, *Europeana* was a significant turning point. Ouředník's intentional authorial impartiality and detachment, which nevertheless function as an emotional catalyst, are undoubtedly close to the method of scenic collages that Mikulášek and Viceníková had experimented with in their previous productions. The success of *Europeana* (the Best Czech Production of 2011) reinforced their artistic approach and the production marked the beginning of the most distinctive aspect of Mikulášek's directorial work—scenic collages on various themes such as Europeanism, Czech identity, childhood, love or death.

When he directed *Europeana*, the 33-year-old director had already earned a reputation as being one of the most promising young talents of Czech theatre. After leaving Janáček Academy of Music and Performing Arts (JAMU) in Brno, where he did not finish his studies in theatre directing, Mikulášek became the artistic director of a small theatre in Brno, Polárka. The critics had noticed him already, when he was working at Petr Bezruč Theatre in Ostrava (since 2005). He drew critical attention by his provocative adaptations of literary and theatre classics: *Three Sisters*, *Eugene Onegin*, *Wild Duck* and so on. The production of *Eugene Onegin* (2008) became a cult production for young audiences. The unusual tension, ambiguity, intense vibrations created by grotesque moments undermining the text, unbecoming gestures, movement not corresponding to the uttered words—all this, together with the set design and costumes (created by Marek Cpin, with whom Mikulášek has been cooperating ever since in almost all his productions), was something brand new in Czech theatre. In the following productions, Mikulášek surprised with his imaginative approach to metaphor, stage hyperbole and scenic design. In *Wild Duck* (2009), the set designer Marek Cpin put a huge model of a duck on a relatively small stage, which was oppressing all the characters and prevented them from any development. In Mikulášek's *Three Sisters* (2006), very stylised, grotesque moments were emphasised not only by the acting style, but also visually. Instead of the typical slow Chekhovian passing of time, there was hysteria, spasm and an exaggerated, tasteless interior that everybody wishes to escape from, be it to Moscow or elsewhere.

The production of *Hedda Gabler* (Moravian-Silesian Theatre in Ostrava, 2008) was a dark vision of human miscommunication and futile desire for perfection. It had a fascinating Art Nouveau set, out-of-proportion hairstyles, three *alter egos* of Hedda, and statuesque postures.

In 2007 Mikulášek left the post of artistic director at Petr Bezruč Theatre, where he would continue to work as a guest director for years, and started to cooperate with other theatres. He directed *Charlie in the Limelight of Modern Times*, a production about Charlie Chaplin, at the City Theatre in Zlín (2008), *Oedipus* at the National Moravian-Silesian Theatre in Ostrava (2009) and *Hamlet* at The Goose on the String Theatre in Brno (2009).

In 2010 Mikulášek directed his first production in Prague: *Macbeth* at the Dlouhá Theatre. In it he accentuated the breaking moments and critical decisions that led Macbeth to his tragic end and made these scenes really memorable: there were several alarm clocks ringing in the hands of the actors, suddenly interrupted stage movements or grotesquely deviated acts by the characters. Power struggles and the fight for the crown took place at one never-ending party, where the royal entourage were drinking tea. Mikulášek's Macbeth (Jan Vondráček) was presented as a man taken by surprise at first by favourable fate and later on by his own behaviour. His uncertainty showed itself by fluctuating between a majestic expression and grotesque grimaces at moments when he was not able to bear the weight of the situation. The cold, rational Lady Macbeth (Klára Sedláčková-Oltová) sometimes surprised with her parodic tone, with which she undermined her own lines. This intentional stylistic disunity of the acting approach of the main protagonists created in the audience the feeling of uncertainty, further enhanced by the elevated, poetic and grotesque moments and the choice of music. In the framework of the story of Macbeth, a certain "play on Macbeth" was simultaneously taking place, mixing Macbeth motifs with openly acknowledged theatricality. Thanks to this approach, in the scene where Macbeth sends the murderers to kill Macduff's wife and children, Macbeth could repeatedly reverse the plot. In horror at his own order, he hid the child in a piano and prevented the

126 K. ČERNÁ

murderers from entering the room—only to watch the unavoidable, dreadful act later on as both its "director" and "spectator."

The dynamic contrast between the text and the acts of the characters played a crucial role in *Macbeth*. Each stylisation of voice and movement was carefully thought out to the smallest detail. Although Shakespeare's text (just like Pushkin's or Ibsen's texts before) was thoroughly transformed, Mikulášek never went against its meaning.

The year 2010 was a turning point for Mikulášek. He started to work with Reduta, one of the venues of the National Theatre in Brno. The artistic director Petr Štědroň and the dramaturg Dora Viceníková were aiming to make it a progressive stage, focusing its repertoire on dramatisations and adaptations of originally non-theatrical texts. Mikulášek directed *Elemental Particles*, an adaptation of the famous novel by the French author Michel Houellebecq. In cooperation with Viceníková on the text of the theatre adaptation, he softened the cynicism, sarcasm and eccentricity of the original and focused the production on the themes of hopeless loneliness and the impossibility of sharing true emotions, relationships and contacts in today's fragmented world. The production emphasised the image of empty social rituals represented, for example, by the repeated procession of advertising logos in a supermarket or by the behaviour of the characters at a funeral; even love or psychotherapy became a ritual. The set consisted of movable desks changing in a precise rhythm according to the carefully choreographed movement of the actors and the musical background, which accompanied the entire production.

Mikulášek's second production at Reduta Theatre, *Correspondence V+W* (2010), was successful among both critics and audiences, and is actually still running to full houses to this day. The letters V+W in the title are an abbreviation of the names of one of the most famous Czech artistic duos, Jiří Voskovec and Jan Werich, exceptionally popular dramatists, actors and singers between the world wars, whose comedy numbers and songs are well known and beloved even today in the Czech Republic. After the Communist coup in 1948, Voskovec emigrated to the United States, while Werich remained in Czechoslovakia and the Iron Curtain stayed between them. Their subsequent correspondence reflects not only the sadness of their separation and their difficult personal life stories, but also the historical circumstances that prevented them from performing together again. The selected letters (the script was again created by Mikulášek and Viceníková) present Voskovec and Werich as two ageing men, two sad clowns, who need a lot of effort and strength to keep their witty, ironic humour. They have troubles with their partners, children, illnesses and old age. Voskovec earns a living by acting in second-rate films, while Werich is forced into humiliating compromises in Communist Czechoslovakia.

There are only three actors in the production—Václav Vašák as Voskovec, Jiří Vyorálek as Werich, both with the iconic black-and-white make-up typical of V+W, and Gabriela Mikulková as Werich's wife. The text, composed only of extracts from their letters, is read by the actors in a matter-of-fact, unemotional manner, yet accompanied by stylised acting—a sad clown show, which sometimes creates an expressionistically grotesque theatrical commentary of what is written in the letters. The set design by Svatopluk Sládeček offers a space for stylised movement: there are two connected illuminated cubes—the bigger one at the front of the stage, the smaller one at the back, functioning as an elevated stage. It is a "liberated space" (Voskovec and Werich's original theatre was called Liberated Theatre), where no laws of gravity are valid—chairs, tables and lights are placed on the floor, walls and even the ceiling. The actors respect the 90 degree–shifted world and sometimes eat while lying on the stage from a table attached to the wall; in other scenes they are back in the horizontal world. The set design appears as if it wants to emphasise the two different dimensions in which V+W ended up and also their two different points of view. Voskovec and Werich are today often sentimentally celebrated as "wise national clowns," which is something Mikulášek's production undermines. Despite the detachment, demythologising and intentional grotesqueness, his *Correspondence V+W* remains deeply theatrical, and in its finale it is a very moving interpretation of the lives and characters of two exceptional personalities.

Mikulášek's third production at the Reduta Theatre was *The Discreet Charm of the Bourgeoisie: Hommage à Buñuel et Carriere* (2012). He used a similar method of scenic collage and combined, developed and transformed various motifs from Buñuel's work. The central metaphor of the famous film—a dinner party as a symbol of awkward existence—was also the basis for the production. In principle, Mikulášek enjoys exploring the anatomy of extreme situations, their birth and often absurd outcome. In this case the result was a stylistically unique production with theatrical etudes based on individual situations intertwined with surreal images. The action took place in a dining room with an enormous table and empty picture frames, where time had stopped. Under the surface of good manners, humorous absurdities or various nasty pranks occurred at first, but

128   K. ČERNÁ

gradually everything escalated into mass murder. The production presented a grotesque, hopeless parable of the state of humankind.

Mikulášek's final production for the Reduta Theatre in Brno was *The Golden Sixties* (2013). Still running to this day, it is based on the diary of Pavel Juráček, a film director and screenwriter, signatory of Charter 77[1] and a key figure of Czech film of the 1960s. According to a review by Vladimír Mikulka in *World and Theatre Magazine*, "The most noteworthy thing about this production is to see the progress of Mikulášek and his team. *The Golden Sixties* is far more visual and theatrically sophisticated than his previous production *Correspondence V+W*. Everything fits logically together and creates a consistent whole, it is less illustrative, and there are more metaphors that do not illustrate the word, but are equal complements,"[2] *The Golden Sixties* won the award for the best production of 2013.

Between 2007 and 2013, the Reduta Theatre in Brno became one of the most respected theatres in the Czech Republic (to a great extent also thanks to Mikulášek's productions). Thus it was not that surprising that the team from Reduta (Štědroň, Viceníková, Mikulášek), whose success culminated with an invitation to the Salzburg festival in 2013 with *The Discreet Charm of the Bourgeoisie*, won the tender to lead Theatre on the Balustrade in Prague.

Theatre on the Balustrade was founded in 1958 and during its history cooperated with many leading figures of modern Czech theatre—Václav Havel, Ivan Vyskočil, Jiří Suchý, Jan Grossman, Otomar Krejča, Evald Schorm, Petr Lébl and others. It is considered to be one of the most prestigious theatre venues in Prague. Jan Mikulášek, together with Petr Štědroň (as managing director) and Dora Viceníková (as artistic director), brought to Prague not only their most successful productions from Reduta, but also a new artistic programme and dramaturgy, which focused exclusively on their own original scripts and dramatisations.

The first production of the new artistic team, *Czech Seventies or Husák's Silence* (2013), however, was not very critically successful. It was composed of two intentionally heterogeneous parts. The first one took place

---

[1] Charter 77 was written in protest against the non-observance of human rights and freedoms in totalitarian Czechoslovakia. The authors of the proclamation and the people around them created an informal opposition group that led the fight against the Communist regime and had to face harsh repression.

[2] Vladimir Mikulka, "Naplivat době do ksichtu," In: *NaDivadlo* (https://nadivadlo. blogspot.com/2013/04/mikulka-zlata-sedesata-reduta.html).

DARK VISIONS OF JAN MIKULÁŠEK   129

in a waiting room with an upholstered door, behind which those in power reside so that those who wait can never reach them. The hopeless waiting symbolised the normalisation era after the Soviet invasion of Czechoslovakia in 1968. There was also a portrait of the Communist President Gustáv Husák on the wall. The waiting people jumped the queue and fought with each other; they were submissive and then passivity turned into aggression; erotic relationships were formed. Later, everybody ate rolls, brushed their teeth with them and combed their hair with them—the roll being a symbol of cheap and accessible "food" for the people in the 1970s. Everything was acted out without words, as in slapstick gags. In the final moment of this part, the door finally opened and there was a roaring lion (the Czech national symbol) and another wall. The waiting crowd massacred the lion and ground him in a meat mincer. Despite the excellently constructed scenes, this portrayal of the 1970s in Czechoslovakia seemed like mere etudes on the motifs of the most characteristic features of the era. *Czech Seventies* did not reach the ease and subtlety of Mikulášek's previous productions, such as *Gottland*,[3] which dealt with a similar topic. The second part of the production provoked very severe criticism. Its "protagonist" was Olga Hepnarová, a woman who in the 1970s drove her car into people waiting for a tram and killed eight of them. She was later executed. The attempt to see Hepnarová as someone protesting against normalisation, or as its victim, seemed very artificial—the woman was mentally ill and would probably have committed murder in any era. Despite the exceptional performance of Magdaléna Sidonová in the role of the murder, there was no connection between the fate of the individual and the times, as in the successful previous productions *Correspondence V+W* or *The Golden Sixties*.

The next production was a dramatisation of *Stranger* by Albert Camus (2014). Mikulášek and Viceníková changed the first-person narrative into a monologue performed by five actors, who take turns in the role of Mersault. The white walls of the almost empty stage were changed by projections and photo sequences. Mikulášek illustrated Mersault's

---

[3] The dramatisation of the novel *Gottland* by Polish journalist Mariusz Szczygiel was directed by Mikulášek at the National Moravian-Silesian Theatre in Ostrava in 2011. Szczygiel creates a mosaic of Czech humour, national character, courage, cowardice and envy, from the point of view of a foreigner. Mikulášek enhanced the dramatisation by adding a Czech perspective and put on stage a number of unified citizens, dressed in brown ugly polyester suits. The "brown zone," an obedient crowd that follows any orders, collective guilt, collective innocence, collective conscience …

detached, as if disinterested, account via a number of scenic images and metaphors or via hectic acts of all five actors.

Mikulášek's first real success at Theatre on the Balustrade was called *The Hedonists* (2014). "Death is my topic" was announced in the prologue. A group of people met in a strange hotel lobby, somewhere between life and death. People disappeared into oblivion in an anteroom and would be forgotten forever. There was a bizarre combination of replicas and characters, heavy topics were discussed next to trashy jokes and speculating about what will be for dinner. The text was again written by Mikulášek and Viceníková, using extracts from Thomas Bernhard, Vítězslav Nezval, Rilke and others. The production was created also as a collective improvisation by the actors; nevertheless, its final shape was very consistent. As the critic Marie Reslová wrote, "Mikulášek's production about death is easy to follow by the audience. They experience something like aesthetic pleasure. Not only thanks to the minutely designed costumes but also thanks to the precise acting performances and surprisingly developed situations and gags which combine high artistry with banality and grotesqueness. Blood spreads over girl's lips—it spurts out after a prick by a pin—as an answer to a request to borrow a lipstick... bizarre murders or suicides at toilets with moulded hospital green tiles."[4] The perfectly flawless red set by Marek Cpin seemed like a much deeper and wider space than the small stage at Theatre on the Balustrade really is. Cpin managed to cram in a room with piano and enormous armchairs, the first floor of the construction on stage offering a view of a corridor with a bathroom and a toilet. Cpin made the stage optically bigger by a glass wall, mirrors and a ceiling with light that seemed like daylight. He won the award for best set design.

In 2015 Mikulášek directed two productions—*Doctor Zhivago* (May) and *Hamlets* (November). The stage adaptation of the famous novel by Pasternak was based not only on the novel, but also on its American film adaptation. Similarly to the film, the plot was made somewhat banal, but intentionally (unlike in the film) focusing mainly on love relationships. The characters of the protagonists were flattened and deformed, the protagonists of the novel becoming self-centred, corrupt and weak human beings. The love entanglement changed into a strange, detached game that the director ridiculed. Marek Cpin's set consisted of several rotating

---

[4] Marie Reslová, "Když na onen svět, tak stylově," *Hospodářské noviny*, November 4, 2014, p. 17.

mirrors, which reflected the actors and the audience from various angles; sometimes even the backstage or the theatre prompter were visible. The production prevented the audience from believing in the emotional depth and fatality of the story from bygone times and showed primarily the present time: disintegration of relationships, strange games we play with each other, sincere feelings crushed by desire for personal gain, the lyrical soul being laughable today and with no chance of success. The love story of the novel was just an excuse for the theatrically impressive expression of total disillusion. This interpretation was rather questionable in relation to the original.

Hamlets was the fourth part of the series of productions comprising *Europeana, The Discreet Charm of the Bourgeoisie* and *The Hedonists*—all created with the same directorial method. It was a thematic scenic collage, this time about acting. Six actors and one actress, all dressed in Hamlet costumes, were fighting with each other in the dressing room to get to the stage. This intentionally simplified image was followed by other ironic scenes that not only explored various faults of the acting profession, but dealt with the frustration and uncertainty of the actors. Twice-told tales from the acting profession were intertwined with powerful scenes; on the one hand there was real terror from the repeated and feared phrase "I don't believe it," rejecting the credibility of the acting performance; on the other hand, there was an actor who literally tore his acting heart out and showed it to the audience. A senile diva, a silly ingénue (both roles played by Jana Plodková), various acting clichés, moments of stardom but also the embarrassing nature and paltriness of the acting profession… The production clearly showed Mikulášek's directorial method—it was devised during rehearsals on the basis of improvisations, and included extracts from texts about acting complemented by music and film citations, references and associations. All this was developed by the actors and mainly by the director. It is this method developed by Mikulášek and Viceníková that has enriched Czech theatre the most and has even drawn international interest.

Mikulášek and Viceníková used the same technique in the two following productions. *Obsession* (2016) deals with love in its various versions. The insignificant stories of the inhabitants of a house, who clash passionately or miss each other tragically, are played out almost without words. Mikulášek manages to condense the latent background stories into short scenes lasting only a couple of minutes and complementing the events on stage. Cpin's two-storey stage set adds rhythm to Mikulášek's brilliant

132   K. ČERNÁ

synthesis of physical gags and actors' performances and enables parallel development of the scenes.

The next production, *AnderSen* (2017), focused on childhood and its nightmares, be it fear of the darkness under the bed, horror moments from Hans Christian Andersen's fairy tales or fear of parents' loud arguments. Authentic memories of the performers were interspersed with extracts from Andersen's diary, where he wrote about his anxiety and uncertainty. The common kitschy, sentimental view of childhood was balanced by rough scenes and dark, depressive motifs from Andersen's fairy tales. Despite the overall positive critical response to this production, some people started to ask whether this repetitively used production method was able to bring something new, or whether its originality would fade away with any subsequent repetition.

Mikulášek reacted to this criticism (perhaps subconsciously) by returning to a classical title: the brothers Mrštík's *Maryša*.

Maryša (1894) is a famous, often performed Czech drama about marriage for money, where the heroine, a village girl, finally kills her unloved older husband. Mikulášek directed the play at the National Theatre in Prague (2017). He suppressed the folklore elements of the Moravian countryside, where the play takes place, and reduced the number of characters. By using stylised movement and expressive acting, and by emphasising the visual aspects of the individual scenes, Mikulášek managed to render the notorious story in a new way, as an analysis of interpersonal relationships in a struggle for fundamental individual freedom. As Marie Reslová wrote in *Theatre Newspaper*, "We more or less know the text, so we can enjoy the nuances, ideas, and be carried away by the creativity of the actors. Sometimes we even paradoxically realize that we experience the meaning of a replica more strongly through the physical expressivity of the actor or the melody and diction of their voice rather than words."[5]

Mikulášek chose very famous texts for his last two productions as well, both at Theatre on the Balustrade. The first was Thomas Bernhard's *Woodcutters* (2018). Mikulášek and the set designer Marek Cpin intensified the suffocating atmosphere of a dinner in a snobbish salon by placing the guests in a relatively small space, overcrowded with furniture and paintings that hang on a poisonously green wallpaper. Mikulášek's dramatisation shifted Bernhard's text to grotesqueness, and the humorous detachment and subtle references to local Czech artistic world made the play surprisingly

[5] Marie Reslová, "Maryša umazaná od mouky," *Divadelní noviny*, No: 21 (2017), p. 4.

alive. The combination of light humour and absurd climaxes of individual situations worked surprisingly well with Bernhard's angry tone. Mikulášek and Cpin managed to keep the dark, existential dimensions of some of the themes—the closeness of art and death, the authenticity and falseness of artistic existence—and at the same time, they undermined with irony the pseudo-philosophical contemplations and snobbish talk about art. Marek Cpin again won the award for best set design (2018).

The latest production by Mikulášek at Theatre on the Balustrade is *Personas* (2018), a scenic collage based on four screenplays by Ingmar Bergman (*Scenes from a Marriage, Autumn Sonata, Persona, Hour of the Wolf*). The replicas from all four films are mixed to create condensed dramas that take place in a non-specific flat. In *Persona* there are most of Mikulášek's directorial attributes—a focus on extreme situations; an intentional contrast between expressive, stylised acting and a matter-of-fact minimalism; the emotive scenes are immediately undermined, questioned and ridiculed (here the ironic effect is created by music). As always, Mikulášek closely cooperates with his set designer, whose concept influences the entire production: in *Personas* they use simple Scandinavian interior design in beige colours, evoking the sand on island beaches, and also bold make-up and costumes.

In his latest productions Mikulášek has been coming back to the texts (dramatic or literary) as starting points, which he then constantly questions, reshuffles, fills with new meanings. Most importantly, he always succeeds in transferring the essence of a text to the stage: the internal struggle of the protagonists (*Maryša* and *Personas*) or the atmosphere and message (*Woodcutters*).

In the context of Czech theatre, Mikulášek is an exceptional personality, a solitaire who found his unique style but is willing and able to change it. He is a director in whose dark stage visions there are echoes of existential anxieties about the present state of the world, but also irony, detachment and humour—something that has made his theatre of importance to audiences not only in the Czech Republic, but also at various festivals worldwide, from Sarajevo through Salzburg, Berlin, Paris, Brussels and New York to Bogotá.

Translation: Hana Pavelková

Image 1 *Golden Sixties* by Pavel Juráček, Jan Mikulášek, Dora Viceníková, directed by Jan Mikulášek, Divadlo Na zábradlí (Theatre on the Balustrade), 2013. (Photo by Viktor Kronbauer)

References

Vladimir Mikulka, "Naplivat době do ksichtu." In: *NaDivadlo* (https://nadivadlo.blogspot.com/2013/04/mikulka-zlata-sedesata-reduta.html).
Marie Reslová, "Když na onen svět, tak stylově," *Hospodářské noviny*, 4. 11. 2014
———, "Maryša umazaná od mouky," *Divadelní noviny*, 21/2017

Alexander Morfov, the Game-Changer, and His Collective Theatre

Kalina Stefanova

Alexander Morfov's productions tend to acquire legendary status. In Bulgaria people go to see them time and again, hum tunes from them, albeit they are not musicals, celebrate their jubilee performances during their usually decades-long runs at the National Theatre. In Northern Macedonia in 2017, he was granted an honorary prize "for his exceptional aesthetic achievements in theatre." In Russia in 2018, the twentieth year of his *Tempest*, at the Komissarzhevskaya Academic Drama Theatre in St Petersburg, was commemorated as "an anniversary of a legend." Back when it premiered, it got him a nomination for the Golden Mask, the most prestigious Russian theatre award, which he later received for another production, *Eclipse*, after Ken Kesey's *One Flew Over the Cuckoo's Nest*, at the Lenkom Theatre in Moscow (2007). Four more nominations for the award, plus many other major awards there, have secured him a unique place in the very high-bar Russian theatre culture, shared only with Declan Donnellan among the foreign directors staging there. His productions in

---

K. Stefanova (✉)
National Academy for Theatre and Film Arts, Sofia, Bulgaria
e-mail: 111@kalina-stefanova.com

© The Author(s), under exclusive license to Springer Nature
Switzerland AG 2021
K. Stefanova, M. Carlson (eds.), *20 Ground-Breaking Directors of Eastern Europe*, https://doi.org/10.1007/978-3-030-52935-2_11

Romania, Israel and Latvia, as well as on their tours all around Europe and also in China, have garnered him critical acclaim and further additions to the roster of awards he has in his native Bulgaria.

How is it so, given that Morfov's theatre is not conceptual, doesn't turn classics upside down (although equally it never follows them strictly), is not in the least shocking or even mildly provocative, or, to sum it up, is not strikingly unusual—that is, it is not a sure bet for critics' accolades or an obvious choice for the festival circuit in most of today's Europe?

The answer is maybe because it is not anything like that. Also, because it is above the fray of the politically correct come-and-go topics, the ephemeral experiments with unusual forms, the avalanche of multimedia burying theatre underneath. Importantly, its focus is never confined within mere pieces of life. It is about life on a large scale and of a large scope. Getting into the very dualism of life, where utopia and pragmatism rub shoulders, it is equally about Don Quixote and Sancho Panza, about Don Juan and Sganarelle—that is, about "the man who dies for his ideas and the man who dies out of hunger."[1] For "in the end we all have a little from the one and from the other. At least in my case it is so," says Morfov.[2] His theatre has the breadth and panache and, at the same time, the humour of the films of Nikita Michalkov. At its best, it is also reminiscent of the unbridled energy and imagination of Gabriel Garcia Marquez's prose, evoking the feeling of witnessing the very march of life through people at large. At the same time, it is imbued with a palpable love for each and every human being. In a time of haste, when we tend to be constantly frustrated for having missed so much, how can one resist such a wealth of experiences just in the course of several hours in the theatre?

A larger-than-life bohemian with a revolutionary streak, Morfov has been leading protests, criticising every government, demanding changes in the poorest and most quickly dwindling nation in the European Union. In theatre, though, he has managed to cause quality changes without radically changing its place, space, configuration, textual springboards, but only by enlarging its territory from within. He does not subvert or sniff at tradition; he upgrades it—with reverence.

Morfov graduated from a Mathematical high school and studied for two years in a Technical University. Then he briefly worked as a stage-hand

---

[1] Giuseppina Manin "My Dom Juan? A Thunderous and Merciless God," *Eventi*, 10 October 2011.

[2] Ibid.

and lights manager in a provincial theatre. In 1984 he enrolled as a student at the National Academy for Theatre and Film Arts in Sofia, where he got an MA in directing for drama and puppet theatre in 1990 and, four years later, another MA in film directing.

The beginning of the 1990s was a time when Bulgarian theatre had, as in the rest of Eastern Europe, lost its audience and its privileged status from before 1989, and was in urgent need of reinvention. In 1994, the National Theatre made an unprecedented move: extended an invitation to Alexander Morfov and seven actors, also puppet theatre graduates, to become members of its company. Together they created the production *Don Quixote*, which premiered the same year.

It turned out to be something unseen both at the National and in Bulgarian theatre at large. Not only did huge puppets dwell on stage next to the actors, as they did later on in the same decade in Julie Taymor's *Lion King* on Broadway; neither were the puppets only interwoven in the texture of the show as they were in 1992, in *Woyzeck on the Highveld* of William Kentridge and the Handspring Puppet Company, a show that travelled the world over two decades later. *Don Quixote* was much more than this: a whole different acting and directing approach was applied. The text was not deprived of its connotations, yet it was handled in a more playful, openly carnival style, not abiding by the canons of psychological theatre and the Method. The actors were making objects on stage come to life as is done in the puppet theatre and, vice versa, characters at times acted in a puppet-like manner. The aesthetics of drama theatre and puppetry melted into a third something.

The essence of the creative approach underlying this in effect new theatre reality and why it made such a big difference are very well explained by Nina Dimitrova, an actress, director and co-founder of CREDO Theatre—one of the several other puppetry graduates who started working on drama stages at about the same time, further reinforcing and enriching the new phenomenon. "There's a different attitude towards the material world in puppetry," she says. "Also, a puppet cannot talk for too long. So we are freer in our dealing with text. We deal more with the playful nature of theatre. In the puppetry education there are several things that are being stressed: imagination, expressiveness, sense of humor, laconism."[3]

---

[3] From a private interview, quoted also in the book *Introduction to Modern Chinese Drama*, editor Kalina Stefanova (Sofia: Bulgarian Bestseller, 2020), p. 19.

Morfov and Dimitrova had as their artistic advisers at the Academy the same renowned directors—Julia Ognyanova and Atanas Ilkov—who taught them that it is of major importance "to have a position, to narrate a story in the simplest possible way, and to look at the world through the eyes of a clown."[4] Ilkov also stressed "the necessity to overcome the weight of the text"[5]—that is, its limits and rationality. Indeed, when watching *Don Quixote,* the CREDO Theatre shows[6] and more of this drama-meets-puppetry type of theatre, one can very clearly understand why the Chinese refer to the usual Western theatre as "spoken drama," confined within the realm of the text.

Don Quixote was an instant hit. And not only because of the unexpected symbiosis of drama and puppetry per se, but for one more reason in effect embedded in this new theatre reality. The stage had acquired magic, fairy-tale dimensions. It was communicating simultaneously on multiple frequency waves, engaging the body of the material and spiritual worlds alike, thus appealing to all the senses. Of course, *Don Quixote,* with its mixture of dreams and reality, illusions-come-true and mirage-like transformations, was the perfect springboard for a distinctly spectacular type of theatre. The thing is that entertainment has traditionally been held in very low esteem on the drama stages in Bulgaria. Having been one of the vehicles for the National Revival in the nineteenth century, Bulgarian theatre has didactics in its very genes and spectacle was for nearly a century predominantly looked down on as something of lesser importance. A production in which entertainment would prevail over philosophy—and this includes pure spectacle too—was rarely considered of merit. Now *Don Quixote* proved that theatre could be incredible fun and pure magic, and yet talk serious stuff at the same time.

Morfov, along with the other puppetry graduates, not only created a new theatre reality. He also helped set Bulgarian theatre free from the deeply ingrained prejudice against spectacle. The audience was back to the National and with a rejuvenated face at that, for the young started flocking to the theatre.

Don Quixote catapulted Morfov to the position of chief director of the National Theatre (which he held till 2000) and tied his destiny to the first

---

[4] Ibid.

[5] Ekaterina Ilkova, *The Tandem* (Sofia: Seven Ways, 2019), p. 55.

[6] *Overcoat* (1992) and *Daddy Always Knows* (2009), which have literally travelled the world over being performed in nine languages, as well as *The Diary of a Madman* (2015).

stage for two decades. Three shows stood out among his productions to the beginning of the millennium: *Midsummer Night's Dream* (1995), *The Tempest* (1996) and *The Lower Depths*, after Maxim Gorky (1997). In 2000 he was appointed also as managing and artistic director of the theatre, but was soon dismissed due to a major conflict with the Ministry of Culture.

During his first stint at the National (in 2004 he went back there), Morfov also started directing in Russia. In 2003, he was invited to become chief stage director at the Komissarzhevskaya Academic Drama Theatre in St Petersburg, which he accepted and where he stayed till 2006. His invariable success in Russia ever since has, of course, been a result of his extraordinary talent. Yet it has also been a result of his stay at the National Theatre in Bulgaria, where he became soaked in a tradition that merits first and foremost the achievement of an organic truth (*правда* in both Bulgarian and Russian) on stage—a term and a tradition brought there directly from Russia by Nikolai Ossipovich Massalitinov.

Massalitinov was one of the main actors with whom Stanislavsky developed his Method and was for several years a director at the Second Studio of the Moscow Art Theatre. He arrived in Bulgaria first in 1920, as head of a touring group of the Moscow Art Theatre that was caught in the chaos of the civil war. Their performances in Sofia caused a furore and, in 1923, he was invited to become head director of the National Theatre. In 1925, he accepted and stayed there for more than thirty years. During his tenure, Massalitinov, in the first place, developed and enriched the already established traditions, sharing the idea of theatre's highly moral role in social life and maintaining the dominance of the classics in the repertoire, while also paying special attention to the discovery and support of Bulgarian playwrights. At the same time, Massalitinov managed to overcome the actors' predisposition for solo performances and created an inner necessity for an ensemble—one of the strongest features of Bulgarian theatre ever since. Also, not only did he teach the Method during rehearsals, he also organised a Theatre Studio affiliated with the National Theatre, which became famous, among other things, for its attendance by some of the most prominent, already middle-aged or even elderly actors.[7]

The remarkable success of Massalitinov in converting Bulgarian actors to the Method resulted from his ability to refer to it as something alive and

---

[7] It was that Studio, changing its names and status over the years, that gradually grew into today's National Academy for Theatre and Film Arts.

flexible. He believed that the actors' talent should be improved but not confined. Rather than teaching the Method as a once-and-for-ever-settled rule, he applied it in harmony with the already existing acting style. Asked about his idea of an acting school figuratively, Massalitinov famously said: "School? Every good actor is A School." Actually it was the presence of many gifted actors at the National Theatre that he pointed out as the main reason for his long stay there.

Himself coming to the National Theatre with a group of likeminded actors, Morfov further developed the rich tradition of ensemble work, upgrading it with a very modern touch. He is famous for never approaching his future work rationally, with a ready-made plan. He always tries to find the way to the production together with the whole cast. It is from their communication that the theatre piece starts coming to life. "My work method is based on improvisation," he says. "I start as if on a blank sheet of paper and aim to provoke and inspire the actors' imagination, so that I can transform them into authors too. For a long time everything looks like we are having fun in our leisure time: we spend time together, talk, go to the cinema, to exhibitions… While at one moment we get to the stage. And everything starts. My actors are my family. I can't live without them. They know everything about me. I too know the problems and passions of each one of them. They are my friends and I can't work without friends."[8]

Of course, this work method can at times result in setbacks: the rehearsal process could hardly be pre-planned in terms of time limit and at times it could even come to a permanent halt. Yet when it works, the feeling is of an authentic naturalness on stage—as if we are endowed with a chance to witness the growth of a tree. It also results in a very strong integrity and wholesomeness of the respective theatre piece, exactly as if a live organism is indeed there. That's why the impact of Morfov's works differs a lot from that of the so-called director's theatre. What we see on stage is not about him in the first place. Not by chance does he like to underline that he wouldn't call his theatre "only my work. It emerges from within the whole team. We are creators of what is to become the next production, constantly provoking one other's minds and souls."[9]

It is exactly because of this collective creative method that Morfov's frequent revisiting of the same classics never results in a conveyor-belt type

[8] Manin, "My Dom Juan?"
[9] See: https://www.morfov.com/ (accessed on 7 March 2020).

of productions. They may look similar, repeating some stunning visual effects, but they never feel the same because of the different actors. This essential difference can very well be experienced in two of his *Don Juans*—at the Komissarzhevskaya Academic Drama Theatre in St Petersburg (2004) and at the National Theatre in Sofia (2006)—both of which are still running. (It was also a *Don Juan*, staged by him at Gesher Theatre in Tel Aviv in 2011, that took Morfov first to China—to the Beijing People's Art Theatre in 2013—and brought him subsequent invitations there.)

Both productions are at once exquisitely beautiful and hilariously funny. Masquerade is also omnipresent here. It is sometimes a part of beauty's extraordinary manifestation—in the ability of beauty to present its impeccability as natural, when everything is actually a matter of make-up. It is in the deliberate stage arrangement at times as *tableaux vivants*. Most importantly, it is in the big theatre *of* Don Juan. For he is not the famed seducer, he *plays* the part of a seducer.

Don Juan's first appearance is in a hilarious theatrical spoof of the films *Coming to America* (John Landis) and *The Siberian Barber* (Nikita Mikhalkov): he is in a bath-tub, servants brush his teeth, cut his nails, dress him, while others play guitar, then give him a glass of an anti-hangover elixir; when he finally manages to stand on his feet, on his shoulder flashes a tattoo: **D.J.** Then, dressed in something like a toreador costume, he sits in front of a mirror, puts on an ugly wig with preposterous whiskers and paints on his face even more preposterous and uglier moustaches. That is, he makes himself *look like* the cliché of a seducer—a cliché brought to at once a laughable and a repulsive extreme.

The Bulgarian Don Juan is closer to the usual cold, even merciless womaniser, in vain seeking freedom in his hedonistic lifestyle and at the other's expense—the production thus hinting at our waste-ridden, selfish times. In Russia, though, because of the different type of actors and especially a distinctly vivacious and warmth-exuding Don Juan, the production delves much deeper into the contemporary existential impasse. There the *theatre in life* is not a whim of Don Juan only. It is the very essence of the world around him: it is not even theatre, nor a masquerade, but a very authentically looking substitute for the real things—were they feelings, relationships, ideals, even faith.

There is a stunning scene in the second act—in both productions. Don Juan, dressed in black, fences with seven swordsmen, all in white and with masks. Four fencing couples, playing perpendicularly to the audience, are formed. From behind, a black-dressed Elvira rushes into their ranks, admonishing Don Juan to repent amid the hissing sound of the swords, while she tries to wade through them. When she manages to overcome the grip of the last couple, all of a sudden, together with her, we realise that all the swordsmen are in white. That is, we haven't noticed that Don Juan has disappeared and, like Elvira herself, we've landed in a world where everyone is without a face and all are alike. When seconds later Don Juan appears, he's the only one without a mask, literally and figuratively. Nothing's left from his role but the inertia: he drags Elvira behind the wings and rapes her—without any joy whatsoever. The over-the-top indulgence has turned him into an ordinary brutal bully. This scene looks like a beautiful focus of an illusionist. De facto, though, it's the essence of the nightmare this world of imitations has turned into. In the process of Don Juan's own theatre, the core of his very being has already been replaced—irrevocably.

At the end, when facing not so much his terrifying host but himself, Don Juan doesn't even manage to die, as if condemned to immortality in that world that for a long time already hasn't been the merry place inhabited by great adventurers, but belongs entirely to the great counterfeiters. While in the Bulgarian production this is a verdict in the first place on the character himself, in the Russian one it is a verdict on our world and all of us who gladly maintain and even relish the false status quo.

In 2012 Morfov created another stunning tour de force, based this time on modern classic: the 1918 *Suicide* by the Russian Nikolai Erdman. He transformed the play into a sweeping tribute to life, appropriately entitling the production *Life Is Beautiful*. He did this together with an equally mighty artist in the title role: Kamen Donev, a playwright, director and actor with a Chaplinesque type of talent, combining lyricism with comedy and commanding 4000-seat halls with his one-man shows, who for the first time joined efforts with the ensemble of the National. To me this production, still among the theatre's sold-out hits, is one of the two peaks in Morfov's oeuvre. It is also the most difficult as an achievement, since it dares to leave the classically dramatic and to enter a territory very rarely accessible to theatre in principle: the territory of bliss dwelt in by our souls when we are at peace with ourselves. It is like an essay on happiness, both in the life of the human spirit and in the small stuff of ordinary life. And, as the Latvian director Alvis Hermanis says, "the hardest task of all is to make a performance about harmonious and happy people. Technically, it is a task on the highest level of complexity."[10]

Not at all about happy people is *On the Edge*, Morfov's so far last production in Bulgaria, which he created in 2015 at the National Theatre, causing yet another quality change in principle on the Bulgarian stage. Like most of Eastern European theatre, soon after 1989 Bulgarian theatre turned its back on politics. However, while by the turn of the millennium political theatre was back in demand nearly everywhere else, in Bulgaria it continued to be generally shied away from, being absurdly considered as a thing from the past, even deemed as something characteristic of totalitarian times—an attitude that persists till today. The only exceptions have been made for some environmental or refugee issues at small, independent theatres.

Morfov's first production, in 1990, in one of the provincial theatres, was actually entitled *Political Cabaret*, yet this was a one-off. Later on, his most popular production at the National Theatre, *Exiles* (2004), after a novel by the national poet and patron of the National Theatre Ivan Vazov, still playing to full houses, touched upon the state of the nation both at the time the action takes place (the pre-liberation era in the nineteenth century) and now, hinting at the rather pessimistic current situation. Yet, although the final scene is literally chilling—with all the much-loved characters becoming a metal monument to be used for scraps—the patriotic spirit associated with the original book has prevailed in the audience's reception.

At the end of 2014, Morfov was rehearsing a non-play-based production about the Trojan horse, when simultaneously the whole cast decided that they would rather do a show about the dire situation in the country— with a huge percentage of hidden unemployment and working poor, the young leaving en masse and most pensioners living below the poverty line. This is how *On the Edge* was born, becoming the first and so far the only mighty act of solidarity of Bulgarian theatre with the Bulgarian people, and making the first stage truly national—that is, the people's theatre, as its name is in the original.

It is an unusual theatre piece: a ninety-minute stunning spectacle with a large cast and huge set, yet with the intimate impact of a poem and as

---

[10] *Theatre and Humanism in a World of Violence* (The Book of the 24th Congress of the IATC), edited by Ian Herbert and Kalina Stefanova (Sofia: St. Kliment Ohridski University Press, 2009), p. 35.

elevating as musical harmony. There are no leading characters, just archetypes of people on the edge (which in Bulgaria includes professions considered in the rest of the world as middle class by default). There is a very sparse text—familiar words in familiar situations, at familiar places—and a powerful music score, part of it live. In the opening scene, people scavenge through garbage bins, then, as if from what they have found there, gradually create the roof of an apartment building, with antennas and chimneys—it slightly rises up and we see the clouds at the back. An invisible character from a nearby balcony is heard announcing his refusal to go on living a life that does not feel like life and his muffled bumping on the ground hushes the audience to a deadly silence. The group decides to jump too and while "flying" down, the full building rises up and we see its inhabitants; then the members of the group lean as if on a balcony and start telling us what they dreamed of being when they were children.

The moment the objects/behaviour/meaning are about to look/sound naturalistic or predictable, the action immediately switches over. The small apartment boxes literally dance; some of the characters dance with the garbage bins on their backs; the walk of a crippled beggar ridiculed by somebody turns into a dance, lifting both him and us above the air of humiliation and anger. The action's tempo unexpectedly intensifies to a breathtaking rhythm, while the everyday routine gets repeated faster and faster to the background of Ravel's *Bolero*. The nth person who throws himself from the balcony comes back home, since he simply lives on the first floor... All that so that we do not get stuck on the wave of despair; so that the show does not enter the sphere of heart-rending melodrama...

The leitmotiv of the flight goes through different variations. A spectacular flight of all the heroes on the roof, picked up by a storm. Airplanes take off carrying away the nth portion of young Bulgarians (the back wing is a huge screen). Banal words fly/soar into a song, choked tears transform into a bout of laughter... Until the final flight from the sphere of the material into the one of the spirit, when, at the end, Bulgarians turn into constellations, while the only remaining grandfather tells the only remaining baby what has happened "once upon a time."

On the Edge is an extraordinary fable for a people and a sky that is related as if only via graphic outlines—of people, objects, pieces of conversations, pieces of events—but contains astounding depths. This is not a usual piece of political theatre. It is akin to the wave of special, so to speak, *politics of the soul* political theatre that started with Alvis Hermanis' *Long*

Life—theatre that is permeated with warmth and that "punches with tenderness."[11]

"*On the Edge* is an emotional improvisation about what is happening in Bulgaria," says Morfov. "It is a requiem for a country, for a disappearing nation. Our nation has existed for over 1300 years but now it is melting… With *On the Edge* we are expressing our sorrow for the lost traditions, celebrations, continuity—anything we tried to teach our children. Those values are lost and we are faced with inclusion in the Red list of extinguished species."[12]

Interestingly, though, deep down the show is not utterly pessimistic. It is like a *revelation*: it overwhelms and shatters in order to "enlighten the eyes of our hearts" (Ephesians 1:18). That's why to me this show translates into hope. Hope that it exists, that we—people on the edge—are not invisible anymore; that in it and with it we are together. The last scene,

Image 1 *On the Edge*, directed by Alexander Morfov, National Theatre, Bulgaria, 2015. (Photo by Elena Nikolaeva)

[11] Ibid., p. 36.
[12] See: https://www.morfov.com/ (accessed on 7 March 2020).

where all the characters celebrate a New Year's Eve, is actually the most important flight in—and of—the show: there people get to "fly" towards each other. *On the Edge* is a revelation about the power of human unity as the only way out of a world on the edge. It's a powerful reminder of Brecht's words, which Morfov says have guided him throughout: "In the dark times will there also be singing? Yes, there will be singing. About the dark times." *On the Edge* is at once like a lump in one's throat and like a hug that makes the lump magically melt—that is, what Morfov's theatre is at its best.

REFERENCES

Ilkova, Ekaterina, *The Tandem* (Sofia: Seven Ways, 2019).

Manin, Giuseppina, "My Dom Juan? A Thunderous and Merciless God," *Eventi*, October 10, 2011.

Herbert, Ian and Kalina Stefanova, eds., *Theatre and Humanism in a World of Violence* (The Book of the 24th Congress of the IATC) (Sofia: St. Kliment Ohridski University Press, 2009).

Stefanova, Kalina, ed. *Introduction to Modern Chinese Drama* (Sofia: Bulgarian Bestseller, 2020).

https://www.morfov.com/ (accessed 7 March 2020).

Eimuntas Nekrošius: The Poetics of Paradise and Hell

Rasa Vasinauskaitė

Numerous reviews have been written about the productions of the Lithuanian theatre director Eimuntas Nekrošius (1952–1918), but there are only a few books or studies on his theatre. Books about a living artist seemed to him to be a monument—the summing up of life and creation, which would mean the end. Nekrošius did experience what it meant to be worshipped, yet with all his being he resisted fame and prominence, and remained committed solely to creating theatre of merit. The theme of creation as a joy and a curse emerged as a focus of his productions in the 1980s, when he was 30 and became the most important theatre director in Lithuania and, after a while, the most famous Lithuanian in Europe and in the world. His productions travelled the world over and he received numerous Lithuanian and foreign awards, among them the prestigious Europe Prize New Theatrical Realities (1994).

R. Vasinauskaitė (✉)
Lithuanian Music and Theatre Academy, Lithuanian Culture Research Institute, Vilnius, Lithuania

© The Author(s), under exclusive license to Springer Nature Switzerland AG 2021
K. Stefanova, M. Carlson (eds.), *20 Ground-Breaking Directors of Eastern Europe*, https://doi.org/10.1007/978-3-030-52935-2_12

148   R. VASINAUSKAITĖ

Nekrošius' oeuvre can be divided into three. A period marked by Anton Chekhov's plays and reflections on Soviet reality: 1980–1995. A period of Shakespeare's tragedies and reflections on human destiny in principle: 1997–2003. A period of turning to Christian texts and "metaphysical dramas," and reflections on creative freedom and the captivity of the creator: 2004–2018. These periods differ not so much in stylistic twists, but rather in the liberating and radicalising of the directorial approach—in its moving beyond the empirical world and getting deeper into the themes of the creator and the condemnation of human beings, the transience of existence and the desacralisation of artistic work.

THE THEATRE OF SOVIET ANTHROPOLOGY

Nekrošius' work at the end of the 1980s was precisely described by the Lithuanian critic Egmontas Jansonas: "His performances are not the model of the world, but the world itself with all its connections, colours, sounds, aromas, dramas, tragedies, past and future. […] The human being in eternity—this is the object of E. Nekrošius' productions."[1] Over the years this stage world changed, the "connections, sounds and aromas" thickened or dissipated, but the image of the lonely and vulnerable human being remained the most important impulse for the director's creative quest and his theatrical life.

In Lithuania, Nekrošius' theatre—which disregards any aesthetic and ideological rules—is called a "metaphorical" theatre. Foreign critics referred to it as "visual" and/or "visionary." Lithuanian critic Ramunė Marcinkevičiūtė called his directing "a dramaturgy of stage images."[2] Many critics focused on the poetic and stylistic features of his theatre, on the director's unique imagination and his particular system of stage metaphorisation. In this system, the boundaries between archaic and modern, fantasy and reality, tradition and postmodernism became blurred.

The roots of Nekrošius' theatre can be found not only in its Lithuanian and peasant essence, which has preserved a special connection with the land and nature, but also in the Soviet experience. The Soviet period "taught" artists to create—and viewers to see, sense and understand—subtext and associations, to widen the space beyond words and open a wider field of interpretation of what is *seen* rather than *heard*. "Why do we

---

[1] E. Jansonas, *Etiudai apie teatrą* (Vilnius: Vaga, 1988), pp. 227–228.
[2] R. Marcinkevičiūtė, *Eimuntas Nekrošius: erdvė už žodžių* (Vilnius: Kultūros barai, 2002).

say, 'I watched the play?'—said Nekrošius.—Here is the strength of the theatre. The director does not do his job if he does not turn the word into action; if the word remains ineffective in his production, he wanders alone."[3]

Nekrošius entered the world of theatre at the age of 25. In 1977, at the State Youth Theatre in Vilnius, he staged his diploma production based on Shelagh Delaney's play *A Taste of Honey*. Behind him he had already years of studies (directing) at the Moscow State Theatre Art Institute, life in the capital of the Soviet Union and service in the Soviet Army.

In 1980, *The Square*[4] at the Youth Theatre became the real beginning of Nekrošius' theatre.

Michel Foucault in his book *Discipline and Punish: The Birth of the Prison* (1975) describes the ideal prison of a disciplinary power—Bentham's Panopticon. A prisoner in such a prison "is seen, but he does not see; he is the object of information, never a subject in communication."[5] Such a panopticon was created by Nekrošius and set designer Adomas Jacovskis in *The Square*, the production that sketched out many of the director's later themes and principles of working with both literary text and actors.

The Square was centred around two episodes. The first was of the silent making of a radio receiver from an empty can and a piece of wire, and it took more than 10 minutes of stage time. Even longer was an episode with a "rain" of small sugar pieces: an almost wordless meeting of the Teacher and the Prisoner culminated in a "rain" of 1002 small squares of sugar—as evidence of anticipation, joy and love. The director demonstrated how rich, contagious and attention-focused a physical action could be, when the actor worked within concrete "specific circumstances" (to use Stanislavski's term), with clear performance goals and objectives. And how

---

[3] E. Nekrošius, "Kokia erdvė už žodžių?" *Kultūros barai*, No.2 (1984), p. 6.

[4] The production was based on a documentary novel by the Soviet Russian author Valentina Yeliseeva. The story was about the correspondence between a teacher and a prisoner; the letters change the prisoner and, upon release, he begins a new life. The ideological subtext of the novel disappeared in the production; the play was rewritten by the playwright Saulius Šaltenis, while observing rehearsals and improvisations of the actors and Nekrošius. The inhumane environment of the prison, as fear and coercion, the warm feelings and the hopeful relation between the Prisoner and the Teacher witnessed a much more dramatic and hopeless sense of totalitarian reality: poverty, bullying, existential emptiness.

[5] M. Foucault, *Disciplinuoti ir bausti. Kalėjimo gimimas* (Vilnius: Baltos lankos, 1998), pp. 237–38.

150   R. VASINAUSKAITĖ

powerful and emotional a "visual metaphor" could be when born out of a well-measured "proportion" of senses, feelings and relationships between the characters.[6]

During the Soviet period, Nekrošius directed at the State Youth Theatre in Vilnius *The Square* (1980), *Pirosmani, Pirosmani* by Vadim Korostyliov[7] (1981), *Love and Death in Verona* inspired by Shakespeare's *Romeo and Juliet* (1982), *The Day Lasts More Than a Hundred Years* by Kyrgyz writer Chingiz Aitmatov (1983), Anton Chekhov's *Uncle Vanya* (1986) and *Nose* by Nikolaj Gogol (1991). The characters of these productions seemed to come from the other side of Soviet slogans—ordinary people who, via their daily work and faith, were endowing their daily existence with sacredness and were thus becoming enlighteners of spirit and morality. They looked "simple" and everyday-like, tempered by nature and harsh living conditions. At first glance, these were people of the post-war period or of some undefined stagnant period, who could be met in the small towns, villages and provinces of Lithuania. A few were wearing a white shirt or a white dress. White clothes as a sign of innocence, spiritual purity, a certain liminal, transitional state went on to be used in many of Nekrošius' later productions.

In general, in Nekrošius' theatre liminality as a transition from the past to the present, from the physical to the metaphysical, or from reality to the world of dreams or visions, was one of the most visible characteristics of the characters, the objects, the stage itself. In this sense, the collisions between a human being and an object, living and inanimate matter, which Nekrošius created through visual image metaphors, marked a transformation, a new becoming that changed both the inner and outer qualities of a person or a thing. But human transformation had its limits in Nekrošius' theatre: it is humanity beyond which the human being loses its meaning.

---

[6] Interestingly, *The Square*, performed at the Youth Theatre from 1980 to 1996, was not banned by censorship. Staged during the Olympic Games in Moscow, the production was also performed during the Soviet war in Afghanistan, the Chernobyl disaster, revolutionary movements in Poland and the "singing revolution" in Lithuania. Over the course of time it did not lose its relevance. It was a testimony, a warning, a search for human feelings and love in a country that was surviving a political, economic, even spiritual crisis. One could also see in it Nekrošius' attitude towards politics and the social relevance of theatre—the off-stage reality did not appear directly in his production, but played the role of a tuning fork for human relations.

[7] As in the case of Yeliseeva, the play by Korostyliov was rewritten by Šaltenis; the two-hour performance used only four pages of text.

This aspect of humanity, honesty, decency sounded very exciting in Nekrošius' productions of the Soviet era: loving and suffering, betraying and sacrificing people were recognised not only by the way they looked, but also by the challenges they faced in life, by how furiously they defended their truth, by how devoted they were to their work.

These productions of Nekrošius, as well as later works on the whole, were characterised by a combination of "poor" and "sacred" theatre. "Poor" because it was he who for the first time in Lithuanian theatre managed to make real, authentic and "everyday life" objects (e.g. tables, chairs, household items, saws, logs, ropes, etc.) change their meanings and acquire new meanings by having actors use them indirectly and unconventionally. "Sacred" or "Holy" because not only human relationships, but also human relations to things, the environment, nature-acquired sacred rituality; that is, the *it* was the "Invisible-Made-Visible" (to paraphrase Peter Brook). The theatre of such non-artificial reality seemed to bring back the image of a lost homeland, its people, their stories and experiences, while also witnessing the heavy burden of a collective trauma. In the face of a standardised, disciplined and outwardly "happy" life in the Soviet Union, the world of Nekrošius' productions seemed like a non-false, non-fake reality. It was not a copied reality, yet it was a reality with a revealed true and profound essence.

Nekrošius' Magical Realism

Nekrošius' theatre was often called visionary; in particular, foreign critics have admired his enchanting, engaging flood of imagination. On the surface his stage language was close to the aesthetics of stage realism, yet it was actually only seemingly material. He achieved the effect of "magical realism" by depicting simple things in unusual ways. It was about looking at those things through the prism of the imagination and visualising what the eyes do not see. It is no accident that his productions consistently presented disturbing, extraordinary images on stage that were difficult to understand. Such images could be attributed to the field of poetic thinking, but could also be regarded as an instantaneous juxtaposition of two realities, two viewpoints. This explains his focus on the time–space continuum rather than the temporal "nature" of theatre: the repeated movements, the "blurring" episodes, the "paused" or extended time in his productions were not governed by intrigue or conflict, but by the creation of new action, situations and circumstances that "exhibited" the

152   R. VASINAUSKAITĖ

protagonist's state and revealed his/her inner life. This invention of new words, micro-scenes, micro-plots, micro-storylines, sub-stories was part of a peculiar transformation on stage. It was achieved through physical action—at first glance simple and quotidian, yet evolving into an artistic/poetic expression of the new story.

Physical action was one of the most important principles of Nekrošius' work with actors. In all his productions, the characters/actors were working, building, carving, pushing, washing, stretching and so on. However, these realistic, even almost naturalistic and physically demanding actions gradually acquired a new quality and meaning. "In the beginning was the Act," says Faust, and Nekrošius began his *Faust* (2006) with the image of God rotating the Earth's axis with a heavy wooden log and Mephistopheles shooting at the celestial bodies flying around. The priest Kristijonas Donelaitis in *The Seasons* (2003) built the church out of real bricks. Othello pulled the ship-tubs (*Othello*, 2000). Macbeth, after a hail-sky curse, took stones and put them in his pockets—the weight of the stones bent him to the ground, but this was how he became non-human/superhuman (*Macbeth*, 1999). Painter Pirosmani carried a huge pile of chairs on his back in reminiscence of the Last Supper ("Pirosmani, Pirosmani..."): the "real" reality of this performance was gradually transformed into the feverish, dreamy reality of Pirosmani on his way to Eternity. And in *A Hunger Artist*, by Franz Kafka (2015), both Nekrošius and the actress Viktorija Kuodytė[8] put their prizes and diplomas on stage as mattresses, pillows or toys, demonstrating the character's incredible skill and flair for exhaustion and self-destruction. The sub-story of Gogol's monument in *The Nose* (1991), which turned into a performance within a performance and made concrete the connection between an artist and an independent "living" work, was repeated in *Dziady* (*Forefathers' Eve*, 2016), by Adam Mickiewicz, at the Teatr Narodowy, Warszawa, Poland, where on a magical night the Poet freed himself from his monument and visited his native land.

The magical, supernatural world intervened with all its power in Nekrošius' take on Shakespeare's tragedies. *Hamlet* (1997), *Macbeth* (1999) and *Othello* (2000) became canonical productions not only in Lithuanian theatre. According to Marcinkevičiūtė, in the case of *Hamlet*, an important aspect characteristic of all three Shakespearean tragedies

---

[8] Nekrošius assigned the role of the Hunger artist to the actress Viktorija Kuodytė, who worked in many of his productions.

could be traced: "the effect of *civilized brutality*, a remarkable combination of archaic signs and modern European culture."[9] For each production Nekrošius created new "stories," new relationships between the characters: for *Hamlet*—the story of children who obey their parents unconditionally and die;[10] for *Macbeth*—the story of a husband and a wife who share a common experience and live as long as they complement each other; for *Othello*—the story of an older venerable general and a young wife both dying for boundless love and blind trust.

In all these productions Nekrošius used the materials and natural elements that corresponded to, and symbolised, the spirit of his artistic ideas: stone, ground, fire, wood, water, metal; heavy and slippery metal balls, iron chairs, shiny and sharp knife or saw blade, ice blocks, hot steam, glowing flame, glass shards and so on. The storm of passions, feelings and nature was not only embodied and endured by the characters/actors and all things on stage, it spilled over into the visual and auditory entity of the productions (i.e. a dense audiovisual semiotics[11]) that affected the audience. Hence, from then on, Nekrošius could be called a theatre phenomenologist who created a unique aesthetics of performativity, where imagination, life, reality and representational/fictional theatre were blended.

After 2000, the intense, expressive actions and movements of the actors in his productions acquired an almost choreographic form. For instance, a group of characters appeared like a chorus, filling the gaps in the

---

[9] R. Marcinkevičiūtė, "Eimuntas Nekrošius: Complex Simplicity," *Contemporary Lithuanian Theatre. Names and Performances* (Vilnius: TKIEC, Tyto Alba, 2019), p. 50.

[10] This motif acquired the significance of a collision between the old and the younger generation; it was no accident that Hamlet was played by a popular rock singer, Andrius Mamontovas. Nekrošius liked to say that he chose actors not by their professionalism but by their human qualities, but the age and psychophysical qualities of the performers/non-actors and their physical presence played an important role in his productions. For example, in *Othello* the prima ballerina from the National Opera and Ballet Theatre Eglė Špokaitė played the role of Desdemona, and her natural constitution and her movement contrasted with that of Vladas Bagdonas, the older actor who played Othello.

[11] Music (rhythm) was another important element of Nekrošius' productions. Music was not only created by actors, playing musical instruments or extracting music from simple objects. Since 1997—that is, since *Hamlet*—music and sounds were involved in the action as a stand-alone acoustic landscape. Lehman calls such use of music in post-dramatic performance musicalisation (see: Lehmann, H.-T. *Postdraminis teatras*, Vilnius: Menų spaustuvė, 2010, p. 138). The Lithuanian composers who most often worked with Nekrošius were Faustas Latėnas, Algirdas Martinaitis and Mindaugas Urbaitis.

story-telling, connecting the scenes, adding or removing props and preparing the stage for the next scene. In turn, the scenes could be described as cinematic shots: a panoramic, long shot when the characters and context of the action are presented; and medium or close-up shot when a character speaks a monologue or experiences a certain state. The director combined these shots and created the effect of a continuous, kaleidoscopic-like action, where phenomenology and imagination, experience and its reflection overlap. This could be observed in *The Seasons* by Donelaitis (2003), *The Song of Songs* after the Old Testament (2004), Dante's *Divine Comedy* (2012), and *Zinc (Zn)*, based on Svetlana Alexievich's books (2017).[12]

Nekrošius was always impressed by "unpredictable," "deep-water" literature, full of air and imaginative possibilities. Magical elements were and are abundant in Lithuanian poetry and novels. One such author is the writer/playwright Saulius Šaltenis, a former dramaturg of the State Youth Theatre, who collaborated with the director in the 1980s. One of Nekrošius' last productions in Lithuania, *The Sons of a Bitch* (2018 at the Klaipėda Drama Theatre), was based closely on a play by Šaltenis. The play's action goes back to the eighteenth century, to Lithuania Minor, the south-western part of ethnographic Lithuania, which at the time was a region of Prussia. There the historical past of the country and the last days of the priest Kristijonas Donelaitis—the pioneer of Lithuanian literature and author of the first poem in Lithuanian—are interwoven with tales, spells and pagan myths. In 2003 Nekrošius staged a work by Donelaitis, *The Seasons*—a fun, bright and transparent production about human life, which depends on natural cycles. In *The Sons of a Bitch* Donelaitis himself is presented on his deathbed; at times the stage plunges into a strange mist and the characters repeat the same movements; it is as if the gaze gets doubled and the focus distorted, and time seems to have stopped.

---

[12] At the State Youth Theatre, 24 years after Nekrošius' diploma work there; in it, after thirty years of staging literary classics, Nekrošius returned to a contemporary text. *Zinc* is based on the 2015 Nobel Prize Laureate in Literature Alexievich's *Boys in Zinc* (1991) and *Voices from Chernobyl* (1997).

Between Paradise and Hell: The Last Modernist World

In Nekrošius' theatre, the connotations of paradise and hell are both direct and metaphorical. It is as if all his characters "walk" through hell—they suffer so much anguish, troubles and pain. When, in 2012, he chose to stage Dante's *Divine Comedy*, he first worked on the *Inferno* and *Purgatory*, creating an "eternal" space filled with strange figures haunted by memories. But he did not emphasise "blackness." He created an intense, moving, even youthfully fresh and witty production about the Poet's journey towards his vision-inspiration: not only the journey described by Dante, but also that of the Poet himself. Nekrošius gave an earthly, human form to this journey, ironising the sins and their enslaved ghosts. One of the most exciting "image metaphors" here was a scene where suddenly headphones descended from the "sky" and the ghosts began to listen, yet what they could hear was only the continuous noise of the universe. Then they tied their bundles onto the headphones and released them upwards—like parcels or greetings. The mood of bereavement, longing, melancholy penetrated the production, but Nekrošius' "metaphysics" was human and concrete—it was in the restoration of the connection between the living and the dead.

Nekrošius staged *Paradise* for the Olimpico Theatre in Vincenzo, Italy, and the stage reality merged with the old sculptures of the theatrical space, with the atmosphere of this old, museum-like building. This fully corresponded to the essence of Nekrošius' *Paradise*—a production of pure poetry. In *Divine Comedy*, Hell was loneliness, unfulfilled desires, wanderings and searching; it was action and creation. Here Paradise was a blissful state, light and love: everyone enters Paradise[13] liberated from everyday objects (things), worries and the past.

The materiality of things on stage and the corporeality and tangible sensuality of people and their relations both with other people and with objects were some of the most striking features of Nekrošius' theatre world. He viewed theatre as a "physical" art of actions and sensations. His actors had to be equally sensual and corporeal. Their characters were

---

[13] Nekrošius staged two separated productions—*Divine Comedy* and *Paradise* (2012)—and managed to transgress the physical nature of theatre and directly address the spectator's feelings, consciousness and even subconsciousness. In 2018 Nekrošius merged the two performances into one and named it *Inferno-Paradiso*.

touching, caressing, shaking hands, covering each other's eyes or mouths, carrying, pushing, squirming, feeling cold, heat and so on. The very essence of being was crystallised through tactile touch. By complementing, expanding and strengthening the relations between objects and human beings on stage, Nekrošius made the objects palpably material and, at the same time, opened a new—metaphorical and magical—meaning of their coexistence with people.

In Nekrošius' theatre everything is transformed at the touch of a human being, turned into a mosaic of emotional impulses and associations. At the same time, through the selection of objects on stage and by using the object as a tool for acting and expression, the process of creation became naked and the idea of pure, archaic, "mimetic" action was realised. That is why, while the text inspired and defined possible meanings and images, these then freed themselves from the text. The "acting" on and with objects, experiencing things and situations through the actor's body and expressing this experience via gesture and movement, represented the cycles and pulsation of nature and life, the creative ups and downs, health and illness, birth and death. And, transformed into visual images, the moments of realised relationships and states of the characters and things in Nekrošius' theatre could be called "crystals-images."

This concept was applied by Gilles Deleuze to modern author's cinema, where, according to him, "what we see in the crystal is no longer the empirical progression of time as succession of presents, nor its indirect representation as an interval or as a whole; it is its direct presentation, its constitutive dividing in two—into a present which is passing and a past which is preserved, the strict contemporaneity of the present with the past that it will be, of the past with the present that it has been. [...] The direct time-image or the transcendental form of time is what we see in the crystal."[14] Importantly, Nekrošius never used any technology and relied only on his imagination and on the creativity of his actors. However, the visuality, aesthetics and composition of his theatre always had crystalline structures.

When Nekrošius' *Forefathers' Eve*, by Mickiewicz, created in Poland, was shown in Vilnius in October 2018, nobody thought it would be his last production to be seen in Lithuania—a production in which the destiny of the creator is so openly and painfully contemplated.

---

[14] G. Deleuze, *Cinema 2. The Time-Image*, translated by Hugh Tomlinson and Robert Caleta (Minneapolis: University of Minnesota Press, 1989), p. 274.

Marriage by Witold Gombrowicz, again at the Teatr Narodowy in Warsaw (premiere 15 June 2018), was Nekrošius' very last work. Several months later, he died at the age of 66, as did Kristijonas Donelaitis (1714–1780). Like Donelaitis, who taught people how to work and live, Nekrošius taught his contemporaries how to create and understand theatre. He had many followers around the world. He taught at the Lithuanian Academy of Music and Theatre. And he taught his students

Image 1 *Hamlet*, directed by Eimuntas Nekrošius, Meno Fortas Theatre, 1997, Hamlet—Andrius Mamontovas. (Photo by Dmitrij Matvejev)

158   R. VASINAUSKAITĖ

one main thing: to release their own imagination and not copy anything. For the past twenty years, his faithful helpers had been his son, the set designer Marius Nekrošius and his wife, the costume designer Nadežda Gultiajeva.

REFERENCES

Deleuze, Gilles, *Cinema 2. The Time-Image*, translated by Hugh Tomlinson and Robert Caleta, Minneapolis: University of Minnesota Press, 1989.

Foucault, Michel, *Disciplinuoti ir bausti. Kalėjimo gimimas*, iš prancūzų kalbos vertė Marius Daškus, Vilnius: Baltos lankos, 1998.

Jansonas, Egmontas, *Etiudai apie teatrą*, Vilnius: Vaga, 1988.

Lehmann, Hans-Thies, *Postdraminis teatras*, iš vokiečių kalbos vertė Jūratė Pieslytė, Vilnius: Menų spaustuvė, 2010.

Marcinkevičiūtė, Ramunė, *Eimuntas Nekrošius: erdvė už žodžių*, Vilnius: Kultūros barai, 2002.

———, "Eimuntas Nekrošius: Complex Simplicity." *Contemporary Lithuanian Theatre. Names and Performances*, edited by Ramunė Marcinkevičiūtė and Ramunė Balevičiūtė, Vilnius: TKIEC, Tyto Alba, 2019.

Nekrošius, Eimuntas, "Kokia erdvė už žodžių?" *Kultūros barai*, 1984, No 2, pp. 6–8.

Béla Pintér and His Postmodern National Theatre

Noémi Herczog

Considering that, when I write these lines, it is almost impossible to get tickets to any of the twenty-one currently running shows by Béla Pintér (b. 1970), there must be some kind of truth in the self-definition offered by the director on the fifteenth anniversary of the company in 2014: "I always thought about my theatre as a 'national institution'." "Béla Pintér and Company" is truly doing popular theatre with a theatrical language that—importantly—appeals to the wider public and theatre professionals alike. The company could not have reached this level of popularity without Pintér's theatre being capable of broadening the notion of the national. I would even say that Béla Pintér has been doing postmodern national theatre, critically framing the cliché of the "national" so as to observe contemporary Hungarian society.

N. Herczog (✉)
Hungarian Journal Színház (Theatre), Film and Theatre Department, Faculty Member, Budapest, Hungary

Babeș-Bolyai University, Film and Theatre Department, Faculty Member, Cluj, Romania

© The Author(s), under exclusive license to Springer Nature Switzerland AG 2021
K. Stefanova, M. Carlson (eds.), *20 Ground-Breaking Directors of Eastern Europe*, https://doi.org/10.1007/978-3-030-52935-2_13

Work Method

Béla Pintér started his career as an actor and this has very much affected his theatrical language. He is an all-round theatre-maker: not only is he the artistic manager of the group called "Béla Pintér and Company" and not only does he direct his own scripts, but he also performs in the shows. So his theatre is *par excellence* an auteur's theatre.

In 2019 "Béla Pintér and Company" was in a unique situation: it had twenty shows in its repertoire out of the twenty-five it had created since 1998. All the twenty-five shows were written and directed by Béla Pintér and he performs in almost every one of them. Pintér has left his company only once in the course of these twenty-one years, which means that only once has he worked with a completely different cast: *The Champion* (2016) is his twenty-sixth work, which runs in the repertoire of the respected Katona József public theatre, with a solely in-house ensemble. This one and his newest piece—*The Apple of My Shining Eye* (2019)—are his only two shows so far in which he does not perform. In 2017, when Pintér was re-invited to Katona, he worked together with his own company and the Katona ensemble, writing and directing the piece, and this time also performing in it, as usual.

Except for four shows, the complete Pintér repertoire of "Béla Pintér and Company" can be seen today more or less with the original cast, even though the company has changed completely since the start. Only three members are exceptions in 2019 Szabolcs Thuróczy, who has played in all the twenty-five shows; Béla Pintér himself, who has performed in twenty-four shows; and Éva Enyedi, who has played in twenty-three shows and has been the dramaturg of the company since 2007 and Pintér's closest working partner. In pieces with music, Pintér's closest work partner is Antal Kéménczy. That there is still interest in shows that premiered in 1999 correlates with the Company's immense popularity and stable audience: it has the unique position of having become more sustainable market-wise than is typical or possible in Hungary, playing about twenty shows in the ten-month season each year, with about 5000 people seeing them monthly. This adds up to a paradoxical status quo, where the Company has to constantly find ways to satisfy the needs of its fans, who buy all the tickets the moment the box office opens each month. So it plays at new venues with 340 seats or, most recently, at a venue that can even host 462 viewers. Yet Pintér's productions work best in small spaces for about 155–160 people.

BÉLA PINTÉR AND HIS POSTMODERN NATIONAL THEATRE   161

Béla Pintér became interested in theatre when studying at Simon Ferenc Vocational Educational and Training School. In 1986 he was accepted in István Somogyi's ensemble, which later became known as Arvisura (1980–1996). It followed the neo-avant-garde theatrical traditions of Jerzy Grotowski, Peter Brook and Eugenio Barba. Arvisura performed in Szkéné theatre at the Budapest University of Technology and Economics, which was an important performing venue for non-state theatres before 1989. The spirit of the space was very important in regard to the actors' training, the concept of Arvisura and its hybrid approach genre-wise.

In 1998 Szkéné Béla Pintér created his first piece, *Common Bondage*, and with it founded "Béla Pintér and Company." The piece was more like a ritual performance with Hungarian folk dance and music motifs and a book (fixed on paper only afterwards) that, according to the Company's dramaturg, Éva Enyedi, more resembled a film script, yet without dialogue. It is from Pintér's second show onwards that the text and the plot became of greater importance and they remain so up to now. Also, the collective working method of the first piece was substituted by the following pattern, which is still valid: Pintér arrives at the first rehearsal with the first twenty pages of the play and writes the rest in the course of the rehearsals, after testing every new scene with the company.

The acting mode has also changed over the years. In the beginning, Pintér had a company of non-professional actors, resulting in a rather crude and brutal means of expression on stage—showing an "imperfect perfectness," as Bettina Brandl-Risi put it.[1] A different process was initiated between 2006 and 2007, when professional actors from the Hungarian Academy of Theatre and Film, Budapest, joined the company. Today they are the majority. This lessened the former roughness and subsequently led to a change of audiences. The former underground subculture audiences, who did not necessarily follow Hungarian theatrical tendencies but did follow this one and only theatre, changed to a wider and mostly middle-class audience. Yet Pintér's critical acknowledgement came much later, which has to do with the literary tradition of drama in Hungary and the generally rigid division between the roles of director, writer and actor in mainstream Hungarian theatre.

---

[1] "The New Virtuosity—Outperforming and Imperfection on German Stages," *Theater* 37:1 (2007), pp. 8–37. Hungarian translation under the title "Az új virtuozitás. Túljátszás és tökéletlenség a német színpadon," *Színház. Magyar Színházi Társaság Országos Színháztörténeti Múzeum és Intézet* 41:11 (2008), pp. 69–84 (translator: Judit Szántó).

POSTMODERN GAME

While Pintér's working method was the main factor in the delay in his critical reception, it also encapsulates one of the major characteristics of his theatre. Being an actor–director–scriptwriter all at once, Béla Pintér has been in a state of a constant postmodern game on stage, with his very own persona as an artist.

Nowhere is this postmodern self-reference as direct as in four of his shows. In *Brilliant Second-Rate* (2010), where Pintér plays a character called Géza Pinczér, a tyrannical idiot who is a company manager. Or in *Tamás Ascher in Háromszék* (2017), where a frustrated theatre director called Béla Pintér is played by the Katona ensemble actor István Dankó. Or in *Common Bondage*, where the letters of the title in Hungarian (Népi rablét) form an anagram of Béla Pintér's name. And in one of the company's latest shows, *Jubilee Talks* (2019), where Pintér yet again plays a tyrannical theatre director and company manager called Béla Pintér, who sometimes—as a slip of the tongue—is addressed by a fictitious reporter as "Viktor," a reference to the contemporary Hungarian Prime Minister, Viktor Orbán. This kind of self-irony is not at all typical of Hungarian theatre.

But even when Pintér plays the most enigmatic Hungarian poet Sándor Petőfi (whose works kids learn at school from a young age), again there is a de-heroisation effect, this time of the symbol of Hungarian patriotism. Seeing Pintér at the top of the ensemble hierarchy playing the poet at the top of the Hungarian literary canon can also be interpreted as a quite direct, self-ironical reference to his very own identity as a theatre artist and a director. There's a list of shows with Pintér playing tyrannical characters, many times tyrannical parents: the despotic father (*The Queen of the Cookies*, 2004) and the despotic mother (*Children of the Demon*, 2008). There again, the tyrannical nature of both the theatrical character and the performed theatre director are available as two parallel strata.

The director as a performer, performing in their own works, has a short tradition in Hungary, mainly as part of the neo-avant-garde theatre of artists like László Najmányi (b. 1946) and the István Kovács Studio, or Péter Halász (1943–2006). The latter, for instance, played his grandmother in his piece *She Who Was Once the Helmet-Maker's Beautiful Wife* (1998) and a dead person in another work of his, *Jack Smith Is Dead* (1994, 2002). In the second decade of the twenty-first century they were followed by artists like Árpád Schilling in *Looser* (2014).

Pintér's works also include postmodern references from pieces of news, literary and artistic works by others (the two major influences for Pintér are Luis Buñuel's films and Bulgakov's *The Master and Margarita*), and even trash motifs. His theatre blends all this into a new entity according to Aristotelian rules, yet combined with surreal and immensely funny elements. This mixture adds up to Pintér's unique, postmodern language within the realm of psychological realism on the Hungarian stage.

Last but not least, Pintér's theatre abounds with references to icons and representatives of contemporary and historical Hungarian culture. This feature relates to and stems from Hungaro-Transylvanian folk culture, from which Pintér also draws inspiration.

POSTMODERN IRONY AND HUNGARO-TRANSYLVANIAN FOLK CULTURE

Pintér first had to deal with folk dance in the Arvisura ensemble. What is of interest to him is how to depict his own culture with less pathos and more sense of humour. (There is only one other Hungarian artistic couple, the Mohácsi brothers, whose aesthetics is centred around this in a similarly postmodern fashion.) Pintér treats folk culture quite freely, certainly not as a sacred entity. On the surreal dissection table of the postmodern, he combines fairy-taleish folk themes with contemporary urban folk material. This postmodern irony towards folk culture comprises also a mixture of the authentic and the kitsch, conservative motifs and liberal values. All of this can be easily described as the "Transylvanian journey" motif. For example, in the second Pintér piece, *Hospital-Bakony* (1999), where the characters are ethnic Hungarians and Yugoslavs, the heroes find a magic fountain that turns out to bring everybody's inner self to the surface; this is how the hyper-macho folk dancer turns out to be gay.

Pintér's first piece was already a Dionysian rampage using the photos of the Szekler photographer Péter Korniss, and presenting a traditional Hungarian wedding with a considerable amount of alcohol where at the end the bride, instead of saying the beatific "Yes," cuts off the groom's head. The only lines belonged to Szabolcs Turóczy, the comic or clown character of the company, who did certain verbal improvisations. Pintér's provocative and subversive way of working with Hungarian folk culture has made him the subject of blasphemy attacks for desacralising national folk themes.

164   N. HERCZOG

One of the central motifs of folk culture is, of course, music, for instance the Moldovian folk music in *My Mother's Nose* (2005), a Szekler couple in *Dievoushka* (2003) and so on—the examples could go on and on. But Pintér reached one of the peaks of this aesthetics in 2002 with his *Peasant Opera*. The structure of this piece is much more closed than what one can generally experience with his work due to the opera-like structure: the contrast between the sublime and the profane; the ironic humour that can be recognised in the harmonic mixture of ethnic Transylvanian-Hungarian songs, baroque and rock (music written by Benedek Darvas).

THE OPERA À LA PINTÉR

Not only is folk music an essential element of Pintér's aesthetics, he has also created three works that are based on postmodern playing with folk culture and the genre of opera in equal measure. The opera tradition inspired altogether four pieces in Pintér's oeuvre before 2019: *Peasant Opera* (2002), *Dievoushka* (2003), *The Champion* (2016) and *The Apple of My Shining Eye* (2019). These operas are in fact musikdramas (a German term), meaning the whole piece is written for singing and music. It was with the *Peasant Opera* in 2002 that this special style of opera-parody genre was actually born.

Peasant Opera takes place in a contemporary Transylvanian village. The structure of the piece follows analytical dramas; *Oedipus Rex* is one of Pintér's favourite plays. The tragic horror ballad's plotline is a popular motif used for instance by Albert Camus in his play *The Misunderstanding*: it is a story about parents who do not recognise their child and kill him out of greed. Yet it is a mixture of tragedy and comedy, where humour comes from the contrast between folk music, baroque and contemporary popular culture (soap operas). In Pintér's theatre in principle, folk is not limited to the past; it lives on in the so-called contemporary folk culture (popular culture). So in *Peasant Opera*, the once naive peasant boy returns to his birth village as a cowboy, thus symbolising how foreign territories are imagined from the perspective of a Transylvanian village. The "Hunglish" articulation of the term "cowboy" has a comic-cabaretesque effect. The use of dialects as a sign of East European is a recurring motif in Pintér's works. It has a partly comic effect and partly gives these heroes an imperfect, thus more lovable character. The aforementioned cowboy then returns wearing a prop-dildo, depicting how the image of the sexy cowboy lives in the little Transylvanian village—the sex scene is stylised: the luminescent dildo is about one metre long.

The other opera-genre peak among Pintér's works is *Dievoushka*, where the terminology of a "unified Europe," which they use in one of the songs, connects the contemporary European Union with the Europe of 1942. *Dievoushka* is about the victims of Don River: the Hungarian army was catastrophically defeated there in the winter of 1942–1943. The work showcases the taboos of the tragic history and an age full of anti-Semitism—the latter being something that has not disappeared in Hungary even now. The set is surreal: with a bold staircase (designed by Péter Horgas, just like the set of the *Peasant Opera*) and music (written by Benedek Darvas again) comprising Puccini-like hits, Hungarian folk songs and soldier marches. In *Dievoushka* the striking contrast of musical genres is part of the irony that deconstructs the icon of the "national."

Subversive Humour: Deconstructing and Re-writing the National

The alpha and omega of Pintér's aesthetics is the sense of humour, and his public knows this so well that it starts laughing at the very first line, or when a character, especially the ones depicted by Szabolcs Thuróczy, has only entered the stage and not even said a word yet. Humour comes combined with cabaret-like elements from the very start, where figures from Hungarian culture, public personalities and historical icons, as well as reversed-sex casting, are represented.

Sometimes this humour and these cabaretesque (postmodern) references have led to political trouble. For example, *The Champion* (2016) is based on Puccini's *Il tabarro* and carries certain resemblances between the family affairs of the main character and that of a Hungarian provincial mayor related to the conservative ruling party (Fidesz). When journalistic articles after the first night tried to discredit Pintér and the theatre, the issue evoked memories of Soviet times,[2] even though the reference was not at all political in the context of the play.

Also, until 2010, Pintér's political references have been always lighter in tone, depicting nationalist attitudes via the viewpoint of the individual and via family narratives (e.g. *The Queen of the Cookies*, depicting domestic

[2] Andrea Tompa, "'You called me, dear Führer!' Béla Pintér: The Champion; Katona József Theater, Budapest," *Theater heute* 7 (July 2016).

violence). Only in 2010 did a figure of an activist of the so-called Hungarian Guard (a martial movement with racist goals, belonging to the radical right-wing party Jobbik in the Hungarian Parliament) appear on Pintér's stage. It was in *Muck* and the racist character's portrayal was much darker (played by Zsófia Szamosi, protagonist of the Oscar-winning short film *Sing*, 2016). It's there that for the first time Pintér's theatre talks about the strengthening of the far right. It should also be noted that *Muck, The Queen of the Cookies* and *Our Secrets* are the three most text-based Pintér pieces.

Muck is a fable about two step-children who are adopted by a couple in their teenage years. One of them—Muck—is called ugly (she has bad teeth), hence feels less loved by the new parents and by the villagers. This is the psychological background for her becoming a right-wing activist. Her step-sister, a Roma girl (played by Éva Enyedi), has the habit of stealing—a common stereotype about the Roma. Still the villagers learn to love her more than her sister despite them being racists too.

Pintér often uses clichés when building up his characters, but in the end they don't become cliché-like and the outcome is free of prejudice. Yet Pintér can reflect on these clichés with postmodern irony—something that happens in Éva Enyedi's lovable Roma portrayal.

Other dark reflections on topical political issues can be seen in *Pheasant Dance* (2015)—on ISIS; and in *Till Heartbreak* (2017)—on immigrants. (*Pheasant Dance* is a funny reference to the Hungarian Prime Minister's hint in his very own political strategy at the so-called peacock dance; meaning mocking his negotiating partners). As Pintér sums it up, this new phase has come about because the previous government gave them money, while the new one gave them topics.

Another important production of his, re-writing not only Hungarian folk culture but also Hungarian national heroes, is *Kaisers TV, Ungarn* (2011). It is based on the premise that the outcome of the Hungarian war of liberty and independence from the Austro-Hungarian empire in 1848–1849 has changed. It is an alternative history in a sense that as a comic effect, Hungarians win the famous battle of Schwechat (1848). Interestingly, Pintér reflects not only on the growth of nationalism, but also on the contemporary media situation. In *Kaisers* there is a royal television channel in the nineteenth century that is occupied by the national icons of war or liberty in a similar fashion to the way national television was occupied during the Romanian revolution in 1989. The nineteenth-century heroes of Hungarian patriotism, Lajos Kossuth and Sándor Petőfi, are thus represented in a desacralised manner: Kossuth, played by the comic actor Szabolcs Thuróczy, becomes a less heroic character and Petőfi, played as already mentioned by Pintér, becomes very touchy and despotic. There is a scene in the loo when a third character, a time-traveller from the twenty-first century, stands between them and his perspective gives a comic contrast between their status in their own time and now, when they are turned into icons in Hungarian history books. The time-traveller is so embarrassed that he is not able to pee. In October 2010 a new media law in Hungary was passed and many people were dismissed from the media for political reasons, so the fact that in 2011, in *Kaisers TV, Ungarn*, Petőfi was on the royal television channel also carried very topical political references.

The music in *Kaisers TV, Ungarn*, by Antal Kéménczy, combines different musical strata from the national collective subconscious. Marches from 1948 get mixed with a Liszt Rhapsody, Schubert, Beethoven and Chopin. At the end of the battle of Schwechat, when the audience thinks all is lost, it hears a Liszt funeral march, but then, when the fictional success story begins, a Liszt Rhapsody resounds.

In 2013, Pintér created another show with the aim of coming to terms with the past: *Our Secrets*. This time the plot takes place in the 1980s, in the time of secret police and secret agents. Yet another secret of the protagonist, played by Zoltán Friedenthal, is that he is struggling with his unrepressable sexual-emotional attraction towards his 10-year old stepdaughter. This helps the state secret service to rope him in. The drama lies in his being too weak to resist temptation - no matter how hard he is trying to. Most of the humorous effects in this show too come from the tradition of cabaret. For instance, the cross-gender casting, applied by Pintér in many of his works, here results in Angéla Stefanovics' bravura, playing a precocious boy. The other reversed-sex role is allotted to Eszter Csákányi, a former Krétakör (Chalk Circle) actress, who plays a police officer. Her appearance on one level refers to the actress herself, imitating the outlook of her father, the iconic actor László Csákányi, with the use of his very own glasses; many people can spot the similarity. On a different level, she represents a gay and lonely officer from the 1980s, trying to seduce his paedophile agent. The child abuse scene makes it evident that even the tragic layer of the show balances between the comic and the morbid.

In *Our Secrets*, Pintér plays a talented but unappreciated folk dancer who longs for the state certificate of merit, but does not get it due to his oppositional activity. Thus the audience sees his struggle as an enemy of the state on two different levels: as a rebel in the 1980s and as a talented theatre-maker in the twenty-first century. So Pintér deconstructs folk culture by his very casting. As a result, his theatre liberates folk dance from the conservative culture and at the same time transforms it into an oppositional power. Folk dancers become young and sexy in *Our Secrets*, without any conservative tone.

Image 1 *Kaisers TV, Ungarn,* directed by Béla Pintér, Béla Pintér and Company, 2011, Béla Pintér in the production. (Photo by Zsuzsa Koncz)

In Pintér's theatre, such postmodern twists help the audience see Hungaro-Transylvanian folk culture in a perspective different from the one in which it is usually presented on the contemporary Hungarian stage. Béla Pintér's theatre is "national" in the truest and the most postmodern sense of the term. The only reason I feel rather uneasy writing this down is that the notion of the "postmodern" sounds too pedantic. And pedantic is everything that Béla Pintér's theatre is not.

REFERENCES

Brandl-Risi, Bettina, "The New Virtuosity—Outperforming and Imperfection on German Stages," *Theater* 37:1 (2007), pp. 8–37.

Enyedi, Éva, "Pintér, the Playwright," in *Béla Pintér—Plays* (Budapest: Saxum, 2013), pp. 359–363.

Pintér, Béla, Round table talk-series held with members of the Hungarian Theatre Critcs' Association, in Szkéné Theatre, 2013

———, Interview, Interviewer: Orsolya Kővári, *Átrium* (Budapest, 2019).

Tompa, Andrea, "'You called me, dear Führer!' Béla Pintér: The Champion; Katona József Theater, Budapest," *Theater heute* 7 (July 2016).

Silviu Purcărete: The Master of Rich Theatre

Octavian Saiu

EXPANSIVE THEATRICALITY

Having been featured in the programme of the Edinburgh International Festival three different times, making a strong impact at the Avignon Festival, currently working all over Europe and in Asia, Silviu Purcărete is arguably Romania's best-known international theatre artist. Beyond any such achievements, it is perhaps his constant presence at the Sibiu International Theatre Festival that accounts for his unparalleled reputation. His iconic *Faust*, a production of monumental proportions, with a cast of more than 100 people, has been the main attraction at every edition of this event since 2008. The show captures the essence of Purcărete's aesthetic and offers a unique insight into his profound philosophy of theatre: it is not only an impressive display of craftsmanship, an exploration of a vast performative space, but a sombre meditation on the destiny of a part of the world where humanity has tasted the Faustian provocations of modern history.[1]

---

[1] It could be said that Purcărete's theatre is one of "resistance," although this concept has led to too many cultural approximations in the performing arts. One relevant example of

---

O. Saiu (✉)
National University of Theatre and Film, Bucharest, Romania

© The Author(s), under exclusive license to Springer Nature Switzerland AG 2021
K. Stefanova, M. Carlson (eds.), *20 Ground-Breaking Directors of Eastern Europe*, https://doi.org/10.1007/978-3-030-52935-2_14

172   O. SAIU

To comprehend *Faust* is to understand Purcărete, an artist whose theatrical vision is at once universal and rooted in the cultural, spiritual ethos of the European East. Everything in his work integrates these two dimensions: a sense of cultural specificity and a style that transcends any geographical identity. The space of this performance is a metaphor for both, more than an apparent postmodern gesture appropriate for the post-industrial age. *Faust* is performed in a former Communist factory, now conquered by theatre, but retaining the traumatic memory of a period for a country once forced into ideological standardisation and brutal massification. Yet beyond the lingering reminiscences of that past, the dominant feel is that of contemporary theatricality. Powerful, intense, complex, Purcărete's *Faust* is a staging that turns a classical text into a visual narrative about the perils of the present. These days, the director seems to say, humankind faces the same challenges that crush Goethe's hero, none of which is more alarming than the loss of spiritual values. The audience watches this mesmerising and immersive performance—during which it is drawn into the centrifugal space of an overflowing Walpurgis Night filled with real fire and conquered by a sort of grotesque reminiscent of Hieronymus Bosch's paintings—and leaves the former factory with a paradoxical feeling of satisfaction and uneasiness. In Purcărete's universe the pleasure of watching theatre is a guilty one, as it entails the questioning of self and the interrogation of pre-established values through the reversed gaze: the spectators gaze, but they feel the gaze of others at the same time. Although a show of sensorial overpowering and rare magnitude, *Faust* is a delicate contemplation of what it means to exist in a world of absurdity, violence and excess. Its message is that we are all as likely to succumb to the lure of evilness as its aged, powerless protagonist.

Covered by many academic publications as well as various European newspapers, *Faust* is not only Purcărete's but Romania's most renowned theatre production.[2] This status, to a certain degree justified by the sheer scale of the show, has turned a contemporary rendition of a classic into a

how vague the category can be is the way in which he is presented by Christopher Innes and Maria Shevtsova in their *Cambridge Introduction to Theatre Directing* (Cambridge and New York: Cambridge University Press, 2013), page 111.

[2] The performance has gained the status of a theatrical cult classic, particularly after the enthusiastic reviews that appeared in some British publications after its Edinburgh tour. BBC also covered the impact of this uniquely large-scale production in the context of the 2009 Edinburgh International Festival, which for the first time in years had to scout for a new venue, capacious enough to accommodate the performance.

cultural phenomenon of adaptation through re-reading and re-writing. It seems to matter less that Goethe's ample text has been reduced to a one-and-a-half-hour experience. It matters even less that many of the play's characters have been eliminated altogether. What is of real importance is that the performance has taken on a life of its own, above and beyond any horizons of expectations surrounding the literary masterpiece. More than its astute interpreter, Purcărete is its new author. This attitude is a trademark of an artist who has sought to re-define stage directing, shifting the focus from construing and interpreting a text to using that text as an imaginative pretext.

To analyse his creations from the point of view of the textual material upon which they are based, to insist on the necessary correlation between the writers' intended meanings and the productions' revealed connotations, is to miss the very essence of a cultural path that has taken Purcărete from the status of an unknown Romanian theatre-maker to international prominence. His journey started immediately after the 1989 Revolution, with an adaptation that portrayed the hideous dictatorial couple who led the country for twenty-five years: *Ubu Rex with Scenes from Macbeth*, a parable about the monstrosity of power beyond the dreams of egalitarianist ideology.

Invited to the Edinburgh International Festival for the first time with this production in 1991, Purcărete was then regarded as an artist who could reveal the hidden creativity of Eastern European theatre, fresher and more exotic than other names from this part of the world already known by that time. Inspired by Jarry's parody, the story was in fact that of Romania's former dictatorial couple: Elena and Nicolae Ceausescu. As in his entire oeuvre, such an allusion was at once clear and subtle, overt and understated. On the huge scaffolds of an abandoned construction site, the Macbeth and Lady Macbeth of the late twentieth century were savouring the delight of their authority in a theatrical caricature of magnified proportions, wrapped in a sort of expansive theatricality. All of a sudden, Purcărete's name became known, respected, sought after.

One of his next successes was a dual adaptation, based on Euripides and Seneca, of the myth of *Phaedra*—another stage story about the moral crisis of humanity and yet another parable suggestive of the same Communist society. The themes of surveillance and manipulation were central and the Chorus consisted of androgynous silhouettes, dressed in long, black raincoats and carrying even longer sticks. Pretending to be old and wise, this amorphous group was in fact listening and plotting behind

174 O. SAIU

the protagonist's back, foreshadowing and facilitating her disaster. In the end, after Phaedra's suicide, they revealed their true face in a triumphant circular dance of joy. Through this group image, which would be recurrent in many of his subsequent works, Purcărete denounced the political police in Communist Romania, a machinery built to spy and control, which functioned for almost half a century in a country where truth was uttered only with fear and reluctance.

THE ACTOR AS A COLLECTIVE ENTITY

Turning individual actors into a collective entity, perfectly homogeneous and coherent, has become the most recognisable feature of Purcărete's style: an attribute that is worthy of a more extensive account. This director, who studied visual arts before venturing into the theatre programmes of Bucharest's National University of Theatre and Film, seems to be apprehensive not about one or other of the actors with whom he works, but about the very idea of working with actors. Their freedom and unpredictability infringe upon his urge to create in the spirit of a true auteur, rather than merely give instructions in the fashion of a typical director. For him, to be able to work freely is to erase their individual characteristics, merging them into a single entity and thus acquiring the much-desired opportunity to control them all. Although graceful and totally unabusive in his interaction with the cast, Purcărete has always striven to control every compartment of his productions—not in the political manner of a dictator, but in the creative style of an auteur. In psychoanalytical terms, such an impetus could be connected to all the traumas of Communist collectivisation, with the gigantic political parades he witnessed in his native country before 1989, but no framework of this kind would suffice. His desire is simply rooted in the vital distinction between the visual and the theatrical, between working alone and working with others.[3]

Purcărete's veritable aesthetic of the collective actor culminated in a production that brought him not only recognition, but also a place in the pantheon of large-scale theatre-makers, alongside Peter Brook or Arianne Mnouchkine. *The Danaids* was co-produced by the Avignon Festival, in partnership with other cultural entities, and staged at the National Theatre

---

[3] For a detailed statement of his theatrical beliefs, see the interview conducted by Aleksandar Saša Dundjero in *Contemporary European Theatre Directors*, edited by Maria M. Delgado and Dan Rebellato (London and New York: Routledge, 2010), p. 87.

of Craiova—the same institution where he had created his *Phaedra* and *Ubu Rex*. *Danaids* involved two components inextricably linked to one another in Purcărete's career: a massive group of actors and an overwhelming sense of stage energy. Aeschylus' story about the women of Danaos chased by Egyptian men became a contemporary fable about exile and asylum, about masculine ideology and feminist resistance, and not least about theatre itself. The size of the cast was impressive: fifty men and fifty women were the Egyptians and the Danaids, respectively, while the proscenium area was occupied by a select few thespians playing the gods of Greek tragedy. Whereas those appearing in the two large groups were virtually indistinguishable from each other, the gods were interpreted by some of Romania's most distinguished actors.[4]

Those gods were talking gracefully about the atrocities they themselves were committing, punishing innocent mortals in order to relish in watching their tragic spectacle. Every line was declaimed with attention and precision. Every gesture was measured and controlled. Behind them, the two groups were fighting in a display of energy released by their mere presence, by their intense movement in a vast, empty space. The contrast between the elegant performers dressed in white, detached and imperturbable, and the high voltage of the two groups carried a message in which Purcărete concentrated his vision of the play and, moreover, his concept of theatricality. For him, the actors' interpretation of lines, their portrayal of characters, matters less than the energy they bring onto the stage. What many considered a sample of visual theatre, placing the Romanian artist in the company of Kantor or Wilson, was in fact an advent of newness, an attempt to re-define the language of the stage—not through the details of individual acting, but through the general impact of the actors merged into a group.[5] No one in the audience could ignore the force of their bodies and no one could deny the strength of their voices. Moving together like a coherent entity, each group of fifty conveyed this message through their presence, in a manner not seen since the very era of Greek theatre.

---

[4] For a more extensive critical account of the production and its space, see Octavian Saiu, *In Search of Lost Space* (Bucharest: UNATC Press, 2010).

[5] An album published when he was running the Theatre of Limoges, titled *Silviu Purcărete: Images de théâtre* (Carnières Belgium: Lansman, 2002), accentuated a certain perception of his work. He has thus been included in the canon of visual theatre, thanks to the power of the images associated with his creative style.

Hauntingly beautiful in its visuality, *The Danaids* contained a political and philosophical statement whose implications resonate today even more than back then.[6] The women chased away from their homes were carrying wooden suitcases, each representing a microcosm of their dislocated identity, hurriedly salvaged. Putting those suitcases one on top of the other, they were trying to form a protective barricade, instantly wrecked by the savage men invading the stage. Exile was the crucial theme of the show, a bitter conclusion to a century in which entire communities were forced to part with their native soil. The first word uttered by the gods gathered in the proscenium was E-U-R-O-P-A, the name of the continent built upon a myth of violent abduction. This part of the world, Purcărete seemed to imply, echoing Derrida, was not only blessed with the great values of culture established by the ancient Greeks, but also riddled with an entire history of violence, displacement and intolerance. Isn't the coexistence of such polar opposites a possible definition of *Homo europaeus*? To deconstruct them on stage became his mission as an artist.

Between Good and Evil

In all his major works, from *Oresteia* in the late 1990s to a recent *Richard III*, Purcărete has been trying to highlight the coexistence of good and evil as a paradox that is inherent to being human. The bitterness of such a conclusion is sometimes disguised in dark humour, coloured by an impressive imagery, but hardly ever absent from his theatre. It was in his *Dom Juan*, a stage version of Molière's play in which the famed philanderer was equally a torturer and a victim, brought upon the stage as a lifeless skeleton in the last scene. It was in his improbable adaptation of Rabelais's *Gargantua and Pantagruel*, a production about the gluttony and also the delicacy of human nature, whose key moment was as visually powerful as it was acoustically impactful: a huge amount of cutlery was dropped from above the stage, like a downpour of matter. This paradox has been there in all his works, which depict the human condition as a fusion of beastliness and spirituality, which one must tell apart, understand, explore.

---

[6] The show proved too challenging, therefore unpalatable for some critics, particularly in the USA. After the performance given at the Lincoln Centre, John Simon wrote a very unfriendly review in *New York Magazine* (28 July 1997). However, other reviewers, such as Ben Brantley, praised it for its lavish theatricality. See *The New York Times* (2 July 1997).

Yet nowhere has this been more acutely present than in another show created in the same period as *Ubu Rex, Phaedra* and *Danaids*, at the same National Theatre of Craiova: *Titus Andronicus*. It is, as specialists conclude, Shakespeare's most cruel play.[7] One scene in particular breaks all boundaries of dramatic correctness, as it contains the most cynical form of revenge imaginable: when Titus wants to punish Queen Tamora for her crimes, he invites her to a dinner party, where he serves food cooked with the flesh of her own children. Beyond the gut-wrenching idea at the core of this gesture, beyond all that can be read and seen in the play, the question that re-surfaces is about the lower limits of individual morality. It is the ethical verdict that one cannot escape, the verdict that Shakespeare formulated without pontificating, but clear enough for all his readers and spectators to comprehend: to be human is to admit that regression into barbarity is as real a possibility as rising above it. For Purcărete, this message was the pretext for a memorable stage rendition. When Titus—played by Romania's then greatest actor, Stefan Iordache—was serving his guests dressed like a chef from a silent movie, the grotesque caricature of that scene was accompanied by the most sublime music. It was Mozart's Piano Concerto nr. 20 in D minor. Between the beauty of what the spectators were listening to and the callousness of what they were watching, one could contemplate the full spectrum of human capabilities.[8] Between good and evil, human nature oscillates permanently and undecidedly: this conclusion was at once derived from, and argued against, Shakespeare. In the play, there does not seem to be any space left for redemption. In the production, there was a sense of sad irony, which was not meant to balance moral perspectives, but to remind the audience that everything is twofold in their own being, that virtuousness and evilness may never be fully reconciled. Few scenes in contemporary theatre have shattered Levinas' notion of the ethics of alterity in a more drastic and penetrating manner.

That same conclusion qualifies all Purcărete's shows, which are theatrical essays about the inextricable mixture of animality and spirituality that is more human than anything else, certainly more than either one or the other. This view is the red line, the link that connects all his performances

---

[7] Today, when Shakespeare's identity is under unprecedented scrutiny, Titus raises issues that are not easy to clarify, as it does not seem to fit in with the rest of the Shakespearean tragedies.

[8] When discussing Titus, Peter Holland praises this paradoxical mixture. In Purcărete's own words, it is an improbable mixture of "horror and splendour." Peter Holland, *English Shakespeares* (Cambridge and New York: Cambridge University Press, 2000), p. 231.

in a fashion that is not emphatic, but rather subtle in its philosophical implications. Dressed in powerful images or delicate symbols, it is always there, because it represents his most fundamental belief, which he expresses not as a director staging plays, but as a creator who addresses the world through the plays he stages. This is why the mere term "director" is perhaps wrong or at least insufficient to capture the vocation of a theatrical auteur who is not preoccupied with the lines of the text, but constantly focused on the spirit of those writers with whom he feels genuinely compatible.[9]

Visual Adaptations

The abundance of imagery, against the necessity of words, is indeed a statement of belief in Purcărete's aesthetic, and not a pose through which the responsibility of painstaking textual interpretation and detailed work with actors can both be evaded. In fact, all his images are born out of the text, distilling its substance through a laborious process: when confronted about a line, about a character, he proves remarkably astute and informed. Understood as an extension of the text itself, nothing can be regarded as whimsical in the visual architecture of any of his productions, even when it appears extravagant and unfounded. This is the case for the visual texture in his daring adaptation of *Gulliver's Travels*.

The eighteenth-century novel seems least likely to be turned into dramatic material, since it includes so many imaginary creatures that pose a serious threat to the very concept of stage representability. When faced with the challenge of this improbable adaptation, Purcărete chose to contradict all possible horizons of expectations, compiling certain parts of the novel with Swift's other writings in a scenario that lends itself to endless contemporary interpretations. His *Gulliver* is about human greed, ambition, lust, all contrasted with the beauty of the world of horses—an idea explicitly present in the fourth, not so known part of the novel. This leads Purcărete to bring a real horse onto the stage, a stage that is simultaneously invaded by the ugliness of human behaviour, by actors trampling over what appears to be a very elegant marble floor.

---

[9] This vocation of being an auteur found its full expression in the only movie that Purcărete has ever directed, a magic-realistic allegory about a small Romanian provincial town in which history, myth and fiction meet: *Somewhere in Palilula* (2012).

SILVIU PURCĂRETE: THE MASTER OF RICH THEATRE 179

The process of adaptation is an endless topic for theatre studies, particularly as the trend in Europe has become more and more obvious with artists like Brook, Castorf and Lupa venturing into the vast territory of prose. In many cases, words are reduced, transformed and even eliminated. Yet not many artists can claim the same ability that Purcărete displays—that of finding words' equivalent in images, reaching the perfect match between language and visuality. *Gulliver's Travels* is a show dominated by two key characters: the splendid black stallion, reminding everyone of nature's perfection as opposed to human faultiness, and a decrepit author-turned-character Jonathan Swift with a long wig, in a wheelchair, telling his own story. Between these two polarities, everything unfolds as a succession of *tableaux* in which humanity is depicted in the least sympathetic of colours, exactly as the eighteenth-century author uncompromisingly saw it. The verbal dimensions of the performance are overwhelmed by the strong imagery, to the degree that the narrative is actually incorporated into them—a perception that lends itself to the broad category defined by Hans-Thies Lehmann as the "postdramatic."[10] A more suitable concept would be that of rich theatre, the opposite of Grotowski's dream of poverty and minimalism. The Polish master wanted to disappear behind his performances, aesthetically defined by humility and austereness. Closer to Kantor in this sense, Purcărete wants to insinuate himself into the texture of his own theatre, and *Gulliver* is a most convincing example.[11] From off-stage, his own recorded voice punctuates the message with copious quotations from the novel, as if the umbilical cord between him and his own rich, full-bodied theatrical creation could not and should not be severed.

SHAKESPEAREAN MEDITATIONS

A totally different way of reinforcing his authorial signature was the decision to stage the same play more than once. It was not just any play, but *The Tempest*, Shakespeare's testament of forgiveness and reconciliation, which for Purcărete is equally a story of intolerance and loneliness. From

[10] In his groundbreaking study, Lehmann himself lists Purcărete among the proponents of the postdramatic paradigm, alongside Jan Lauwers, Robert Lepage and Heiner Goebbels. Hans-Thies Lehmann, *Postdramatic Theatre* (London and New York: Routledge, 2006).

[11] Much like Kantor, Purcărete introduces elements of the grotesque into his shows. They are not merely aesthetic elements, however, but symbols meant to remind his spectators of the baseness of human existence.

180   O. SAIU

the first version, which he directed in Nottingham, to the most recent one, created in Craiova, his relationship with the text has become more and more personal. The British show included comic accents and enough lightness to be considered hopeful. The latest Romanian staging takes place in a single room, the dilapidated residence of an old and tired Prospero, whose magic skills have long faded. It is a sad meditation on the limits of hopefulness. In all his attempts at the play, Purcărete has used Shakespeare as a pretext for a very subjective meditation on humankind, whose contradictory nature he has associated with both Ariel and Caliban, as expressions of spiritual aspiration and utter savageness, respectively. Also, in all three of his versions he tried to make it clear to the audience that they were not watching a faithful rendition of the text, although it is kept almost entirely, but a rather idiosyncratic perspective belonging to an artist who believes Shakespeare is "our contemporary" for the most uncomfortable of reasons.[12] According to Purcărete's reading of *The Tempest* and *Titus Andronicus*, Shakespeare is the author who painted human nature not with mild forbearance, but with fierce cynicism.

Another proof of this dark scrutiny of Shakespeare is Purcărete's take on *Richard III* in the context of a special collaboration with Tokyo Metropolitan Theatre. No other Romanian theatre artist has been invited by this prestigious Japanese institution to stage a show, and the opportunity occurred for him after a series of cultural exchanges between Romania and Japan, centred around his works. After the tours of his *Lulu* and *Oedipus* in Tokyo in 2013 and 2015, respectively, his reputation was cemented by waves of critical and public acclaim, all the more so as some Japanese theatre-goers could still remember the revelation of seeing his *Titus* in the 1990s.[13] In a country where the broad cultural reception of Shakespeare has been markedly influenced by masters like Akira Kurosawa in cinema and Yukio Ninagawa in theatre, the task of the Eastern European director was not an easy one. Surrounded by his constant team—set designer Dragos Bugahiar and composer Vasile Sirli—Purcărete chose an unorthodox approach to the play and its central character. Not long after Ostermeier's version prompted headlines throughout the theatrical world,

---

[12] It is worth highlighting the fact that Jan Kott's book *Shakespeare, Our Contemporary* was enormously popular in Romania, and it influenced many generations of theatre artists, including the one to which Purcărete belongs.

[13] The only book published in Japan, in Japanese, on Romanian theatre is for the most part dedicated to Purcărete's works, one of which is featured on its cover. See *Rumania Engeki-ni Miserarete* (*Lured by Romanian Theatre*) (Tokyo: Serika Shobo, 2013).

the premiere of *Richard III* at Tokyo Metropolitan Theatre made another type of statement.

It is worth mentioning that this was not the director's first encounter with the play. He had staged it before, in the 1980s, during the harshest times of Romanian Communism. One scene was more evocative than any other in that production, and it caused a stir that almost led to the immediate banning of the show: Richard, played by the same actor who would later be cast as Titus, was making love to the throne. The obsession with power, which is recognised as the central theme of the text, was more than a part of Kott's "grand mechanism of history." It was an uncontrollable desire of a madman. The same theme of absurdity and madness, dressed in different imagery, was pivotal in the Japanese stage rendition, and the single element of continuity between the Romanian version and the new one was that scene in which Richard tries to impregnate the throne. The major difference? In Tokyo, the character was nothing but an insensitive clown, who in the end dies alone in a wheelchair. What a metaphor for the weakness and vulnerability of power, and what a way to describe death as the ultimate jest of a consummate actor who plays with fire until he gets burnt and burnt out at the same time! His self-destructiveness is not the effect, but the cause of everything.

GLOBAL PERFORMANCE AND TRANSNATIONAL IDENTITY

Working in many countries, with engagements in opera as well as in theatre,[14] living in France as a naturalised French citizen and constantly travelling for new projects, drawn to the universal themes of humanity and history, hardly ever approaching Romanian texts, Purcărete epitomises the status of the contemporary director with no fixed abode and thus with no discernible national identity. According to certain classifications, he could be seen as a global artist, transgressing boundaries.

Nevertheless, he has never abandoned his Romanian roots, and nowhere else has he been more present and more at home than in his country of origin. Even when he was the Director of the National Dramatic Centre of Limoges (1996–2002), Purcărete maintained a close and deep connection with the Romanian theatrical movement, which he could not

---

[14] He is one of the few Eastern European directors invited to work at Scottish Opera as well as Vienna State Opera. His career as an opera director started after 1989, and has continued uninterrupted ever since.

completely leave behind. In his style, in his method, in all that constitutes his artistic personality, there are vibes of Romanian culture, which in turn is part of an Eastern European ethos unmistakably affirmed by his theatre.[15] Nothing obvious places his work in the theatrical tradition of this part of the world, where Stanislavskyian realism still dominates the curriculum of all acting schools and stage naturalism has never been deserted. In fact, in many ways, everything about Purcărete contradicts this tradition. And yet…

When asked at a press conference about the composition of the Walpurgis Night of his *Faust*—a polyphonic and multi-sensorial experience of true immersive theatre, reminiscent of Fellini's portrayal of Trimalchio's Banquet in *Satyricon*—Purcărete's reply was bewildering.[16] Rather than pedantically elaborating on such high cultural sources, he confessed that the origin of that breathtaking scene, in which the spectators are invited to follow the actors through the unsuspected vastness of the former industrial factory, is personal and perhaps mundane. It was inspired by the boisterous, crude atmosphere of the Cattle Fair of Bolintin, a small rural settlement not far from Bucharest. At that fair, he witnessed the aggressiveness of kitsch, the jarring cacophony of fake traditionalism and genuine commercialism combined. In an instant, he discovered the obliteration of all the values of the Romanian village and the instauration of a hybrid, grotesque form of progress infused with socialist collectivisation. This was the direct result of an ideology that sought to alter the essence of tradition by destabilising its spiritual values. At the press conference, Purcărete did not go into any details about all these intricacies of recent Romanian history, nor did he claim that the complex cultural references prompted by his staging of *Faust* are unfounded. He simply acknowledged that the dark visual symphony of Walpurgis Night had its origin in that haunting memory. To make that admission, to associate Goethe's play with such an episode of personal biography, is to accept the anthropological contradictions of one's own being, if one comes from a corner of the Balkans where everything is mixed and hardly anything is pure. It is for this reason, because of this impurity of selfhood permeating his theatre,

---

[15] Purcărete is often described in these terms, between his native roots and a very cosmopolitan, global sense of identity. See Jozefina Komporaly, *Radical Revival as Adaptation: Theatre, Politics, Society,* (London: Palgrave Macmillan, 2017), p. 69.

[16] This was at one of the daily press conferences of the Sibiu International Festival, which is in fact a series of panel sessions with the most prominent artists included in the programme of the event.

Image 1 *Faust*, directed by Silviu Purcărete, 'Radu Stanca' National Theatre, 2007. (Photo by Mihaela Marin)

that Purcărete is a Romanian, Eastern European director before being a global one. And indeed, it is for the very same reason that he is not only global, but truly universal.

References

Delgado, Maria M. and Dan Rebellato, *Contemporary European Theatre Directors* (London and New York: Routledge, 2010).
Fabre, Patrick and Sean Hudson, *Silviu Purcărete: Images de théâtre* (Carnières, Belgium: Lansman, 2002).
Holland, Peter, *English Shakespeares* (Cambridge and New York: Cambridge University Press, New York, 2000).
Innes, Christopher and Maria Shevtsova, *The Cambridge Introduction to Theatre Directing* (Cambridge and New York: Cambridge University Press, 2013).
Komporaly, Jozefina, *Radical Revival as Adaptation: Theatre, Politics, Society* (London: Palgrave Macmillan, 2017).
Lehmann, Hans-Thies, *Postdramatic Theatre* (London and New York: Routledge, 2006).

184   O. SAIU

Saiu, Octavian, *In Search of Lost Space* (Bucharest: UNATC Press, 2010).
Shichiji, Eisuke, *Rumania Engeki-ni Miserarete (Lured by Romanian Theatre)* (Tokyo: Serika Shobo, 2013).
New York Magazine, 28 July 1997
The New York Times, 2 July 1997

From the Theatron to the Agora: Changing Concepts of Theatricality in Schilling Árpád's Oeuvre

Gabriella Schuller

THE SUBVERSIVE THEATRE-MAKER (1995–2008)

Árpád Schilling founded the Krétakör Színház (Chalk Circle Theatre) in 1995, shortly before he was accepted into the Theatre and Film Academy. By 2008, when he announced the re-organisation of the Krétakör Theatre, he had directed nineteen productions in total with it, besides his guest directing at other theatres. The originality of his directorial style during this period stemmed from a certain elusiveness: each of his productions displayed a distinct stage language. Some of them brought about a paradigm shift in Hungarian theatre and sealed the director's international reputation.

The turn of the millennium saw the end of an important decade for Hungarian theatre. During the 1990s, many directors worked on deconstructing the canonised dramatic texts and their acting tradition, which

---

G. Schuller (✉)
Artpool Art Research Center—Museum of Fine Arts, Budapest, Hungary

© The Author(s), under exclusive license to Springer Nature
Switzerland AG 2021
K. Stefanova, M. Carlson (eds.), *20 Ground-Breaking Directors of Eastern Europe*, https://doi.org/10.1007/978-3-030-52935-2_15

was the beginning of the postmodern theatrical era—an era severely delayed due to the strict control of theatres during Communism. After 2002, it became once again important for the theatre to reflect on social issues and the events of public life, only now it was done via the postmodern stage language of the so-called director's theatre instead of 1980s realism and "reading between the lines." Árpád Schilling played an important part in this process.

Schilling first got involved in theatre-making as an actor. He was a member of Kerekasztal Színházi Társulás (Roundtable Theatre Association, one of the oldest organisations working in the field of drama education in Hungary) and Arvisura (an amateur theatre group that experimented with ritual and non-verbal theatre in the 1980s, but had lost much of its credibility by the 1990s—as Schilling later recounted in interviews).

Amateur theatre and drama education have a unique history in Hungary. During the Communist era, professional theatres (with some notable exceptions) were obliged to safeguard the literary tradition and that of psychological realism, while the so-called amateur theatres enjoyed a freedom of sorts: they were able to experiment with different acting styles and perform texts that were prohibited in professional theatres. For this reason, the amateur movement brought about many innovations and, even after the change of political system, it remained an inspiring circle.

Schilling founded the Krétakör Theatre without a permanent cast. He maintained it while studying directing at the Theatre and Film Academy, from where he graduated in 2000. Although he had the opportunity to join a public theatre and follow the conventional path of young directors working in the system, he decided to strike out on his own and create his own company that at times would question the system itself. From this time on he worked with a (typically) fixed group. Following the initial success in 2002 that lead to increased financial support, the group was joined by actors who had already made their names in the theatre world: Eszter Csákányi, József Gyabronka and Zoltán Mucsi. Besides them, Annamária Láng, Lilla Sárosdi, Borbála Péterfy, Sándor Terhes, Zsolt Nagy, Gergely Bánki, Zoltán Katona and Roland Rába were the core members of the group; Viktor Bodó and Sándor Csányi also played important roles in the first successful productions.

Schilling had a unique method of working with actors, inspired by the methods of István Somogyi, the leader of Arvisura. The group would go to the countryside and stay secluded from the outside world, and he would train the actors by means of improvisational exercises to be more creative,

FROM THE THEATRON TO THE AGORA: CHANGING CONCEPTS... **187**

to explore their physical and psychical limits, and take responsibility for the final form of the performance. This fruitful relationship led to many remarkable moments for the audience.

It is also important to mention Máté Gáspár, who joined the group in 1998 and played a very important role in its operations and growing success. As a cultural manager with a wealth of practical experience in the field of theatre, he began to use a new model of cooperating with foreign partners and handling productions as projects that had to be successful both artistically and financially. This was a completely new concept and method in Hungary, and one that is widely used by many groups nowadays.

The first big success came with Brecht's *Baal* (1998). It stemmed from the untamed nature of the production: the physical and acrobatic ability of the actors, the explicit and yet natural nudity on the stage, and the cruel portrayal of female and male sexual desire. Since the members of the Apartment theatre on Dohány Street (the first and only group that has experimented with the physical and psychical transgression of intimacy in a theatrical context) had been forced to leave the country at the end of the 1970s, this kind of theatre was a complete novelty to the Hungarian stage. Moreover, *Baal* paved the way for Schilling and Krétakör Theatre to work in the international arena due to its warm reception abroad.

W—Workers' Circus (2001), based on Büchner's *Woyzeck*, followed the same line (though displaying greater maturity) and could be deemed as a performative turning point in Hungarian theatre history in principle. The production incorporated a simple, minimalistic set and props. The actors occupied a small space covered with sand behind a metal grid and all wore the same costume: black trousers/skirt with a white vest. In Schilling's reading of the play, the protagonist (whose name was reduced to a letter) was taken away from "a family paradise" and placed in the hierarchical structure of the military. There he was systematically robbed of his individuality, and he finally took back his freedom through the act of killing his adulterous wife. The storyline and the relationship between the characters were characterised by actions that pushed the performers to their physical limits. For example, the Fool, played by Lilla Sárosdi (naked during the whole performance), ate sand and later popped soap bubbles from her mouth. At the height of his suffering, W (Zsolt Nagy) ran around in circles with heavy stones fixed to the soles of his shoes by tape, his features contorted by a piece of string; the Doctor (Gergely Bánky) was born into the world from a large liquid-filled bag hanging from the ceiling. Finally, W and his wife's intercourse was performed as a kind of acrobatic stunt.

188   G. SCHULLER

The physicality of the actors and their brave or dangerous actions were just as important as the story and characters represented on stage. This raw and energetic style of acting was previously unknown in Hungary and earned the group an international reputation. This production brought about a turning point in the history of the language of Hungarian theatre criticism too: in a roundtable discussion, the invited critics acknowledged that, in order to articulate this kind of theatre, they needed new words and methods.

In 2002, *Hazámhazám* (*Fatherland, My All*—the title in Hungarian is also a wordplay on a famous line from a nineteenth-century patriotic opera) was a revival of the genre of agitprop political theatre. István Tasnádi's play (based on the company's improvisations) provided an overview of Hungarian history between the fall of the Iron Curtain (1989) and the beginning of the new millennium. The events were presented via the life of an average family living on the breadline and via characters representing the state and political parties. The production was highly stylised and easily decodable in its use of simple signs and music. The production was performed in the Capital Circus of Budapest and portrayed the entire history of Hungary in the post-socialist period as a farce. The country was symbolised by a car that was stuck in one spot not only because of the circular-shaped space of the arena, but also thanks to the incompetence of its drivers; that is, the existing ruling parties. This humorous and satirical production (which was equally critical of both political left and right, and ended with a caricature of the politics of the conservative ruling party and its leader) captured the attention of politically committed right-wing supporters, who took the opportunity to throw rotten tomatoes at the actors. For this reason, it can be said that *Hazámhazám* transgressed the lives of ordinary people and the intellectual theatre-going elite, becoming a political act in itself.

In 2003, *Siráj* (*The Seagull*, with a misspelling in the Hungarian title to show the detachment from tradition) played with the inheritance of psychological realism. The production was performed in a small hall of a semi-bohemian club of the socialist era, lending the debate between Kostya (Zsolt Nagy) and his mother (Eszter Csákányi) over new and old forms a resonance outside of the story as well. The acting generally followed the tradition of representing characters in a fictitious story on stage. Yet on numerous occasions, the actors broke the fourth wall by speaking directly to the audience and focusing on the "theatre of everyday life" in minute detail. The chamber-like size of the space and the actors' wearing their own clothes and speaking and gesturing like our contemporaries made the hyperbolism of the situation very apparent.

This deconstructive approach towards Chekhov and realism in principle was not without precedent in Hungary. András Jeles had directed an important *Three Sisters* adaptation with the title *Somewhere in Russia* in 1990, combining the language of psychological realism with his own cruel, archaic and ritual directorial language. However, Schilling's *Seagull* clearly showed that he and his actors could use the language of realism perfectly and touch on important themes that concern the meaning of life and art, and the generational tensions between artists. Also, some minor changes in the text helped to bring the audience closer to the story and the inner lives of the characters.

While the historical perspective of *Fatherland, My All* represented many of the most important historical turning points after the system change in Hungary, *Black Land* (2004) used political theatre to reflect on contemporary issues. The production was framed as a revue where actors in formal evening wear performed small sketches based on pieces of news sent to Schilling's phone by SMS. During the rehearsals the company used these SMSs as a starting point for improvisation. In the production at the end of each scene, often replete with humorous and grotesque episodes, the respective piece of news got displayed on a screen in its original form—in many cases, to shocking effect. For instance, a folk song performed as a choreographed duet provoked much laughter; only later did the audience learn, though, that the original stories concerned suicide by self-immolation. The title was taken from a well-known Hungarian symbolist poem by Mihály Babits published in 1909. In the production it was interpreted in direct reference to Hungary: a black land of corruption where the healthcare system was decimated, the victims of domestic violence were not protected by the judicial system and so on. Every month the audience was invited to speak about the stories and issues in the production by means of a forum, which was an important step in re-politicising Hungarian theatre. Krétakör Theatre performed the play for only two years in Hungary (eighty-eight times), because the original stories began to lose their relevance, making the production less dynamic and meaningful. Nonetheless, it was performed abroad for a further two years, demonstrating both the production's direct political importance and its brilliance as a theatre piece.

In 2007, Schilling directed *hamlet.ws* (with a small "h;" "ws" is an abbreviation for workshop and Shakespeare's name) at Burgtheater,

Vienna. Afterwards the production was (re-)performed in Hungary, by three actors from Krétakör: Roland Rába, József Gyabronkai and Zsolt Nagy. *hamlet.ws* can be considered as a new experience with another form, namely Theatre in Education: though it was—and is—occasionally shown to adult audiences (it was still performed in 2019), it has been mainly performed in secondary schools and universities. Schilling used the translation by Ádám Nádasdy, one of the most brilliant translators of Shakespeare who uses contemporary language to create the same effect on the audience as the Bard did with his original plays. In the production, the three male actors play all the roles, changing parts from time to time; there are neither props nor costumes, nor a set. *hamlet.ws* can be seen as a journey to the origin of theatre: a joyful play, existing for its own sake and devoid of intellectual or humanist "burden" (as in the case of modernist directors). This was Schilling's last directing stint with Krétakör Theatre and stands as a statement about the essence of his theatre.

During this first period, besides his work as a director, Schilling, through his statements and interviews (in many cases together with Máté Gáspár), was also a part of Hungarian intellectual and theatrical public life. In 2002, *W—Workers' Circus* won the prize for best alternative performance, but Schilling refused to accept the prize. He criticised the tradition whereby different prizes go to the best performance shown in "stone theatres" (i.e. public theatres with a permanent building, cast and subsidy) and in independent theatres, arguing that all performances should be nominated in the same category. Via this act of protest, he drew attention to the anomalies of a system where the meaning of words like "alternative theatre," "independent theatre" and "stone theatre," the inheritance of these categories from Communism, as well as their aesthetical or financial context remain unclarified.

In 2002, Schilling and Gáspár applied to the National Theatre, and then withdrew. In an open letter, they criticised the phenomenon and concept of a national theatre that has a representative political function without artistic quality, while at the same time many innovative groups exist from one day to the next.

From 2001 on, Schilling attempted to get a permanent building for Krétakör Theatre, but failed. Though they were able to use this situation to their advantage, performing in a wide variety of places, thereby enriching the interpretation of their productions, it is clear that this was unjust from the perspective of their growing success. Schilling's credibility increased when he criticised the system in which the heads of theatres get appointed on the base of their political loyalty, while independent theatres face increasing financial difficulties from year to year.

As indicated earlier, Schilling's career was in constant ascendency from 1998 until 2008: he was recognised as one of the most innovative directors and he was forthright in his opinion about the financial and organisational structure of post-socialist Hungarian theatre. He was hugely successful with Krétakör Theatre, not only in Hungary but abroad too. Therefore it came as a shock for everyone when, in 2008, Schilling decided to "re-draw" the chalk circle and delete the word "theatre" from the name of the company, choosing to work on projects with invited creators rather than make theatre productions with a permanent cast. In hindsight, it can be seen that this was indeed a very important step in terms of widening our perspective—as an audience and even a society—and searching for new forms of engaging with reality through the medium of arts.

THE SOCIALLY ENGAGED ARTIST (2008–2018)

From 2008 until the end of 2014, Krétakör worked as a foundation supporting cultural projects, many of which took place at its base, a large flat in the centre of Budapest. From the beginning of 2015, Krétakör left this space, reduced the number of staff and announced its intention to concentrate more on international projects. Even so, from the point of view of its performances, this did not constitute a real watershed compared to 2018, when Schilling made public his emigration to France.

When it comes to the 2008–2018 decade, it is essential to take into account the changing political and social context in Hungary. Nowadays it is clear that since the fall of the Iron Curtain none of the ruling parties has contributed substantially to the country's prosperity—that is, the change of system has largely failed to meet citizens' expectations. However, since 2010, when FIDESZ became the governing party for the second time, for many people the social and economic climate has turned even harsher. Besides the cuts in healthcare and public education—sectors that were already struggling—there is an increase in inequality in terms of the re-distribution of resources, resulting in a re-structuring of society. There is an extremely wealthy stratum of society making a fortune from the state, while an increasing number of people from the intelligentsia and the precariat live in worse conditions than before. The judiciary and the media (due to heavy centralisation) are no longer independent;

192   G. SCHULLER

non-governmental organisations are increasingly under threat; while in cultural life funding is provided on the basis of political loyalty.

Schilling and Krétakör took it upon themselves to analyse and protest against these changes, resulting in their constant persecution. At one point Schilling and two other activists were named as a threat to national security by the parliament's special committee.

During this period of his work, Schilling's ideas and creativity were more collaborative in nature. The ensuing productions ran under the name "Krétakör," but this represented a brand rather than a personal stage language. This was an unusual step in contemporary Hungarian theatre, where most directors are eager to make a name for themselves and find a style of their own.

The productions and projects Schilling worked on during this period can be divided into four main categories, although in some cases there is overlap. The first one occurred beyond the concept of theatre: these were events more akin to happenings or rituals for a contemporary audience. In many cases, they involved ordinary people as performers. In spite of the political facet of these performances (concerning memory, cultural identity and relationships within a given group), most of them did not target specific political issues. For the most part, an emphasis was placed on subverting the conventions of theatre. Most of the projects in this category were created at the beginning of the period. As the political situation became increasingly severe, Schilling and Krétakör began to focus on more direct political questions. The productions used theatre as a kind of therapy—a means of healing the alienation in society. For example, in the performative video installation entitled *Gap* (2009), Schilling spoke about his marriage to the actress Lilla Sárosdi, and the expectation and birth of their first children. In *Artproletarz* (2009), he asked three female directors to create community theatre performances on birth, adulthood and old age. In *Mayday* (2009), they dealt with the former cultural inheritance of the mining industry in Pécs through a sci-fi story involving local inhabitants as performers.

Also, Krétakör developed projects in the field of Theatre in Education, aimed at youngsters or underprivileged groups. Schilling cooperated with experts: drama educators and sociologists, of which the Káva Cultural Workshop, AnBlokk Cultural and Social Scientists' Association were the most important partners. In this category, the theatrical devices were mere tools that helped people to understand hierarchical situations and develop critical thinking, taught participants how to represent themselves and so

FROM THE THEATRON TO THE AGORA: CHANGING CONCEPTS... **193**

on. Moreover, the pedagogical role of theatre was emphasised: the enablement and empowerment of the participants (who in many cases reported the effectiveness of the programmes). Working in Theatre in Education productions was a courageous step, because applied theatre had little prestige at the time. However, since 2012 it has enjoyed growing popularity and there is increasing financial support in the field—which is a rare exception in the trend of shrinking subsidies for independent initiatives. And Schilling's activity has largely contributed to this. In *New Spectator Programme* (2010), the members of Káva and Krétakör travelled to Szomolya and Ároktő, two villages in one of the poorest regions of the country, where there is a tension between Hungarians and Romani. They interacted with local inhabitants: besides creating an enjoyable atmosphere, they acted out situations in which Romani people had been humiliated in daily life.

The third category was the closest to conventional theatre, since Schilling did still go on directing theatre productions. Yet they were far from orthodox and had a marked focus on social engagement, dealing with topics such as racism, poverty, exploitation, migration, social tension and inequality. Other features of these productions were the blending of reality and fiction, different kinds of media (film, theatre and circus) and, on occasion, direct communication with the audience. In contrast to other projects, the aesthetic function of theatre was of key importance here. For instance in *Loser* (2014), Schilling's starting point was autobiographical but with a fictional add-on: in the story, he loses his wife and livelihood, eventually deciding to be on good terms with those in power as a way out of his difficulties.

The fourth category of projects was deeply involved in everyday politics and brought an augmented notion of theatricality. Krétakör was involved (not always with Schilling in person) in many performative interventions in public spaces, whether in protest speeches or by making their opinions known in interviews or articles. When the government sent out a questionnaire to citizens (ostensibly asking their opinion on politics), Schilling responded with a series of short videos posted on Facebook in which he played (respectively) a working-class man, an academic and a young person of the intelligentsia. When the Ministry of Culture eventually cut its financial support to Krétakör, Schilling tore up the contract outside of the building, stating (as a speech act) that he would no longer apply for state funding and posting the event on social media. In terms of historical context, these videos exemplify a revival of political performances combined now with social media. Faced with the impossibility of acts "in real life," symbolic ones become increasingly important. Such theatrical events foreground the political function of theatre and theatricality.

Krétakör's last performance in Hungary was *The Day of Fury—the Song of a Foolish Heart* (2015). It tells the story of a nurse whose protests against low salaries and bad working conditions lead to her dismissal. Her life unravels and she commits suicide on her 40th birthday, acknowledging the deleterious effects of her material insecurity on the lives of her mother and daughter. The production also highlighted the topic of unpaid female domestic work, cleaning, nursing, childcare and so on.

Image 1 *Pansion Eden*, directed by Árpád Schilling, Zagrebačko kazalište mladih (Zagreb Youth Theatre), 2018. (Photo by Marco Ercegovic)

What Is Next? (2018–)

It was on 6 May 2018 when the news arrived that Schilling and his family were leaving Hungary due to the lack of solidarity and ongoing persecution. Since then he has directed plays and operas in several other countries and no longer in Hungary. How this nomadic lifestyle and globalisation will influence his directorial language and its reception is still an open question. Yet there can be no doubt that he counts among those who have brought substantial changes to Hungarian theatre and society. Moreover, in 2009 Schilling was awarded the European Theatre Prize for New Theatrical Realities as an acknowledgement of his being one of the most innovative contemporary directors. His commitment to pedagogy, social work and political activism was recognised by the international community when, in 2016, the Krétakör Foundation received the ECF Princess Margaret Award for Culture for "engaging with the changing landscape and social urgencies in today's Hungary and Europe."[1]

References

Bérczes, László, "Critical Theatre in Hungary 1945–1989" in Dragan Klaic (ed), *The Dissident Muse. Critical Theatre in Eastern and Central Europe 1945–1989* (Amsterdam: Theater Instituut Nederland, 1995), pp. 41–73.
https://catalogue.boekman.nl/pub/96-112.pdf (accessed 6 August 2020).
https://www.culturalfoundation.eu/pma-2016 (accessed 6 August 2020).
https://kretakor.eu/en/home-en/ (accessed 6 August 2020).

[1] https://www.culturalfoundation.eu/pma-2016 (accessed 8 February 2020.)

Andrei Şerban: The Search for 'New Forms'

Ion M. Tomuş

Andrei Şerban is definitely one of the most important theatre directors of the second half of the twentieth century. He belongs to theatre's universal heritage by virtue of his artistic strategies as a director and his constant preoccupation with the interpreting of text. In 2006, I had an amazing opportunity to witness an open rehearsal of *The Seagull* at Radu Stanca National Theatre in Sibiu (Romania), directed by Şerban. The production was part of the Sibiu 2007 European Capital of Culture programme and was considered the highlight of the season, together with Goethe's *Faust*, directed by Silviu Purcărete. This particular open rehearsal stays in my theatre emotional memory for two reasons.

The first was the director's vision and concept: Şerban proved to be extraordinarily thorough and meticulous in his search for the play's subtext in order to identify certain specific themes. Theatre within theatre was the foundation on which he had built his production, together with all possible implications that this particular approach could entail: for example, the deconstruction of the theatre mechanism that allowed the audience and the actors to access difficult meanings in the text, context,

---

I. M. Tomuş (✉)
Lucian Blaga University of Sibiu, Sibiu, Romania
e-mail: ion.tomus@ulbsibiu.ro

© The Author(s), under exclusive license to Springer Nature Switzerland AG 2021
K. Stefanova, M. Carlson (eds.), *20 Ground-Breaking Directors of Eastern Europe*, https://doi.org/10.1007/978-3-030-52935-2_16

characters and situations. Also, by using this approach Şerban opened a generous window towards other areas tangential to or interrelated with *The Seagull*: Shakespeare's *Hamlet*, the Oedipus complex, the artists' social status and so on.

Second, since it was an open rehearsal supervised by Andrei Şerban, I had the chance of witnessing another deconstruction of the theatre mechanism: the audience experienced the times when the director stopped the actors and gave spontaneous instructions, demanding more and more elaborate nuances in acting and/or polishing specific moments and scenes. Following these interruptions (there weren't that many), it became obvious that all Şerban wanted from the actors in terms of aesthetics was nothing more than a good old-fashioned expression and uncovering of the subtle nuances in the text and all the subtexts of the play. What made him insist on reading and uncovering the subtexts, on having references and elaborate visual metaphors, on abandoning preconceived apprehensions, on establishing similarities with the present time and pinpointing them through acting, was the specific artistic and social context in which he had placed his *Seagull*: the strong censorship in Romania before 1989 and the Communist dictates on how artists should express themselves.

There are two distinct premises for discussing and studying the work of Şerban: the social and politically specific context of the 1960s in Romania, when he started his career, and the Romanian exile culture in the second half of the twentieth century.

The 1950s were particularly tough years, as the Communist regime recently established to the East of the Iron Curtain was preoccupied with the extermination of all the intellectual, moral and aesthetic values that existed outside of its official propaganda. The 1960s came together with a certain relief and ease, and also with a certain opening towards other countries in Europe. The last years of the decade became a breath of fresh air for all Romanian art and culture. Theatre and the performing arts were granted more freedom by the Communist party and it seemed that the official propaganda and the strict principles of socialist realism were beginning to ease off. Romanian theatre started to become more liberal and somehow to distance itself from the political and social establishment also thanks to a new generation of artists. In the 1960s, they had already been working for about a decade and started to organise themselves into a new "liberal" artistic infrastructure, a fresh, solid and healthy foundation for the new Romanian performing arts.

ANDREI ŞERBAN: THE SEARCH FOR 'NEW FORMS' 199

The most important theatre university in Romania—the Academy for Theatre in Bucharest—was at that time training its students for the specificities of the market: its graduates were rapidly making their names known throughout the country and were becoming important figures in Romanian theatre. It was also famous for its remarkably prescient tutoring of students. Şerban started studying acting there, but after just a year was advised to shift to theatre directing. The famous theatre critic George Banu, one of the most important critical voices in the twentieth century, experienced a similar "detour:" he also started studying acting (in the same class as Andrei Şerban), but was later guided towards theatre studies and theatre criticism.[1]

There is quite an impressive bibliography on Şerban, so there is no urgent need to review his career and his most important works. It may be far more interesting to prove that Şerban's theatre's main focus is on the continuous (re-)interpretation of texts, on the search for new nuances and also on making use of each possible subtext.

Given that in the background of Şerban's formation as a theatre director were the dogmas of socialist realism, the stereotypes of an old bourgeoisie from between the wars and the empty ambitions of a new bourgeoisie preoccupied by the formal aspects of culture and the arts, he had to escape and to seek refuge and a "safe haven" in discovering new means of expression.

Hence, it is important to emphasise Şerban's preoccupation with travelling and discovering different cultures. One of his first productions (*I Am Not the Eiffel Tower*) was part of a festival in Zagreb, in former Yugoslavia. This proved to be an excellent chance for the very young director, as La MaMa's Ellen Stewart saw the show. For the political and cultural context of the 1960s, such a trip abroad, even only to the East of the Iron Curtain, represented an extraordinary opportunity. Such was also the case with Şerban's visit to Wrocław in 1967, when he met Jerzy Grotowski.

During those years an important part of the Romanian intellectual elite chose the hard path of exile, as happened all over Eastern Europe. Beyond the personal life-jacket exile can offer, it granted Şerban the extraordinary chance to reach creative freedom, to get to know new artistic environments, to meet some of the most iconic names in the performing arts and to take part in artistic dialogue. In brief, exile granted him the chance to achieve intellectual and artistic effervescence and project his own vision

---

[1] Andrei Şerban, *O biografie* (Iaşi: Polirom, 2006) p. 30.

200 I. M. TOMUŞ

before a daring audience. The popular culture of the twentieth century created a certain cliché of an exiled artist: lonely, without strong contacts with the new cultural environment, and preoccupied with creating a "closet" type of literature and art. Thanks to the nature of his profession, Şerban did not become part of this cliché and cultural pattern. His exile was communicative, as he was very preoccupied with the social sphere of his existence.

His first productions in the USA (*Medea* in 1972, *Electra* in 1973, *The Trojan Women* in 1974 and *Fragments of a Greek Trilogy* in 1974) generated a lot of questions related to the specificity of the cultural context of the 1970s. Would the ancient Greek universe still be up to date for the American audience? Would the actors and the audience consider the tragedy as a personal experience, not only an intellectual one? Of course, these questions were not all new, but they proved to be challenging. Şerban's strategy of creating his shows at La MaMa was to make the actors look at the text like a musical score that needs interpretation. He demanded from them discipline and commitment in communicating the inner mythical essence of the characters. Using an ancient language on stage made them reach a condensed type of acting and generated new possibilities for performing. Thus, the premise of interpreting the text as a possibility for bypassing and getting rid of the Romanian socialist realism propaganda of the 1960s proved to be a very useful tool for Şerban just a decade later, in the free artistic world of the USA. American multiculturalism, on the other hand, opened new and useful doors for working with actors, for discovering hidden but fundamental meanings in Greek tragedies—and led to success. Audiences were enthusiastic and it seemed that the fundamental truths in the ancient tragedies were being (re-)discovered.

I'd like to again emphasise Şerban's interest in travelling. After the huge success of his *Medea* in New York at the beginning of 1973, he travelled for three months to and in remote and exotic places and cultural environments: Japan and Bali attracted him, as others before, because of the large number of hidden and old meanings in these specific cultures.

Many theatre reviews from the 1970s note the impact *The Greek Trilogy* had on Şerban's relation to ancient theatre. Reading them, one can get a glimpse of that specific feeling of novelty and freshness the reviewers had. For instance, Ed Menta's *Behind the Curtain: Andrei Şerban in the American Theatre* focuses on two fundamental issues. First, the impact of the plays on the American avant-garde: the function of speech is described as being of crucial importance. At the same time, the *Trilogy* is seen as having helped the actors to improve their standards in training, since despite their good physical and vocal training they had the propensity for outperforming and going beyond the American system of creating realistic theatre conventions on stage. Second, according to Ed Menta, the *Trilogy* is—deliberately or not—a coherent apogee of the disparate theories of Antonin Artaud regarding sound, music, gesture, dance and violent stage image. Thus, Artaud's theories seem to have been implemented in practice: theatre becoming ceremonial rather than psychological, creating poetry by abstracting life itself rather than imitating it. Șerban's exploration of the strange sounds of dead ancient languages is perceived as excellent proof of this poetical mutation and also of his constant preoccupation with interpretation.

During the 1980s, the theatre critic and reviewer Mel Gussow talked about *new fabulism* as the contemporary attempt to transform the ancient myths into sapient stories.[2] Ed Menta also mentions new fabulism in regard with Șerban's work. Back in the 1980s, new fabulism meant using ancient myths and stories and encapsulating them in a bright, colourful style, altogether with masks, dance and also elements from circus.[3] This resulted in a mix of theatre conventions from cultural and geographical areas that seemed to be incompatible (kabuki, bunraku, commedia dell'arte, etc.). Now, more than thirty years later, re-evaluating the concept is unavoidable, since Șerban's theatre has become more complex and diverse, and also because art and society have been subject to many changes and transformations. We know very well that in 2020 the world is a global village and physical distances hardly have any impact on art. Now, when I write this text during the COVID-19 pandemic, we are living in a strange truth: people are isolated in their homes, but they have never been more connected, although they are worlds (or blocks) apart. (Online) communication breaks all the cultural boundaries. This special mix of the new fabulism is something we now take for granted. In the 1980s, postmodernism was going hand in hand with all the complex agglutination of trends in theatre and was saying that the truth is not truly

---

[2] Mel Gussow, Fabulist 'Serpent Woman,' *The New York Times*, 30 December 1988, https://www.nytimes.com/1988/12/30/theater/review-theater-fabulist-serpent-woman.html (accessed on 8 August 2020)

[3] Ed Menta, Andrei Șerban. *Lumea magică din spatele cortinei* (Bucharest: Unitext Publishing House, 1999), p. 100.

202   I. M. TOMUȘ

knowable. The audience and the artists alike were looking for their own personal truth.

For Șerban, the process of searching for his own personal truth was a journey that consisted (and consists) not of the overall productions, but of the daily rehearsals and also of the continuous quest for finding and keeping the sacred truths of life. It seems that his predisposition for minutely interpreting all the layers of a specific text can be viewed in the context of postmodernism. The interpretation itself is a process that contains improvisation, resuming specific key moments and highlighting some details or nuances, overlaying the different individual truths of the actors. In this context, everything is about overlapping artistic truths, such as kabuki and commedia dell'arte, as two different cultural layers that will be assumed by the actor. Andrei Șerban knows very well how to juggle all these layers and, most importantly, he knows how to make the actors look deep into their interior layers of significations. His theatre is even ampler, as sometimes all these layers comprise dead languages in which the actors need to act in order to create strong emotions in the audience.

If a common denominator (or more than just one) of Andrei Șerban's achievements in theatre is to be found, special attention has to be paid to what he has created since 1990, when he returned to Romania. As in the rest of Eastern Europe, in the first part of the 1990s the theatres were empty, contrary to the expectation that with the newly conquered freedom and the finally departed censorship they would be full. Instead, Romanians had moved their social dialogue to the streets and the media. Only towards the end of the 1990s did the artistic and social freedom start to be understood and assumed by the society with all its inner implications of responsibility.

In 1990 Andrei Șerban became general manager of the Romanian National Theatre in Bucharest. He was new to the Romanian post-Communist realities (as we all were back then), but he was full of enthusiasm, had a world-wide reputation and was always surrounded by the world's greatest artists. His programme was very ambitious and courageous, especially against the background of the then artistic establishment. In the long term, he wanted to hold workshops in which young actors, directors and set designers would collaborate and work together. He wanted to open a secondary small venue for young and bold artists, and had a plan to create a theatre school and affiliate it with the theatre. In the short term, he revived *The Greek Trilogy*. It was a huge success in Bucharest and became a reference for Romanian and European theatre. It was the first major Romanian theatre project after forty years of Communism and was quite innovative: the actors left the stage and played in dark, strange, forgotten hallways in the huge building of the National Theatre in Bucharest. Priscilla Smith and Valois Mickens came to Bucharest and worked with the Romanian cast: they passed on the vocal techniques so imperative for the project.

The reasons for having *The Greek Trilogy* in Bucharest were scarcely personal. Of course, the production was the highlight of Şerban's oeuvre, yet now, three decades later, the trilogy seems like a true re-start of contemporary Romanian theatre. The project was a return to particular origins. It was a re-interpretation of a personal reference point from the beginning of his career, only this time he was back home in a presumably familiar cultural environment. Then, in a wider and deeper sense, it was a journey back to the origins of theatre, to its essential and intimate truths, as they were put together by the ancients. The Romanian audience embraced the project and it is still considered the best production since 1990. At the same time, though, the new freedom in Romania was poorly understood and assimilated. Şerban realised that he could not change the situation as general manager of the Romanian National Theatre, so he decided to pursue his international career further. The productions he directed later on in Romania have their own stories and represent a certain landmark.

So one possible common denominator for Şerban's work after 1990 in Romania is the special environment he had to face in the local artistic establishment. For sure, the theatres here usually have smaller budgets than in the West. Accordingly, he knew very well how to manage this apparent disadvantage: he continued to be interested in the interpretation of texts and in looking for "new forms." Thus, this is not a reference just to Treplev, Chekhov's famous character, as it gains new, wider meanings.

Şerban's preoccupation with the text's interpretation goes along with a particular kind of fine and discrete theatricality. This may be the reason why the special technique of theatre within theatre in *The Seagull* I had the pleasure to see in Sibiu in 2006 was larger than just the scene in which Nina acts Treplev's bizarre play. Şerban's many adaptations of *The Seagull* (he directed it five times: in Tokyo, Japan, at the Shiki Theatre Company, 1980; at the Public Theater in New York, 1981; at "Radu Stanca" National Theater in Sibiu, Romania, 2007; at the Lenfest Center for the Arts of Columbia University, 2017; and in Bucharest, at Unteatru, 2018) may be justified not only by his apparent reluctance to view the play as a "comedy,"

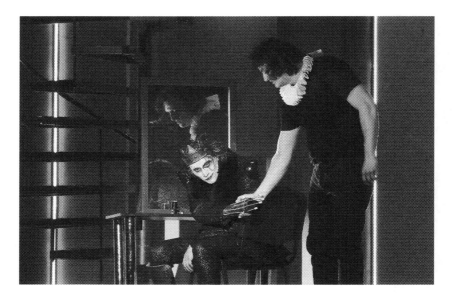

Image 1 *Richard III*, directed by Andrei Șerban, Bulandra, 2019. (Photo by Mihaela Marin)

according to its strange subtitle. Theatre within theatre is a mechanism that generates maximum attention in the audience, who need to concentrate on the viewers on stage rather than on the performers in the play within the play. So Treplev is far more interested in his mother's reaction, since he expects some kind of confirmation of his identity as a human being (son) and as an artist.

In fact, in Șerban's work there is a constant search for a certain artistic "beyond," difficult to access but potentially generous in meaning. His long exile, together with his life story, may be another key to understanding his amazing work. He recently donated all his archive to the Museum of Romanian Books and Exile in Craiova, Romania. This is not a sign that his work may be over. Not a chance! It is rather an acknowledgement that spiritually he belongs to Eastern Europe, with all its peculiarities and specific problems. Andrei Șerban's permanent search for and concern with texts' interpretation is similar to the way all the great characters in his productions are searching for their inner truths.

REFERENCES

Gussow, Mel (1988). *Fabulist 'Serpent Woman,'* The New York Times (Dec. 30, 1988).

Menta, Ed (1995). *The Magic World Behind the Curtain: Andrei Serban in the American Theatre (Artists and Issues in the Theatre)* (New York: Peter Lang, 1955).

Şerban, Andrei (2006). O *biografie* (Iaşi: Polirom, 2006).

Beauty by Instinct or Daniel Špinar's Theatre of Style

Michal Zahálka

Few buildings in Prague stand out as much as the National Theatre's New Stage: an imposing structure of pure 1980s brutalism, all glass and steel, planted in the city's glamorous historic centre right next to the National's neorenaissance main venue. Its interiors are filled with ridiculous amounts of green Cuban marble, supposedly received as payment for Cuba's debt to Czechoslovakia. It was meant to be a triumph of theatre architecture, a brilliantly equipped venue easily transformable from proscenium stage to arena and back, but ever since its 1983 opening it has been proving itself a battleground for all theatre-makers: technical problems aplenty, including lousy acoustics, and chairs in the auditorium that are so soft and comfortable that it's nearly impossible not to fall asleep. These chairs, upholstered in dark green leatherette to match all the marble, and the very nature of this space are a fitting backdrop to *For Beauty* (2019), the latest production by the artistic director of the National Theatre's Drama Company—Daniel Špinar (b.1979).

M. Zahálka (✉)
Arts and Theatre Institute, Prague, Czech Republic

© The Author(s), under exclusive license to Springer Nature Switzerland AG 2021
K. Stefanova, M. Carlson (eds.), *20 Ground-Breaking Directors of Eastern Europe*, https://doi.org/10.1007/978-3-030-52935-2_17

Špinar divides public opinion, not unlike the aforementioned building: more conservative audiences tend to consider his aesthetics too radical for the National Theatre's solemn stature. *For Beauty*—among other themes—addresses just these claims. It is a love/hate letter to theatre itself, drawing from essays and remarks by the legendary director Karel Hugo Hilar, who headed the National Theatre's Drama Company in the 1920s and 1930s and was a pioneer of expressionism and modernism in Czech theatre. The audience is seated on-stage, facing the sea of those chairs, patched over the years with bits of leather in various other shades of green. On top of the chairs, a replica of the huge chandelier from the National's historic auditorium lies half-broken, tilted, but still capable of glowing. From under the chairs, a number of actresses gradually appear, all dressed up to resemble Hilar, with his trademark hat and suit: the director multiplied, fighting various fights—against his collaborators, the theatre, society and, not least, himself. It is more than clear that Špinar sees himself as Hilar's spiritual successor. Both share a reputation of a violent temper, obsession with detail and total devotion to the theatre. And while it is not easy to draw a direct parallel between two directors set apart by almost a century, Špinar does find—in Hilar's writings—places that exactly pertain to his own works. A considerable part of the script effectively consists of a Hilarian manifesto, with lines such as:

> *Theatre should not be a "teacher of mankind", its nanny,*
> *the witness to its silliness,*
> *but its spark, its impulse and its fire!*
> *[…]*
> *The spectator needs no dictionaries,*
> *no rules,*
> *he seeks great BEAUTY by instinct.*[1]

These words are particularly fitting as a description of Špinar's aesthetic roots. Unlike his predecessor Michal Dočekal, who directed plays like Lucy Prebble's *ENRON* during his 12-year tenure, and unlike a number of his own-generation peers, like Jan Frič, Jiří Havelka, Jiří Adámek or

---

[1] Karel Hugo Hilar and Daniel Špinar, *Za krásu* (Prague: Národní divadlo, 2019), p. 83. [Script published in a programme book. Transl. by M.Z.]

Petra Tejnorová, Špinar is manifestly uninterested in overtly political theatre. When, on a rare occasion, he did stage a distinctly political text—Moira Buffini's *Welcome to Thebes* (2018) or, to a lesser extent, Mike Bartlett's *Earthquakes in London* (2015)—the productions were far from his best. He is, first and foremost, a director of style and emotion.

AN ACTORS' DIRECTOR?

"He wasn't easy on the actors. He always demanded the impossible. Actors would say he only uses them as material," says Špinar about Hilar in *For Beauty*. "His best instinct was for women. He could inspire actresses to extraordinary performances."[2] Again, speaking of Hilar he also speaks of himself: while not all actors necessarily enjoy being in a Špinar production, he decidedly has the ability to put the actor in the centre, even in very stylised pieces of theatre. As a result, a number of actors (and especially actresses) have garnered awards and nominations for their work with him. There is a reason for Špinar's sensibility for acting. Before he studied Directing at Prague's DAMU (Theatre Faculty of the Academy of Performing Arts), he graduated as an actor and was even awarded for his role in Mark Ravenhill's *Some Explicit Polaroids* (2002). Still, having already directed his first production (a three-character adaptation of *Dangerous Liaisons*), he decided not to pursue an acting career. He studied together with a number of his subsequent collaborators, such as the director Jan Frič (currently a resident director at the National Theatre), the playwright Petr Kolečko or the dramaturg Jana Slouková. Their chief pedagogue was the director Jan Nebeský, a key figure in postmodernist Czech theatre of the 1980s and 1990s, who continues to create his wild, daring and strangely spiritual productions. Parallel to his studies, Špinar also ran an independent theatre company, Valmet, where he would collaborate with his fellow students as well as with artists from other generations, and his first major breakthrough as a director came even before his graduation project. With Valmet, he staged Sophocles' *Electra* (2006) in a new translation that he co-authored with classical philologist Alena Sarkissian and dramaturg Lenka Chválová. It was well received and foreshadowed the key qualities of Špinar's productions of classical drama in general: a distinctive single set providing a strong metaphorical backdrop (in *Electra*, it was a white upholstered cell in a psychiatric ward), a focus

[2] Ibid., p. 82.

210   M. ZAHÁLKA

on the emotionality of dramatic situations, and a daring work with a text that nevertheless retains its spirit.

After *Electra*, Špinar began to work in various theatres across the country as a guest director. Still as a student, he was invited to the Petr Bezruč Theatre in the eastern, industrial city of Ostrava to stage Petr Kolečko's original play *Britney Goes to Heaven* (2006). Here he could give vent to his penchant for pop culture, something he and Kolečko definitely share: Špinar's productions in general tend to feature pop songs or quote iconic movies, no matter whether they are based on a new play or on a literary classic. Such was the case with his graduation project at the Academy's theatre DISK: *Brothers (Karamazov)* (2007), an adaptation he himself made of Dostoyevsky's novel. Much praised for its stellar acting ensemble (with the character of Father Karamazov omitted in favour of a single-generation cast) and noted for Špinar's abundance of ideas, the production drew the critics' attention to an extent very rare for a student's work.

What followed was perhaps the production least characteristic of Špinar's directorial style: in 2007, on the National Theatre's small stage, he staged Marguerite Duras' *L'Amante anglaise* to rave reviews. The play consists of two hour-long dialogues at a single table and he did just that, abstaining from any explicit visual metaphors or wild ideas and concentrating on the actors, words and emotions. Špinar revealed himself—for once—as an actors' director in the most literal sense. Usually, it is somewhat more complicated.

Staging Heartbreak

Before joining the National Theatre as resident director in 2014, Špinar spent most of his career freelancing. The singular exception was his brief, yet notable stint at Prague's Vinohrady Theatre, a large drama theatre well known for its conservative staging tradition and audiences, mostly accustomed to drawing-room comedies. Špinar had a two-year contract, but ended up directing only two productions before a somewhat bitter departure. Nevertheless, the first one—Büchner's jarring *Woyzeck* (2009)—was a major critical success and secured him the position of a top-league director. The stage was almost bare, dominated by a huge, brightly lit billboard showing the face of a mindlessly cheerful blonde beauty with red lips, a telephone and a catchword saying: "Hello, everyone." It was a paradoxical metaphor for a world in which the lead character seeks in vain anyone who would listen to him, a world of a timeless, yet contemporary periphery,

BEAUTY BY INSTINCT OR DANIEL ŠPINAR'S THEATRE OF STYLE   211

where human wrecks hang around aimlessly. Woyzeck came across as an almost philosophical character, seeking some sense in a world ruled by ugliness and cruelty. There were rave reviews (one went so far as to state that the production was a "resurrection for the Vinohrady theatre").[3] Yet, when Špinar accepted the Alfréd Radok Award for Best Production of 2009, he announced that the show would close within weeks, about a year and some fourteen performances after it opened. His second production— of Schiller's *Mary Stuart*—was a modest commercial success (chiefly thanks to the popularity of its leading lady). While he has repeatedly proclaimed his love for grand theatre, gilded arches and the like, Špinar didn't find his audience at the Vinohrady Theatre and went back to freelancing, citing his disappointment with a theatre that asked him to stage a radical production, but backed off when the audience's reactions were, expectedly, underwhelming.

As is the custom in Czech theatre, much of this freelance work was done outside of Prague. Actually, some regional theatres have nation-wide importance, often surpassing the ambitions of theatres in larger centres. This has long been the case for the Klicpera Theatre in Hradec Králové. Špinar's first production there was before his departure from the Vinohrady Theatre: a flamboyant staging of Shakespeare's *The Winter's Tale* (2008), all in furs and on skis, wild ideas and disco music aplenty. Since then he has become a frequent collaborator of Klicpera, teaming up with Jana Slouková, who became the theatre's dramaturg and then artistic head. The results were Lermontov's *Masquerade* (2009), deemed by a reviewer to have "ambition, opinion, and style;"[4] a haunting, surreally psychological horror called *Morgiana* (2012, based on the eponymous novel by Alexander Grin and its film adaptation by Juraj Herz); and finally—and most importantly—*The Beggar's Opera* (2013) by Václav Havel.

Even in his homeland, Havel's plays are rarely staged by directors from Špinar's generation, since their verbose nature and the author's wish that they be performed in a simple, text-based manner provide very little material for visual and metaphorical interpretations. Updating the story from the eighteenth century to the 1970s (when Havel wrote his play), Špinar found a fitting style that played with the 1970s of the capitalist USA (with Macheath stylised as half-Travolta, half-Elvis; an overall well-to-do Mafioso

---

[3] Marie Reslová, "Vojcek je zmrtvýchvstání Vinohrad," *Hospodářské noviny*, 14: 4 (2009), p. 9.

[4] Petr Mareček, "Panoptikum lačných hyen," *MF Dnes*, 31: 10(2009), p. 35.

style for the Peachum family; and a jazzy soundtrack) and of the Communist Czechoslovakia (with chief of police Lockit dressed in a period uniform and playing with a remote-control Communist police toy car). The backdrop, made from concrete with visible bullet holes, had a neon sign as its centrepiece: *LOVE*, which is also a Czech slang word (of Romani origin) meaning "money." Špinar managed to transform the clash of various principles of amorality, depicted in the text, into an image, and thus showcased his ability to retain the spirit and content of a play without necessarily heeding every direction and wish of the author. In the case of an author as iconic as Václav Havel, this is something quite rare.

Another regional playhouse Špinar often visited was the City Theatre in Kladno. After Zoltán Egressy's contemporary play *Portugal* (2009), he staged yet another classic—Chekhov's *Seagull* (2010). Cutting the text to a bare minimum, Špinar focused on non-psychological means of expression. Marie Reslová wrote: "All one needs is an intonation, a gesture, a posture, a look—and we see a character bare naked, stripped from their illusion or socially masked lie."[5] This *Seagull* was immensely theatrical—stressing the fact that theatre itself is one of the key subjects of the play. As is unrequited love in many forms: at one point, the plywood backdrop (dominated once again by a set of shining letters saying Чайка—seagull—in Russian) got sprayed over with Trigorin's famous line: "If you ever need my life, come and take it." The production was a major critical success and was featured at important festivals, but local audiences were much less enthusiastic and it closed fairly quickly. Špinar's next production there, *Bel-Ami* (2013), his own adaptation of the famous Maupassant novel, was another critical and festival hit. A simple, yet enthralling portrayal of a cynical social climber, it was set in the modern day—and thus spoke volumes about our own cynicism and careerism. The main scenographical metaphor was a photographer's studio: the entire story was played out for the lenses of a camera, setting the overall theme of the importance of media and self-presentation in today's world. In a typically ironical gesture, Špinar gave his loveless lead character a massive fluffy cushion in the shape of a heart, and his selection of obscure French 1970s and 1980s pop songs was equally fitting. Then came *Marie Antoinette* by David Adjmi (2014)—a tour de force of style—and *The Night Butterfly* (2014), based on a 1941 Czech movie of the same name—light, entertaining, parodical, yet retaining some real emotions.

[5] Marie Reslová, "Racek," *Hospodářské noviny*, 9: 6 (2010), p. 1.

At a time when Brno's Reduta Theatre (then a separate unit of Brno's National Theatre, independent of its drama company) was gaining renown for the productions of its resident director Jan Mikulášek, Špinar was also invited to direct. After revisiting Laclos's novel with *Valmont* (2011), he staged *Anna Karenina* (2012) in a contemporary adaptation by Armin Petras. Done in a semi-cabaret style, it was a cruel, ironic look at modern-day relationships, portraying love as a succession of selfish acts and as an ultimately fatal obsession. All of the characters' extreme emotions were given equally extreme expressions: Anna swinging on a huge chandelier, or stripped only to her stockings, or digging in a pile of mud. Her infatuation with Vronsky happened at a drunken party in a disco bar, with music (played by a live DJ present on-stage) so loud that it was almost impossible to speak. For her final monologue, she was surrounded by a number of microphones on stands, providing the feeling of a tragic stand-up gig. In the end, she slammed herself against a seemingly solid white wall in the background (with inscriptions, much like walls in the lavatories of cheap pubs)—and disappeared. This haunting, touching, daring production (decidedly among Špinar's very best) was, however, somewhat overshadowed by Mikulášek's successes at the Reduta. Soon afterwards, Špinar returned for the third and final time with *Cabaret Kafka* (2012), an uncharacteristically abstract production based on Kafka's *Letter to My Father*, subsequently given the Josef Balvín Award, handed out to the best productions of a German-language text. But while the latter two productions transferred to Prague's Balustrade Theatre when Reduta's team moved there, Špinar himself never directed there again.

Upon leaving the Vinohrady ensemble, Špinar began collaborating with another Prague venue, the 300-seat Švanda Theatre. Already established as an apt, daring director of classical drama with a penchant for strong female characters, he first staged *Hedda Gabler* (2010). Ironically set in a room with a kitschy fjord-themed wallpaper, the production was just as light and not immersed in traditional Ibsenian psychologism as the stagings of Špinar's teacher Jan Nebeský and was deemed "positively mesmerizing."[6] Špinar's 2011 return to the National Theatre, staging an adaptation of the Ernst Lubitsch wartime comedy *To Be or Not to Be*

---

[6] James Waling, "Riveting realism," *The Prague Post*, 10: 3 (2010), p. B5.

(2011), was less convincing, with critics judging that the material's nature was ill-suited to Špinar's much more avant-garde theatrical style.[7]

Špinar's second (and, as of today, final) production at the Švanda Theatre was perhaps his greatest hit: *Hamlet* (2013), which is still playing to full houses. Set in a chateau-turned-museum, Denmark seems to have become a stale exhibition of itself. Hamlet (played by actor and TV teen idol Patrik Děrgel) is a thoroughly modern young man—not unphilosophical, but just as much immersed in the emotional and sexual issues of his age. In fact, the entire production is highly accessible for a young audience, while the spirit of the text is retained. Even when Špinar's jokes appear light-headed at first glance, there tends to be a strategy behind them: for instance, when Hamlet and Horatio famously discuss that "Time is out of joint," they share a joint of marijuana. What follows is the apparition of Hamlet's father's ghost. Another cleverly twisted scene has Hamlet distribute the texts of the play-within-the-play to the members of the court, with Gertrude and Claudius forced to stage-read the lines of their fictional counterparts. Upon seeing *Hamlet* at the Pilsen Divadlo festival, Kalina Stefanova wrote that Špinar's work has mastered something she calls "constructive deconstruction."[8] Even though Špinar may play with the text, and sometimes even rather radically, he always takes care to tell the story and convey emotion—an aspect that has made *Hamlet* a particularly powerful production, explaining its longevity.

Fun and Games

Špinar also has a record of staging contemporary texts, working with independent theatres and even collaborating on original creations. While still a student at DAMU, he collaborated with Jana Slouková on an original script called *HOMO 06* (2006, revived in 2008 at A Studio Rubín, a tiny, fashionable, independent venue in Prague's historic centre). Discussing contemporary queer life, topics and aesthetics, often taken to extremes, is in general a frequent feature of Špinar's productions. Especially in his early years, he was also a frequent collaborator of the Letí Theatre, an independent company founded in 2005 to promote contemporary drama—his

[7] Jana Machalická, "Špinarovo nedorozumění v Národním," *Lidové noviny*, 1: 3 (2011), p. 10.

[8] Kalina Stefanova, "To Be Or Not To Be .... At Once," MASKA 175–176 (winter-spring 2015/2016).

particular hit there was Mark Ravenhill's notorious *Mother Clap's Molly House*.

Špinar had a particularly notable collaboration with A Studio Rubín. During Petr Kolečko's stint as Rubín's artistic director (2008–2015), Špinar directed numerous times there. He co-authored Kolečko's trilogy dedicated to three female characters of classic drama and mythology: *Causa Salome* (from the Bible; 2009), *Causa Medea* (2010) and *Causa Maryša* (from the eponymous Czech classical drama by the Mrštík Brothers; 2011). *Causa Medea* was particularly clever, relocating the story of Medea's revenge into a current Czech apartment and mixing contemporary language with the elevated Euripidesian verse. At once hilariously funny and heartbreakingly sad, this one-act show demonstrated Špinar's and Kolečko's shared penchant for strong female heroines and a mix of seriousness and humour, even when approaching dark matters.

AT THE HELM

When, in 2014, the position of artistic director of the National Theatre's Drama Company was vacated, Daniel Špinar applied with a concept entitled New Blood and was seen as the most daring option among the three candidates. After he was appointed to the post, in close collaboration, among others, with his dramaturg-in-chief Marta Ljubková, they fairly swiftly changed the dramaturgy, much of the company and—first and foremost—the selection of invited directors. Since the 2015/16 season, the roster of guest directors has been made up exclusively of Špinar's generation of peers, which did not necessarily mean the theatre would lack variety.

There were three productions Špinar directed in the National Theatre during the final seasons of his predecessor's tenure. In the Čapek Brothers' 1921 expressionist allegory *The World We Live In* (2014),[9] he remained fairly faithful to the original play, only slightly updating it to have the various kinds of insects portray contemporary society. Set in a modern indoor location but featuring 1920s costumes, his *Othello* (2014) showcased his forte primarily as a director of strong acting performances, especially female ones. Magdaléna Borová's self-confident, active Desdemona, well aware of her female charms, was a revealing departure from the character's

---

[9] Incidentally (or perhaps not really), the play was first produced at the National Theatre by Špinar's role model today, the aforementioned Karel Hugo Hilar.

216 M. ZAHÁLKA

usual timidity, but also from Borová's frequent, almost stereotypical good-girl stage persona. Less convincing was Špinar's attempt at a commentary on common-day racism, present in the added character of a clown who stumbled around the stage half-drunkenly shouting racist jokes and remarks. The idea behind this addition didn't seem quite clear, especially since Othello (as portrayed by Karel Dobrý) was white. Marie Reslová still judged the production to have "European parametres," stating that it "shows the way the National's Drama Company could and should be heading."[10] The third one, Mike Bartlett's *Earthquakes in London* (2015), was less of a success—Radmila Hrdinová claimed that Špinar seemed to miss the point of the text, which was drastically reduced to the extent that it was hard to follow even basic relationships between characters, and that the characters' lack of motivation made the production politically much more straightforward than Bartlett's play.[11]

Špinar's first production as the company's head was another contemporary text, yet it was not political but much more intimate: Anja Hilling's *Protection*, given a new Czech title that translates as *Together/Alone* (2015). Špinar, along with set designer Lucia Škandíková, placed the action of the three stories about strange romantic encounters between three couples inside a plexiglass box, providing a strange voyeuristic experience and contrasting with the intimate content of the dialogues. Even though the production was quite compact and the text obviously more suitable for Špinar's needs, it opened to lukewarm reviews. It is, in fact, a sort of tradition that once a critically revered artist becomes head of the National, they very quickly lose support and credit, and have to fight to prove themselves worthy all over again. This was the case for Dočekal, Špinar's predecessor, as well as a long line of previous artistic directors, including—unsurprisingly—Karel Hugo Hilar.[12] I myself have to admit that to me Špinar hasn't quite topped the significant successes of his pre-National Theatre era, most notably *Hamlet* or *Anna Karenina*.

Not that there haven't been exceptions. In 2016 came *Manon Lescaut* (2016), a staging of the 1940 verse-drama by poet Vítězslav Nezval, based on the eponymous novel by Abbé Prévost. Once again after his Čapek production, Špinar found himself in the sacrosanct historic building of the National staging a national classic, this time even more iconic—the play's

[10] Marie Reslová, "Anatomie zločinu," *Hospodářské noviny*, 7: 1 (2014), p. 18.
[11] Radmila Hrdinová, "Ekologické tři sestry na Nové scéně," *Právo*, 4: 4 (2015).
[12] This, too, is naturally also a topic of *For Beauty*.

popularity in the Czech Republic is equally comparable to that of *Romeo and Juliet* and some of the verses can be recited by just about everyone. Telling the story of a young nobleman's fatal infatuation with a beautiful, yet ultimately treacherous girl, Nezval's text is essentially an extremely well-crafted bit of kitsch, designed as a crowd-pleaser for a nation in the hard times of the Nazi oppression. It seems to me that Špinar also aimed to create an audience favourite, with a lavish set and a popular young cast. In many ways, he succeeded: the production still sells out and while it is obviously not meant to be too provocative, some of the choices are very clever in finding just the right amount of novelty (including queer topics and visuality) not to turn away too many viewers, yet remaining loyal to the director's general aesthetics.

Špinar's own adaptation of Austen's *Pride and Prejudice* (2016) also drew the public's attention (more so than critical praise), as—to a lesser extent—did his staging of *A Midsummer Night's Dream* (2016), featuring an enormous trampoline and exchanging the Players for accident-prone employees of a modern-day wedding agency.

Chekhov's *Three Sisters* (2016), directed in just a couple of weeks after the show's original director Štěpán Pácl fell ill during rehearsals,[13] was a departure from the Chekhovian staging tradition towards a highly expressionistic style. Given that the cast included some of the country's finest actors facing a new stylistic challenge, this was in itself a treat. At the same time the production included multiple nods at previous stagings of *Three Sisters*. The final scene consisted of all the characters listening to a recording of Olga's final monologue from a celebrated 1982 production by Ivan Rajmont, a well-loved director and one of Špinar's predecessors who had recently died (as had Marie Spurná who had played Olga).

Returning to contemporary British drama, in 2017 Špinar staged Rebecca Lenkiewicz's somewhat neo-Chekhovian relationship drama *The Night Season*, providing a long-deserved starring part to Jana Preissová, one of the ensemble's doyennes.[14] His next was Moira Buffini's *Welcome to Thebes* (2018), a production that garnered a number of rave reviews,

---

[13] Pácl's planned production was, paradoxically, itself a replacement. The originally announced show was meant to be a project called *Kafka* by Kirill Serebrennikov, withdrawn from the plan with little explanation; budget disputes were alleged, but it also shows that unlike Dočekal (who regularly invited foreign directors and who was also originally behind Serebrennikov's invitation), Špinar doesn't see international collaborations as much of a priority.

[14] Also in 2017 came *Frailty, Thy Name Is Woman*, an unusual production starring five of the theatre's ageing female stars—with Špinar writing a script using their own public personas.

Image 1 *Hamlet*, directed by Daniel Špinar, Švanda Theatre, 2013, Patrik Děrgel as Hamlet and Marek Pospíchal as Horatio, (Photo by Alena Hrbková)

praising its presentation of political topics—personally, though, I tend to agree with Radmila Hrdinová's less enthusiastic view that it ends up merely repeating superficially sketched themes.[15] Those two productions seem to show quite clearly that Špinar is much more at ease with the intimate than the political.

Luckily, his following production was also highly emotional. It was an adaptation of Stephan Zweig's novel *Beware of Pity* (2018).[16] This story of a young soldier's tragic relationship with a handicapped girl, motivated partly by pity and partly by prospects of social climbing, serves as the basis for an emotionally strong, highly stylised, at times almost horror-like show; in particular the girl, as portrayed by Pavlína Štorková, is stylised almost as a freaky doll, while not lacking in emotional depth. The set

---

[15] Radmila Hrdinová, "Vítejte ve zpustošeném světě," *Právo*, 1: 6 (2018).
[16] The original German title as well as its Czech translation, however, translate into English as *The Heart's Impatience*.

makes full use of the theatre's revolving stage, while the costumes suggest the atmosphere of pre-World War I Vienna (not unlike *The Night Butterfly*), creating a visually stunning experience. Indeed a piece of theatre of style and theatre of beauty—leading to Špinar's latest show and therefore to the starting point of this chapter.[17]

It is too early to give an overall judgement of Daniel Špinar's National Theatre era (recently his contract was renewed for three additional seasons). It is, however, safe to say that, at the age of 40, he is one of the most distinctive creators of contemporary Czech theatre, for reasons this chapter has attempted to convey.[18]

REFERENCES

Hrdinová, Radmila, "Ekologické tři sestry na Nové scéně," *Právo*, 4. 4. 2015.
———, "Vítejte ve zpustošeném světě," *Právo*, 1. 6. 2018.
Hilar, Karel Hugo and Daniel Špinar, *Za krásu* (Prague: Národní divadlo, 2019).
Machalická, Jana, "Špinarovo nedorozumění v Národním," *Lidové noviny*, 1. 3. 2011.
Mareček, Petr, "Panoptikum lačných hyen," *MF Dnes*, 31. 10. 2009.
Reslová, Marie, "Anatomie zločinu," *Hospodářské noviny*, 7. 1. 2014.
———, "Racek," *Hospodářské noviny*, 9. 6. 2010.
———, "Vojcek je zmrtvýchvstání Vinohrad," *Hospodářské noviny*, 14. 4. 2009.
Stefanova, Kalina, "To Be Or Not To Be…. At Once," *Maska*, winter/spring 2015/16.
Waling, James, "Riveting realism," *The Prague Post*, 10. 3. 2010.

---

[17] It should also be noted that during his time at the National, Špinar has also twice worked with its Opera Company, directing Janáček's *From the House of the Dead* (2015) and Britten's *Billy Budd* (2018). Both productions were highly successful.

[18] Those interested in Daniel Špinar's work are encouraged to visit his personal presentation at www.danielspinar.cz, featuring a comprehensive archive of his productions, including photographs. Also in English.

Włodzimierz Staniewski: (Re-)Constructing Traditions and Archetypes

Tomasz Wiśniewski

STANIEWSKI'S SPECIAL STATUS

Unlike most other directors discussed in this volume, Włodzimierz Staniewski was already a widely recognised figure in theatrical circles around the world at the fall of the Iron Curtain in 1989. With his "Gardzienice" Theatre[1] he had developed an innovative method of actor training, proposed an original concept of rural *Expeditions*, and argued for the origins of theatrical practices in the so-called *Gatherings*. Established in the eponymous village of Gardzienice in eastern Poland, the company comprised a collective that blended together a nearly ethnographical fascination with verbal, vocal and folk music traditions, with a strong sense of alternative performativity. Between 1977, when the company was founded,

---

[1] It is generally assumed in Polish scholarship that in order to distinguish the name of the village Gardzienice from "Gardzienice" Theatre the former should be used without—and the latter with—quotation marks.

T. Wiśniewski (✉)
University of Gdańsk, Gdańsk, Poland
e-mail: tomasz.wisniewski@ug.edu.pl

© The Author(s), under exclusive license to Springer Nature Switzerland AG 2021
K. Stefanova, M. Carlson (eds.), *20 Ground-Breaking Directors of Eastern Europe*, https://doi.org/10.1007/978-3-030-52935-2_18

222   T. WIŚNIEWSKI

and 1989, Staniewski directed only three productions, but they were all praised for their intensity of creative vision. It is symptomatic that throughout the initial twelve years of its existence, "Gardzienice" Theatre not only visited culturally undervalued villages in Poland, Italy and Ukraine, but also toured in major urban centres such as New York, Baltimore, Stockholm, Amsterdam, Toronto and others.[2] At that time Staniewski had also formulated his major artistic manifestos, including *Towards the New Natural Environment for Theatre* (1979).[3]

It is not surprising, then, that the social and political reality after 1989 mounted something of a challenge for the alternative formula of theatrical practices developed by the early Staniewski. Paul Allain's conclusion to his book *Gardzienice: Polish Theatre in Transition* concisely formulates this problem:

> Staniewski now faces challenges of another order. The burden of managing a larger, older and more unwieldy group, the pressures of touring, combined with the stresses of sustaining success on the international festival market, take their toll. To confront these problems and respond to rapid changes perhaps demands more strength than the previous battle with Communism which had a clear agenda. From the present transitional confusion a clarity and strength might grow [...]. Gardzienice's artistic practices and theorising now lack the coherence and purpose they formerly possessed as they move towards more open structures. [...] Theatre is formed in response to the social and political environment in which it exists. As yet, Gardzienice have not fully defined their place in contemporary Poland, but the process has begun and the seeds have been planted.[4]

Published in 1997, the manuscript of Allain's book was completed by November 1995, so its argument captures some of the most urgent matters of the early years of transformation. It should be stressed, however, that what seemed unresolved at that time is clarified at present. We now know that, even though his early principles have evolved a lot by 2019, Staniewski has managed to successfully accommodate himself to the new

---

[2] A detailed chronology of Staniewski's activities between 1976 and 1996 is presented in Zbigniew Taranienko, *Gardzienice: Praktyki teatralne Włodzimierza Staniewskiego* (Lublin: Test, 1997), pp. 409–24. See also: gardzienice.org/en/Calendar.html (accessed on 30 August 2019).

[3] Staniewski's *Towards the New Natural Environment for Theatre* was delivered at the Congress of ITI that was held in Sofia (Bulgaria) in 1979.

[4] Paul Allain, *Gardzienice: Polish Theatre in Transition* (London: Routledge, 1997), p. 136.

economic, social and political situation. He has staged new productions, has collaborated with national and international institutions and, above all, has established what he claims to be his lifetime achievement: the European Centre for Theatrical Practices "Gardzienice." His successful implementation of European Union funding exemplifies the transformations that have been underway in this part of Europe since 1989.[5]

Artistic ideas developed in a world that no longer exists—and I mean by this both rural Poland of the late 1970s and 1980s and the Communist regime in general—have found their ultimate expression in a completely re-built palace that is now a part of the spectacular Centre. A film, entitled *Carrying GARDZIENICE from the Ruins*[6] documents Staniewski's strenuous work when re-constructing the palace. Aware of controversies caused by the stark contrast between the harsh conditions that originally inspired his work and the comfort offered by the premises of "Gardzienice" at present, Staniewski seems annoyed by nostalgic glorification of the past. For him, material gentrification does not necessarily condition diminishing spiritual creativity.[7]

BIOGRAPHICAL BACKGROUND[8]

Staniewski was born in 1950 in Bardo Śląskie, a small town located some eighty kilometres south of Wrocław. Between 1969 and 1971, as a student of the Jagiellonian University in Kraków, he got involved in the alternative student theatre circles of Teatr Stu. Staniewski's leading role in the famous production of *Spadanie [Falling]*, directed by Krzysztof Jasiński, attracted Jerzy Grotowski's attention. The subsequent invitation to Staniewski—to join Teatr Laboratorium—was a significant turning point in his career, as he moved from an ambitious student theatre to a company headed by one of the leading figures in global alternative theatre. Between 1971 and 1975 Staniewski was involved in the work of Grotowski's Teatr Laboratorium in Wrocław, where he contributed to para-theatrical

---

[5] See: pois.gardzienice.org/en/ and http://gardzienice.org/en/Carrying-GARDZIENICE-from-the-ruins.html (Both accessed on 30 September 2019).

[6] http://gardzienice.org/en/Carrying-GARDZIENICE-from-the-ruins.html (accessed on 20 November 2019).

[7] See Tomasz Wiśniewski and Dominik Gac, "Three conversations with Włodzimierz Staniewski," *Konteksty*, 1–2 (2018), especially pp. 330–33.

[8] Based on culture.pl (Accessed on 30 August 2019), Taranienko, *Gardzienice* and Allain, *Gardzienice*.

224   T. WIŚNIEWSKI

research, including actions conducted within the framework of the Complex Research Program (e.g. *Święto [Holiday]*). In 1975 Staniewski was the leader in one of *Ule [Beehives]* that offered one day para-theatrical activities open to the general public.[9] He turned into one of the closest collaborators of Grotowski and was considered his successor. However, dissatisfied with the hermetic style of Grotowski's work, Staniewski decided to quit the company and pursue an independent artistic career. At the time, this was considered a rather controversial choice.

Several months afterwards, in August 1977, Staniewski presented the results of his theatre workshop to the local community of Gardzienice and on 18 January 1978 formally registered the Theatre Association "Gardzienice."[10] The provincial character of the formation allowed for experiments that were immediately recognised as innovative, since they merged strong physical and vocal training with *Expeditions* to rural communities that quickly developed into a trademark of his company. The scale of Staniewski's success could well be illustrated by the praise expressed by Richard Gough and Judie Christie in 1989:

> We believe the Gardzienice Theatre Association is one of the most extraordinary theatre companies in the world today; working at odds with any current trend—post modern, autobiographic, dispassionate—pursuing an artistic endeavour that merges with a "Life-Project," they seek the naturally creative and responsive act where the human being taps all its resources and radiates an incandescent energy.[11]

Indeed, at the time of the failing Communist regime, Staniewski provided the ground for provocative, collective and autonomous creativity. Not only did he challenge the overall stagnancy of the time, he also managed to attain an international renown that depended neither on petrifying well-established patterns nor on fulfilling expectations of Western audiences. Yet, as the above quotation proves, his artistic voice was generally perceived as genuine and autonomous.

---

[9] http://www.grotowski.net/en/encyclopedia/ule-beehives   (Accessed   on   30 August 2019)

[10] Taranienko, *Gardzienice*, pp. 409–10.

[11] Richard Gough and Judie Christie, "Gardzienice," a brochure issued by the Centre for Performance Research, Cardiff in 1989, p. 3.

Isolation from major cultural centres was vital for developing the specificity of "Gardzienice."[12] On the one hand, the geographical remoteness allowed for more liberal treatment of the artistic experiments by the political authorities and, on the other hand, it helped the formation of an ensemble not exposed to the cultural or economic temptations that are the norm in an urban environment. At the same time, such remoteness was never an obstacle for carrying out collaboration with international institutions, including the Royal Shakespeare Company, the Meyerhold Centre in Moscow, Yale University, Stanford University, the Getty Center in Los Angeles, the Barbican Centre in London and Rose Bruford College.[13] This has certainly been a rare achievement for an Eastern European theatre-maker detached from metropolitan life. Yet, such remoteness incited some dangers to the ethical conduct within this rigidly hierarchical company.

EXPEDITIONS AND GATHERINGS[14]

There is a general consensus among scholars that the original understanding of the *Expeditions* and *Gatherings* undertaken by "Gardzienice" as theatrical practices was not only formative for all its later activities, but also decisive for establishing its international status.[15] The idea of *Expeditions* was quite simple. Rooted in the Romantic tradition of searching for the real in native culture,[16] it was additionally inspired by Mikhail Bakhtin's concept of the carnival.[17] These were physically demanding, if collectively rewarding, walking tours through rural areas. Organised on a monthly basis, they would last a few days. In principle, the selection of areas to be explored was motivated by the cultural remoteness of a destination, since

[12] Paul Allain notes that the telephone was installed in the theatre space of "Gardzienice" as late as 1991 (*Gardzienice*, p. 23).

[13] See: gardzienice.org/en/Completed-projects.html (Accessed on 30 August 2019).

[14] This part is based on Taranienko, *Gardzienice*, pp. 52–129 and Allain, *Gardzienice*, pp. 21–44.

[15] Taranienko, *Gardzienice*, p. 52.

[16] For further discussion of impact of the Polish Romantic tradition on Staniewski see: Allain, *Gardzienice*, pp. 9–20.

[17] "The company therefore organised Expeditions to rural areas which became a time of carnival—a microcosmic existence separated from the everyday, with its own laws, priorities and forms. They used the carnival's images, objectives and anti-structures in a practical way, recognising how its philosophical frames embraced their marginal oppositional stance" (Allain, *Gardzienice*, p. 35).

the company intended to preserve native songs, stories and gestures that were in danger of extinction. Although they were meticulously planned, the *Expeditions* were generally open to a variety of events that might occur on a journey. As numerous testimonies illustrate, practical activities, such as preparing food, contacts with locals, organising *Gatherings* and above all cross-country walking, were accompanied by singing, training and other activities that helped to establish professional relations within the ensemble.

Taranienko claims that, even if it passed unnoticed by those involved in the *Expeditions*, their motivation was of a strictly theatrical character.[18] Staniewski probed the genuine communicative potential preserved in closed societies in which conventionalised theatrical forms were simply unknown. For this reason, the *Expeditions* culminated in *Gatherings*. These meetings aimed at mutual cultural exchange between the company and the villagers. On the one hand, "Gardzienice" offered a more or less improvised performance—full of singing, dancing and robust jokes—and, on the other hand, the villagers, especially the older ones, were asked to share songs they knew from the past. Needless to say, these were unprecedented events for the local community, so the reactions would range from enthusiasm through disinterest to hostility.

It is vital to differentiate the *Expeditions* and *Gatherings* that were conducted in eastern Poland between 1977 and 1979 from later similar undertakings by "Gardzienice." The latter adapted by then conventionalised structures to international and urban contexts.[19] Originally, "Gardzienice" aimed at "discovering an archaic gesture, an expression of genuine emotion, a source of the voice and unusual singing"[20] so as to use the gathered material for performative purposes by the company and individual actors. Notably, the early *Expeditions* and *Gatherings* were conducted in the Polish language, which significantly increased immediate contact between all involved parties and diminished the sense of cultural exploitation. For obvious reasons, their *Expeditions* in other parts of the world required a translator and those conducted in an urban environment acquired a more conventional explanatory character.

---

[18] Taranienko, *Gardzienice*, p. 52.

[19] Allain discusses the distinction between rural and urban *Gatherings* (*Gardzienice*, p. 40).

[20] Taranienko, *Gardzienice*, p. 55.

Evening Performance[21]

Physical and vocal mastery of the ensemble gathered by Staniewski was most evident in the culminating event of each *Gathering*, namely a presentation of the provocative, ever evolving and loosely structured *Spektakl wieczorny* (*Evening Performance*). Conceived in 1977 and performed till 1986, it provided the basis for a presentation of short etudes, inspired by *The Life of Gargantua and of Pantagruel* by François Rabelais, that were mixed with folk and religious songs, chants, as well as quotations from Polish Romantic drama. The *Evening Performance* was enormously physical, energetic and visually spectacular, and some episodes required circus acrobatics. Its main intention was to provoke an active response from the villagers, so it explored emotional rather than intellectual communication. These fluctuating performances would intentionally differ from one evening to another, which not only cultivated the actors' alertness, but also responded to the conditions dominating on a particular day.

The *Evening Performance* started at dusk and was usually presented outdoors in carefully adapted venues, such as meadows, homesteads or hills. As part of a *Gathering*, the spectacle was framed by the arrival and departure of performers carrying a cart that in the course of an *Expedition* "was used to transport belongings."[22] The playing area was demarcated by the light of a fire and an audience remained in darkness. There were standard elements of scenography, such as a large canvas and wooden platforms, but in general the performance was exposed to the natural scenery that was well known to the villagers. Such a spatio-temporal arrangement revealed the predilection of "Gardzienice" for communicative immediacy, structural fluctuation and the carnivalesque. Indeed, critics univocally stress that the *Evening Performance*'s subject matter, acting style and structure were profoundly indebted to the concept of laughter as understood by Mikhail Bakhtin. Staniewski, in turn, underlined that he found its annihilating power particularly attractive at a time of gloomily fossilised official hierarchies imposed by the Communist regime.

---

[21] Details on *Evening Performance* after Taranienko, *Gardzienice*, pp. 190–205, and Allain, *Gardzienice*. pp. 80–82.

[22] Allain, *Gardzienice*, p. 80.

228   T. WIŚNIEWSKI

SORCERY[23]

Gusła [Sorcery] was a short performance of between twenty and forty minutes that premiered in May 1981 in a hermitage in Italy. Based on the masterpiece of Polish Romanticism *Dziady [Forefathers' Eve]*, by Adam Mickiewicz, it canonised major features of the performative style of "Gardzienice." While exploring contrasting rhythms of all sorts, *Sorcery* interweaved sparse excerpts of the play with folk songs, dances and other sounds and movements that had been gathered during *Expeditions* or adapted from various traditions. Such a combination referred to the multicultural heritage of the region and corresponded to the rite of meeting the dead. A particular function was given to Hasidic spinning, which epitomised the overwhelming pulsation and ecstatic vitality of the collective body formed by the ensemble. Staniewski attempted to reflect the cultural context that inspired Mickiewicz.

Devised for an indoor space, *Sorcery* was addressed to rural and urban audiences alike. Whereas in the former case it would accompany an *Evening Performance* as the climax of a *Gathering*, in the latter one it was presented to sophisticated spectators at international festivals and usually contributed to a general presentation of the company's work. Critics stressed the role of Staniewski, whose directions contributed to the actual shape of the performance and mediated between the realities of the stage and of the audience. The episodic composition allowed for stylistic and semantic fluctuation—its ecstatic corporeal joviality was gradually replaced by manifestations of darker imagery and black humour. As Taranienko concludes, *Sorcery* was a kind of performance that "immensely engaged emotions, imagination and intellect of an audience" and "long afterwards remained with its spectators."[24] This has certainly remained true in other works by the company.

AVVAKUM[25]

In 1983, "Gardzienice" presented *Żywot protopopa Awwakuma (The Life of Archpriest Avvakum)*—a gloomy, ecstatic and frightening performance inspired by an autobiographical account of Avvakum Petrovich, a

[23] Details on *Sorcery* after Taranienko, *Gardzienice*, pp. 205–225, and Allain, *Gardzienice*, pp. 82–84.
[24] Taranienko, *Gardzienice*, p. 225.
[25] Details after Taranienko, *Gardzienice*, pp. 225–266, and Allain, *Gardzienice*, pp. 85–92.

seventeenth-century religious orthodox archpriest from Russia who fought for the preservation of old rituals and was imprisoned, exiled and finally burnt at the stake. Abundant in "confusion, ambiguity and violence,"[26] the performance was devised at the time of Martial Law in Poland, but premiered in a remote church in Italy. *Avvakum* lasted between thirty-five and forty-five minutes and was performed till the mid-1990s, when its tone became lighter and more carnivalesque.[27] Divided into "thirteen segments of action,"[28] the performance was more rigorously composed than the previous ones, and yet left room for fluctuations. At the time it was an innovative type of adaptation, as verbal and narrative accuracy gave ground to physical explication of the anguish and suffering that characterised the original.

Claustrophobic as it was, the playing area alluded to the sacred space of an orthodox church where the "closeness effect" achieved its peak. Scarce, if powerful, visuals made extensive use of Russian Orthodox imagery, including *iconostasis*, a cross, a wheel, a ladder, a gate, bread and candles. The latter provided the only light in this overwhelmingly dark performance. Intensified "contrastive rhythm" developed into the compositional dominant, unifying all aspects of the performance.

At this point it was clear that Staniewski's artistic language was fully developed. It was idiosyncratic and communicative, physical and emotional, straightforward but rooted in intellectual exploration, and made use of all available means of performative expression—be they of sonic, visual or verbal provenance.

CARMINA BURANA[29]

Carmina Burana was first presented in 1990, after the fall of the Iron Curtain, in a newly re-built "outhouse" (*szopa*) in Gardzienice, which as few as sixty spectators could attend. In this performance Staniewski shifted his interests to Western medieval culture and searched for inspiration in *Carmina Burana*, a volume comprising thirteenth-century secular and religious poems in Latin and German, the Celtic story of Tristan and Isolde, and the story of Merlin and Vivian that was part of the Arthurian

---

[26] Allain, *Gardzienice*, p. 88.
[27] Michał Boni quoted in Taranienko, *Gardzienice*, p.257.
[28] Allain, *Gardzienice*, p. 86.
[29] Details after Taranienko, *Gardzienice*, pp. 266–292, and Allain, *Gardzienice*, pp. 92–100.

230   T. WIŚNIEWSKI

cycle. The performance explored all aspects of passionate, physical and spiritual love in a rather universal manner, and included additional allusions to *Macbeth* and the Bible. Spatial imagery was structured upon the sign of a cross, alluded to a church interior, explored the juxtaposition between the vertical and the horizontal, and was visually dominated by a wooden wheel of fortune/torture that determined the lot of the characters.

Burdened with enormous semiotic potential, the world model was confronted with the surrounding reality of Gardzienice by a compositional framework. In the opening scene, a live horse was brought onto the stage by Merlin through the main doors, and at the end the audience was made to leave into the surrounding grassy fields through the same entrance. Powerful ensemble acting included elements of physical acrobatics and further proved the mastery of the cast's individual and collective performative skills. Allain succinctly describes its main features: "*Carmina Burana* is lyrical and moving, rousing and comic, is paced with variety and speed and builds to a thrilling conclusion. It has a dynamic physical score and acrobatic sequences."[30] As in other performances by "Gardzienice," the sonic dimension was decisive for the integrity of diverse and at times kaleidoscopic elements of all sorts. In an attempt to artistically recreate "the spirit of medieval music," Staniewski not only collaborated with his usual partners, led by Tomasz Rodowicz, but also arranged collaboration with a multi-instrumental musician, Maciej Rychły.

VISIONS OF ANTIQUITY

The spectacular success of *Carmina Burana* led to yet another significant turning point in the evolution of "Gardzienice." With the next five productions Staniewski offered creative explorations of various artefacts from Ancient Greek and Roman cultures. Although the selection of the material was motivated by the previously established methods of work—with a clear predilection for intermingling ludic and official elements—the focus on European cultural roots had far-reaching consequences for the artistic techniques and aesthetic aspirations of "Gardzienice."

During the winter of 1994 an international ensemble (which in the company's jargon is referred to as a "Constellation") started rehearsing *Metamorfozy albo złoty osioł (Metamorphosis or the Golden Ass)*—a text by Apuleius of Madarus, written in Latin at the time when Christianity was

---

[30] Allain, *Gardzienice*, p. 98.

about to subdue ancient culture.[31] The initial version of the performance was presented in public in 1997. Described as "a theatrical essay"—a genre that was indebted to the convention of "work in progress"—*Metamorphosis* used an episodic structure in which strongly musical etudes were supported by vocal and dance elements and framed by meta-theatrical commentary. The musical score was a result of a creative "re-construction" of ancient scales and rhythms by Maciej Rychły, which marked a departure from the company's earlier practices. Although it spurred an intense academic and critical dispute concerning research accuracy, the production was generally praised for its "organic acting" (Wyka), "ecstatic joyfulness" (Benedykowicz) and inventive capturing of the spirit of ancient music and culture (Lengauer).[32]

In *Electra*, which premiered in January 2004 in Berlin, Staniewski further explored the possibilities opened up by the genre of "theatrical essay."[33] Inspired by Euripides' tragedy, the production developed a language of gestures, called *cheironomia*, which was re-constructed from images of figures on Ancient Greek vases and other kinds of artwork. Yet again, it was music that was the driving force of the production. It was created by Maciej Rychły, whose premise was that antique vigour should be found in its echoes that have been preserved in the contemporary music of the Balkans, the Carpathian Mountains and Ukraine. Whereas Alison Hodge found that the main protagonist in *Electra* was "Euripides himself with his obsessions about the secret of the woman's nature and the mystery of the way in which a crime spiral gets wound." Michael Billington concluded that "Gardzienice" "remind us that Greek tragedy was intended as an all-out, total theatre experience rather than a restrained poetic event."[34]

The premiere performances of *Ifigenia w A…* (*Iphigenia in A[ulis]*), another production inspired by Euripides, further proved the international

---

[31] For a more detailed discussion of *Metamorphosis*, see the whole volume of *Konteksty* 1–4, 2001. See also the CD *Matamorfozy. Music of Ancient Greece* issued by "Gardzienice" in 2001.

[32] Quotations from "A Conversation about 'Gardzienice' and *Metamorphoses*" published in *Konteksty* 1–4 (2001) pp. 194–239.

[33] For a detailed discussion of *Electra*, see gardzienice.org/en/ELEKTRA.html (accessed on 30 August 2019) and Krzysztof Bieliński, *Staniewski—Gardzienice,—Antyk* (Wołowiec: Czarne, 2015), pp. 64–101.

[34] Both quotations after: gardzienice.org/en/ELEKTRA.html (accessed on 30 August 2019).

renown of "Gardzienice," as it took place in October 2007 in the celebrated La MaMa Theatre in New York.[35] The music was composed by Zygmunt Konieczny, a famous Polish composer, and ancient songs were adapted by Maciej Rychły. The cast included famous Polish actors, such as Andrzej Seweryn and Krzysztof Globisz. In this multi-lingual production, in which Polish, English and Ancient Greek languages intertwined, the main theme was sacrifice as a means to preserve human values. In his director's note, Staniewski laid emphasis on the contemporary relevance of the ancient tragedy and this was one of the most important traces of the piece:

> When we push aside the antiquarian historicity, we shall see characters which seem to have been taken from today's life. The final ritual of sacrifice is an act of blind violence, a forced faith behind which stands indoctrination, poisonous instigation, a defeat of those strong in words and postures but weak in spirit.[36]

The contemporary relevance of myth was further explored in the next production of "Gardzienice": *Ifigenia w T...* (*Iphigenia in T[auris]*), first presented in 2010 in Warsaw.[37] Staniewski referred to the historical prominence of Crimea—that is, Tauris—for his concept of Euro-Asian tensions, which became startlingly relevant after the annexation of the peninsula in 2014 by Russia. Another contemporary critical reference was the plane crash of 10 April 2010, when ninety-six members of a Polish official delegation to Katyń, including the Polish president, died. The production's immediate sociological and political engagement was as unusual for Staniewski's theatre language as the extensive use of audiovisual projections. Yet, as Edith Hall's observation proves, the production achieved a more universal dimension:

> The concept of the ritual journey is [...] integral to *Iphigenia in Tauris*. [...] And the journeys of this play are not only between physical spaces. The audience is invited to ponder the connection between the idea of surviving psychological ordeals and surviving hazardous journeys; in ritual terms, the

---

[35] For a further discussion on *Iphigenia in A...*, see: http://gardzienice.org/en/IPHIGENIA-AT-A....html (accessed on 30 August 2019) and Bieliński, *Gardzienice*, pp. 14–63.

[36] In: Bieliński, *Gardzienice*, p. 63.

[37] For details on *Iphigenia in T...* see: gardzienice.org/en/IPHIGENIA-IN-T....html (accessed on 30 August 2019) and Bieliński, *Gardzienice*, pp. 170–221.

journey also represents the transition from childhood to adulthood for both sexes, a journey which in the cases of Iphigenia and Orestes can now finally be achieved despite its previous cruel disruptions.[38]

In 2013 Staniewski presented *Oratorium pytyjskie (Pythian Oratorio)*,[39] the last part of the cycle exploring ancient culture. Inspired by the myth of Pythia/Sibyl/Cassandra, it used phrases from "The Commandments of the Seven," which as "the earliest known didactic collection of Greek wisdom [...] served Greek education for more than twenty full centuries."[40] Archetypal juxtaposition of male and female parts of the chorus culminated in a ritualistic, if orgiastic, dance "around the *omphalos*, the carved navel-stone marking the centre of the known world at Delphi."[41] Set at the roots of Ancient Greek culture, around the sixth century BC, *Pythian Oratorio* reveals Staniewski's fascination with the "mantic perspective" and other forms of witchcraft and sorcery.[42]

THE WEDDING, OR "GARDZIENICE" TODAY

After a one-off presentation of *Tagore, Tagore*—a chronological sequence of "scenic sketches" depicting the life and work of Rabindranath Tagore—during a festival celebrating the links between India and Poland, organised by "Gardzienice" in September 2014,[43] Staniewski directed *The Wedding: Wyspiański—Malczewski—Konieczny*. It premiered on 29 September 2017 as part of an event devoted to the fortieth anniversary of the company's founding.[44] Culminating many of his previous achievements, *Staniewski* integrated textual, visual and sonic elements in a vigorous and densely structured theatre piece, which endowed the literary masterpiece of Polish modernism, by Stanisław Wyspiański, with a mythical dimension rooted in Greek antiquity. Wyspiański's *The Wedding* has an oneiric plotline with a

---

[38] In: Bieliński, *Gardzienice*, p. 12.

[39] For further discussion on *Pythian Oratorio*, see: gardzienice.org/en/PYTHIAN-ORATORIO.html (accessed on 30 August, 2019) and Bieliński, *Gardzienice*, pp. 126–169.

[40] http://gardzienice.org/en/PYTHIAN-ORATORIO.html (accessed on 30 August 2019).

[41] Edith Hall, "'Only what is lost can be possessed for ever:' The Transcendent Theatre of Gardzienice," in Bieliński, *Gardzienice*, p. 13.

[42] See: http://gardzienice.org/en/Mantic-Perspectives.html (accessed on 30 August 2019).

[43] See: gardzienice.org/en/2014-IV-F.W.T..html (accessed on 30 August 2019).

[44] See: gardzienice.org/en/40th-Anniversary-Festival.html and thetheatretimes.com/celebrating-40th-anniversary-gardzienice/ (Both accessed on 30 August 2019).

central theme devoted to the artistic fascination with peasant culture. Endowed with auto-referential elements, Staniewski's production is an interesting retrospective commentary on his own artistic programme and original postulate to find a natural environment for contemporary theatre in the native culture preserved in rural Poland and other parts of the world.

Image 1 *The Wedding*, directed by Włodzimierz Staniewski, "Gardzienice," 2017, Photo by Bartłomiej Górniak

The cast of *The Wedding* exemplifies an increasing contribution of graduates of the Academy for Theatre Practices.[45] Established by "Gardzienice" in September 1997 and coordinated by Mariusz Gołaj, the Academy provides young enthusiasts of alternative theatre from Poland and abroad with experience of training methods and theatrical techniques developed over the years by Włodzimierz Staniewski and his company. As the present "Constellation" of "Gardzienice" proves, some graduates are invited to become members of the ensemble, while others contribute to numerous festivals, symposia and other events organised by the company.

A retrospective overview of the over forty-year long history of "Gardzienice" confirms the collective character of Staniewski's theatrical enterprise. In such an environment, a confrontation of strong personalities was intrinsic, if at times controversial, in each phase of the company's evolution. Artists such as Mariusz Gołaj, Tomasz Rodowicz, Jadwiga Rodowicz, Dorota Porowska, Elżbieta Rojek, Anna Zubrzycki, Grzegorz Bral, Krzysztof Czyżewski, Piotr Borowski, Henryk Andruszko, Mariusz Mrowca, Joanna Holcgreber, Jarosław Fret, Anna Dąbrowska, Maciej Gorczyński and others contributed significantly to the development of the idiosyncratic performative language of "Gardzienice." Some of them left the company to successfully pursue their own professional paths. Examples abound: the "Borderland of Arts, Cultures and Nations" Centre was established by Czyżewski in Sejny, Theatre Association "Chorea" by Rodowicz, Porowska and Rojek in Łódź, "Song of the Goat Theatre" by Bral and Zubrzycki in Wrocław, Theatre "ZAR" by Fret in Wrocław, and Theatre Studium by Borowski in Warsaw. Notwithstanding such impressive development of these careers, one should be aware of the recently revealed accusations concerning ethical conduct of Staniewski in approach to the female members of the company. Serious as they are, these testimonies not only point to significant transformations in functioning of theatre companies but also contribute to the forthcoming re-evaluation of the history of alternative theatre in Poland.[46]

---

[45] See: "Praktyki edukacyjne 'Gardzienic'" in Wojciech Dudzik and Zbigniew Taranienko (eds.), *Teatr obiecany*, (Warsaw: Academica, 2008), pp.107–130.

[46] For details of the ongoing case see: https://e-teatr.pl/mobbing-i-molestowanie-w-opt-gardzienice-i371 (accessed on 1 December 2020).

REFERENCES

Allain, Paul, *Gardzienice: Polish Theatre in Transition* (London: Routledge, 1997).

Bieliński, Krzysztof, *Staniewski—Gardzienice,—Antyk* (Wołowiec: Czarne, 2015).

Dudzik, Wojciech and Zbigniew Taranienko (eds.), *Teatr obiecany*, (Warsaw: Academica, 2008).

"Gardzienice," Official Website, www.gardzienice.org/en (accessed on 30 August 2019).

Gough, Richard and Judie Christie, "Gardzienice," a brochure issued by the Centre for Performance Research, Cardiff in 1989.

Hall, Edith, "'Only what is lost can be possessed for ever:' The Transcendent Theatre of Gardzienice," in Bieliński, *Gardzienice*, p. 13.

Hodge, Allison, and Włodzimierz Staniewski, *Hidden Territories: The Theatre of Gardzienice*, (London: Routledge, 2003).

Taranienko, Zbigniew, *Gardzienice: Praktyki teatralne Włodzimierza Staniewskie*go (Lublin: Test, 1997).

Wiśniewski, Tomasz and Dominik Gac, "Three conversations with Włodzimierz Staniewski," *Konteksty*, 1–2 (2018).

Rimas Tuminas: A Poetic View of Theatre

Dmitry Trubotchkin

The career of the Lithuanian director Rimas Tuminas (born on 20 January 1952) is connected with two countries and two cultures—Lithuania and Russia. It happened that in the second half of the 1970s, as a student who was making his first steps in the profession, Tuminas had to take regular long-distance train journeys: from Vilnius to Moscow and back. It was along this road, connecting two different capitals and two different cultures, that his theatre world-view was formed. It is not by accident that in the majority of Tuminas' productions the journey motif is personified in a character with a large, weathered suitcase.

The ability to see the new and unknown in the ordinary, to leave settled life and embark on a voyage for the sake of acquiring knowledge, is still valid for Tuminas. Also, similarly to the founders of Lithuanian theatre, he preserves the time-honoured connection with Lithuanian mythology and a belief in the spirituality of nature. A man of refined taste, Tuminas at the same time resembles a farm owner—with his affinity for the soil, for the things which begin in it, grow and flourish, which need care and tactful commitment. A farm owner is like a large-crowned thick tree, deeply rooted in the ground yet looking into the sky and delicately reacting with

---

D. Trubotchkin (✉)
State Institute for Art Studies, Graduate School of Performing Arts, Russian Institute of Theatre Arts (GITIS), Moscow, Russia

© The Author(s), under exclusive license to Springer Nature Switzerland AG 2021
K. Stefanova, M. Carlson (eds.), *20 Ground-Breaking Directors of Eastern Europe*, https://doi.org/10.1007/978-3-030-52935-2_19

its thick branches to any gust of the wind. Even in a modern megapolis, Tuminas lives according to the ancient calendar cycles. He has in his house a miniature portrait of the entire earthly world and has no doubt that taking care of his small garden is the path to turning the entire Earth into a large, flourishing garden.

Immediately after graduating from the Department of Acting of the Lithuanian Conservatory in Vilnius (currently the Lithuanian Academy of Music and Theatre) in 1974, Tuminas came to Moscow and entered the Department of Directing of the State Institute of Theatre Arts (GITIS). In 1978, a year before finishing his studies there, he directed his first production in the Vilnius Drama Theatre: *January* by the Bulgarian writer and playwright Jordan Radickov. In 1979, having already graduated from GITIS, he directed his first production in Moscow: *Peacock Melody* by the Slovakian Osvald Zahradník, at the Stanislavsky Drama Theatre.

The same year Tuminas went back to Vilnius, started working as a director in the State Drama Theatre of Lithuania (called since 1998 the Lithuanian National Drama Theatre) and began teaching at the Department of Acting of the Lithuanian Conservatory.

During the tumultuous second half of the 1980s, a group of actors from the State Drama Theatre of Lithuania gathered around him. They were his students, graduates of the Lithuanian Conservatory. Tuminas wanted to attract people with artistic rather than political ideas in order to realise his dream for a new theatre. So the group was, in fact, a new fellowship of like-minded people brought together by the desire to create a new, poetic theatre—theatre that was relevant to the contemporary reality, but did not forget about the artistic nature of the events on stage, about the text, irony and theatricality.

The ideas that inspired Tuminas and his actors at the end of the 1980s were very similar to those that brought about the European "free theatres" movement of the end of the nineteenth century, later on the first studios of the Moscow Art Theatre, and after World War II the "theatres for people," according to Giorgio Strehler's formulation, when in 1946 he created his Teatro Piccolo. Actually, Tuminas' company was also called "small" (*maži* in Lithuanian): because of the small number of members and also because from morning to night they could be found on the Small Stage of the State Drama Theatre of Lithuania, endlessly rehearsing, speaking, reading and discussing the material for their future collaborative work. In the group there were not only actors: in the second half of the

1980s Tuminas' fruitful creative cooperation with theatre composer Faustas Latenas (1956–2020) began.

The first work of the "small" group was the production *There Will Be No Death Here* (1988), based on a play written by Tuminas himself and the poet Valdas Kukulas. The play was about the famous Lithuanian poet Paulus Širvys; it combined his poetry with fragments of Jack London's "Martin Eden" and historical chronicles of the life of provincial Lithuanian towns after World War II.[1]

With this production Tuminas and his actors in practice introduced the new company to the theatre community and clearly showed their original and memorable creative style, which is still recognisable today. What the authors of the production chose to address was not the official history—the heroic history of the capital—but the history hidden from the superficial glance, the history of the inner land. Not only did Tuminas combine poetry and history, he also looked at historical documents with a poet's eye. He saw a philosophical dimension in simple provincial stories, turned real facts into testaments of people's memory, striking with the richness of poetic associations and the freedom of moving from fact to fantasy and legend. Tuminas seemed to have chosen as the basis of his work an old thesis of classical culture: poetry is more serious and philosophical than history because history speaks about the specific (the things that happened), whereas poetry speaks about the general (the things that happened and might have happened).[2]

The audience, critics and officials alike appreciated the professional accomplishment, self-sustainability and potential of the new company. So on 2 March 1990 in Vilnius, a new state theatre led by Tuminas was established (of course, this became possible thanks to the persistent requests sent by him to the Ministry of Culture). All the members of the "small" group became actors of the new theatre. It was named the Small Theatre (Mažasis teatras), so to speak confirming the mock (and at the same time meaningful) title of the artistic group. These were tumultuous days: on 11 March the Supreme Soviet of the Lithuanian Republic passed the Act of the Re-Establishment of the State of Lithuania. The Small Theatre led by Tuminas was destined to become nothing short of an artistic prologue to the new period of the history of the State of Lithuania. It became the first

---

[1] In the 1940–1950s Širvys worked as a journalist and newspaper editor in small towns of the Rokiškis area of Panevėžys district.

[2] See Aristotle, *Poetics* 1451b, 3–12.

240   D. TRUBOTCHKIN

of the three most famous new Lithuanian theatres of the first decade after the collapse of the USSR.[3]

Lithuanian audiences still consider as "legendary" four of the Small Theatre's productions, directed by Tuminas during that period. Three of them were based on classical drama and the fourth on modern prose: *The Cherry Orchard* by Anton Chekhov (1990); *Smile Upon Us, Lord*, based on the 1989 novel by Grigory Kanovich *A Baby Goat for Pennies* (1994); *Masquerade* by Mikhail Lermontov (1997); and *The Government Inspector* by Nikolai Gogol (2001). Together they contain the most significant characteristics of Tuminas' viewpoint on theatre and his way of directing. It is important to note that, starting with *Smile Upon Us, Lord*, Tuminas has been working exclusively with set designer Adomas Jacovskis. Thus, his style, which is so recognisable today, is the result of an impressive creative cooperation and co-authorship of three theatre masters: himself as director, composer Latenas and stage designer Jacovskis—a cooperation that continues.

From Tuminas' point of view, every plot conveys the story of the wanderings of a human soul that unravels as a life's path, as a journey from one corner of the world to another. This explains why there are so many travellers and images of journeys in his productions. In *The Cherry Orchard*, a whole mountain of suitcases stood on stage, by the left wing, as if reminding the characters that they would not be able to find tranquillity and therefore they already need to prepare for travel. At the end of *The Cherry Orchard* Ranevskaya's family has to leave, having lost their beautiful orchard and heading for a vague, uncomfortable future. In *Smile Upon Us, Lord*, the central plotline is the road trip of three Jews from the Lithuanian *shtetl* of Miškiné to Vilnius aboard a cart, pulled by an old mare. Various meetings await them on their way; for all three of them this journey has the meaning of a pilgrimage, because they see Vilnius as "the Lithuanian Jerusalem."

The world in Tuminas' theatre is the world of art, living not according to the laws of mundane everyday life, but according to the laws of the imagination. In this world the border between reality and dream is indiscernible, the images of the past and present mix, and imagination gives a fantastic and paradoxical form to any, no matter how simple, manifestation of life.

---

[3] In 1998, the Meno Fortas Theatre of Eimuntas Nekrošius and Theatre of Oskaras Koršunovas (OKT) were founded.

RIMAS TUMINAS: A POETIC VIEW OF THEATRE   241

In *Masquerade*, after the curtain rises, the audience sees the stage, covered with artificial snow: a winter garden with a lonely statue of a naked Aphrodite solemnly illuminated with evening lights. The backdrop and wings are made of thick black fabric, so the stage looks surrounded by the blind night. In this bottomless space, a direct path from the Earth to the Moon is hidden (it is there that young prince Zvezdich aspires to go, starting to ascend the invisible staircase), as well as all kinds of visual miracles (a huge shining chandelier unexpectedly flies across the entire stage from the right wing to the left over the group of extras).

In this world, where dream, fantasy, memory and reality are merged, there are characters personifying the light and the dark sides. Grotesque holy fools come from the dark, whereas dancing girls in pastel dresses emerge from the light (Nina in *Masquerade* looks like a star of a romantic ballet). Tuminas introduces such characters even when they were not present in the original plays. In *Masquerade* there is a certain "Winter man," who lives in the winter garden and for the sake of entertainment rolls a big snowball; the ball gets bigger and bigger, growing together with Arbenin's jealousy; at the very end it turns into a huge white ball and rolls over the jealous Arbenin, who has killed his wife and gone mad with grief.

Tuminas and Jacovskis prefer building sets and props inside the black-box of the stage without changing them with the changes of scenes. Instead, they enrich the performance with expressive visual symbols, which remain in the memory of the audience for a long time.

In *The Government Inspector*, a huge ghost lives in the provincial town. It is so tall that it can reach the gridiron. It looks like an unfinished chapel with a small tower and a dome with a cross, and, at the same time, like a pagan doll with a blurred face, wrapped in grey cloth. This giant, eerie ghost, invisible to the characters but visible to the audience, is a reminder of the worst crime committed by local officials: they have not finished the church, stealing the funds allocated to its construction. It seems that in the entire long production history of *The Government Inspector*, Tuminas is the first and only director who has emphasised in such an expressive way the subject of the crime, committed by the town in front of God: Khlestakov's visit is a punishment for this crime. "The ghost" is tied with a cable to a round rail on the gridiron (Jacovskis' idea). From time to time it unties itself and starts moving around, filling the entire space with itself, sweeping on its way through all the deeds, all the sins of the people. Faustas Latenas composed incidental music for the movement of a ghostly church: in this music we can hear both loud keyboard chords in the register of the organ and Slavic polyphony, which was used in villages to accompany a bride to the altar, a ritual moaning, and a farewell cry of a flock of cranes flying south in the rainy autumn.

Despite all this boundless freedom of imagination displayed on stage, Tuminas puts the text of the playwright above himself as a director and accepts this as a law. He likes to repeat that directing a production "separately from the drama" or "against the drama" equals immediately declaring one's superiority over authors like Shakespeare, Gogol and Chekhov. The creative process is the process of growth: if you are "great" from the very start, there is nowhere for you to grow; it is better to grow, fathoming the greatness of genius ideas, reaching their height with your own imagination.

The middle and second half of the 1990s were marked by Tuminas' productions in the theatres of Northern Europe (Finland, Iceland) and the dynamic European tours of the Vilnius Small Theatre. This new journey reinforced in Tuminas the feeling of the vastness of the world, the breadth of the creative space even when productions are created for small stages. During that period Tuminas' specific approach towards the classics was formed; the director sometimes describes this approach as "the foreigner's view" or "the look from the outside," allowing him to find non-trivial methods of interpreting well-known texts.

This approach, moving the audience away from the automatism of perception, became known in the history of art as "alienation" or "defamiliarisation." The Russian equivalent to "defamiliarisation," "*ostraneniye*" (which literally means "making something look strange"), was introduced by the Petrograd literary scholar Viktor Shklovsky in 1916.[4] In theatre a similar method is known in the interpretation of Bertolt Brecht as the "alienation effect" or "estrangement effect" (*Verfremdungseffekt*). For Tuminas, "alienation" does not mean "distortion." It is more of a careful touch from afar, a distance necessary for co-creation, poetic contemplation and interaction, as well as a desire to look from a distant point in order to discern new configurations of symbols, already indiscernible at a short distance.

The artistic authority of Tuminas in Lithuania in the beginning of the 1990s was so great that he, the artistic director of the Small Theatre, was

---

[4] Shklovsky was also the author of the first description of the "ostraneniye" method using the examples from Russian literature in his work *Art as Device* (1917); see Alexandra Berlina (ed.), *Viktor Shklovsky. A Reader* (London: Bloomsbury, 2017), p. 73.

invited in 1994 to become the principal director of the State Drama Theatre. He accepted the position (without leaving his post at the Small Theatre), but left it after five years of work.

This change coincided with the beginning of a new chapter of his work: at the turn of the twenty-first century Tuminas and his Small Theatre were receiving rave reviews in the theatre capitals of Russia—Moscow and St Petersburg. For the first time the Small Theatre was on tour in Moscow in 1998, where on the stage of the Vakhtangov Theatre they performed *Masquerade* in Lithuanian with great success. The next year, in 1999, the very same production was performed at the Golden Mask Festival and received the award for the best foreign production. This was the first international award in the history of the Moscow festival, which is very famous today.

In 2000 Tuminas directed his first production in Moscow with Russian actors: *Playing…Schiller!* after *Maria Stuart*, at the Sovremennik Theatre. In 2002 he directed the Russian version of his *Government Inspector* after Gogol at the Vakhtangov Theatre.

At the same time he continued working in the Small Theatre of Vilnius, remaining faithful to his habit of alternating classics and modern drama. The creative peak of the Small Theatre coincided with an outstanding event in its history: the company was granted the rights to use a historic building in Vilnius, after its 14-year reconstruction: an empire-style pavilion of the early twentieth century at Gediminas Avenue, 22. Its ceiling is unique: it is faced with transparent green tiles made of glass fibre–reinforced concrete. Today this building, thanks to the architecture and glory of the Small Theatre, is recognised as one of the landmarks of Vilnius.

In 2007 Tuminas became the artistic director of one of the most famous Russian theatres: the Vakhtangov Theatre in Moscow. For the first time in the history of Russia, a foreign citizen was appointed as the head of a theatre company. As time proved, the essence of the theatre as a creative organism and the essence of Tuminas as a director coincided and reinforced one another.

Convincing proof of the synergy of the Vakhtangov Theatre and its artistic director are the productions *Uncle Vanya* after Anton Chekhov (2009), the number one playwright in Russia, and *Eugene Onegin* (2013), based on the novel in verse by Alexander Pushkin, the number one poet in Russia. Both productions continue to be performed with great success, including at festivals and on tours; many audience members still describe them as the best modern Russian-language productions of Chekhov's and Pushkin's works.

In *Uncle Vanya* Tuminas rejected the mundane "Chekhovian" setting, which we are so accustomed to seeing in the theatre: basket chairs, swings, samovars, the pastoral idyll of Russian intelligentsia, philosophising in the autumn on their country estates. Tuminas and Jacovskis replaced this with a mystical space: huge, wide wooden portals are constructed on the stage, and in the background there is a big statue of a lion with a lonely yellow moon above it. The space of *Eugene Onegin*, in turn, is a giant ballet class-room with a bar and a huge foggy mirror, hanging on the backdrop: this mirror "lives"—that is, from time to time it changes its angle of slope, moving slightly, creating ghostly copies of what is happening on the stage.

In both productions there are images of memory mixed with fantasy that we are used to seeing in Tuminas' work. In *Eugene Onegin* they are taken to the point of paradox. There are two Onegins: the young one (a participant in events) and the old one (whose memoirs keep the events progressing). And two Lenskys: the young one (a participant in the events that led to his death in a duel) and the older one (the one Lensky would have become had he not been killed in a duel). Next to them there are characters that did not exist in Pushkin's original: a hussar, wounded in the war—the drinking buddy of Onegin in an empty room, a grotesque silent wanderer—dishevelled, in torn canvas clothes with a stringed musical instrument, a *domra*, in his hands, who once ended up in Onegin's abandoned house. Besides that, there are some unexpected episodes: Pushkinian in their essence, yet not taken directly from the text, but born via playing with a poetic line. They include a striking silent scene, explaining why young Tatyana married the old general. This scene leads to a beautiful episode that has become the visual symbol of the production: seven girls (Tatyana among them) are lifted above the stage on metal swings; they look sad and lifeless, their white dresses and white chiffon capes are fluttering in the air. This flight means they are saying farewell to love right in the course of the wedding: they were all brought by their parents to the capital to a bride "fair;" they were not marrying out of love, but had arranged marriages, each of them marrying her own "old general."

Since 2007, Tuminas has directed at the Vakhtangov Theatre eleven productions featuring celebrated actors of different generations. Two more of them deserve special mention.

On the occasion of the ninetieth anniversary of the Vakhtangov Theatre in 2011, he created a production, *Quayside*, that brought together fragments of works by various writers (from Fyodor Dostoyevsky to Arthur

Miller), all centred around an important role. Legendary actors of the older generation of the theatre were cast in the roles and their performances were real examples of virtuosity. Then, if the principal actor of an episode passed away, the entire episode would be removed, because the director did not want to replace the actor. Today this living collective testament of theatre memory has been suspended until the theatre finds the energy to fill it with new episodes.

In 2016, Tuminas directed *Oedipus Rex* by Sophocles—a co-production of the Vakhtangov Theatre and the National Theatre of Greece (Athens). It opened on the stage of the ancient Epidaurus Theatre and later on, with a slight change of mise-en-scène, it was added to the repertoire of the Vakhtangov Theatre. The Russian actors performed the roles of the characters in Russian, while the Greek actors were part of the chorus and performed in Modern Greek. Today Russian and Greek actors still perform it, cherishing the memory of the large open-air theatre with a capacity of 11,000 people, where, together with the audience, the stars looked down at the stage. Sophocles' story about the greatness of characters who no longer exist, characters who did not forgive themselves for their crimes, absorbed the energy of Epidaurus that it is so rarely possible to accumulate in traditional European theatres with a proscenium arch.

If the essence of the creative method of Rimas Tuminas were to be distilled down to several concrete characteristics, of course in view of the fact that his career is continuing, they would be the following.

He is a director who begins his work firmly based on the author's story and the actors' nature and only then moves to improvisations, sometimes utterly limitless, but never betraying the idea belonging to the author of the literary text. He is a romantic and a surrealist, enthusiastically filling his productions with nocturnal pagan imagery, with elements of nature (snow, rain, stars, wind, moon) and with ancient animalistic symbols (dog, fish, bear). He tries to preserve the mysteries of the universe and senses the mystique even in the most mundane life stories. He is inclined to read almost any word of the author as poetry. He looks for, and accentuates, the rhythm and the aphoristic nature of every line, demanding that his actors deliver the text as precise thoughts elaborated in advance and expressed in an exact form, hence the constant impression that the speech in his productions is poetic. Tuminas is a director who admits the primacy of the actor, rejoicing in any actor's relevant improvisation, yet always reminding the actors of the mysterious "pressure of heaven," the invisible divine glance, which is meant to make an actor ask him- or herself the question: "Who gave me the right to walk on the stage in this manner?"

He is also a director for whom the actor's source material is non-mundane gestures, dance movements and pantomime. He insists on the musicality of stage manifestations (similarly to Meyerhold and Vakhtangov), but at the same time demands that even the most whimsical action be identifiable in meaning and purpose.

For Rimas Tuminas the auditorium symbolises a cumulative view of the world. Heaven joins the Earth there, so angels watch the performance together with the audience. They, as Tuminas likes to repeat, "are either above the gridiron or at the gallery."[5] In such elevated surroundings, the poetry of theatre is purified to the point of ultimate clarity and is guided by the two oldest laws of art, named "harmony" and "rhythm." Directors, creating their work according to these laws (Tuminas included), reach the peak of happiness when they understand that they have managed to touch a hidden nerve in the souls of their audience, bringing together time and eternity.

Image 1 *Eugene Onegin*, directed by Rimas Tuminas, Vakhtangov Theatre, Moscow, 2013. (Photo by Valery Myasnikov, Courtesy of the Vakhtangov Theatre, Moscow)

[5] From the conversations of Rimas Tuminas with actors at the rehearsals of *Eugene Onegin* at the Vakhtangov Theatre, February 2013; recorded by Dmitry Trubotchkin (unpublished).

REFERENCES

Aleknonis, G. and H. Šabasebičius (eds.). *Lithuanian Theater*. Vilnius: Kultūros, filosofijos is meno institutas, 2009.

Aristotle, *Poetics*. Translated with an Introduction and Notes by A. Kenny. Oxford: University Press, 2013.

Berlina, Alexandra (ed.). *Viktor Shklovsky. A Reader*. London: Bloomsbury, 2017.

Trubotchkin, D. *Rimas Tuminas. Moskovskie spektakli* [*Rimas Tuminas. Moscow Productions*]. Moscow: Teatralis, 2015.

Krzysztof Warlikowski: A Beautiful Shock Therapy

Małgorzata Jarmułowicz

A Child of His Era

Krzysztof Warlikowski is one of those directors who turned out to be among the most renowned architects of change in Polish theatre following the fall of Communism in 1989. Scandal and a firm rejection of calcified traditions and conventions have become his hallmarks; establishing a lively, risky, European and provocative theatre, emancipated from the shackles of national duty—his primary ambition. Piotr Gruszczyński, a theatre critic and playwright cooperating with Warlikowski, in his book *The Patricides: The Younger and More Talented in Polish Theatre* includes in this circle Grzegorz Jarzyna, Anna Augustynowicz, Piotr Cieplak and Zbigniew Brzoza as well.[1] He names Krystian Lupa as their "founding father," since, as a teacher at the Krakow Theatre School, he was a charismatic mentor and guru of sorts for many of them. Following Lupa, who sought the

---

[1] P. Gruszczyński, *Ojcobójcy (The Patricides) Młodsi zdolniejsi w teatrze polskim* (Warsaw: Wyd W.A.B.,2003).

M. Jarmułowicz (✉)
University of Gdańsk, Gdańsk, Poland

© The Author(s), under exclusive license to Springer Nature Switzerland AG 2021
K. Stefanova, M. Carlson (eds.), *20 Ground-Breaking Directors of Eastern Europe*, https://doi.org/10.1007/978-3-030-52935-2_20

250 M. JARMUŁOWICZ

"symptoms of the spiritual crisis of our epoch,"[2] they went on the prowl for difficult and contentious subjects, discovering shameful and repressed aspects of contemporary reality.

Taking advantage of the benefits of the new political order, Warlikowski bravely chose the most vitriolic and heavy-hitting themes. It was his decision to turn the stage into a means of confronting what is socially rejected and repressed that signalled the dawn of his great theatre. As Grzegorz Niziołek wrote: "The temperature in Warlikowski's theatre began to rise when he ceased to conceal the fact he was fighting with society and dared to hit, condemn and loudly denounce what was bothering him."[3] Such a harsh assessment of social reality already began to percolate the director's earliest productions: *White Nights* by F. Dostoyevsky (1992), *The Marquise of O* by H. von Kleist (1993), *Tancerz mecenasa Kraykowskiego* (Dancer of the Lawyer Kraykowski) by W. Gombrowicz (1997) or *The Barred Window* by Klaus Mann (1994). As Niziołek noted: "All these works appear to bring to the fore the willingness of society to condemn all manner of nonconformists, excoriate eccentricity and stifle forbidden passions. Ever present are the motifs of stigma, guilt and humiliation. This sheds new light on the commonly accepted order, turning it upside down."[4]

In the eyes of critics, Warlikowski cheekily pulled back the curtain on the dark side of our social and individual lives. Piotr Gruszczyński placed his theatre "on the edge of the abyss, beyond which you can no longer formulate any questions in human language."[5] Rafał Węgrzyniak called him an "esthete in hell."[6] Grzegorz Niziołek placed his performances in the "zone of the shadow archetype—that, which is culturally rejected, condemned, subordinated to the mechanisms of internal censorship and depicted as 'evil.'"[7] As a matter of fact, the subject of evil has become one of the trademarks of Warlikowski's theatre, which simultaneously attacks socially prevalent taboos and hypocrisy. In his productions, the dominant, normative order is manifested through violence and humiliation, there are no happy endings, no promise of a better world, while evil grows to such

---

[2] G. Niziołek, *Sobowtór i utopia. Teatr Krystiana Lupy* (Cracow: Universitas, 1996), p. 42.

[3] G. Niziołek, *Warlikowski. Extra ecclesiam* (Cracow: Wydawn Homini, 2008), pp. 19–20.

[4] Ibid., p. 16.

[5] P. Gruszczyński, *Ojcobójcy*, p. 137.

[6] R. Węgrzyniak, "Esteta w piekle. Od 'auto da fé' do 'Burzy'," *Notatnik Teatralny* 28–29 (2003).

[7] G. Niziołek, *Warlikowski*, p. 21.

unreal proportions that it becomes a gruesome metaphor for humanity itself.[8]

What is Warlikowski looking for in such a dark theatrical world? In one interview, he answered a similar question: "An escape from guilt. I always felt guilty. In puberty, guilty of leaving someone I loved. Later, of leaving my family; all my life I tried to escape from a blue-collar environment. Next: of being a homosexual. Finally: of being Polish. Once I became an adult, I was able to create myself by accepting my Polish identity, though it took a lot of time."[9] His theatre is obviously a reflection of his personal battles with inner darkness.

Szczecin and Beyond

Non-conformist rebelliousness has been part of his life from an early age. It first manifested itself when, as a high school graduate, Warlikowski ran away from familiar, yet alien Szczecin to distant Cracow. Refusing to become a truck driver, according to his family's background and pleas, Warlikowski went on to study history, philosophy and French philology at the Jagiellonian University. Yet he did not graduate and decided to flee to Paris in 1983, once martial law ended in Poland. Paris reassured the young rebel regarding his life choices. His independent intellectual development, stimulated by forays into intellectual circles and theatres there, as well as his further studies yielded results that helped him once he came back. In 1989, a memorable date for Poland, 27-year-old Warlikowski embarked on a vital part of his artistic journey, undertaking stage director studies at the National Theatre School in Cracow. However, he did not limit himself to studying solely under the tutelage of the master, Krystian Lupa. He gained invaluable experience during laborious internships abroad: in Stockholm he studied Ingmar Bergman's rehearsals, in Vienna and Paris he practised with Peter Brook, at Piccolo Teatro di Milano he participated in Georgio Strehler's workshops.

[8] I devoted one of the chapters of my book *Teatralność zła: antropologiczne wędrówki po współczesnej dramaturgii i teatrze* (Theatricality of Evil: Anthropological Journeys across Contemporary Theatre and Drama) to the issue of evil in Warlikowski's theatre (Gdańsk: Wydawnictwo Uniwerstetu Gdánskiego, 2012), pp. 186–195.

[9] F. Pascaud, "Piękny potwór" (Interview with Krzysztof Warlikowski, in: dwutygodnik. com, 07/2009, https://www.dwutygodnik.com/artykul/347-piekny-potwor.html (accessed 31 July 2019).

252   M. JARMUŁOWICZ

Foreign acquaintances and world-wide travels influenced the director's later career, granting him access to theatrical scenes and festivals all over Europe, where he earned many accolades. His plays appeared at the Avignon Festival, Prensa de Otoño Festival in Madrid, Edinburgh International Festival, Wiener Festwochen, Next Wave Festival BAM in New York, Athens Festival, International Theatre Festival Santiago and Mil in Chile, International Theatre Festival PoNTI in Porto, XXI Seoul Performing Arts Festival in South Korea, BITEF Festival in Belgrade. His fame was solidified also thanks to his productions abroad. In Germany he staged *Śmierć króla* (in Hamburg, 1994), *Twelfth Night* (1999) and *The Tempest* (in Stuttgart, 2000), Proust's *In Search of Lost Time* (in Bonn, 2002), *Macbeth* (in Hanover, 2004). In Croatia: Koltès' *West Coast* (1998) and Euripides' *The Bacchae* (2001). In France: *A Midsummer Night's Dream* (2003); in the Netherlands: Andrew Bovell's *Speaking in Tongues* (2004), Yukio Mishima's *Madame de Sade* (2006); in Italy: *Pericles* (1998); in Israel: Kafka's *Process* (1995), *Hamlet* (1997), Euripides' *The Phoenician Women* (1998). While working abroad, he met artists who later joined his crew: Renate Jett and Felice Ross.

Ironically for a well-travelled man like Warlikowski, he found himself a stranger in the city where he gained his directorial credentials. A rather cold reception of his debut at the Old Theatre in Cracow (a production of *The Marquise of O.* based on a short story by Heinrich von Kleist, 1993), and later the failure of a production based on Matei Vișniec's *We Will Employ an Old Clown* (1996), effectively discouraged Warlikowski from trying to appease Cracow. His work turned out to be completely at odds with the conservative, bourgeois tastes of the city's audience, so his need for artistic autonomy drove him to places more open to disobedience and rebellion. After several years of travelling around various Polish and foreign stages, in 1999 Warlikowski became a full-time director at the Rozmaitości Theatre in Warsaw, which at the turn of the twentieth and the twenty-first centuries gained the nickname "Martens theatre" (from the shoe brand worn by teenagers). He stayed there for nine years and, working in an atmosphere of rebellion successfully maintained by the then artistic director Grzegorz Jarzyna, directed his most famous productions: *Hamlet* (1999), *The Bacchae* (2001), *Cleansed* by Sarah Kane (2002), *The Tempest* (2003), Szymon Anski and Hanna Krall's *Dybbuk* (2003), Hanoch Levin's *Krum* (2005) and Tony Kuschner's *Angels in America* (2007).

In 2008, looking for a creative space that corresponded exactly to his artistic needs and visions, Warlikowski left Rozmaitości and, together with a group of permanent collaborators, founded Nowy Teatr in the facilities of the Municipal Services Company in Warsaw, Mokotów district. His most daring and independent projects flourished there. He directed *(A) pollonia* (2009), *Koniec* (The End; 2010), *Opowieści afrykańskie według Szekspira* (African Stories According to Shakespeare; 2011), *Kabaret warszawski* (Warsaw Cabaret; 2012), *Francuzi* (Frenchmen; 2015). The theatre was designed from scratch and was/is meant to elicit an emotionally and intellectually provocative dialogue with the audience. As described on the theatre's current webpage, its aim is to change routine modes of thinking and unearth the hidden and repressed parts of memory. Indeed, Warlikowski, the "child of darkness," never ceases to brazenly disrupt the audience's mood.

ANTIQUITY, SHAKESPEARE, HOLOCAUST, OPERA

Both modern and classical plays are vehicles for Warlikowski's acerbic output, though he tends to exclude Polish works from the latter category. In 2003 Piotr Gruszczyński counted three "stages" in total in Warlikowski's theatre: "On one, they play Shakespeare, on the second, Greek tragedies, on the third, Koltès and Sarah Kane."[10] These stages, however, cannot be separated—they are connected through the common thread of evil. "From the very beginning I felt," the director claims, "that from her [Sarah Kane's] dramatic texts you have to do Shakespeare, and from Shakespeare's you have to do Sarah Kane. Conversely, Sarah Kane can be done from Euripides and Euripides has to be made from Koltès."[11] The crisscrossing of various authors is also a result of Warlikowski's ripping them from the original historical contexts. Due to these bold interpretive operations of his, they gain universal meaning, touching on matters related both to Poles and to humanity in general. In Warlikowski's productions, myth and history go hand and hand, timeless truth connects with lived experience, although there is no intrusive modernisation of the very texts of the classical dramas. The director explicitly declares his aversion to "particular problems, closed groups and environments, the everyday humdrum of

---

[10] P. Gruszczyński, "Świątynia/rzeźnia," *Notatnik Teatralny* 28–29 (2003), p. 102.

[11] A. Fryz-Więcek, "Skondensowany strach" (Interview with Krzysztof Warlikowski), *Didaskalia* 47 (2002), p. 6.

tomorrow and yesterday."[12] Instead of depicting bits of reality, his theatre takes place "always and everywhere." His fascination with antiquity, Shakespeare and the works of Koltès and Sarah Kane is largely derived from his need to feel and interact with the universe.

The type of modernity that permeates Warlikowski's productions of the classics often appears in the shape of violent outbursts of our collective conscience. This was the case in his *Electra* by Sophocles: by means of the set design and costumes he shifted the action to the war-torn Balkans where, in 1997, he heard the echo of an ancient story of a fratricidal struggle prompted by a vendetta. In *The Taming of the Shrew* (1998), the violence of the patriarchal system, which allows Petruchio to strip rebellious Katherine of her dignity and brutally subordinate her, appeared in the modern form of a drunken audience member (who then played Petruchio) humiliating an usher (who then played Katherine). In Shakespeare's *The Tempest* (2003), the topic of Polish responsibility for the murder of Jews in Jedwabne emerged, prompted by a powerful book by Jan Tomasz Gross, *Neighbors*, which had recently been published at the time and had caused a very heated dispute. The main theme of the production revolving around collective memory was the inability to understand, forgive and reconcile. The trauma of the Holocaust reflected in *The Tempest* turned out to be one of the most frequently recurring leitmotifs of Warlikowski's theatre: variations on it appeared in *Dybbuk*, *(A)pollonia* and *Opowieści afrykańskie według Szekspira* (African Stories According to Shakespeare). Again, however, this subject is taken up not as a historical nightmare but— as Grzegorz Niziołek claims—"in the context of identity issues" and "personal sensitivity regarding social acts of aggression against otherness."[13]

Starting in 2009, Warlikowski began to look for new works of literature for his productions. At the same time he was writing his own authorial scripts. Combined and intertwined, these materials form a thick web of associations that adds dramatic depth to personal and social themes. Such an artistic strategy was to become a hallmark of his productions realised at Nowy Teatr, a prime example being *(A)pollonia*—a monumental work on the subject of innocent sacrifice. It utilised, among others, fragments of Aeschylus' tragedy *Oresteia*, Euripides' *Alkestis*, *Iphigenia in Aulis* and *Herakles*, Hanna Krall's story *Pola*, Jonathan Littell's novel *The Kindly*

---

[12] K. Mieszkowski, "Do jutra" (Interview with Krzysztof Warlikowski), *Notatnik Teatralny* 28–29 (2003), p. 231.

[13] G. Niziołek, *Polski teatr Zagłady* (Warsaw: Instytut Teatralny, 2013), p. 70.

Ones, John Maxwell Coetzee's *Elizabeth Costello*, Rabindranath Tagore's drama *The Post Office* and Marcin Świetlicki's poem *Pobojowisko*. Warlikowski's directing activity is not limited to drama theatre. In 2000, he made his debut as an opera director. In the Grand Theatre in Warsaw he prepared a one-act chamber music concert, *The Music Program* by Roxanna Panufnik. On the same stage, he also directed, among others, *Don Carlos* by Giuseppe Verdi (2000), *Ignorant i szaleniec* (Ignorant and Madman) by Paweł Mykietyn based on *Der Ignorant und der Wahsinnige* by Thomas Bernhardt (2001), *Ubu Rex* by Krzysztof Penderecki (2003) and Alban Berg's *Wozzeck* based on Georg Büchner's play (2006). Then he directed *Iphigénie en Tauride* by Christoph Willibald Gluck (2006) and Leoš Janaček's *The Makropulos Affair* (2007) at the Paris Opéra, and Richard Wagner's *Parsifal* (2008) at Opéra Bastille. Even in this extremely conventionalised stage genre, Warlikowski has been trying to create enclaves of artistic freedom by freely re-interpreting opera, playing with librettos and even adding his own elements. It is true that Warlikowski's ideas are often subversive enough to disturb or downright shock the spectator. For instance, the lead character of Mozart's *Don Giovanni* (2004) was portrayed as a pornography-addicted sex maniac inspired by the 30-year-old protagonist of Steve McQueen's movie *Shame*. Still, Warlikowski is considered one of the most influential creators of contemporary European opera.

STAGE AS LABORATORY

The peculiar language of Warlikowski's theatre stems from his close cooperation with certain artists. In addition to the composer Paweł Mykietyn and lighting director Felice Ross, he has been working with the set designer Małgorzata Szczęśniak, his spouse. They have been a duo right from the start, their cooperative debut being a production of Elias Canetti's play *Auto da fé* in 1992. Their subsequent work shows they are mutually complementary personalities endowed with similar tastes and sensibility. The "monopolisation" of Warlikowski's theatre by one set designer means also that her work has acquired the characteristics of a very specific process. Małgorzata Szczęśniak sees it as a journey through a maze of recurring motifs and associations: "Actually, I still keep doing the same thing. Of course, I make progress, but I find myself coming back to the same subjects. [...] These experiences 'travel' from one performance to the next. I

256 M. JARMUŁOWICZ

often use elements and ideas that I've already used somewhere, which means I'm still searching, looking, wandering."[14]

The theatrical worlds of Warlikowski and Szczęśniak are ever indeterminable, built upon murky, ambiguous notions and perched between realism and metaphor. This is the case, for example, in *Cleansed*, where the place of action—the university campus—becomes a zone of multiple significations: a gymnasium, a hospital, a mortuary, a bath or even a concentration camp (a campus is, obviously, close to a camp). The action in Warlikowski's productions takes place in unknown areas at an unknown time, making his theatre semantically open, laced with secrecy and posing a challenge to the imagination. Małgorzata Szczęśniak, conversely, adheres to minimalism, consistently avoiding decorativeness that would obscure the sense of the theatrical image. The human universe is usually denoted by an open, homogeneous, often empty space, and the possible meanings born within this cleansed, imaginary territory are automatically universalised and hence gain clarity.

A chief feature of such a peculiar stage world is its structural artificiality. It is emphasised by the use of contemporary industrial materials: glass, mirrors, plastic, foil and metal. Warlikowski's theatre is built only from human-made elements, products of civilisation not of nature. Whenever nature is imitated, it is done conspicuously: in *The Winter's Tale* (1997) artificial flowers sprout from the stage boards, in *Merchant of Venice* (1994) glass imitates water canals, and in *Twelfth Night* real sand is combined with shimmering foil. Humankind is the sole creator of Warlikowski's theatrical universe. It is the only force pulling its strings and the only one responsible for the evil dwelling within it. Metaphysical justifications simply do not exist.

The stage microcosm reflects this vision: cold, bathed in bright light, dehumanised. The characters roaming this hostile landscape remind one of hapless test subjects submitted to thorough dissection. The sense of alienation is exacerbated by the sterility of stage light, sharply contrasted with the filth of ever-present violence. In *The Bacchae*, the torn-apart remains of Pentaeus are brought to the stage in a "hygienic" bucket, Agamemnon's corpse lies in a purity-evoking bathtub, the bloody scenes in *Cleansed* are heavily conventionalised and unfold in a pristine tiled shower room. In this aseptic, laboratory space, every gesture, grimace or

---

[14] K. Łuszczyk, "Przestrzeń jako miejsce spotkania" (Interview with Małgorzata Szczęśniak), *Notatnik Teatralny* 28/29 (2003), p. 78.

intonation is doubly expressive, as if magnified under a microscope. Nothing distracts the protagonists: they are focused on themselves, devoid of unnecessary contexts. After all, they are the only ones who matter here. Empty space and people are the only ingredients of this stage reality.

"We burn people"

Nobody who enters Warlikowski's theatre is innocent. It's a theatre that refuses to make and take any compromise, ruthlessly expounding the grim and bitter conclusions it reaches. There is no fourth wall protecting the audience, which in turn loses its safe status of an ignored observer. The stage world catches the spectators in the act of voyeurism and unceremoniously engulfs them, thus turning them into additional subjects of close scrutiny.

In other stage situations the audience is the witness of specific confessions addressed directly at it. For example in *Cleansed*, facing the audience, Renate Jett performs his initial monologue with touching frankness, confessing love via words taken from S. Kane's *Crave*—love that will soon turn into torture. The weight of a public confession that hits the viewer is also felt in the final monologue of Danuta Stenka in the role of Katherine in *Taming of the Shrew*. As a victim of male violence, she speaks from the proscenium, again directly addressing the audience. She's finally totally submissive, yet blaming everyone around for her humiliation. In *Cleansed*, Grace's words hit the audience like a bullwhip: "Kill them all." At this point, the lights are on and all the actors stand on the stage and stare intently at the audience. The invisible boundary between the two worlds breaks and, through this crack, the disturbing darkness of the stage reality pours out onto the spectators. There is a disturbing impression that Grace was quoting the viewers' thoughts. In *(A)pollonia*, at the end of a Nazi criminal monologue adapted from Littell's *The Kindly Ones*, Agamemnon reaches a shocking conclusion: "I am just like you!" Warlikowski personally instructs technicians on how long they should keep the lights on above the spectators. He closely surveys their reactions, their struggles with the words assailing them from the stage. "Only when he achieves a satisfactory level of havoc can the lights be dimmed."[15] Olga Śmiechowicz noted. Summoning the power of social frustration and repressed, traumatic expe-

---

[15] O. Śmiechowicz, *Lupa, Warlikowski, Klata. Polski teatr po upadku komunizmu* (Warsaw: Wydawnictwo Naukowe PWN, 2018), p. 158.

riences, Warlikowski's shock therapy demolishes the ethical well-being of viewers. "You got what you deserved," says the director to those who visit his theatre and gullibly believe that by following certain rules of conduct they are capable of distinguishing good and evil.

In Warlikowski's productions, it is the outsiders, foreigners and other extraordinary individuals who bear the full brunt of a "healthy" society's wrath. With their help, he asks the most difficult and uncomfortable questions and highlights those things we prefer to keep secret. The actors also pay the price of such extreme mental identification. "I am terrible, especially towards actors," admits the director. "I split roles; I tell them to relive their traumas. I poison them with pessimism, with my predilection for dust. Only pain can give birth to art. If you're happy, you better have a picnic than go to the theatre."[16] When he gave his actors the play *Roberto Zucco* (the story of a teenage serial killer who murders his parents and eventually commits suicide), the crew unanimously refused to work: "The actresses cried: 'How can we play it, we have children!' But a few months later, wrapping up rehearsals, we felt we're on a mission,"[17] Proposing Kane's *Cleansed*, Warlikowski was able to persuade actresses reluctant to enter such a cruel and dangerous world. Ultimately, in a production brimming with sadistic perversion, loathing, death and brutal sacrifice, everyone played phenomenally, "accurately and without emotional involvement. Cool yet sharp. Like a razor cut across the eye."[18]

Warlikowski is a "master of disgust" (Grzegorz Niziołek's term) also because he tends to transgress the boundaries of cultural taboos, whether it's intimacy, corporeality or sexuality. He caused a frenzy that wracked Polish theatre at the turn of the twenty-first century. Heated discussions regarding nakedness erupted in the wake of Warlikowski's *Hamlet*. One female audience member stood up during a scene, where the prince (played by Jacek Poniedziałek) stands naked in Gertruda's bedroom, and demanded he put on his pants. Even stronger reactions of decency defenders were triggered by *Cleansed*, in which the nakedness of homosexual lovers, pointing penises at the front row, clashed with the "overbearingly

[16] F. Pascaud, "Piękny potwór" (Interview with Krzysztof Warlikowski, in: dwutygodnik. com, 07/2009, https://www.dwutygodnik.com/artykul/347-piekny-potwor.html (accessed 31 July 2019).

[17] R. Pawłowski, "Burza we mnie" (Interview with K. Warlikowski). *Gazeta Wyborcza*, 55 (2003), in: "Duży Format" supplement, no 10.

[18] P. Gruszczyński, *Ojcobójcy. Młodsi zdolniejsi w teatrze polskim* (Warsaw: Wydawn W.A.B., 2003), p. 143.

horrid nudity" of a middle-aged, overweight actress (Stanisława Celińska), playing with much flair and panache the role of a peep-show dancer. The moral and aesthetic scandal so effectively occupied the minds of critics and viewers alike that few asked about the purpose of this provocation. People refused to acknowledge that Warlikowski was venturing into forbidden territory in order to show the oppressiveness of a social norm and the helplessness of those standing against it. On the other hand, once the timidity of the Polish audiences was overcome, they became less outraged by similar provocations. Reviewers of *Angels in America*, directed by Warlikowski just five years after *Cleansed*, said, "there is no scandal anymore;" "Nobody is shocked by a naked Joe Pitt or by a pair of guys hugging."[19]

Reviews notwithstanding, moral provocation, thematic brutality and radical critique of society reign supreme in Warlikowski's theatre. The ostentatious beauty of sets meticulously designed by Małgorzata Szczęśniak and Felice Ross evinces that. Cruelty and perversion appear in the guise of refined charm. Spaces filled with evil possess the enchanting allure of picturesque textures, colours and light. In *Roberto Zucco*, *Macbeth* or *Cleansed*, cruelty and disgust are enshrined in tasteful stage compositions, while the feeling of dread collides with the feeling of the sublime. Each production is a series of beautiful frames seemingly contradicting the bitterness and fear they represent. "You can't express dirt and unhappiness with dirt and unhappiness. [...] In order to make dirt tangible, it first must be cleansed and elevated to the highest echelons of art,"[20] explains Piotr Gruszczyński, who sees in Warlikowski's artistic strategy a "kind of beautiful anesthesia" injected into viewers in order to make them receptive to meaning. It's a very tricky manoeuvre, since the pristine cleanliness of the stage images renders Warlikowski's theatre and its shock therapy even more cruel. Still, if one believes in the power of theatre, perhaps one should believe that beauty can save the world?

Translated by Filip Cieślak

---

[19] Ł. Drewniak, "Wciąż ten sam pokój," *Dziennik* 46 (2008).
[20] P. Gruszczyński, "Świątynia/rzeźnia," *Notatnik Teatralny* 28/29 (2003), p. 110.

Image 1 *We Are Leaving*, directed by Krzysztof Warlikowski, Nowy Teatr, 2018. (Photo by Magda Hueckel)

References

Drewniak, Łukasz, "Wciąż ten sam pokój," *Dziennik* 46 (2008).
Fryz-Więcek, Agnieszka, "Skondensowany strach" (Interview with Krzysztof Warlikowski), *Didaskalia* 47 (2002).
Gruszczyński, Piotr, "Świątynia/rzeźnia," *Notatnik Teatralny*, 28–29 (2003a).
———, *Ojcobójcy* (The Patricides) *Młodsi zdolniejsi w teatrze polskim* (Warsaw: Wyd. W.A.B., 2003b).
Jarmułowicz, Małgorzata, *Teatralność zła: antropologiczne wędrówki po współczesnej dramaturgii i teatrze* (Theatricality of evil: anthropological journeys across contemporary theatre and drama to the issue of evil in Warlikowski's theatre) (Gdańsk: Wyd. Uniwersytetu Gdańskiego, 2012).
Łuszczyk, Katarzyna, "Przestrzeń jako miejsce spotkania" (Interview with Małgorzata Szczęśniak). *Notatnik Teatralny* 28/29 (2003).
Mieszkowski, Krzysztof, "Do jutra" (Interview with Krzysztof Warlikowski). *Notatnik Teatralny*, 28–29 (2003).
Niziołek, Grzegorz, *Warlikowski. Extra ecclesiam.* (Cracow: Wyd. Homini, 2008).
———, *Sobowtór i utopia. Teatr Krystiana Lupy* (Cracow: Universitas, 1996).
———, *Polski teatr Zagłady*. (Warsaw: Wydawnictwo Krytyki Politycznej, 2013).

Pascaud, Fabienne, "Piękny potwór" (Interview with Krzysztof Warlikowski). dwutygodnik.com, 07 2009, https://www.dwutygodnik.com/artykul/347-piekny-potwor.html (accessed 31 July 2019).

Pawłowski, Roman. "Burza we mnie" (Interview with Krzysztof Warlikowski). *Gazeta Wyborcza*, 55 in: "Duży Format" supplement, no 10 (2003).

Śmiechowicz, Olga, *Lupa, Warlikowski, Klata. Polski teatr po upadku komunizmu.* (Warsaw: Wydawnictwo Naukowe PWN, 2018).

Węgrzyniak, Rafał, "Esteta w piekle. Od 'auto da fé' do 'Burzy'." *Notatnik Teatralny*, 28–29 (2003).

An Attempt at Drawing an Artistic Family Tree

Marvin Carlson, Kamila Černá, Kim Cuculić, Artur Duda, Katarzyna Kręglewska, Blaž Lukan, Octavian Saiu, Kalina Stefanova, Edīte Tišheizere, Dmitry Trubotchkin, Rasa Vasinauskaitė, Tomasz Wiśniewski, and Michal Zahálka

We asked the directors included in the book to share with the readers what the major influences they have experienced as artists are and, if they had to draw an artistic family tree, whom they would include on it. Only in the case of the late Lithuanian director Eimuntas Nekrošius is an excerpt of an existing interview used. Here is what all the rest had to say.

M. Carlson (✉)
City University of New York, New York, NY, USA

K. Černá • M. Zahálka
Arts and Theatre Institute, Prague, Czech Republic
e-mail: kamila.cerna@idu.cz

K. Cuculić
Novi List Newspaper, Rijeka, Croatia

© The Author(s), under exclusive license to Springer Nature Switzerland AG 2021
K. Stefanova, M. Carlson (eds.), *20 Ground-Breaking Directors of Eastern Europe*, https://doi.org/10.1007/978-3-030-52935-2_21

264 M. CARLSON ET AL.

Grzegorz Bral: Living in a deeply Communist regime made me long for some islands of free speech, free expression and free thinking. By a so-called coincidence I went to see *Apocalypsis Cum Figuris* by Grotowski's Laboratory Theatre. At that time I was 15 years old. I hadn't seen any other forms of theatre before that, but this experience was in many ways... shocking! I'd never in my life before experienced such an extreme expression. I don't think I understood any of the underlying ideas, but it didn't matter. That experience made me look for a similar type of theatre. I thought if this was what people call "Theatre" I'd also want to be part of it. For about the next ten years I went to see different performances and most of the time I felt more and more disappointed. I couldn't understand

A. Duda
Nicolaus Copernicus University, Toruń, Poland
e-mail: dudaart@umk.pl

K. Kręglewska • T. Wiśniewski
University of Gdańsk, Gdańsk, Poland
e-mail: katarzyna.kreglewska@ug.edu.pl; tomasz.wisniewski@ug.edu.pl

B. Lukan
Academy for Theatre, Radio, Film and Television, University of Ljubljana, Ljubljana, Slovenia
e-mail: blaz.lukan@guest.arnes.si

O. Saiu
National University of Theatre and Film, Bucharest, Romania

K . Stefanova
National Academy for Theatre and Film Arts, Sofia, Bulgaria
e-mail: 111@kalina-stefanova.com

E. Tišheizere
Institute of Literature, Folklore and Arts of the University of Latvia, Riga, Latvia

D. Trubotchkin
State Institute for Art Studies, Graduate School of Performing Arts, Russian Institute of Theatre Arts (GITIS), Moscow, Russia

R. Vasinauskaitė
Lithuanian Music and Theatre Academy, Lithuanian Culture Research Institute, Vilnius, Lithuania

AN ATTEMPT AT DRAWING AN ARTISTIC FAMILY TREE   265

why in Poland, despite having such a stunning example of free art as the Laboratory Theatre, no one else was exploring this. In the meantime I encountered Tadeusz Kantor's productions at Cricot 2 Theatre. That was also a powerful and nourishing experience. I knew I wouldn't explore his way as I didn't have any of his fine art skills. I couldn't even draw. There was another theatre company that touched me at different times and they were a kind of a legend of anti-Communist theatre: 8th Day Theatre, under the direction of the amazing Lech Raczak. Later on I visited "Gardzienice Theatre," which became my first theatre "school" for four-and-a-half years. But my experience with "Gardzienice" very soon felt rather limited. Włodzimierz Staniewski does not carry in his vision any of the profundity of Grotowski. I had to leave and seek my own way. So summing it up, I was inspired by the strongest of the Polish avant-garde theatres, that of Grotowski. And although I was neither his actor, nor his student, that first impression is still living in me even today.

Gianina Cărbunariu: For me the major influences do not come from other artists. Or, to put it differently: all artists whom I admire are important for me as a spectator/reader etc., but it was not their influence that made me insist on doing theatre. The vital experience for me was to meet and enter into a dialogue with people coming from anthropology, sociology, journalism or history and science. The meetings with such people from different generations and with their works and studies were a great source of inspiration on how to look at the world around me, how to articulate some perspectives on a theme or a subject. I will only name a few of them; all are Romanian anthropologists: Zoltan Rostas, Ruxandra Cesereanu, Vintilă Mihăilescu and Valer Simion Cosma (with Valer I've already collaborated on three of my performances that were touching subjects like cheap labour in the EU, the public shaming of the poor, the traffic of toxic waste from West Europe to East Europe in the last few years).

Still, I wouldn't include myself as a 100% member in the group of documentary theatre makers (even if I am interested in and I deeply admire their work). The research through interviews is just one of the steps in creating the concept for my performances. Usually after the research period I spend a lot of time with my team of actors, set designer, choreographer, etc., trying to make a selection from the whole material, doing improvisations, having a lot of discussions. A performance is therefore a translation on stage of our meeting with reality and not the reality itself. That is why the productions I have created are quite different as ways of expression; they are inspired by very different situations, images, contexts.

The work of Svetlana Alexievich is very inspiring for me, but also novels by other women writers such as Lucia Berlin, Olga Tokarczuk, Zadie Smith, etc., and from Romania I would name Tatiana Țibuleac, Lavinia Braniște, Elena Vlădăreanu.

As for my education in arts, I guess I was very lucky to meet at the university two professors, Valeriu Moisescu and Nicu Mandea, who, most of the time, gave me a lot of freedom and made the education in theatre look like an adventure into the unknown of both "the master" and the "student." Unfortunately, the reality of the art world, of the theatre system and also of art education nowadays in Romania has nothing to do with the experience I had while being a student in directing in Bucharest.

The art world and especially the theatre world can become extremely suffocating and toxic for an artist. As for me, if I didn't have the chance to "go out," to do research and meet other people, to spend time in the archives and discover other worlds, probably I would have given up making theatre by now. So, yes, I think the best part of my work as a theatre artist happens mostly far away from the stage, in these situations of being in touch with different realities and human experiences. These moments give me inspiration, they disturb me and shake my prejudices, they help me become part of the world I am observing and, in the end, make me the artist I am. If I think of a family tree in the theatre field, probably the fact that I am doing my own research and writing my own scenarios for performances puts me in the family of artists who are creating author-performances. I started like this when I finished my theatre studies and I always thought of myself as a director-playwright, not a playwright-director. This means I do not write a play and then direct it on stage, but rather the concept of a performance and a text are developed at the same time during the rehearsal process.

Oliver Frljić: I would say that Tadeusz Kantor is definitely part of this artistic family tree. Beside him: Forced Entertainment, Goat Island and The Wooster Group.

Alvis Hermanis: I'm Latvian, and I have been educated and raised in the Latvian theatre environment. To be exact, it was still the theatre environment of Soviet Latvia. I must separate two things. The acting school, which stems from the Russian tradition, is definitely at the base of everything. I still think that the best actors I've encountered have been in Russia. Therefore, I've been influenced by the Russian acting school of the 1970s and 1980s, which

AN ATTEMPT AT DRAWING AN ARTISTIC FAMILY TREE   267

came through my teachers at the Faculty of Theatre of the Latvian State Conservatory. It depends greatly on the people interpreting it. My teacher was the director Māra Ķimele, who herself was a student of Anatoly Efros. I've been influenced by actors who worked in about the same way as Meryl Streep and Dustin Hoffman do. The one who inherited Stanislavsky's traditions in the most authentic way was, in my opinion, Georgy Tovstonogov. He has described it best—as a method, as a recipe of sorts, just like making meatballs. Anyone can work by the method the way he has described it.

From the point of view of directing, it must be said that the Latvian theatre, or, more accurately, the Soviet theatre, affected me not as an inspiration, but as the very opposite of that: it pushed me to do something in order to oppose it. I cannot name a single director whom I have wanted to emulate or copy.

I was in time to see Efros' last productions. They were already at the highest level. Or Vasiliev in the late 1980s, who also moved the Russian school into the so-called playful theatre, which toys with… the lousy realism, as it were. As a result, realism gets raised to a higher level. When Vasiliev decided to advance the playful theatre to what I believe was an ever higher level, up to the metaphysics of the form, he, unfortunately, remained misunderstood, because the audience was simply not able to appreciate it. I believe this was the tragedy of his life, since he started going along this trajectory where he became more and more lonely.

This is something I have also felt while walking along my own path: there are these crossroads and you can take either way. I have tried going down the more delicate and refined way, but the understanding of the audience diminishes in proportion as well. I, however, am one of those directors who like it when the audience does understand, when there is dialogue with the audience.

Just like all my generation, I was frustrated with the directing around me and that is why I took a sort of antagonistic track against the mainstream early on. My role models and inspirations came from elsewhere— from people who do not come from the theatre, like Pina Bausch and Christoph Marthaler. I was more likely to seek out how to organise a story, which theatre language to use exactly from people who do not come from the theatre at all. Visual arts, cinema—that seemed to influence me a lot more. And, of course, around this part of the world and among my generation, a major influence was most certainly the Lithuanian director Eimuntas Nekrošius. The linear theatre, staging plays, especially with our youthful go-getter attitude—it all seemed so senile and boring. Nekrošius offered a whole new ball game! Yes, we had extremely little trust in theatre as simply speaking text. The talking heads to us were just so yesterday.

Pina Bausch was the first one to introduce me to a metaphorical theatre, where each situation is abstracted down to a trick—a trick that also gains some of the poetic meaning of a metaphor. That, oh, that—yes, that is cool! We want to do that too! We all saw the process of analysing texts as a waste of time. All we've got to do is just come up with tricks! I have to say, the audience was tired of speaking texts as well. You could feel that the audience was also craving some new theatre language.

By now, of course, all of it has changed seven times over. I, for example, have been focused on speaking texts for several years now. That's when the text is exactly absolutised. That is something that will definitely end, and a new thing will come along.

I want to underline the Russian acting school as the cornerstone. At the end of the day, it has always served as a beacon for me, so I can maintain my course. One can do conceptual theatre, documentary theatre or melodrama, do any type of genre, but the actor must never be bored on stage. The actor must be given as much work as possible; they must be loaded with tasks that are as complex as possible, so that they always have several dimensions. The actor must, after all, be at the centre of the stage; well, yes, they must be the most important thing.[1]

Grzegorz Jarzyna: (1) Before studies: Stanisław Ignacy Witkiewicz—life and works, his original Unity-in-Multiplicity Theory; journeys and research on Asian and Central American cultures from the perspective of Antonin Artaud's and Jerzy Grotowski's books. (2) Study period: performances and education under the guidance of Krystian Lupa at the Theatre Academy in Cracow. (3) First three years of creative work after debut: movies directed by Alfred Hitchcock and Quentin Tarantino, David Lynch and Lars von Trier in the last a dozen or so years; residual and casual inspirations from the area of art house cinema and new technologies. It is very inspiring in my work to be open and share ideas with all creators engaged in the process of realising performance.[2]

Jan Klata: Euripides, Sun Ra, Lew Kuleszow, Captain Beefheart, Philip K. Dick, Fela Kuti, John Cage, Andrzej Żuławski, Claudio Monteverdi, Muhammad Ali, Brian Eno, Iggy Pop, John Coltrane, Tadeusz Kantor, Rei Kawakubo, Serge Gainsbourg, Holger Czukay, William Shakespeare,

---

[1] Translated by Kristina Guste.
[2] Translated by Artur Duda.

AN ATTEMPT AT DRAWING AN ARTISTIC FAMILY TREE   269

Joseph Beuys, Glenn Gould, Alfred Korzybski, Alan Moore, Martin Margiela, Aby Warburg, Iggy Pop, Andriej Płatonow, Alejandro Jodorowsky, Miles Davis, Robert Wyatt, Ayrton Senna, Francis Bacon, Charles Mingus, Rick Owens, David Bowie, Lee "Scratch" Perry, Fernand Braudel, Scott Walker.

Oskaras Koršunovas: First: Eimuntas Nekrošius. I saw his performances at a very young age. I was maybe 16 years old. It was the golden period at the Youth Theatre when he staged *The Square, Pirosmani, Pirosmani...* I was especially impressed by *The Day Lasts More Than a Hundred Years.*

Then came a time when I became very interested in Jurgis Mačiūnas and the Fluxus movement. But it rather affected my life philosophy. If we talk about a family tree in this respect, then I was very influenced by the punk movement, which at that time was also an anti-system movement in Soviet Lithuania. The punk dress was a direct protest against the Soviet rule; the punk rock made an indelible influence on me.

My direct teacher was the Lithuanian theatre director Jonas Vaitkus, with whom I studied. He affected both me and the Lithuanian theatre. He created a completely non-Russian, but rather a Western type of theatre. He was a classical modernist and, at the same time, a non-conformist in the theatre and life; a person who understands the roots and laws of theatre.

My first performance was *There to Be Here* by Daniil Kharms. Afterwards, I built a trilogy based on the works of Kharms. In total, I have staged about ten performances based on the work of Kharms and Alexander Vvedensky. They and the OBERIU association were the radical avant-garde of the first half of the twentieth century. Kharms wrote that a poem needs to be written in such a way that if you throw it at the window the glass would shatter. He also spoke of the "inverted arithmetic of faith." It shaped my understanding that art has its own reality and its own laws, and that those laws have nothing to do with life: art has a different physics and the reality of art is stronger than the reality of life. It is not that art is created from life; it is life that is created from art. It means that we live as much as we are creative. As Hamlet inspects the rotten Kingdom of Denmark through the theatre, so I began to analyse the world and myself in theatre.

There was a time when I really admired Antonin Artaud. I admired Jerzy Grotowski, Anatolij Vasilyev less, but delved deeper into their work. When the Poles saw my *There to Be Here*, they said that it is

Image 1 A drawing by Krystian Lupa of his artistic family tree

unbelievable—they recognised Tadeusz Kantor. From my wide open eyes, they gathered that I didn't know who Kantor was. They were stunned and then arranged for me a trip to Poland, to the Kantor Museum, to his homeland. There I saw *The Dead Class* and was very impressed. I am also interested in Christoph Marthaler and Frank Castorf. Of course, a lot of persons affected me. Also: Pina Bausch and especially the personal meetings with her at the festival in Wuppertal.

I started directing very early and tried to break down all possible stereotypes. Already in my first performance *There to Be Here* I ironised Eimuntas Nekrošius. At the age of 21, I had already worked at the National Theatre as a director and had looked at everything critically. In general, influences are only relevant in youth. Let's say I couldn't watch any theatre in Lithuania at that time except for Nekrošius. I expected pure art from the theatre. For me, Joseph Beuys, for instance, was the theatre. I don't think about it now and yet, I feel everything still lives in me.

Jernej Lorenci: Ritual, religious beliefs, religious practices, sacred texts, mythology, epics. *The Iliad*, the *Epic of Gilgamesh, Mahabharata,*

AN ATTEMPT AT DRAWING AN ARTISTIC FAMILY TREE   271

Metamorphoses, Das Nibelungenlied, the Bible. Also C. G. Jung, C. L. Strauss, Mircea Eliade.

Novels, first and foremost and for a long time: from Cervantes, Laclos, Dostoevsky and Tolstoy to Mann, Kafka, Butor, Duras, Fuentes, Rushdie, Llosa, Kazantzakis, Bruckner, Kiš, Bernhard and Knausgard.

To this day I still look for inspiration in images, structures and atmospheres from epics and novels. Rarely from theatre itself, even less so from dramatic texts. Maybe from the Polish branch of theatre practices (only as an example): Witkiewicz, Gombrowitcz, Kantor, Grotowsky, Kott.

Old Testament of Artaud and New Testament of Brook.

A few examples of my first theatre memories in terms of performances: as a 14-year-old—La Fura dels Baus (*Tier Mon*), as a 15-year-old—Tomaž Pandur (*Scheherezade*), as a 16-year-old: Roberto Ciulli (*Kaspar Hauser*). Also: Emile M. Cioran. Hannah Arendt. William Blake.

Krystian Lupa: (Image 1)

Jan Mikulášek: As a student, I was mesmerised by the works of the director Jan Antonín Pitínský, later on also Vladimír Morávek. In both cases I saw a distinct sense of rhythm of the show and emphasis on the visual aspects. I was influenced by their work with stylised acting and by their ability to switch between the poetic and the expressive, the ironic and the sincere. Nowadays, I mostly follow the works of my generation of peers: Jiří Havelka, Anna Davidová, Daniel Špinar or Jan Frič. A new source of inspiration has been my three years of teaching acting classes at DAMU: I try to follow which subjects students seek out and which, on the other hand, they find trivial.[3]

Alexander Morfov: I've never been inspired by theatre. A formative role for me has been played by classicism, the paradox, irony, anti-classicism, dreams, hatred and love, egotism, altruism, empathy, misanthropy and the feeling of how important and unnecessary I am in this world! My inspirations are... I will enumerate them as they come to me at that very moment: Chaplin, Fellini, Mozart, Raphael, Caravaggio, Michelangelo, the baroque, Georg Gross, expressionism, the 7th Symphony, surrealism, Buñuel, Marquez, Monty Python, the sea, death, my childhood, rock-and-roll, Pergolesi and the wind in the reeds (according to *Becket*), Don Quixote and Winnie the Pooh... and more and more...

---

[3] Translated by Michal Zahálka.

Eimuntas Nekrošius:[4] Perhaps I stand out among my colleagues for not following the rules. I do not follow the traditions or the rules when I create a production or analyse a text. It seems to me that any rules and schemes restrict one's personality, lead to self-expression in stagnation. I respect Stanislavski, other theatre teachers, but I ignore them, I do as I want, not as it is accepted or needed.

When I interact with actors, I do not interact with employees, but with personalities. I like not to turn an actor into a character, but to show the character through unique, interesting, unusual traits of the actor's character and personality.

I never thought about applying the themes of a performance to something that is relevant to the audience at one time or another. I chose artwork for a performance driven by an inner search, but… I think our time is longing for sincerity, reluctance and inability to lie, it is longing for love, for relationships based on people… Apparently, I am longing for it. That is why I'm talking about it. Frankly, I don't even need public recognition. The basic satisfaction comes from within, not from the outside.

If I feel that I have done what I wanted to do, if I know that it is a big and powerful thing, then no one matters—the audience can be blown away, the critics can laugh, and I will still be happy. For this is my victory. Well, if you know you have done nothing, neither trophies nor popularity will help you. From praise, the inner resentment will only increase. An artist can put his conscience to sleep but only for a short time. Someday the conscience will still wake up and name things by their real names.

You need to be yourself. You will not learn much from books, from other people's life experiences. You will still have to experience it all, to walk all mountains with your feet. You must experience everything yourself, you must yourself overcome all mountains. Only in this way true knowledge can be acquired. Therefore, you never need to save yourself because it's the same as saving yourself from life.

Béla Pintér: My starting point is always personal. Many of my pieces treat autobiographical issues, motives. And, naturally, on a broader scale my country's problems influence and inspire my thoughts. In the last few years (culture) politics and overall social behaviour have come more into focus.

---

[4] *Vakarų ekspresas*, 21 November 2018; https://www.ve.lt/naujienos/visuomene/zmones/eimuntas-nekrosius-nereikia-savo-kailio-tausoti1-1676271/ [accessed 2 March 2019] Interview with the director, first published on 26 April 2010.

I started my professional life as an actor, so in my first few years my main goal was to become a "perfect" actor—to learn all the skills—vocal, physical, mental... My idol was at that time the Russian company Derevo. Their metaphysical presence on stage was astonishing. Since I write and direct, I have seen many contemporary performances, and I am happy to be enchanted, but I cannot single out anybody.

Silviu Purcărete: My grandfather, Ilarian, a man without too much formal education, totally devoid of artistic interests, was the overwhelming, quintessential personality who pushed me—in a way unclear to me at that stage—and, of course, against his will, towards the field of art. When I was 3 years old, he would hold my hand with a pencil in it and make me draw fleas with Egyptian anthropomorphic figures. When I was 5 years old, he enjoyed listening to my theories about the mysteries of cinema: I suspected that some dwarfs hidden behind the screen would move the actors, like in a sophisticated shadow play. Later, when I was already a student at the Theatre Institute in Bucharest, he would say to my grandmother, with a sense of disappointment in his voice, that the job of director for which I was just preparing would mean "some kind of whore entrepreneur!" It's true that he could say such outrageous things because, at that time, there were no feminist movements, no "me too" or anything of the kind.

Then, when I discovered culture, on the trunk provided by my grandfather grew all sorts of branches: Bulgakov, Kubrik, Roy Andersson, Louis de Funès, Richard Strauss, Apuleius, de Sade, Euripides, Caragiale, Ionesco, Schubert, Cezar Joao Monteiro, Marquez, Dostoevsky, Borges, Benedict Erofeev, Dante Alighieri, Peter Bruegel the Elder, Desiderio Monsù, Tarkovski, Munch, Böcklin, Lucian Pintilie, Brook, Valeriu Moisescu, Fellini... let's stop, because there are too many to mention, but not before I mention a few books from the Septuagint and the New Testament.

Árpád Schilling: I was influenced by several major artists. The first name to mention is Gábor Székely, who was my head teacher at the University of Budapest for five years. It was from him that I could learn how to respect a dramatic text. How do we analyse it? What do we look for behind the sentences? How do we interpret conflicts and characters? Bertolt Brecht (from whom I borrowed the name of my company: Chalk Circle) captivated me with his clear thinking, his "laboratory art" and his social commitment. I was greatly impressed by Peter Brook's works in his old age for their clarity, simplicity and minimalism. Ariane Mnouchkine's community commitment and the social mission of her theatre also fascinated me, despite the fact that the performances she produced were not stylistically captivating for me. My encounter with TIE (Theatre In Education) as a genre of art education was especially important. The complex task of drama teachers (paying attention to students as a teacher and to the play as an actor) had a strong impact on me in my work with actors. *Gaudeamus* by Lev Dodin, as a good example for poetic theatre and for common creativity, often floated in my mind.

However, I learnt the most about theatre from Chekhov and Shakespeare by reading, interpreting and staging their plays. From Chekhov I learnt how to be a good judge of human character and from Shakespeare—the poetry of theatre.

I was also intrigued by the aesthetics of the new French circus, the language of German and British contemporary drama, and the libertine world and ruthless politics of happenings of the 1960s and 1970s. I was also influenced by film-makers—by their dramaturgy, their methods for leading actors and their consistent visual world: Fassbinder, Tarkovsky, Trier, Cassavetes, the Dardenne brothers, Mike Leigh, Buñuel, Cristi Puiu, Andrey Zvyagintsev and so on.

Paintings by Francis Bacon, Hieronymus Bosch and Caravaggio, photographs by Richard Avedon, music by Ligeti, John Cage and Miles Davis complement the theatre and film horizons.

And, generally speaking, any new discovery. The family tree is not finished.

Andrei Șerban: First, it was my education at the Romanian Theatre Academy and my first few years as a young director in Romania. The good practice there of being open both to Stanislavski and Meyerhold was great, since I was able to use these two powerful systems that at once contradict and complement each other. This was the advantage of studying during Communism, which is opposite to what is happening now in Romania. Then, when I arrived in New York in my mid-20s, I faced a completely different situation: the avant-garde was very strong. But it was also shocking to me, as a person coming from such a rigorous and strict academic background. So I went through a series of art shocks. Yet I profited from working with the radical and free artists who worked at La MaMa, since I got from them a sense of freedom in improvisation and breaking the rules. They had no discipline and rigour, but they had incredible courage to try anything. The boundaries of theatre were not clear anymore. This provoked a kind of anarchy in me, which I needed very much because in Communist Romania nothing was anarchic, everything was way too

AN ATTEMPT AT DRAWING AN ARTISTIC FAMILY TREE   275

structured. So that influence from downtown experimental Theatre La MaMa, the Open Theatre of Joseph Chaikin, the Living Theatre was very strong.

I was also very interested in the new music. I went to many concerts. Meeting John Cage was an extraordinary shock. I further understood what freedom means and how art has no boundaries and how you can be sensitive to new possibilities. Also, I went to see the performances of Merce Cunningham. Andy Warhol had his famous Factory Studio next to La MaMa and I could see all these avant-garde artists working with him every day, when I was going to my rehearsals. All this had a strong influence on me.

The big luck I had was that Peter Brook came to New York, saw my very first production which I did at La MaMa, and the same evening he invited me to join him in Paris, at the International Centre that was just getting started. It was 1970. This, of course, changed my life. I spent a whole year there and went to the Shiraz Festival as part of the assistant directors' team working on the historical play *Orghast at Persepolis*. That made me question everything I was doing in the theatre. For, until that moment, I was working just out of the joy of being at the theatre. I didn't know what my responsibility was. It was pure, young joy. And suddenly, after meeting Brook, I had only question marks. The joy was gone. No more joy, only pain. I was asking myself why am I doing things so easily, why am I accepting and enjoying such superficial decisions? Why am I not going deeper? Why am I not putting more obstacles and challenges in front of me to see what my potential was? The whole year I spent there was a year of great search into myself as an artist and a human being. I was trying to see who I am, what I'm here for, why am I doing theatre, what is my aim and responsibility. Now fifty years later I have not found any answers. There are no answers to any of these questions. It's just a very long search, which continues even now as I'm saying this.

Daniel Špinar: I'm not going to be very original. Our generation was mostly influenced by the directors of the late 1990s. I went to see Petr Lébl's productions often, of course, Michal Dočekal's, and most of all those of Jan Nebeský, who later became my teacher and shaped my way of thinking about the theatre immensely. Vladimír Morávek was another director who interested me at that time, along with—not to forget—Jan Antonín Pitínský. All these are directors with very original approaches to a given material and I was always interested in strong directors. Even from the beginning, as a spectator, I wanted to see some personal approach to the texts. To these days there are spectators who claim that we rape the great classic plays and that we don't honour the author's intentions. Whereas what I always like to see is an original, fresh take on everything: what's new and contemporary about Chekhov, about Shakespeare. This generation was also very visual; they were directors who focused on a visual style, on an image of the production.

As for the foreign directors, I remember those huge Marthaler shows during the Prague German Language Theatre Festival and, of course, the works of Thomas Ostermeier. René Pollesch has always been a favourite of mine, with his slightly weird aesthetics... Currently I always try to follow Martin Kušej, he is—for me—perhaps the most interesting director today, even though he mostly does opera. I could name more, but these were most important for me—also very visual and also breaking conventions, something especially important in the somewhat stale environment of Czech theatre, which I would at times compare to a small museum.

I'm also very much interested in visual arts, especially in contemporary painting. I do like museums, but what's happening right now is what fascinates me. Overall, in pop culture, I'm fond of artists who push the limits of show business. I've been a long-time fan of Madonna, for instance. Her stage shows are highly theatrical. I really enjoy American quality TV today, because I feel that a lot of contemporary plays come from the same source, such as *The Night Season*, which I staged a few years ago.

I read quite a lot. Lately I've come back to reading lots of novels, because it stimulates the fantasy and also provides great material for stage works. I think that any director needs to be very receptive all the time.

When I travel, I'm always interested in seeing theatre abroad, not only productions, but also the overall context. I'd say that on a global scale, theatres tend to focus on spectators as parts of productions, even to the point when audiences are more important than directors. This is quite different compared to how it was before. Telling stories is turning away from constructed situations towards documentary stuff, no longer even needing actors and rather using people who've actually lived through the given problem.[5]

Włodzimierz Staniewski: I perceive myself as a creator self-excluded from artistic families. I am inventing and practising my life-in-art in seclusion. I convoke people to work in seclusion, I build a material theatre in seclusion, I convoke an audience in seclusion and this is where, in seclusion, I present my theatrical works. There is a clear provenance with the "separateness" of Miron Białoszewski.

---

[5] Translated by Michal Zahálka.

I identify with life (without any restrictions) and I transform this life. In the book *Hidden Territories*, I coined the motto "identify and transform," which I still practise.

I gaze on average people and play tricks so as to explore their hidden beauty and enliven their suppressed powers. I mingle with natural phenomena and by the means of thought I attempt to grasp them as events presenting transfiguration (transformation) of natural phenomena. It is the enjoinment of space and time that is searched for. In art I am most probably a tramp. A wanderer.

When I was a student in Kraków, the academic family was the most magnificent. In my directorial work I have been referring to self-directing laws and rituals of the seven liberal arts, to ancient, medieval and renaissance schools as the quintessence of a theatre family. I'm inclined to do so even today. What you discover should be disseminated. The Theatrical Centre should follow the pattern established by the gymnasium of Athens and the Platonic Academy and the disciples of Sais…

Taken for questioning and tortured, I would have to confess to the inspiration I take from Meyerhold. And Euripides is the ultimate oracle in all aspects of theatre.[6]

Rimas Tuminas: In Lithuania it was Juozas Miltinis, the artistic and general director of the Panevėžys State Drama Theatre. People are still debating whether he was a great director or a great philosopher. He expressed his philosophy through performance. His performances were followed by meetings with him. I was very much influenced by his reflections on the world, the place of humans and their mission in art.

The second major influence was Anatoly Efros in Moscow: productions, rehearsals, meetings with him. At the same time, Giorgio Strehler—from a distance: his works and reflections on theatre. Speaking of contemporary directors who are working today: Anatoly Vasiliev.[7]

Reference

Vakarų ekspresas, 2018 11 21; https://www.ve.lt/naujienos/visuomene/zmones/eimuntas-nekrosius-nereikia-savo-kailio-tausoti1-1676271/ [accessed 2 March 2019] Interview with Eimuntas Nekrošius, first published on 26 April 2010.

[6] E-mail correspondence. The night of 3–4 February 2020. Translated by Tomasz Wiśniewski.

[7] Translated by Anna Shulgat.

The Stakes Today

*Marvin Carlson, Kamila Černá, Kim Cuculić,
Artur Duda, Katarzyna Kręglewska, Blaž Lukan,
Octavian Saiu, Kalina Stefanova, Edīte Tišheizere,
Dmitry Trubotchkin, Rasa Vasinauskaitė,
Tomasz Wiśniewski, and Michal Zahálka*

We asked the directors included in the book to try to define the issues that contemporary theatre faces today, especially in its relationship with the new off-stage realities. We also asked them to dwell on how theatre retains, develops and re-imagines its role of a defender of humanity and harmony in an increasingly disharmonious society. Again, only in the case of the late Lithuanian director Eimuntas Nekrošius are excerpts of existing interviews with him and about him used. Here is what all the rest had to say.

M. Carlson (✉)
City University of New York, New York, NY, USA

K. Černá • M. Zahálka
Arts and Theatre Institute, Prague, Czech Republic
e-mail: kamila.cerna@idu.cz

K. Cuculić
Novi List Newspaper, Rijeka, Croatia

© The Author(s), under exclusive license to Springer Nature
Switzerland AG 2021
K. Stefanova, M. Carlson (eds.), *20 Ground-Breaking Directors of
Eastern Europe*, https://doi.org/10.1007/978-3-030-52935-2_22

280   M. CARLSON ET AL.

Grzegorz Bral: In my own work I'm focused on understanding acting, directing, text, and everything on stage as a particular craft. I'd like to use a term: MINDFUL ACTING. I would often associate theatre with music and acting with the craft of a musician. Training in music is a gradual process, so is training in acting. It is a step-by-step way to recognise what is one delivering from stage to audience. Walking in life and walking on stage are two different ways of being. Speaking in life and speaking on stage are two different ways of being. And so on. Everything we do on stage has a purpose and must be imbued with extreme awareness, and therefore *mindful*. In these days of our human existence I believe being aware of one's own *actions* is vital and most important. Acting can teach

---

A. Duda
Nicolaus Copernicus University, Toruń, Poland
e-mail: dudaart@umk.pl

K. Kręglewska • T. Wiśniewski
University of Gdańsk, Gdańsk, Poland
e-mail: katarzyna.kreglewska@ug.edu.pl; tomasz.wisniewski@ug.edu.pl

B. Lukan
Academy for Theatre, Radio, Film and Television, University of Ljubljana, Ljubljana, Slovenia
e-mail: blaz.lukan@guest.arnes.si

O. Saiu
National University of Theatre and Film, Bucharest, Romania

K . Stefanova
National Academy for Theatre and Film Arts, Sofia, Bulgaria
e-mail: 111@kalina-stefanova.com

E. Tišheizere
Institute of Literature, Folklore and Arts of the University of Latvia, Riga, Latvia

D. Trubotchkin
State Institute for Art Studies, Graduate School of Performing Arts, Russian Institute of Theatre Arts (GITIS), Moscow, Russia

R. Vasinauskaitė
Lithuanian Music and Theatre Academy, Lithuanian Culture Research Institute, Vilnius, Lithuania

people to be *mindful*. Acting can teach people to understand that all one does on stage must be full of respect for the others there. Acting can teach that one is not alone on stage and therefore one needs to collaborate with all partners in order to achieve a proper performance. Acting can't leave a mess on stage. There will be others entering the stage tomorrow. If one leaves a mess, no one else will be able to perform on the same stage. Acting is about understanding of the basic principles of life and this I see as its main role in the future and for future generations.

Gianina Cărbunariu: Theatre has always had as its mission to change the official agenda, to try to bring to the viewers subjects and ideas that are otherwise put in the second plan, ignored or hidden by those in power. For even if the media are touching upon subjects such as social inequity, racism, global warming or people's lives in war zones, the way television is dealing with important topics is not an inclusive one. On the contrary, it is a sad and derisory simulation of a dialogue that is actually never happening. That is why theatre has now (as always) the potential to offer a place for a real dialogue, for reflection, for the confrontation of different perspectives in a safe environment. The interactions that social media offer to online participants give the false feeling that a dialogue is taking place. But the violence and the polarisation of different discourses in the last years show so clearly that this is not a real and meaningful communication. That is why for me theatre remains the place where people with different ideas can meet, share an experience and sometimes reflect on it together in post-performance discussions (private discussions with friends or public discussions with the artistic team and the other spectators).

The challenge for the theatre and for theatre people is to give themselves time to understand what happens outside the rehearsal room, to be in touch with spectators with different backgrounds (not only with the intellectual elite or spectators who can afford to buy a theatre ticket) and to try to imagine global answers to global problems. It is obvious that the world we are living in now has become unbearably unjust, cynical, led by cartoon-like politicians, and that we, as humanity, have to leave behind the practices of today and dare to create new models of thinking. As a creator of original scenarios, theatre could be a place of imagining new possibilities—a "rehearsal for revolution," as Augusto Boal said.

Oliver Frljić: There are at least two possible paths that theatre can take in a time when reality is constantly shaped, re-shaped and distorted by all those new media and unprecedented forms of surveillance introduced by the same media. Theatre can either try to imitate those media and their respective strategies and representations or insist on its own essence, which somehow opposes the world where everything is already mediatised. The former is most of the time expressed in theatre's return to the live co-presence of a performer and the audience. But we should keep in mind that both of those paths have ethical implications as well. To make theatre compete with new media means to put it in the same ideological arena—either by trying to participate in the same promise of omnipresence and instant-ness, or by turning to conservative essentialist politics. I have never believed in theatre trying to create harmony. Theatre should not unify the audience, it should rather antagonise it, show how their gender, class or any other identity participates in the general economy of inclusion and exclusion. Theatre is the place where invisible social division and structural violence should come under a lens and create respective actions.

Alvis Hermanis: Culture is the one thing that harmonises everything, which is wonderful, but art is still somewhat of a destructive charge. Artists are still, as the marvellous Latvian painter Jānis Pauluks put it, supposed to be slightly reeking of piss at all times. Working in theatre to harmonise the world—we shouldn't be worrying and thinking about that. In fact, we should be thinking about the opposite. Over the past few seasons, I've had this new discovery for myself, it's like an indicator of whether or not a performance has been a success—it's when people who haven't seen it argue and talk about it. This means that the topic hits society in a weak spot where everyone gets nervous and anxious... And that is, of course, also done with the purpose of harmonising something, but it's more of a nasty act. That's why I like it when we have productions that the audiences view and get nervous afterwards. Asking the most disgusting questions in a completely politically incorrect manner. If the theatre becomes a politically correct area, that's the end of it all.

It is for this reason that I look upon the new generation with great interest—they lack this instinct completely. They do not possess the instinct of stepping on mines. They constantly avoid the mines. Our generation had this principle: if there is a mine somewhere, you must absolutely step on it. This new generation is more of a feel-good one. It's important for them to have everything nice, cute and stylish. We were the

THE STAKES TODAY   **283**

opposite: we were always worried in case anyone ever thought we were softies or something.[1]

Grzegorz Jarzyna: The role of theatre is to be involved in transforming the hierarchic paradigm of thinking about the art and artists. The empowerment of all performers engaged in creating the final piece of work. The empowerment of the audience: the emotional, energetic and intellectual exchange between the artists and the audience. It's about theatre-makers sharing ideas and their mission with other people or different cultural communities. Theatre has been a place of social debates. It should still function as an active and culture-creating institution, having impact on the social transformations of our age, especially regarding the equal rights of women, LGBT communities, outsiders and immigrants. Theatre has to oppose all forms of intolerance, limitations of people's rights and freedom without regard for their nationality or cultural identity. Issues of race—white race supremacy—seem to be particularly significant for me. My newest performance will be devoted to the criticism of anthropocentric attitudes in the context of Shakespeare's *Tempest*.[2]

Ian Klata: I don't know, but I keep trying to find that out.

Oskaras Koršunovas: Theatre is becoming more and more social, but it is not as critical as it was in Soviet times. Then good theatre was in opposition to the system and the society. It was the place of resistance. Now theatre has become mainstream. Its sociality and positivity are often just clichés. Theatre has lost its critique and elitism, and is increasingly becoming a non-artistic venue, a place for non-art. Art becomes a part of social processes, but sociality kills art. Today, a new generation of creators and spectators are coming to the theatre. They do not accept any authoritarianism. The director is no longer an authority, nor is the author. These are natural processes, but with them the art of theatre seems to dissolve.

Theatre should be contradictory in nature. But theatre will survive not because it will compete with the flow of knowledge (internet, Google, social networks), but because of the presence of the live actor and as a place for real meetings. Theatre becomes needed as a living source and can become very important again.

Jernej Lorenci: Theatre does not want a performance, it wants an event. It does not want to present, it wants to be. Fully present.

It wants to happen here and now, in this fragile, empty and merciless intersection between the stage and the auditorium. In absolute present.

---

[1] Translated by Kristina Guste.
[2] Translated by Artur Duda.

It is against repetition and predictability. It is against moralising and preaching. It despises the new for the sake of the new.

It wants to be uncertain, unforeseeable, risky.

It wants to seduce and repel. To caress and to mangle. To bore and to enchant. And often all of that at the same time.

Theatre wants us to look at familiar, well-known things and see them differently.

It is obsessed with love, death, solitude, fear, with the individual and the community. And with endless combinations and variations of them all.

Theatre knows that there is no right variation, no variation is final or finite. But, at the same time, it is aware that phony combinations and covert imitations are the end of its magic.

But mostly it knows when we are together. Or when we are each for ourselves.

Actors make me a director. My wife makes me a husband. Pipa and Jakob make me a father. My students make me a professor. Peter Brook makes me young. Susanne Kennedy makes me old. Jan Klata makes me overweight. Sidi Larbi Cherkaoui makes me tall. People smarter than me make me dumb. And I am intelligent because I'm not the dumbest. The religious make me an atheist. The Germans, Chileans and Syrians make me a Slovenian. I exist only through relation. I am a sum of relations. As oneself I am nothing.

Under the magnifying glass of theatre—in theatre everything small becomes big—my nothingness becomes even more null, when I don't anchor myself to the net of relations. When I misuse the stage to exhibit myself. When as a spectator I sit in the stalls only because it's befitting.

Theatre wants all of me, with everything that I am. It doesn't make differences and judgements, it doesn't moralise. Theatre wants me to crave, to crave truly. And it also wants me to indulge, almost to the point of dispersion. Therefore to be totally myself and simultaneously some kind of not-me who is also you and him and them.

Once upon a time within man there appeared a crack. Which eventually became a void. From this void theatre was born. It generously offers to us this void, its empty space—the theatrical stage—where we can gather, meet and settle in. And sometimes, when a performance becomes an event, to fill it in.

Krystian Lupa: Perhaps theatre retains certain secrets in the area of the truth which has been disappearing from our reality, from the public dis-

THE STAKES TODAY   285

course? Not only through what it is saying, affirming or asking about—> but in the context of relationships. What is happening to us when we are trying to talk with one another—>both in theatre and real life. Our relationships undergo intangible processes of destruction. What is happening in the field of politics stems from the deterioration of us as a society and the degradation of reality created by people. The eagerness of our civilization condemns human beings to terminal moral and spiritual passivity.

The hidden truth of dignity and identity being lost in social relationships may be retouched in theatrical rites—>in the mystery of common participation. I'm aware that what I am trying to say is quite vague.

I want to say that if you feel anxiety, fear, despair, dismay or rebel against what you are spotting in your world and yourself, and in other people, in more and more mendacious people who you are governed by—> you will be able to find [the truth] in the increasingly intense ritual of performances created in cooperation with artistic partners, in discovering the most complex human gestures within these works. Whether we regain our artistic truth in the reality, in which this truth has been devalued, depends on the fact to what extent you are able to sacrifice your humanity in your performances.

This is the question of exploring a new language, narration or acting [methods]. In what forms, what signs we will convert our profound and most poignant feelings? This is not only the necessity of searching for the revival of our artistic activity, but also the need for the resurrection of our humanity that has been still declining. We cannot hide our poverty and helplessness. Simply expressing our views is not sufficient. We have to work on our fears and anxieties to generate an underlying message. Not to be content with just hysterical expressions of it. Maybe theatre is the place where we can face all that we have recently learnt to avoid.

… Maybe theatre, the venue of human (religious) ritual, is the place where something is to be revealed…

What shall we do in particular?

Each of us [should follow] extremely our deepest intuition. Alas, what a cliché. What if we tried to consider theatre as creating the world from scratch, with the whole incompleteness of basic ingredients. If we tried not to miss the moments that we constantly overlook in our real life. The performative theatre as a process of discovering lost paths of human suffering…

Not to settle for the mere message conveyed by texts invented to follow our needs and our intuition. What is most significant nowadays is: to discover and complete ourselves—>consider rehearsals and performances—>as an opportunity for common investigation. Only the most extreme personal message will retain something deeply true. Let's try to generate a dilemma on which we are working in its most drastic, personal and difficult shape. We do have it—>the capability to fight—>but we have to pose the most strenuous challenge for ourselves in order to get it. The struggle to prevent the world from collapsing, the fight against the vague and intangible human catastrophe, demands an extremely creative sacrifice from each of us. Theatre is a seance, it is necessary to express within it everything unreadable that is inscribed in us.

Theatre is a place where the illegible writing is being deciphered constantly.[3]

Jan Mikulášek: Compared to the really serious problems that theatre-makers in Hungary or in Russia have to face, we don't have much to complain about in the Czech Republic. Our main problem is the long-time underfinancing of culture as a whole. Actors, set designers, directors have to stage several productions in very short periods of time throughout the year. Such a mad tempo may over the years lead to a feeling of disillusion and burn-out. Czech audiences, as well as theatre critics, seem to me rather conservative. I don't know why, but over the past few years there's a demand for theatre in a style reminiscent of the 1970s. In such an atmosphere, any even slightly radical approach is seen as disrespect for the author, as a self-centred effort to present oneself and as a gratuitous shock.

In a time dominated by social media, manipulating and dividing us, and leading us to a state of deadly apathy, theatre is one of the last places of direct human contact, live dialogue and confrontation. In a world of digital friendships and fake news, theatre should offer authenticity and sincerity; it should be able to challenge established truths and positions. More and more often I hear demands for greater accessibility of theatrical language and for some kind of hope we should be offering our spectators. If, however, theatre should reflect the fluid nature of our times, it must also be a space where theatre-goers face uncertainty, doubt, incomprehensibility, complexity, abstraction. Theatre could also be a space where we wonder about the very sense of theatre.

In the beginning of the staging process of a devised production, I tend to deliver as diverse a mixture of materials as possible, in order to help the actors navigate through the given topic. We work with literary texts,

---

[3] Translated by Katarzyna Grabowska.

essays, newspaper articles, photos, documentaries, etc. As clichéd as this might sound, my greatest source of inspiration is the actors and the entire production team. I try to stay open to any notion, any impulse that may arrive. It happens to me from time to time that some ideas that appear shallow or naive can actually turn out to be powerful on stage. When interpreting a classic text, I am most inspired by the stage designs of Marek Cpin, my creative partner of almost twenty years.

When I sit at home with a text, my imagination is most stimulated by music, which is also a means of disconnecting from the outside world. When working on a complex scene with the actors, I often put on music to let them get an intuitive grasp of the intended atmosphere, instead of describing it at length.[4]

Alexander Morfov: The problem a director faces is one and only: the director themselves.

Eimuntas Nekrošius: We have empty years, empty days and empty months alike in our lives. We only have a handful of real life. Almost everything is wasted time. However, we all imitate that we are in a hurry, that we do not have time, and that we are and will be very busy for a few years ahead. This is not true. This is how we deceive ourselves and others. Theatre directing is a primitive, simple profession. It is just the organisation of a particular action.[5]

Theatre artists want comfort and say that if they had another hall, another building, the theatre would be better and work would be easier. It won't be better. First and foremost, you need to insist on yourself. A young person has many new ideas, yet over time he begins to feel hunger for ideas. And no book, no method will help to gain them. I am not saying that one cannot improve until the end of one's life. But I think that is not true. Time is coming and nature itself does not allow one to progress. What you read yesterday you have forgotten today. Once upon a time we were told "Learn, learn, learn." No. This is nonsense. We lack good, exciting, new ideas today. Theatre lacks good ideas.[6]

[4] Translated by Michal Zahálka.

[5] https://www.lrt.lt/naujienos/kultura/12/1117360/metai-po-eimunto-nekrosiaus-mirties-to-tikro-gyvenimo-buvo-tik-saujele [accessed 24 July 2019]. The interview was shown for the first time on 9 January 2017.

[6] *Bernardinai.lt*, 23 November 2018; http://www.bernardinai.lt/straipsnis/2018-11-23-teatro-amziaus-mohikanai/172989 [accessed 4 February 2020]. From a meeting with directors Eimuntas Nekrošius, Jonas Vaitkus, Gintaras Varnas on 15 November 2018 at the Vilnius Small Theatre.

Rolandas Kazlas (an actor) about Eimuntas Nekrošius' theatre: Now that the Director is gone, we can confirm that he was the Man who made the permanent Paradise on the Theatre stage. Eimuntas Nekrošius, one of the very few who have managed to transcend the boundaries of the profession, of theatre and of art in general, and to look at the earthly human life from the other, the Divine side. Like his character Dante,[7] the Director tried—and succeeded!—to connect the earth and the sky, proving that the human being could do it. It was the Director who was able to raise humanity to Divinity.[8]

Béla Pintér: I believe in my profession, I want to do it as best as is possible. I have to go into social problems as deeply and cruelly as I can, I have to be self-critical all the time, and if I succeed and find the sharpest language to tell what I felt, then the audience will follow me and together we create something new and liberating. I believe in story, in the mixture of tragedy and comedy. Our performances can be of mental help to our audience.

Silviu Purcărete: I do not know to what extent my opinion in this regard could count today. I belong to a generation that has almost finished its mission. And anyway, as a European artist, a man, a "Caucasian," heterosexual man and, above all, an Orthodox Christian, my voice should have no legitimacy.

There is a famous phrase: if we forget the lessons of history, we risk repeating the same mistakes. It's what the human race has been doing for thousands of years, repeating the same mistakes. Only the costumes and make-up are changed according to the whims of fashion, but the gestures remain the same. Society has been disharmonious since the time of Cain and Abel. Nothing essentially new is happening with humanity today, in my opinion.

I don't remember ever finding out that theatre had the power to improve human nature or society as such. If the theatre has any virtue, that would be the celebration of human wickedness. If there is any point for theatre to exist in the world, it is not to make it better, but to fight to leave it as it is.

I believe in education, but I don't believe in progress. I believe in culture as the only palliative to our fear of death. Theatre is also a palliative,

---

[7] In *Divine Comedy* and *Paradise* (2012).

[8] *Kultūrpolis.lt* 19 February 2019; https://www.kulturpolis.lt/scena/teatras-2/eimunto-nekrosiaus-spektaklis-inferno-paradiso-palangoje/ [accessed 3 March 2020].

nothing more. A small, more subtle pleasure, it is true, but quite ambiguous and paradoxical: it is an absolutely useless but still indispensable human occupation. This paradox, it seems to me, is the only argument that would give it some nobility and meaning. From here to thinking that theatre can be an instrument of emancipation, of progress, that it can define society, that it can change minds... the distance is huge.

Árpád Schilling: I have a Syrian friend, Oussama Ghanam, who lived through the civil war in Damascus. He did not leave his hometown and makes theatre with local artists. They play Harold Pinter or Tennessee Williams, trying to focus on the humanity that has still remained and seeking what is common and connects people rather than what separates them. Theatre during the civil war and after the war. There is no money, no support, no festivals, no successes, just a concern for the human spirit, the fragility of the human being, the complexity of conflicts and the hidden truth behind the sentences. The future of the theatre lies in our determination. Do we want it to exist? Do we want people to experience their humanity not only superficially but as deep as possible through stories that can happen to all of us, completely free of any ideology or religion? Do we want that? Then let's do it!

The biggest threats to theatre are the puffed-up cultural businessmen—directors and cultural organisers—who do not represent art but prestige, power, and the façade.

We have to fight for cultural support, for the state's decisive role in culture. We have to fight for the real art that presents itself even for free in order to reach its goal: the human being.

We must fight to prevent ourselves from being strangled by snobbery, fake art, conferences about nothing at all, the cynicism of wealth. All must die: egoism, the theatre festival life similar to a fresh vegetable market. (Fresh tomatoes here, that's two for the price of one!)

We need some kind of deepening, of getting an insight into ourselves, a correct understanding of the social and political processes, solidarity without any doubt, a loud affirmation of life without shame.

As always, what blooms on stage is the art hungry for success, political favour-seeking, traditional and suppressing true talent flat (meaning in Hungarian: boring). Theatre is a factory that is rewarded for its productivity and dominated by performance and competition restraints. Immediate and loud success is expected. Critics also reward only what they already know well enough to put their hands on. If theatre wants to fight with the cinema, the media, the Internet, it will be like the king who showed himself naked to the crowd, believing he was in his most fashionable clothing.

The only meaning of theatre is the living human being on stage. The Human Being. Everything other than that is no more than simple ornamentation, unnecessary nonsense on which we spend a lot of money, but in this way we only hide our own emptiness. Have more human being and less technology on stage! This is the pledge to the survival of theatre.

But it doesn't bother me at all if there's finally no more theatre in the future. Just let life flourish; everything else is, anyway, an apology.

Andrei Șerban: At the moment everything is at a big stop—not only in the theatre but in the whole life of the planet. This coronavirus forced all of us to stop everything. Besides the tragedy of so many people dying, this is a great opportunity for the lucky ones like us who are staying at home and are still healthy. It's an opportunity to ask the big question: Why are we doing what we are doing? Everybody is wondering about the future: what it will be, how will the change happen. And, of course, nobody is a prophet to have the answer. But for sure, we all need a radical change and this change will imply our attitude towards theatre and how to approach theatre.

My problem is: How can we do theatre in a new way? Because if I look now at the projects I've done, I ask myself which ones will be valuable to be presented after this crisis is over and the theatres are re-opened. Am I proud to bring any of my shows back again, after this radical experience of seeing death at every corner, of facing the fact that we are not going to be here for much longer? All the time, as an artist one feels very special, unique, one feels one's talent is so much needed; and now, when this stopped happening, I realised that I'm not the centre of the universe, that I'm not so special. Therefore, working in the theatre, we have to see what theatre should do to reach another level, another quality of communication. This is something very urgent. The question is: How can we do theatre that is totally new and not bring back the old stereotypes? I'm thinking of all the movements that happened: the fall of political theatre, the social problems, the conflict between the generations, the young ones who are always trying to rebel against society and the political systems that are betraying all they have promised to deliver—the young ones who bring frustration and hate and negativity, which is understandable... So I'm thinking whether all this will come back again and what is more important.

And I think that what's more important is to find something that is absolutely positive, a feeling of togetherness, of unity, of asking altogether

THE STAKES TODAY   **291**

how we can have a relationship with the audience. If someone asks me at which particular moment in the theatre I feel accomplished, I say in the very rare moments that a viewer says: "Ah, look, this is like me; I recognise my life." This happens so rarely and I hope this happens more in the future.

So I have this deep wish that something will change, that we are all ready because of this gravity of facing death and this lack of real communication now. And real touch is part of the basic human need. We all stay in front of the big dilemma: Who Am I? Like the first line in *Hamlet*: Who's there? This is the big question: Who am I? Who are you? And: Why are we doing theatre? These questions that I had as a young artist are the same now. I want all of us to get more interested in what is essential— beyond politics, style, beyond everything which becomes a cliché, which becomes old tomorrow. What is it that is deeper than that, closer to our essence as human beings and artists?

Daniel Špinar: The problem of today's theatre in Prague is the sheer number of theatres, which is quite absurd and frankly insupportable. Everyone is kind of "in" the theatre—as amateurs or as professionals— everyone knows someone in the theatre. This means that the focus is blurred. Interestingly, there are fewer theatres in Berlin than there are in Prague. That's also connected to quality. Theatre craft has lost its value. We're coming into an era when actors will no longer be members of permanent ensembles—everyone is getting to be a freelancer, acting here and there, in the theatre, in cinema, on TV.

Another problem of Czech theatre in general is the audience. Still a large portion of theatre-goers are the generation who have lived through a vacuum during Communism, with a somewhat deformed perception. People tend to feel that theatre should be more noble than it is, almost like a museum. Whereas it should in reality be the freshest of arts because it has the unique power of immediate contact. This may sound a little sceptical, but to make full use of this freshness, you need a cooperating audience, and that's something that's not quite happening.

Theatre, in my opinion, lacks a definition—or a re-definition—of what it should be today. It used to be a solitary means of entertainment; nowadays you have many other ways. You can experience a lot without even leaving your living room. We have to find some juiciness in the theatre.

I think all good theatre is political in the sense that it shows some models of communication, some kind of moral credit. Even in a play about love, you have politics. I'm not a documentary-maker or a political theatremaker in the sense of putting my finger on individual problems of a given place and time. I prefer the grander themes—love, death, fate—to texts that are purely topical. Perhaps the most political play that I've staged was Havel's *Beggars' Opera*, but even that I staged as a highly theatrical piece based on a story.[9]

Włodzimierz Staniewski: For the last eighty years, theatre has become a means of numerous and various revolutions all around the globe. The strength of screaming objection has been the measure of the weight and prominence of various theatrical phenomena. The cry and scream of disobedience against the ruling authorities, against customs and norms, against injustice and—paradoxically—justice, disobedience against the human being as a prodigious being (as portrayed in ancient myths) and, finally, disobedience against the very essence of theatre.

Theatre has challenged itself. It has started to eat its own tail. The mirror that reflects the images of theatre is a crooked mirror, scratched, broken and occupied with endosperm, because the epoch is crooked, scratched, broken and occupied with endosperm. Theatre looks in the epoch like in the mirror and, since it can SEE LITTLE, it cries and gets panic-stricken.

Theatre has become a *tool*. I am saying this with pain, observing as it has been exploited for decades now by demagogy and demagogues (ideologies and movements) and as it has been losing its creative integrity. Disobedience and rebellion that are not endangered by the gallows of sanctions but are subject to the applause of the nurturing mob turn into mockery.

Theatre annihilates itself by immersing into mimesis. The sense of its functioning may be restored solely through creating art work, through fighting for life and death for grand art and extraordinary forms, through energies renewing the covenants with art.[10]

Rimas Tuminas: Today beauty comes as no surprise to anyone. We behave as if beauty had no relation to us, or perhaps we are so overfed with beauty in culture—we used to speak about it so much… As if beauty had been killed a long time ago and we knew of it only from history: once upon a time there was a certain era of beauty and now it is no longer with us because we are surrounded by squalor, war.

---

[9] Translated by Michal Zahálka.
[10] Email correspondence, the night of 3–4 February 2020. Translated by Tomasz Wiśniewski.

THE STAKES TODAY **293**

I wholeheartedly believe in beauty: it is revealed in an era, an author, life, in the attitude towards life, childhood, mother, father, family and death. Beauty is all around.

It is not easy to reveal it. When they tell me that beauty is in some beautiful drawings, or a beautiful costume, or a beautiful, light play devoid of any serious meaning, I recall Auguste Rodin at this point: in his works there was beauty along with some brokenness; he was searching for beauty in ugliness. So I am telling people today: if you want ugliness on stage, look for beauty in ugliness!

Auguste Rodin lived in an era when life was hard, dirty, when there was a war, people were dying. How was it even possible to celebrate beauty? What if beauty is particularly in demand when humanity is facing great challenges? Disasters, catastrophes, cataclysms...

There is power in beauty. In the art of acting, the art of theatre there is power, too. This power is not the same as taking possession of beauty. Through beauty we approach God, we feel connected to Heaven: it is beautiful there, so it should be beautiful here as well. Beauty has power over the powers that be: over politics, over information. Perhaps due to the lack of culture, we try to hide in the flow of information and do not want to rise above it: the flow of information is a good hiding place for anyone—killers, fools, poets, politicians. Or perhaps today we have got no strength to resist the flow of information.

What is the place of theatre today? I think about this every day and I have a feeling that theatre should be able to distance itself from the so-called direct contact with the audience. They say: "We exist for the audience, we are nothing without the audience." Yes. But, being a creative organism, we mean something even without the audience's gaze, we mean something on our own.

Sometimes you have to choose solitude in order to preserve yourself and survive. Theatre, too, should be able, for the sake of our audience, to move away from serving the audience's interests. Instead of approaching the audience, theatre should be able to vanish from the audience's gaze, but not in the way ageing actors vanish from the stage being unable to act. Theatre vanishes with love, respect and care, bidding a big farewell; it vanishes to leave the audiences' surroundings empty for a couple of moments, to live in its own land, its paradise, of which we know that it is good there, theatre will rest there... and we will come back again.

When we return to the audience after vanishing, we regain distance. In order to say important things, we need distance. We should not open up, confess, pour our soul onto the stage. This is not because we do not want that, but because it no longer works. Distancing can work. Only through distance can we find a clear, graphic aesthetics, can we work through a light touch.[11]

REFERENCES

https://www.lrt.lt/naujienos/kultura/12/1117360/metai-po-eimunto-nekrosiaus-mirties-to-tikro-gyvenimo-buvo-tik-saujele [accessed 4 July 2019]. The interview with Eimuntas Nekrošius was shown for the first time on 9 January 2017.

Bernardinai.lt, 23 November 2018; http://www.bernardinai.lt/straipsnis/2018-11-23-teatro-amziaus-mohikanai/172989 [accessed 4 February 2020]. From a meeting with directors Eimuntas Nekrošius, Jonas Vaitkus, Gintaras Varnas on 15 November 2018 at the Vilnius Small Theatre.

Kultūrpolis.lt, 19 February 2019; https://www.kulturpolis.lt/scena/teatras-2/eimunto-nekrosiaus-spektaklis-inferno-paradiso-palangoje/ [accessed 3 March 2020].

[11] Translated by Anna Shulgat.

INDEX

A

Abramović, Marina, 59
Acquaviva, Jean-Claude, ix, 10
Adámek, Jiří, 208
Adjmi, David, 212
Aeschylus, 98, 102, 175, 254
The Aesthetics of Resistance, 39
Agamben, Giorgio, 99, 100
Aitmatov, Chingiz, 150
Aleksandra Zec, 33, 35, 37
Alexievich, Svetlana, 154, 266
Ali, Muhammad, 268
Alkestis, 254
Allain, Paul, 222, 230
Amerika, 82
Anatoly, 82
An Anatomy Class, 38
AnBlokk Cultural and Social Scientists'
    Association, 192
Andersen, Hans Christian, 132
AnderSen, 132
Andersson, Roy, 273
Andruszko, Henryk, 235
Angels in America, 252, 259
Anna Karenina, 213

Anouilh, Jean, 86
Anski, Szymon, 252
Anty-Gone, 2, 12, 13
Apartment theatre, 187
Apocalypsis Cum Figuris, 2, 264
The Apple of My Shining Eye,
    160, 164
Apuleius of Madarus, 230, 273
Arcadia, 47
Arendt, Hannah, 271
Aristotelian, 100, 104
Artaud, Antonin, 201, 268, 269, 271
Artists Talk, 23–26
Artproletarz, 192
Arvisura, 186
Athens Festival, 252
Augustynowicz, Anna, 249
Austen, Jane, 217
Auto da fé, 255
Autumn, Chertanovo, 44
Autumn Sonata, 133
Avedon, Richard, 274
Avignon Festival, 21, 22, 171,
    174, 252
Avvakum Petrovich, 228, 229

© The Author(s), under exclusive license to Springer Nature
Switzerland AG 2021
K. Stefanova, M. Carlson (eds.), *20 Ground-Breaking Directors of
Eastern Europe*, https://doi.org/10.1007/978-3-030-52935-2

296 INDEX

B

Baal, 98, 187
Babits, Mihály, 189
A Baby Goat for Pennies, 240
The Bacchae, 6, 35, 36, 58, 98, 99, 252, 256
Bacon, Francis, 269, 274
Bailey, Brett, xvi
Bakhtin, Mikhail, 227
Bánki, Gergely, 186, 187
Banu, George, 199
Barba, Eugenio, 161
Bārda, Fricis, 53
Bartlett, Mike, 209, 216
Baryshnikov, Mikhail, 53
Bash, 65
Baudrillard, Jean, 89
Bausch, Pina, 52, 267, 268, 270
Beckettian, 101
Bedbug, 105
Beefheart, Captain, 268
Beethoven, Ludwig van, 167
Beggars' Opéra, 292
Behind the Curtain: Andrei Şerban in the American Theatre, 200
Bel-Ami, 212
Benedict Erofeev, 273
Bentham, Jeremy, 149
Berg, Alban, 255
Bergman, Ingmar, 133, 251
Berlin, Lucia, 266
Berlioz, Hector, 52
Bernhard, Thomas, 113, 117, 118, 130, 132, 133, 255, 271
Beuys, Joseph, 269, 270
Beware of Pity, 218
Bible, vi, 105, 106, 230, 271
Bible, *first attempt*, 105
Biennale, Wiesbaden, 19
Billington, Michael, 231
BITEF Festival, 252
Black Land, xvi, 189

Black Milk, 49
Blake, William, 271
Blanchot, Maurice, 100
Blažević, Marin, 35–37, 39
Boal, Augusto, 281
Böcklin, Arnold, 273
Bodó, Viktor, 186
Bolero, 144
Book of Job, 106
Borges, Jorge Luis, 273
Borová, Magdaléna, 215
Borowski, Piotr, 235
Bosch, Hieronymus, 172, 274
Bovell, Andrew, 252
Bowie, David, 269
Bral, Alicja, x, 11
Bral, Grzegorz, ix–xiii, 1–13, 235, 264–265, 280
Brandl-Risi, Bettina, 161
Branişte, Lavinia, 266
Braškytė, Alma, 93
Braudel, Fernand, 269
Brave Festival, 3
Brecht, Bertolt, 39, 146, 187, 242, 273
Brilliant Second-Rate, 162
Britney Goes to Heaven, 210
Broch, Hermann, 113
Brodsky, Joseph, 53
Brodsky/Baryshnikov, 53, 54
Brook, Peter, 161, 174, 179, 251, 271, 273, 275, 284
Brothers (Karamazov), 12, 210
Brown, Mark, 8
Bruckner, Anton, 271
Brzoza, Zbigniew, 249
Büchner, Georg, 67, 187, 210, 255
Buffini, Moira, 209, 217
Bugahiar, Dragos, 180
Bulgakov, Mikhail, 88, 90, 163, 273
Buljan, Ivica, 97
Buñuel, Luis, 127, 163, 271, 274

INDEX   297

Bute, Neil La, 65
Butor, Michel, 271
By Gorky, 48, 49

C

Cabaret Kafka, 213
Cage, John, 268, 274, 275
California/Grace Slick, 68
Callas, Maria, 63
Camus, Albert, 129, 164
Canetti, Elias, 255
Čapek, Karel, 216
Capri—the Island of Fugitives, 120
Caragiale, Ion Luca, 273
Caravaggio, Michelangelo Merisi da, 271, 274
Cărbunariu, Gianina, xvi, 17–29, 265–266, 281
Carmina Burana, 229, 230
Carrying GARDZIENICE from the Ruins, 223
Caspar Hauser, 47
Cassandra's Report, 13
Cassavetes, John, 274
Cassiers, Guy, 82
Castorf, Frank, 73, 179, 270
The Cathedral, 92
Causa Maryša, 215
Causa Salome, 215
Ceausescu, Elena, 173
Ceausescu, Nicolae, 173
Celińska, Stanisława, 58, 259
Cesereanu, Ruxandra, 265
Chaikin, Joseph, 275
The Champion, 160, 164, 165
Chaplin, Charlie, 125, 271
Chaplinesque, 85, 142
Chekhov, Anton, 12, 24, 50, 89, 148, 189, 203, 217, 240, 242–244, 274, 276
Chekhovian, 217

Cherkaoui, Sidi Larbi, 284
The Cherry Orchard, 240
Children of the Demon, 162
Chopin, Frédéric François, 167
Christie, Judie, 224
Christmas at the Ivanovs, 86
Chronicles—A Tradition of Mourning (Kroniki—Obyczaj lamentacyjny), 6, 7, 9
Chválová, Lenka, 209
Chyra, Andrzej, 64
Cielecka, Magdalena, 59, 61, 62, 64
Cieplak, Piotr, 249
Cioran, Emile M., 271
The City of Sleep, 109, 110, 112, 117, 118
Ciulei, Liviu, xxi
Ciulli, Roberto (*Kaspar Hauser*), 271
C.K. Norwid Theatre, 111
Cleansed, 58, 100, 252, 256–259
Coetzee, John Maxwell, 255
Cole, Nat King, 63
Coltrane, John, 268
Coming to America, 141
Common Bondage, 161, 162
Complex, 38
Córka Fizdejki (The Daughter of Fizdejka), 80
Correspondence V+W, 126–129
Cosma, Valer Simion, 265
Cowardice, 32
Cpin, Marek, 124, 130–133, 287
Crave, 257
Crazy God, 11
The Crazy Locomotive, 98, 103
Creangă, Ion, 27
Crime and Punishment, 82
The Croatian Association of Dramatic Artists, 35, 37–39
Csákányi, Eszter, 167, 186, 188
Csákányi, László, 167
Csányi, Sándor, 186

298 INDEX

Cunningham, Merce, 275
Czech Seventies or Husák's Silence,
128, 129
Czukay, Holger, 268
Czyżewski, Krzysztof, 235

D

Dąbrowska, Anna, 235
*Dainty Shapes and Hairy Apes, or
The Green Pill*, 111
*Damned Be the Traitor to His
Homeland!*, 32
The Danaids, 174–177
Dangerous Liaisons, 209
Dankó, István, 162
Dante Alighieri, 155, 273
The Danton Case, 80
The Dardenne brothers, 274
Darvas, Benedek, 164, 165
Das Gemüse, 63
Das Nibelungenlied, 271
Davidová, Anna, 271
Davis, Miles, 269, 274
*The Day Lasts More Than a Hundred
Years*, 150, 269
*The Day of Fury—the Song of a Foolish
Heart*, 194
de Brea, Diego, 97
de Dines, Andrew, 116
De Sade, Marquis, 273
The Dead Class, 270
*The Dead Man Comes for His
Sweetheart*, 103
Debt: The First 5000 Years, 82
Delacroix, Ferdinand Victor
Eugène, 38
Delaney, Shelagh, 149
Deleuze, Gilles, 156
Demirski, Paweł, 6
Derevo, 273
Děrgel, Patrik, viii, 214

Der Ignorant und der Wahsinnige, 255
Derrida, Jaques, 176
Dessecker, Eva, 52
Dialog, 72, 73
Dick, Philip K., 268
*Die schönsten Sterbeszenen in der
Geschichte der Oper*, 49
Die Soldaten, 47, 51, 52
Dievoushka, 164, 165
Dimitrova, Nina, 137, 138
*Discipline and Punish: The Birth of the
Prison*, 149
*The Discreet Charm of the Bourgeoisie:
Hommage à Buñuel et Carriere*,
127, 131
Divine Comedy, 155
Dług (Debt), 82
Dobrý, Karel, 216
Dočekal, Michal, 208, 216
Doctor Faustus, 63, 64
Dodin, Lev, 274
Dom Juan, 99, 176
Don Carlos, 63, 255
Donelaitis, Kristijonas, 154, 157
Donev, Kamen, 142
Don Giovanni, 255
Don Juans, 141
Donnellan, Declan, 135
Don Quixote, 137, 138
Dostoyevsky, Fyodor, 4, 12, 64, 210,
244, 250, 271, 273
DramAcum, 20, 21, 23
Dravnel, Jan, 65
The Dreamers, 113
Drewniak, Łukasz, 66
Duras, Marguerite, 210, 271
*Dwoje biednych Rumunów
mówiących po polsku* (*A Couple
of Poor Polish-speaking
Romanians*), 65
Dybbuk, 252, 254
Dziady [*Forefathers' Eve*], 152, 228

INDEX 299

E

Earthquakes in London, 209, 216
Eclipse, 135
Eco, Umberto, 88
Ecstasy, 12
Edinburgh Fringe, 2, 6
Edinburgh International Festival, 171, 173, 252
Efros, Anatoly, 267, 277
Egressy, Zoltán, 212
Electra, 57, 200, 210, 231
Elemental Particles, 126
Eliade, Mircea, 271
Eliot, 98
Elixir of Love, 63
Elizabeth Costello, 255
Elvis, 211
An Enemy of the People, 81
Eno, Brian, 268
ENRON, 208
Enter Enea Festival, 13
Enyedi, Éva, 160, 161, 166
Ephesians, xiii
The Epic of Gilgamesh, 98, 100, 101, 270
Epîngeac, Alina, 21
Erdman, Nikolai, 142
Erml, Richard, viii
Etchells, Tim, 106
Eugene Onegin, 50, 124, 243, 244
Euripides, 6, 35, 36, 58, 98, 173, 231, 252–254, 268, 273
Euripidesian, 215
Europeana, 123, 124, 131
European Centre for Theatrical Practices "Gardzienice," 223
Europe Theatre Prize for (New) Theatrical Realities, 47
Eurypides, 82
Evening Performance, 227, 228

Eve's Garden of Paradise, 44
Exhibit B, xvi
Exiles, 143
Expeditions, 224–228
Expulsion, 92, 93

F

Fabbricone, Teatro, xxii
Fabre, Jan, 46
The Face of Fire, 88
Factory 2, 114–117
Fassbinder, Rainer Wender, 274
Fatherland, My All, 189
Fathers, xvi, xvii
Faust, 82, 152, 171, 172, 182
Fellini, Federico, 182, 271, 273
Féral, Josette, 75
Festen, 63
Festival de Liège, 23
Festwochen, Wiener, 39, 252
For Beauty, 207–209
Forced Entertainment, 266
Forefathers' Eve, 156
For Sale, 28
Fortas, Meno, vi
Foucault, Michel, 149
4:48 Psychosis, 59, 60, 68
Fragments of a Greek Trilogy, 200
Francuzi (Frenchmen), 253
Fraser, Brad, 58
Freibergs, Andris, 47
Fret, Jarosław, 235
Fricis Bārda. Poetry. Ambient, 53
Frič, Jan, 208, 209, 271
Friedenthal, Zoltán, 167
Frljić, Oliver, xvi, 31–39, 41, 282
Frogs, 103
Frontal, 27
Fuentes, Carlos, 271
Funès, Louis de, 273

300 INDEX

G

Gainsbourg, Serge, 268
Gańczarczyk, Iga, 114, 117
Gap, 192
Garbaczewski, Krzysztof, 6
Garcia Marquez, Gabriel, 136
Gardzienice, 2–4, 9, 221–223,
    225–228, 230–233, 235, 265
"Gardzienice": *Ifigenia w T...*
    (*Iphigenia in T[auris]*), 232
Gardzienice: Polish Theatre in
    Transition, 222
Gardzienice Theatre, 265
Gardzienice Theatre Association, 224
Gargantua and Pantagruel, 176
Gáspár, Máté, 187, 190
Gatherings, 225–228
Ghanam, Oussama, 289
Gide, André, 73
Gierek, Edward, 73
Gilgamesh, 7, 101
Globisz, Krzysztof, 232
Gluck, Christoph Willibald, 255
Goat Island, 266
Goethe, Johann Wolfgang von, 82,
    172, 173, 182, 197
Gogol, Nikolai, 47, 71, 73, 150, 152,
    240, 243
Gołaj, Mariusz, 235
Golden Mask Festival, 243
The Golden Sixties, 128
Gombrowitcz, Witold, 58, 59, 100,
    157, 250, 271
Goncharov, Ivan, 50
Gorczyński, Maciej, 235
Gorky, Maxim, 48, 50, 89, 139
Gotesmanas, Arkadijus, 90
Gottland, 129
Gough, Richard, 224
Gould, Glenn, 269
The Government Inspector, 71, 73, 76,
    240, 241, 243

Graeber, David, 82
Grandfather, Martha from the Blue
    Hill, 49
The Grand Inquisitor, 12
The Greek Trilogy, 200, 202, 203
Greenson, Ralph, 116
The Gripefruit's Smile, 73
Grishkovets, Evgeny, 106
Gross, Georg, 271
Grossman, Jan, 128
Grotowski, Jerzy, xxi, 1, 2, 6,
    161, 179, 199, 224, 264, 265,
    268, 269, 271
Gruber-Ballehr, Uta, 52
Gruszczyński, Piotr, 249, 250,
    253, 259
Grzegorzewski, Jerzy, 73
Guczalska, Beata, 59
Gulliver's Travels, 178, 179
Gultiajeva, Nadežda, 158
Gurdjieff, George, 115
Gusła [Sorcery], 228
Gussow, Mel, 201
Gyabronka, József, 186, 190

H

H., 74–76, 78, 79
Hadžihafizbegović, Emir, 33
Hajewska-Krzysztofik,
    Małgorzata, 113
Halász, Péter, 162
Hall, Edith, 232
Hamlet, vi, viii, ix, xxii, 34, 35, 58, 74,
    75, 77, 82, 88, 89, 92, 125, 130,
    131, 152, 153, 198, 214, 216,
    252, 258, 291
Hamlet: A Commentary, ix, xi, 12
Hamlet.ws, 189, 190
Havel, Václav, xxi, 128, 211, 292
Havelka, Jiří, 208, 271
Hawking, Stephen, 52

INDEX   301

Hazámhazám (*Fatherland, My All*), 188
Haze, 63
Hazlitt, William, xix
Hedda Gabler, 125
The Hedonists, 130, 131
Hello Sonia New Year, 86
Hepnarová, Olga, 129
Herakles, 254
Hermanis, Alvis, xiii–xvii, 25, 43–55, 82, 106, 142, 266–268, 282
Herz, Juraj, 211
Hidden Territories, 277
Hilar, Karel Hugo, 208, 209, 216
Hilling, Anja, 216
Hirst, Michael, 13
Hitchcock, Alfred, 268
Hitler, Adolf, 38
Hodge, Alison, 231
Hoffman, Dustin, 267
Hojnik, Branko, 101
Holcgreber, Joanna, 235
Hollywood, 116
Homer, xi, 98, 103, 104
HOMO 06, 214
Horgas, Péter, 165
Horvat, Sebastijan, 97
Hospital-Bakony, 163
Hotel Europa, 90
Houellebecq, Michel, 126
Hour of the Wolf, 133
Hrdinová, Radmila, 216, 218
H7, 63
Hudziak, Andrzej, 113
The Human Circle 3:1, 116
A Hunger Artist, 152
Husák, Gustáv, 129

I
I Am Not the Eiffel Tower, 199
Ibsen, Henrik, 81, 126

The Ice. Collective Rreadinfg of the Book with the Help of Imagination, 47, 50
The Idiot, 4
I Due Foscari, 51
Ignorant i szaleniec (Ignorant and Madman), 255
I Hate the Truth!, 33
Ilarian, 273
The Iliad, xi, xii, xviii, 98, 100, 104, 105, 270
Ilkov, Atanas, 138
Il tabarro, 165
Inferno, 155
INNE, 11
Inni ludzie (*Other People*), 68
In Search of Lost Time, 252
Insgeheim Lohengrin, 49
The Inspector General, 47
The International Small Scene Theatre Festival, 35
International Theatre Festival Divadelna Nitra, 21
International Theatre Festival "Kontakt," 58
International Theatre Festival PoNTI, 252
International Theatre Festival Santiago, 252
International Theatre Institute (ITI), 2
Ionesco, Eugene, 4, 273
Iordache, Stefan, 177
Iphigenia in Aulis, 254
Iphigenia in Tauris, 232
Iphigénie en Tauride, 255
Island, xiii, 11
Ivaškevičius, Marius, 92, 93
Ivona, the Princess of Burgundia, 58, 59

302 INDEX

J

Jack Smith Is Dead, 162
Jacovskis, Adomas, 149, 240,
 241, 244
Janáček, Leoš, 51, 52, 255
Janežič, Tomi, 97
Jansonas, Egmontas, 148
January, 238
Jaremko, Grzegorz, 67
Jarocki, Jerzy, 73
Jarry, Alfred, 105, 173
Jarzyna, Grzegorz, 57–68, 73, 249,
 252, 268, 283
Jasiński, Krzysztof, 223
Jeles, András, 189
Jelinek, Elfriede, 67
Jenůfa, 51, 52
Jett, Renate, 252, 257
Jodorowsky, Alejandro, 269
Jubilee Talks, 162
Jung, C. G., 271
Jupither, Sofia, 22
Jupither Josephsson Theatre
 Company, 22
Juráček, Pavel, 128

K

Kabaret warszawski (Warsaw
 Cabaret), 253
Kafka, Franz, 82, 119, 152, 213,
 252, 271
Kaisers TV, 166, 167
Kalwat, Katarzyna, 67
Kan'ami, 98
Kane, Sarah, 58, 59, 100, 252–254,
 257, 258
Kanovich, Grigory, 240
Kantor, Tadeusz, xxi, 175, 176, 179,
 265, 268, 270, 271
Kaufmann, Jonas, 52
Káva Cultural Workshop, 192

Kawakubo, Rei, 268
Kazantzakis, Nikos, 271
Kazlas, Rolandas, 288
Kebab, 19
Kéménczy, Antal, 160, 167
Kempinas, Žilvinas, 86
Kennedy, Susanne, 284
Kentridge, William, 137
Kerekasztal Színházi Társulás, 186
Kesey, Ken, 135
Kharms, Daniil, 85, 86, 88, 269
Kimele, Māra, 267
The Kindly Ones, 254–255, 257
King Lear, 81
Kiš, Danilo, 38, 271
Klata, Ian, 283
Klata, Jan, vi, 6, 64, 71–82,
 268–269, 284
Knausgard, Karl Ove, 271
Kocur, Mirosław, 13
Kohout, Michal, xxi
Kolečko, Petr, 209, 215
Koležnik, Mateja, 97
Kölner Affäre, 49
Koltès, Bernard-Marie, 88, 252, 253
Koniec (The End), 253
Konieczny, Zygmunt, 232
Konrad Wolf Award, 47
Kopciński, Jacek, 62
Korniss, Péter, 163
Korostyliov, Vadim, 150
Koršunovas, Oskaras, vi, 58, 82,
 85–95, 269–270, 283
Korzeniak, Sandra, 116
Korzybski, Alfred, 269
Kosiński, Cezary, 61
Kosiński, Dariusz, 8, 9
Kossuth, Lajos, 166, 167
Kott, Jan, viii, 181, 271
Krall, Hanna, 252, 254
Krasinski, Zygmunt, 33
Krejča, Otomar, 128

INDEX

Krétakör Foundation, 195
Krétakör Theatre (Krétakör Színház),
  xvi, 185–187, 189–194
Krievs, A., 44
Kroll, Jack, x
Krum, 252
Kubin, Alfred, 110, 112, 117
Kubrik, Stanley, 273
Kukulas, Valdas, 239
Kuleszow, Lew, 268
Kuodyté, Viktorija, 152
Kurosawa, Akira, 180
Kuschner, Tony, 252
Kušej, Martin, 276
Kuta, Magdalena, 66
Kuti, Fela, 268

L
Laclos, Pierre Choderlos de, 213, 271
Lacrimosa, 6, 8, 9
La Damnation de Faust, 51, 52
La Fura dels Baus (*Tier Mon*), 271
La MaMa, 274, 275
L'Amante anglaise, 210
Landis, John, 141
Láng, Annamária, 186
The Lark, 86
Latenas, Faustas, 239–241
Latvian Love, 49
Lear, 10
Learned Women, 105
Lébl, Petr, 128, 275
Le Cheval, 32
Lehmann, Hans-Thies, 87, 179
Leigh, Mike, 274
Lenkiewicz, Rebecca, 217
Lermontov, Mikhail, 240
Letter from 1920, 33
Levar, Milan, 36
Levinas, Emmanuel, 177
The Lexicon of Yu Mythology, 32

Life Is Beautiful, 142
Ligers, Roberts, 44
Ligeti, György Sándor, 274
*Like a Calm and Peaceful River Iis the
  Homecoming*, 44
The Lime Works, 113
Lion King, 137
Liszt funeral march, 167
Liszt Rhapsody, 167
Littell, Jonathan, 254, 257
Living Theatre, 2, 275
Ljubková, Marta, 215
Llosa, Mario Vargas, 271
London, Jack, 239
Lonenci, Jernej, xi
Long Life, xiii, xv–xvii, 48,
  49, 144–145
Looser, 162
Lorenci, Jernej, xi, xii, xviii, 97–107,
  270–271, 283
Loser, 193
Love and Death in Verona, 150
The Lower Depths, 48, 89, 92, 93, 139
Lubitsch, Ernst, 213
Lucius Annaeus Seneca the
  Younger, 173
Lulu, 180
Lupa, Krystian, 58, 60, 63, 73,
  110–120, 179, 249, 251,
  271, 284
Lynch, David, 58, 268

M
Macbeth, xii, 9, 10, 82, 125, 126, 152,
  153, 230, 252, 259
Mačiūnas, Jurgis, 269
Madama Butterfly, 51–52
Madame de Sade, 45, 252
Madonna, Louise Ciccone, 276
Madrid, 252
Mahabharata, 270

304 INDEX

Maj, Maria, 109
Makarovič, Svetlana, 103
Malaparte, Curzio, 120
Male Fantasies, 100
Malinowski, Bronisław, 60
Mandea, Nicu, 266
Mann, Klaus, 250
Mann, Thomas, 63, 271
Marcinkevičius, Justinas, 92
Marcinkevičiūtė, Ramunė, 148, 152
Margiela, Martin, 269
Maria Stuart, 243
Maribor Theatre Festival, 32
Marie Antoinette, 212
Marquez, Gabriel Garcia, 271, 273
The Marquise of O, 250, 252
The Marriage, 100, 157
Marthaler, Christoph, 46, 267, 270
Martin Eden, 239
Maryša, 132, 133
Mary Stuart, 211
Masłowska, Dorota, 65, 67, 68
Masquerade, 211, 240, 241, 243
Massalitinov, Nikolai Ossipovich, 139, 140
A Mass for Arras, 8
The Master and Margarita, 88, 90, 92
Matjašec, Nataša, 103
Maupassant, Henri René Albert Guy de, 212
Max Reinhardt Pen, 47
Mayakovsky, Vladimir Vladimirovich, 105
Mayday, 192
Mayenburg, Marius von, 88
McQueen, Steve, 255
Measure for Measure, 82
Medea, 200
Menta, Ed, 200, 201
The Merchant of Venice, 82, 256
Mercy, Dominique, 52

MESS, 33
MESS Festival, 2
Metamorfozy albo złoty osioł (*Metamorphosis or the Golden Ass*), 230
Metamorphoses, 231, 271
Meyerhold, Vsevolod, 246, 274, 277
Michelangelo, 271
Mickens, Valois, 203
Mickiewicz, Adam, 152, 156, 228
Midsummer Night's Dream, 88, 139, 217, 252
Między nami dobrze jest (*We Are Pretty Good*), 65
Mihaela, the Tiger of Our Town (*A Mockumentary Play*), 22
Mihăilescu, Vintilă, 265
Mikhalkov, Nikita, 141
Mikulášek, Jan, 123–133, 213, 271, 286
Mikulka, Vladimír, 128
Mikulková, Gabriela, 127
Mil, 252
Miller, Arthur, 244–245
Miltinis, Juozas, 277
Mingus, Charles, 269
Mishima, Yukio, 45, 252
Missa in A-Minor, 38
The Misunderstanding, 164
Mitchell, Katie, 82
Mnouchkine, Ariane, 174, 273
Modes of thinking, 253
Modreanu, Cristina, 18, 29
Mohácsi brothers, 163
Moisescu, Valeriu, 273
Molière, 94, 99, 105, 176
Monroe, Marilyn, 63, 115, 116
Monsù, Desiderio, 273
Monteiro, Cezar Joao, 273
Monteverdi, Claudio, 268
Monty Python, 271
Moore, Alan, 269

INDEX   305

Morávek, Vladimír, 271, 275
Morfov, Alexander, xv, 136–143, 145, 146, 271, 287
Morgiana, 211
Mother Clap's Molly House, 215
Mozart, Wolfgang Amadeus, 8, 177, 255, 271
Możdżer, Leszek, 13
Mr. Lonely, viii
Mrowca, Mariusz, 235
Mrozek, xxi
Mrštík, Vilém, 132
Muck, 166
Mucsi, Zoltán, 186
Munch, Edvard, 11, 273
Murder in the Cathedral, 98
The Music Program, 255
Musil, Robert, 113
Mykietyn, Paweł, 255
My Life with Mozart, xii
My Mother's Nose, 164
My Name Is Isborg. I'm a Lioness, 18

N
Nagy, Zsolt, 186–188, 190
Najmányi, László, 162
National Theatre Ivan Vazov, 143
Natural Born Killers, 63
Naumanis, Normunds, 50
Nebeský, Jan, 209, 213, 275
Neibarts, Aivars, 53
Neighbors, 254
Nekrošius, Eimuntas, vi, xi, xiii, xxii, 82, 85–87, 92, 147–157, 267, 269, 270, 272, 287, 288
Nekrošius, Marius, 158
Némirovsky, Irène, 25
Neshat, Shirin, 40
Nestroy-Preis, 47
The New Life, v
New Spectator Programme, 193

New Testament, 273
The New Theatre, 64
Next Wave Festival BAM, 252
Nezval, Vítězslav, 130, 216, 217
The Night Butterfly, 212, 219
The Night Season, 217
Ninagawa, Yukio, 180
Niziołek, Grzegorz, 60, 112, 250, 254, 258
Non-Divine Comedy, 33
Noren, Lars, 116
The Nose, 150, 152
Novalis, vi

O
OBERIU, 87, 91
Obidniak, Alina, 111
Oblomow, 50
Obsession, 131
Oedipus, 125, 180
Oedipus Rex, 88, 90, 164, 245
Ognyanova, Julia, 138
Old Testament, 154
The Old Woman, 86
The Old Woman 2, 86
On Actors and Acting, xix
One Flew Over the Cuckoo's Nest, 135
O'Neill, Eugene, 4
On Hearing, 113
On the Edge, xv, 143–146
Opowieści afrykańskie według Szekspira (African Stories According to Shakespeare), 253, 254
Oratorium pytyjskie (Pythian Oratorio), 233
Orbán, Viktor, 162
Oresteia, 98, 101–103, 176, 254
Orghast at Persepolis, 275
Ostaszewska, Maja, 59, 64
Ostermeier, Thomas, 58, 180, 276

306 INDEX

Ostrovsky, Alexander Nikolayevich, 103
Othello, 103, 152, 153, 215
The Other Side, 110, 112
Our Class, 94
Ouředník, Patrik, 123
Our Secrets, 166–168
Our Violence and Your Violence, 33, 39, 40
Owens, Rick, 269
Oxygen, 65

P

Pamuk, Orhan, v, vi, xvii, xviii
Pandur, Tomaž (*Scheherezade*), 271
Pantagruel's Sister-in-Law, xv
Panufnik, Roxanna, 255
Papuczys, Jakub, 116
Paradise, 155
Parsifal, 52, 255
Parulskis, Sigitas, 88, 93
Passolini, Pier Paolo, 61
Pasternak, Boris Leonidovich, 130
The Patricides: The Younger and More Talented in Polish Theatre, 249
Paulékaité, Jūraté, 89
Pauļuks, Jānis, 282
Pawłowski, Roman, 60, 73
Peacock Melody, 238
Peasant Opéra, 164, 165
Penderecki, Krzysztof, 255
Pérez, Iván, 11, 12
Pergolesi, Giovanni Battista, 271
Pericles, 252
Perry, Lee "Scratch," 269
Personas, 133
Persona. Simone's Body, 116
Persona. Triptych/Marilyn, 115, 116
Peter Bruegel the Elder, 273
Péterfy, Borbála, 186

Petőfi, Sándor, 162, 166, 167
Petras, Armin, 213
Phaedra, 173, 175, 177
Pheasant Dance, 166
The Phoenician Women, 252
A Photo of a Woman and a Wild Boar, 44
Piano Concerto nr. 20 in D minor, 177
Picasso, x
Pilsen Divadlo festival, 214
Pintér, Béla, 159–169, 272–273, 288
Pinter, Harold, 289
Pintér, Szkéné Béla, 161
Pintilie, Lucian, 273
Pirandello, Luigi, 33
Pirosmani, Niko, 152
Pirosmani, Pirosmani, 150
Pitínský, Jan Antonín, 271, 275
Plastic Jesus, 38
Platonov, 50
Płatonow, Andriej, 269
Plodková, Jana, 131
Pobojowisko, 255
Pola, 254
Political Cabaret, 143
Pollesch, Rene, 68, 276
(*A*)*pollonia*, 253, 254, 257
Poniedziałek, Jacek, 57, 64, 258
Pop, Iggy, 268, 269
Popkin, Henry, xxi
Popławska, Magdalena, 66
Popovici, Iulia, 19, 20
Pormale, Monika, 48–50
Porowska, Dorota, 235
Portraits of the Cherry Orchard, 12
Portugal, 212
Postić, Višnja, 38
The Post Office, 255
Prebble, Lucy, 208
Preissová, Jana, 217
Prensa de Otoño Festival, 252

INDEX 307

Prévost, Abbé, 216
Pride and Prejudice, 217
The Prince Myshkin, 64
Process, 252
Protection, 216
Proust, Valentin Louis Georges
    Eugène Marcel, 252
Przybyszewska, Stanisława, 80
P.S. File O.K., 87, 93
Puccini, Giacomo, 51, 165
Puiu, Cristi, 274
Pulka, xiii
Purcărete, Silviu, 171–183, 197,
    273, 288
Purgatory, 155
Pushkin, Alexander, 50, 243, 244
Pythian Oratorio, 233

Q

The Queen of the Cookies, 162,
    165, 166

R

Rába, Roland, 186, 190
Rabelais, François, xv, 105, 176, 227
Raczak, Lech, 265
Radickov, Jordan, 238
Radu Stanca National Theatre
    Sibiu, xv
Rajmont, Ivan, 217
Rammstein, 63
Raphael, 271
Ravel, Joseph Maurice, 144
Ravenhill, Mark, 82, 88, 215
*Rechnitz.Opéra—The Angel of
    Holocaust*, 67
Reihl-Kir, Josip, 36
Requiem, 8
Reslová, Marie, 130, 132, 212, 216
Return to the Voice, 2, 12

Rhythm 0, 59
Richard III, 176, 180, 181
Rijn, Rembrandt
    Harmenszoon van, 38
Rilke, René Karl Wilhelm Johann Josef
    Maria, 130
Rinpoche, Akong Tulku, 3, 4
Risk It All, 65
Ristić, Ljubiša, 37, 38
The Ristić Complex, 37–39
The Robbers, 82
Roberto Zucco, 88, 258, 259
Rodin, Auguste, 293
Rodowicz, Jadwiga, 235
Rodowicz, Tomasz, 230, 235
Rojek, Elżbieta, 235
ROKPA, 3, 4
Romanian Association of Theatre
    Professionals UNITER, 28
Romeo and Juliet, 150, 217
Ross, Felice, 252, 255, 259
Rostas, Zoltan, 265
Royal Shakespeare Company, 2, 9
Rožman, Branko, 101
Różewicz, Tadeusz, xxi
Rushdie, Salman, 271
Rychły, Maciej, ix, 10, 230–232

S

Saavedra, Miguel de Cervantes, 271
Šaltenis, Saulius, 154
Salzburg Festival, 47
Sanader, Ivo, 35
Sanctuary, xvi
Sarkissian, Alena, 209
Sartre, Jean-Paul Charles Aymard, 23
Sárosdi, Lilla, 186, 187, 192
Satyricon, 182
Scenes from a Marriage, 133
Schauspielhaus, Zurich, xvi
Schiller, Friedrich, 82, 211

308 INDEX

Schilling, Árpád, xvi, 162, 185–187, 189–193, 195, 273–274, 289
Schmidt, Erik-Emanuel, xii
Schorm, Evald, 128
Schubert, Franz Peter, 167, 273
The Scream, 11
The Seagull, 89, 92, 93, 189, 197, 198, 203, 212
The Seasons, 152, 154
Sedláčková-Oltová, Klára, 125
Šeligo, Rudi, 103
Senna, Ayrton, 269
Septuagint, 273
Sepultura, 63
Şerban, Andrei, 197–204, 274–275, 290
Seven Gates of Thebes, 12
Seweryn, Andrzej, 232
Shakespeare, William, x, xii, xiii, xv, 9–11, 34, 35, 64, 72, 74, 75, 77, 82, 88, 92, 103, 105, 126, 148, 150, 152, 177, 179, 180, 189, 190, 198, 211, 253, 254, 268, 274, 276, 283
Shame, 255
She Who Was Once the Helmet-Maker's Beautiful Wife, 162
Shklovsky, Viktor, 242
Shoot/Get Treasure/Repeat, 82
Shopping and Fucking, 88, 89
The Siberian Barber, 141
The Sibian Tiger, 22
Sibiu International Theatre Festival, 22, 171
Sidonová, Magdaléna, 129
Sidran, Abdulah, 32
Siekiera (The Axe), 66
Sienkiewicz, Henryk, 80
Sieradzki, Jacek, 113
Sigurjónsson, Hávar, 18
Sing, 166
Sipunova, Ineta, 52

Siráj (*The Seagull*), 188
Sirli, Vasile, 180
Škandíková, Lucia, 216
Skiba, Piotr, 111
Sládeček, Svatopluk, 127
Sleepwalkers, 58
Słobodzianek, Tadeusz, 94
Słoń zielony (*The Green Elephant*), 72
Slouková, Jana, 209, 211, 214
Śmiechowicz, Olga, 257
Śmierć króla, 252
Smile Upon Us, Lord, 240
Smith, Priscilla, 203
Smith, Zadie, 266
Sodeika, Gintaras, 86, 89, 90
Solitarity, 21, 25
Some Explicit Polaroids, 209
Somewhere in Russia, 189
Sommergäste, 50
Somogyi, István, 161, 186
The Song of Songs, 154
Song of the Goat—Dithyramb, 6, 7, 9
Song of the Goat Theatre, ix, xiii, xv, 1–4, 6–8, 10–13
Songs of Lear, xii, 10
The Sons of a Bitch, 154
Sophocles, 57, 88, 90, 209, 245, 254
Sorcery, 228
The Sound of Silence, 53, 54
Speaking in Tongues, 252
Spektakl wieczorny (*Evening Performance*), 227
Špinar, Daniel, vii, viii, 207–219, 271, 275–276, 291
SPI->RA->LA, 118
Sprawa Dantona, 80
Spring Awakening, 32
Spurná, Marie, 217
The Square, 149, 150
The Square, Pirosmani, Pirosmani, 269
Stalin, Joseph, 38

Staniewski, Włodzimierz, xiv, 2, 3, 221–224, 226–235, 265, 292
Stanislavski, Konstantin Sergeievich, 139, 149, 182, 267, 274
Štědroň, Petr, 126, 128
Stefanova, Kalina, 10, 214
Stefanovics, Angéla, 167
Stenka, Danuta, 257
Stewart, Ellen, 199
Stojanović, Lazar, 38
Stojowska, Magda, 114
Stone, Oliver, 63
Stoppard, Tom, 47
Stop the Tempo, 18, 19
Štorková, Pavlína, 218
The Storm, 103
The Story of a Lazy Man, 27
The Story of Caspar Hauser, 47
Strasberg, Paula, 115–116
Strauss, C. L., 271
Strauss, Richard, 273
Streep, Meryl, 267
Strehler, Giorgio, 238, 251, 277
Strindberg, August, 81
Strniša, Gregor, 103
Strzempka, Monika, 6
Studium o Hamlecie (A Study of Hamlet), 75
Suchý, Jiří, 128
Šugman, Jernej, 105
Suicide, 142
Sun Ra, 268
Švanda Theatre, vii
Svoboda, Robert, xxi
Świetlicki, Marcin, 255
Święto [*Holiday*], 224
Swift, Jonathan, 178, 179
Szamosi, Zsófia, 166
Szczęśniak, Małgorzata, 255, 256, 259
Szczypiorski, Andrzej, 8
Székely, Gábor, 273
Szewcy, 80

Szewcy u bram (The Shoemakers at the Gates), 80
Sztarbowski, Paweł, 77

T
Tagore, Tagore, 233
Talankin, I., 44
Tamás Ascher in Háromszék, 162
The Taming of the Shrew, 254, 257
Tancerz mecenasa Kraykowskiego (Dancer of the Lawyer Kraykowski), 250
Taranienko, Zbigniew, 226, 228
Tarantino, Quentin, 58, 268
Tarkovsky, Andrei Arsenyevich, xiv, 273, 274
Tarnowska, Anna, 10
Tartuffe, 94
Tasnádi, István, 188
A Taste of Honey, 149
Tavčar, Ivan, 105
Taymor, Julie, 137
Tchrimekundan or The Unblinded, 100
Teatr, 58, 61
Teatr Pieśń Kozła, 1
Teatr Polski, 73
Teatr Rozmaitości (Theatre of Rarities) (TR), 57, 62, 64, 65, 67, 68
Teatr Studio, 4
Tejnorová, Petra, 209
The Tempest, xiii, 11, 135, 139, 179, 180, 252, 254, 283
Terhes, Sándor, 186
Theatre Association "Gardzienice," 224
The Theatre of Youth, 18
Theorem, 90
T.H.E.O.R.E.M., 61
There to Be Here, 85, 269, 270
There Will Be No Death Here, 239
Third World Bunfight, xvi
Three Sisters, 124, 125, 189, 217

310 INDEX

365 Days/365 Plays, 80
Thuróczy, Szabolcs, 160, 165, 167
Țibuleac, Tatiana, 266
Tigern, 22
Till Heartbreak, 166
The Tipsy God, 53, 54
Tito, Josip Broz, 38
Titus Andronicus, 12, 177, 180
To Be or Not to Be, 213
To Damascus, 81
Together/Alone, 216
Tokarczuk, Olga, 266
Tolstoy, Count Lev Nikolayevich, 271
A Tomb for Boris Davidovič, 38
Tovstonogov, Georgy, 267
Towards the New Natural Environment for Theatre, 222
Tragos, 3
Transfer!, 80
The Trial, 119, 120
Triennale, Ruhr, 47, 50
The Trilogy, 35, 37, 80, 200, 201
The Trilogy of Croatian Fascism, 35
The Trojan Women, 82, 200
Tropical Craze, 57–59
The Tropical Haze, 60, 63
TR Warsaw, 64, 67
TR Warszawa Theatre, 110
Trylogia, 80
Tulane Drama Review, xxi
Tuminas, Rimas, 87, 237–246, 277, 292
Turbofolk, 32
Turóczy, Szabolcs, 163
Twelfth Night, 252, 256
2007: Macbeth, 64
Typographic Capital Letters, 21

U

Ubu Rex, 175, 177, 255
Ubu Rex with Scenes from Macbeth, 173

Ubu the King, 105
Ule [*Beehives*], 224
Ulysses, x
Uncle Vanya, 150, 243, 244
Ungarn, 166, 167
Unidentified Human Remains and the True Nature of Love, 58
Unidentified Remains, 63
Uśmiech grejpruta (The Gripefruit's Smile), 73

V

Vaitkus, Jonas, 87, 269
Vakhtangov, Yevgeny Bagrationovich, 246
Valmet, 209
Valmont, 213
Vanagaité, Rūta, 86
Varga, Dario, 101
Vašák, Václav, 127
Vasiliauskas, Valdas, 88, 89
Vasiliev, Anatoly, 267, 277
Vasilyev, Anatolij, 269
Väter, 49
The Vatican Cellars, 73
Verdi, Giuseppe, 51, 63, 255
Viceníková, Dora, 124, 126, 128–131
Vikings, 13
Vinterberg, Thomas, 63
Vinton, Bobby, viii
Vișniec, Matei, 252
The Visoko Chronicle, 105–107
Vlădăreanu, Elena, 266
von Kleist, H., 250, 252
von Trier, Lars, 268, 274
Vondráček, Jan, 125
Voskovec, Jiří, 126, 127
Vvedensky, Alexander, 86, 269
Vyrypaev, Ivan, 65
Vyskočil, Ivan, 128

INDEX 311

W

Wagner, Richard, 52, 255
The Waiting Room, 116, 117
Waiting Room.0, 116, 117
Walentynowicz, Anna, 75
Walker, Scott, 269
Warburg, Aby, 269
Warhol, Andy, 114, 115, 275
Warlikowski, Krzysztof, 57, 58, 60, 64, 249–259
The Warrior, 13
Wassa, 50
We Are Pretty Good, 67
The Wedding, 103, 233, 235
The Wedding: Wyspiański—Malczewski—Konieczny, 233
Węgrzyniak, Rafał, 63, 250
Weil, Simone, 115
Weiss, Peter, 39
Welcome to Thebes, 209
Werich, Jan, 126, 127
Wesele (The Wedding), 81
West Coast, 252
We Will Employ an Old Clown, 252
When Father Was Away on Business, 32
When I Fall in Love, 63
White Nights, 250
Wichowska, Joanna, 117
Wielki Fryderyk (Fryderyk the Great), 82
Wild Duck, 124
Williams, Tennessee, 289
Wilson, Robert, 175
Wind in the Pines, 98, 101–103
The Winter's Tale, 211, 256
Witaj/Żegnaj (Greetings/Farewell), 80
Witkacy, 59, 60
Witkiewicz, Stanisław Ignacy, 57, 63, 80, 103, 268, 271
Wojcieszek, Przemysław, 65

Wojna polsko-ruska pod flagą biało-czerwoną (*White and Red*), 65
Woodcutters, 117, 118, 132, 133
The Wooster Group, 266
Woyzeck on the Highveld, 67, 137, 187, 210
Wozzeck, 255
Wuttke, Martin, 50–51
W—Workers' Circus, 190
Wyatt, Robert, 269
Wybreze, Teatr, vi
Wyspiański, Stanisław, 75, 81, 233

X

XX Century. Поезд-призрак. Vision Express, 46
XXI Seoul Performing Arts Festival, 252

Y

Years of Deception, 33

Z

Zahradník, Osvald, 238
Zariņa, Guna, 53
Zec, Aleksandra, 36, 37
Zenchiku, Konparu, 98
Zieda, Margarita, 51
Ziemia obiecana (The Promised Land), 80
Zimmermann, Alois Berndt, 51
Zinc (*Zn*), 154
Żółkoś, Monika, 114
Zoran Đinđić, 33
Zubrzycki, Anna, 1, 3, 4, 9, 235
Żuławski, Andrzej, 268
Zvyagintsev, Andrey, 274
Żywot protopopa Awwakuma (The Life of Archpriest Avvakum), 228

Printed in the United States
by Baker & Taylor Publisher Services